MY FAMILY,
MY FRIENDS,
and ME

By

Tom Wade, Jr.

ISBN: 1-4140-1576-3 (e-book)
ISBN: 1-4140-1574-7 (Paperback)
ISBN: 1-4140-1575-5 (Dust Jacket)

Library of Congress Control Number: 2003097688

This book is printed on acid free paper.

Printed in the United States of America
Bloomington, IN

1stBooks — rev. 12/16/03

TABLE OF CONTENTS

INTRODUCTION

After it's too late most of us eventually realize that we wish we knew more about the lives of our parents, grandparents, and other older relatives. Certainly I'm one of those folks. Writing this book will be helpful in that regard to Pat's and my children and grandchildren and generations to follow.

This autobiography contains a good deal about Kenton, Union City, The University of Tennessee, the Pi Kappa Alpha Fraternity, McCallie School, our travels, our businesses, and a great deal about my family and friends. It was, however, written primarily for my family, and some of it will hold little interest for others. Details of our house, art, furnishings, and other personal and business type information are strictly for the benefit of Pat's and my family and future generations. A considerable amount has been written about our present and former employees which should be interesting to them and/or their families. The index includes the names of the people who are an integral part of this book. The names of many Kenton/Mason Hall and Union City folks who are not mentioned in a specific way are found in Chapter 36.

I have elected to keep the writing of this book secret from almost everyone except for my son Will, Julie Parker, a few cousins, and my UT fraternity brothers. Will, of course, works with me, and Julie is Will's and my assistant. It would have been extraordinarily difficult to write this book without Julie's outstanding help. Certain parts of the book would have been a little more complete if I had not kept it secret from my family, but I simply wanted to surprise them with it. For some reason this was important to me. I have resorted to a little subterfuge to get some information, but hopefully the book will be a total surprise to my family and most others.

I urge you readers before it's too late to write information about your own families for future generations. Just think about how great it would be if you had a book similar to this one written by one of your parents or grandparents.

DUST JACKET

Descriptions of the pictures on the dust jacket, from top to bottom from left to right, follow:

FRONT: Home of C. R & Lyda Belle Wade, my grandparents (standing together); my Dad, Tom Wade, on his pony; Auntie Moselle Wade Tucker, Dad's sister, seated; my great grandmother, Rachel Moselle Elder Watkins on the right, ca 1905.

Pat and me and our family: Lolly and Don Bearden, and Meg and Ellen Bearden; Patti and Rance Barnes and Rance, Jr., Walker, and Thomas Barnes; Will and Kim Wade and Wilton and John Wade at the Bearden's Shreveport home, spring 2002.

Tom Wade, ca. 1910

The C. R. Wade family and employees in the rubble of Wade's burned store in Kenton, ca. 1902. Little boy is Tom Wade.

Tom Wade and Eugene Wade in C. R. Wade store, ca 1916.

My Mother, Patti Walker Wade, ca. 1903.

Tom Wade and his parents at Red Boiling Springs, ca. 1912.

BACK: Tom Wade, 1945.

Dr. Joe Johnson, Dr. Ed Boling, and me, UT Annual Giving totals, 1983.

Patti, ca. 1986.

David Roberts, head of UT alumni, Pat and me at bowl game party, ca. 1985.

Pat, ca 1961.

Will and me, cover of September, 1993 PiKA magazine.

Lolly, ca 1970.

Mother, 1945.

Will and me, strawberry patch, ca. 2000.

Sally Wade Tomlinson and Tom Wade's long-time herdsman, Dewey Bradley, with a Tom Wade championship heifer at the Obion County Fair (part of the grandstand of Union City's Class D Kitty League baseball team in the background), ca 1958.

William E. Wade, my great, great, great grandfather, ca. 1845.

Will, ca 1990.

My maternal grandmother, Kate Smith (Walker), with the guitar, and her sister, Martha Smith (Craig), ca 1891.

Pat, ca 1985.

LEFT FLAP: Tom and Patti Wade home (now Will's and my offices).

Lolly, ca 1999.

A Kenton White Squirrel.

Lolly and me, November, 1963.

Kenton Brand strawberry label.

Will and me at a Fiesta Bowl party, probably 1988.

Patti, ca. 1971.

RIGHT FLAP: UT McCallie Pikes in Knoxville, 2002: John Hoff, Malcolm Colditz, Malcolm's wife, Harriet, Bill McDonald, Bill Monin, Bob Greer, and me (standing).

Pat and me, Don and Lolly, Pitt Tomlinson IV, Patti and Rance, and Kim and Will at The Palm in New York, 1996.

A few of the Supergroupers at the 2000 Pike reunion in Knoxville, standing left to right: Bob Seyfried, John Michels, Roger Bradley, Dick Kidwell, Bill Taylor (kissing Dream Girl Fran Dominick Shackelford), Bill Monin, Jim Johnson, Jim Paulus, Henry Davis, Gene Totri, Bob Greer, Ron Taylor, Gary Caylor, Bill Weller, John T. O'Connor, Randy Mansfield, Dave McSween, Tim Sullivan; sitting left to right: Howard Hinds, Bill McDonald, Joe Taylor, me, Malcolm Colditz.

Sally, Mother, Dad and me at a PiKA function, ca 1958.

These photographs represent in a cursory way the history of our family from 1845 to the date of the printing of this book, 2003. Hope the dust jacket isn't better than the book!

Tom Wade, Jr.

Chapter One

Growing Up In Kenton

When I was an infant Mother carried me around in a little
basket. I've always thought that I could remember lying in
my basket and looking up at some ladies looking down at me. My
recollection was that this took place in either our living room or dining
room. This was my first memory. Or at least I think it was.

I consider myself indeed fortunate to have been brought up in the
small West Tennessee town of Kenton. Almost all of us Kenton
children were reared in God-fearing families who, along with our
preachers, Sunday School teachers, school teachers, scout leaders, and
other local adults, taught us the Christian way of life. In the case of my
sister, Sarah Katherine (Sally), and me, when the doors to the Kenton
Cumberland Presbyterian Church opened, we were there! No ifs,
ands, or buts about it.

In my early years the prayer we always said at night was, "Now I lay
me down to sleep, I pray the Lord my soul to keep. If I should die
before I wake, I pray the Lord my soul to take. Amen." When I was
real young I said "Amen" twice, once with a broad "A" and once with a
long "A." To me this added considerable weight to my nightly prayer
and it was hard to understand why Mother was not totally enthusiastic
about my approach to covering all the bases. Dad's meal blessing,
"Father, make us thankful for these and all thy blessings. For Christ's
sake, Amen" is still said at meals at home by me and by our son, Will,
at his home. A friend of my wife, Pat, had an even shorter blessing.
She always said, at breakfast, lunch, and dinner, "God bless breakfast.
Amen."

When Mother was pregnant with Sally she and Dad decided that if
the baby were a girl they would name her Sarah Katherine. Our
maternal Grandmother Walker suggested that if the baby girl had curly
hair they'd call her Sarah and if she had straight hair she'd be called
Sally. Well, we all know what kind of hair Sally had.

1

One time when Sally must have been one or two years old, Mother was feeding her in her high chair in the kitchen as she usually did. Somehow Sally tipped the high chair over backwards and fell and hit her head hard enough that she was knocked out cold. It scared Mother to death, and she picked Sally up and ran out the front door onto the sidewalk crying and yelling for help. A passerby picked her up and drove her down to Dr. Gray's office. As it turned out no damage was done. I can just imagine how panicked Mother must have been after having had little Patti, her first child, die in her arms at the age of 22 months (more about little Patti later). Sally's incident may have been the only time I ever saw Mother out of control. She was always very much of an in-control person.

When I was young I went through a period of wanting a little brother to play with. It never happened, of course, and I grew out of that phase.

Since there was not a whole lot to do in Kenton we youngsters had to make our own fun. And we did a mighty good job of that! I seemed to be the main organizer of the neighborhood (and you might even say that all of Kenton <u>was</u> the neighborhood). Some of those in the gang were Jackie Glisson, Jackie Hollandsworth, Paul Jenkins, Freddy Jordon, Bobby Keathley, Jamie (Pig) Norton, Howard Duncan Taylor, Truett Tilghman, John and Betty Wells, and Ikey Witherspoon. Sometimes Cuddin' Tommy Hamilton, who was a little older, would play with us. And occasionally his older brother James, and Charlie Freeman, another older cousin, would join us. In fact one winter Charlie stopped by on his way home from school to play a little basketball with our gang and blew out his knee. I couldn't help but feel responsible. That was a bad day.

We had what was to us a big "side yard" north of our house where we played softball or baseball in the summer, football in the fall, and basketball in the winter. This was long before the new garage and office were built onto the house. The basketball goal was in the northeast corner of the yard, and baseball was played with home plate on the south side next to a concrete abutment of the gravel driveway which ran into the old garage. There was no street on the north side of the side yard; instead there was a dormant alley with a hedge beside it.

Also there was a hedge that ran beside the sidewalk on the west side of the side yard. Football also was played from north to south. Another game that we enjoyed was Kick-the-Can which we played at night.

Another game we played was marbles which was played at the southwest corner of the house. That grass was pretty well beaten down to pure dirt. We marked off a rectangle, in which we placed the marbles, and a line from which we started play. Mother would not let us play "for keeps;" that was too much like gambling. Those who had big "steelies" usually won.

When we were young Sally played all sports just like the boys. She even boxed and played football. I used to tell Mother and Dad that it was not fair for both of us to be on the same team; we were too good. I also told Dad that one reason my team usually won was that we used "strategy."

Dad loved to tell the story about Sally coming home from her first day in school and telling him that she could whip everybody in the first grade, boys included, except for Mary Lee Cody. (I saw Mary Lee at the recent Kenton School reunion, and she is, as she always was, a delightful person. She has long lived in Richmond, Virginia.)

Jack Barton, the husband of Laura Joyce Howell Barton and the father of Kay Carroll Barton Dement and Laura Lisa Barton Clark, married Laura Joyce soon after World War II. (Laura said that as a little fellow I once said, "I can't say 'tuttle,' but I can say 'fwog.' Auntie Moselle said that I referred to my pants as "panchies." A Phi Beta Kappa I wasn't! And ain't.) Early on Jack worked for Lanzer Printing Company in Union City and after work more often than not he would join us in the side yard for our baseball games. It was a real treat to have a grown man play with us. I always wished Dad would do that, but he was always too busy. And he was busy — no doubt about that. One time my cousins from Greenwich, Connecticut were visiting. The two boys, Dick and Bill, and their Dad, Herman Bevis, were playing with us when Dad came home. Dad joined the game. How wonderful it was to have one's own dad join the game! We adults just simply do not know how important it is to our children to participate with them in their activities. My own children (especially Will) probably often wished that their Dad would play with them more.

Laura and Jack lived with her mother, Karon Carroll Howell, and Miss Karon's sister, Hattye Carroll Connell. Both Miss Karon and Miss Hattye were widowed. Laura still lives in that same house.

Mrs. Vade McNeely and her son Carthel lived in the house just north of our side yard. As mentioned there was a hedge that ran the length of our yard on that side. After some high flying baseballs broke windows of their house, Dad, who was tired of apologizing to the McNeelys and replacing windows, insisted that we make a rule that any ball hit over the hedge on the fly was an out. We quickly learned to be line drive hitters. Sally was murder on pitches that were shoulder high. But throw them anywhere else and you could whiff her every time. You see, she always swung shoulder high. Sally was also a pretty good boxer 'til one time a friend from Dyersburg, Tommy Rosser, later of the United States Naval Academy, cleaned her plow. After that whippin' she hung up the gloves for good. In fact a short while later she gave up all sports and started primpin' and doin' girl things. Suddenly she quit playing one day, and that was it. She never played again, no matter how much I begged. At that point it was hard to imagine that in earlier times when some of us boys would head out to the country southwest of St. Mary's Street on one of our "Junior Commandos" expeditions up the creek and through the woods on the Carroll farm to hunt birds and fish, Sally wanted to be with us and would tag along at a safe distance. I'd throw rocks at her to try to get her to go back home. I wish I hadn't done that. I was just lucky that she didn't tell Dad. (The Carroll farm later belonged to Mark and Margaret Lumpkin. I bought it from them about 20 years ago.) The only time Dad ever whipped me was once when he saw me hit Sally. He used a rolled up newspaper! Mother was the "enforcer" in our family. She would take me into the bathroom and whip me with a yardstick. Once I got into trouble with Mother and ran to the north side of the hedge and hid in Jack Glisson's daddy's Model T (that was before the McNeelys bought that house) all day long. At dusk I finally accepted the inevitable and headed home. Mother met me at the back porch, ran me into the bathroom, and absolutely wore me out.

I had asthma pretty badly until the age of ten. One fall I played in a pile of leaves with some of the gang and an asthma attack hit me. I headed for the back steps which led up to the back porch and started calling for Mother. Just as she reached me at the back porch I blacked out; I simply could not breathe. She rushed me into my room and set fire to a medicinal powder that we used to burn for relief from asthma. The resulting smoke quickly roused me. That was the worst attack I ever had, and I believe to this day that if Mother had not been at home that day I would have died.

Despite my bad allergies as a youngster I had ponies and dogs. My first pony was a Shetland named Tony. One time I was riding him in town up what is now Hillwood Street. At that time there were no houses on that street which was really little more than a lane out into the country. Tommy Hamilton and I were riding. It was a rainy, wet day, and for some reason Tony ran away with me. Tommy ran behind, and finally Tony stopped dead in his tracks several hundred yards up the hill. Tommy finally caught up with us, worn out and very upset. He took off one of his rubber boots and hit Tony in the rear with it. Tony took off again and ran a long way out into a farm. When Tommy was finally catching up with us again I hollered at him, "Don't hit 'im!"

Another Tony story involved his ability to swell up his belly when we saddled him so that the cinch would not be too tight. Then after he was saddled he would relax and the saddle would not be secure. One day I was riding Tony hard in a pasture on the Railroad farm, and I cut him quickly to the left. The saddle flew around and directly underneath Tony, and he stopped on a dime — with me on the ground directly underneath him! Tony was an old pony and his "smarts" may well have saved me from serious injury, or worse. This more than repaid me for his having run away with me. Later I learned to drive a standard shift car in the "Tony" pasture.

My next horse was larger than a Shetland but was not real big. She was white with reddish- brown spots. Every spot was outlined with about a half inch of mixed reddish brown and white hair. She was a beauty.

My first dog was a stray that just showed up. He was solid white and I named him Snowball. He was bad about chasing cars. We tried to break him from doing it but were unsuccessful. One day he was chasing a car when another car met the car that Snowball was chasing and the second car ran over him. He yelped and yelped and ran underneath the Witherspoon's house where he died. I was heartbroken, so Dad bought a collie for me. We picked him up at a barn just west of Paris. A Hereford breeder whom Dad knew sold him to Dad. We took the puppy from his mother and headed back to Kenton. Sally was with us and she played with Laddie on the way home to the extent that he seemed to like her better than me. This broke my heart again, but pretty soon he liked me better than he liked her. All was well with the world.

During elementary school years Mother and Dad talked me into taking piano lessons from Kenton's extraordinary teacher, Miss Verne Tomlinson. She taught in her home which was just east of the Kenton Elementary School. Mother and Dad had bought a Steinway Baby Grand, so we had a wonderful piano at home. Dad told me that I could stop for strawberry season, which would begin in about three months, and then if taking piano lessons no longer appealed to me after berry season was over, it would be all right. That seemed to be a fair proposition. My lessons were during recess at school, and some of the boys teased me about taking piano lessons instead of playing ball or whatever. Playing the piano was kind of fun, and Miss Verne told me that I had a good deal of talent. But when berry season was over I chose not to go back to Miss Verne's. That wound up my piano career. Later on in college one of my fraternity brothers taught me some chords, and playing around on the chapter's Steinway was fun. I think it would be really neat to be able to play, especially when friends gather.

When Sally was young she started taking piano lessons from Miss Verne. Many a Saturday morning her piano practicing woke me. Her constant practicing was not my favorite thing to hear, but as she continued studying piano and improving I grew to be very proud of her accomplishments. The best score you could have in piano competitions was Superior Plus. She scored Superior Plus for something like ten straight years. In later years she seemed to lose interest in playing and, in fact, gave me the mint-condition Steinway years ago. We love having it in our home, and it is one of our most prized possessions. It constantly brings back tender memories.

Sally did not talk real well when she was very young. For some reason she called chewing gum "bue." Old Mr. Ben McCullough who lived west of town thought this was cute and he always had gum for Sally. Another example of her baby talk was one time when somebody came to the front door and asked for Mother, and Sally said, "My mama he gone to da booty pahluh."

No tellin' how many birds I killed with my BB guns. We knew not to kill mockingbirds (after all, they were the state bird), cardinals (they were too pretty to kill, and besides, our favorite baseball team was named the Cardinals), blue jays (some killed them, but despite the raucous sounds they made I thought they also were mighty pretty), blue birds and wrens (we rarely saw them anyway), and robins (apparently we didn't want to interrupt their walk to Missouri). We killed sparrows and black birds primarily, though you had to hit black birds just right to kill them. However, unlike lots of the boys, especially those from "the country," I never was very accurate with my slingshot. Until one day I came around the corner of the house (now my office) and saw a sparrow sitting in the walnut tree that is still here. I loaded my slingshot with a big rock from the gravel driveway and shot in the general direction of the unsuspecting bird. The rock after a very high trajectory hit the sparrow squarely on the breast and he dropped dead. For some reason that kill kind of bothered me. Oftentimes we would dress and cook the birds we killed and little fish we caught and feed them to the dogs that roamed the neighborhood. We didn't know that those small bones could injure dogs. To my knowledge, however, none of those dogs ever had any problems after those feasts which they loved.

We fished primarily in the little creek that runs through Kenton. Back then it had lots of trees and pools with fairly deep water and a good number of fish. One of our favorite adventures was to follow the creek back out of town toward the southwest. This territory was real junglely in those days, and we had a lot of fun pretending that we were "Junior Commandos." This was a popular expression for young people during World War II. Sometimes we fished in the farm ponds and in the "old riverbed" (the remaining courses of the original Rutherford Fork of the Obion River). About 55 to 60 years ago, there were many snakes in the Obion River bottoms. When I was a child it was very

7

seldom that you would walk down to the bottom without seeing some snakes. One day a bunch of us headed for the old riverbed on Dad's Railroad farm (which incidentally has now been in the family for nearly 100 years). We crawled through a three-strand barbed wire fence and got set up at a bend in the river. I stepped on a big clump of grass, and the biggest snake I had ever seen (a giant water moccasin) slithered out from underneath that grass and into the water. We cleared that fence in one leap and didn't stop running until we had crossed a big field almost halfway to town. We never went back for the fishing tackle and never again fished in that area of the river. Dad said that when he first bought the land you could hardly take a step without seeing snakes. Snakes really shouldn't have scared me. Sally and I went swimming with snakes in ponds plenty of times. Mother, who could not swim, sat on the side of the pond and watched us. (The ponds we swam in were pretty shallow.) Another of my favorite pastimes was shooting snakes in ponds with my pellet gun.

The neighborhood gang had more talent than just for sports. One time we decided to produce and stage a show in our garage which was a free standing building just northeast of the house. We took an old swing frame and made a stage out of it with a plank floor and curtains. The hit of the show was Paul Jenkins who was the butler. He was dressed in tails and brought one of us a tray of food or drink or something and bent over as he handed it to whomever. As he bent over one of the backstage crew tore a piece of cloth as if Paul's pants had split. Paul grabbed his rear end and quickly left the stage profusely apologizing. We charged five cents, and our audience of three or four thought this was a scream. So did the rest of the cast.

Paul and his sister, Peggy Jenkins, and Sally and I produced, directed and starred in the show. I can't remember who else was in the show, but the cast was two or three times as large as the audience. To start with none of the audience had any money with them. They all had to go home to get a nickel. Some couldn't persuade their mothers to part with a nickel which severely impacted our box office take.

Halloween might have been my favorite holiday. At least it was a close second to Christmas. We'd never heard of "Trick or Treat." We were just into trickin'. The gang would gather at my house as dusk approached and we would map out the night. We tried to touch every house in our part of town street by street. Our main activity was to soap windows. We had a rule never to do anything really damaging. For instance we never soaped screens, as soap on screens would cause them to rust. We also moved lots of porch furniture into yards and tools and such out of sheds.

We had great success in our endeavors and were never caught. Maybe we all should have been spies. We seemed to have that sort of talent. At the very least we saw to it that Kenton had much cleaner windows than it would have had, had not our soap brigade come its way.

One Easter Sally and I received baby chicks, mine colored blue and hers pink. Mine developed into a gregarious white Leghorn rooster which I named Doodle. Doodle was a real pet. I could snap my fingers over my head, and Doodle would fly up, land on my head, face the front, and crow majestically. Doodle roosted at night on the rafters of our garage. It seemed that he saved up all day so that he could continuously go to the bathroom all night on the cars parked below. I drove nails into the rafters thinking that they would persuade Doodle to roost elsewhere, but that didn't work. I nailed nails between the nails and nails between those nails. It seemed that there were not enough nails in Kenton to stop his roosting. I became proficient at car washing. Some ladies who walked to work on our sidewalk left sticks at each end of our sidewalk in order to fend off Doodle. At this age I had asthma pretty badly and fairly often was sick in bed. Mother would let Doodle come in, and he would lie on his side beside me in my bed while I rubbed him. One day our preacher's wife, Mrs. John Stammer Smith, came to visit and left her infant son in his stroller on our front porch, and Doodle spurred him on his temple. That wound up Doodle's idyllic life as Mother and Dad gave him to Margaret Dodson (more about Margaret later) who had some chickens. I have always suspected that Doodle ended up in some sort of chicken casserole or other chicken concoction. Odds are he was plenty tough.

I mowed our yard with an old fashioned push mower. Our septic tank lines ran underneath the east end of the side yard back in the days before Kenton had a sewer system. The grass above the lines grew so thick and tall that it had to be mowed regularly. One hot summer it got away from me, and trying to push my mower through that tough grass almost caused me to have a heat stroke. I never again got behind on my mowing.

I remember when Kenton got its first neon sign. It was very small, but it was neon. Kenton was becoming a cosmopolitan city. Come to think of it just about the only neon signs that we now have advertise beer and cigarettes. Some folks might think that Kenton would be better off if it still had no neon signs.

In the old days all the streets in Kenton were gravel. The dust in the summertime was really bad, so an afternoon ritual with many of the people in town, including Mother and later me, was to sprinkle down the street that ran in front of our houses. This kept the dust down for several hours. We usually did this late in the afternoon when it was cooler, and the results would hold overnight and pretty well into the next day. Another of my chores was to fill up the stoker in the winter. As was the case with many houses back then we had a coal furnace in the basement which was fed by a stoker. The coal truck would come down our driveway and pull up to a window at our coal bin in the basement and men would shovel in the coal. I would shovel it from the storage area into the stoker. Dad had men who worked for him who would come periodically and remove the clinkers from the furnace. This was not a job for a little boy. Besides, the smoke created by this task was hard on my asthma.

Our gravel street was a great battleground in my young eyes. I would break apart little twigs and build tiny cannons facing each other at a distance apart of four or five feet. Then I would get on one side and toss rocks at the cannons on the other side, alternating back and forth, all the time narrating the battle. After a certain amount of time the side with the fewest destroyed cannons was declared the winner of the battle. My goodness how little it takes to entertain a child.

At an early age I was asked to be in the Kenton School's Amateur Hour which was a big deal back then. The recitation of a poem was my assignment. At a certain point backstage my nerves got the best of me, and I slipped out and ran home. My remembrance is that my scheduled time came and went and Mother and Dad left the gym and went home where they found me, and they persuaded me to go back and "perform." For years afterward public speaking in some situations was very hard for me to do. (Later on this problem will be discussed in some detail.)

In addition to the Amateur Hours we had at school, once every year or two we would have a "Womanless Wedding" in which old and young men would dress up like women, all prim and proper but with heavy makeup, and glide down the aisle to the alter. Each man had a funny feminine name which would be printed in the program. For a change of pace sometimes they staged "Womanless Beauty Revues" which were just as hilarious. One of the funniest "ladies" was Johnny Bogle who was pretty much of a clown anyway. These shows were great fun and drew large crowds. Before the days of television we found many wonderful ways to entertain ourselves.

During my single digit years one fall Dad's and customers' vehicles were experiencing more flat tires than usual on our gravel gin lot. Dad told me that he would give me a penny for every nail I picked up on the lot. After a couple of hours of careful searching I had found only a small handful of nails which was disappointing. The gin platform was constructed of wood and was raised four or five feet off the ground. I decided to look underneath the platform, reasoning that it was a part of the gin lot. Nails were everywhere, apparently having been dropped during the construction of the platform and maybe even from earlier platform constructions. I wound up with almost 2,000 nails and presented them to Dad. Some customers were in the office when I carted in all those nails for Dad's inspection, and these men kidded Dad unmercifully for allowing his young son to outsmart him. The $20.00 that Dad paid me that day was the equivalent of two weeks of hard work on the strawberry platform. I was one happy little fellow whose Dad was actually mighty proud of him.

Sometimes I would pick cotton for Mr. Columbus (Lum) Bradley, Dewey's father, who, along with most of the men who worked on Dad's farms, sharecropped cotton with Dad. One day my total reached 100 pounds; I was on the way to being one of the world's great pickers! However, this lofty plateau was never again reached and soon thereafter my pick sack was hung up forever. A talent for cotton pickin' wasn't in the cards for me. Good pickers picked 300 pounds and up. Great pickers picked 500 pounds and up.

At age twelve or thirteen I had an FFA project of two acres of strawberries on the Brick House farm. The patch was in the field across the highway from Dewey and Modine Bradley's house. We decided to try a new University of Tennessee-developed variety called Tennessee Shippers. They were supposed to be hardy berries that would stand up better to normal abuse, ship well, and have good shelf life. Well, they probably did have all those attributes, but the problem was that they were very poor yielders. I helped set out those berries, chopped them, pinched the blooms, and trained the runners that first summer. The next spring my sales did not cover my expenses. Furthermore, no payment was received for my hundreds of hours of hard labor under the hot sun. Tennessee Shippers taught me the hard way that a farmer doesn't always make money. Unfortunately we farmers continue to experience all too often this unpleasant fact of the agrarian life.

One of the neat things about living in Kenton was that you could walk anywhere if you decided not to ride your bicycle. I walked to the picture show at the Horse Opera many a night. Mother and Dad didn't think it was safe to ride my bike at night. The Horse Opera, a small wooden building with imitation brick siding, was a little movie theater in Kenton next to old Dr. Capps' house. We liked to sit on the front row despite the fact that half the people who came in crossed over in front of us. The theater goers came into the building on the end where the screen was located, and to get to the north aisle you had to walk bending over so that the crowd could see the screen. We sweltered in the summer (no air conditioning, of course) and froze in the winter depending on how close we sat to the big pot-bellied stove that sat in the front south corner. Many Saturday nights found me listening to Mr. Dan Schwab, the owner, standing in front of the screen and describing coming attractions. Cowboy movies were my favorites, and Bob Steele was my favorite cowboy despite the fact that Gene Autry and Roy Rogers were more famous. All famous cowboy stars had sidekicks. Gene Autry's was Smiley Burnett. Two other popular sidekicks were Andy Devine and Gabby Hays. Another sidekick was a Mexican man whose favorite saying was "me too also." The Horse Opera was an important part of my young life. We usually started Saturday night off at the John Deere place which was almost next door to the theater. Dad would give me a quarter. My ticket was a dime and my bag of popcorn was a nickel, and I always brought the dime change back to Dad. The men hanging around (everybody hung around somewhere in town on Saturday nights but that's another story) often teased me about giving Dad his change, but that made perfect sense to me. Dad would always be there when money — or anything else — was needed. I had a good Daddy.

One crowded Saturday night at the Horse Opera I was sitting about six or seven rows back from the front when wind was unexpectedly but quietly broken by yours truly. The resulting flatulence was considerably less than what one might call "odoriferous." My internal situation got worse and worse, and people in my vicinity were obviously becoming a little uneasy. A couple, apparently dating, sitting directly in front of me looked at each other a time or two, then laughed, then moved. Another person excused himself and moved. As time went on others moved. Finally I was sitting almost by myself, and rather than be conspicuous I also moved. That Saturday night was the most fun I ever had at the Horse Opera. It wasn't for dozens of others.

Sally and I walked to and from school as well as back home for lunch and then back to school for afternoon classes. In my early years in school in Kenton we did not have a cafeteria. The country children who came to school in buses brought their own lunches. They often had biscuits with ham and sausage as well as fried pies. It was hard not to be a little envious of them. Nevertheless the fact was that my Mother was a wonderful cook, and all her meals were great. A typical breakfast for us was bacon or country ham or sausage and eggs with toast. Often we had oatmeal or Cream of Wheat or Ralston with bacon. We usually had a big meal at noon with a meat and several vegetables. Often at night we had broiled steak and French fries or mashed potatoes. Fairly often we had breakfast food at night. We killed hogs and cured our own hams. We also killed fat steers and Mother supervised the cutting and aging of her prime beef. Our hams and beef and sausage were as good as you could get. Man, we ate good at our house! Condiments that added a great deal to my enjoyment of Mother's cooking were redeye gravy, steak gravy, and Mother's own strawberry preserves. I'm gettin' hungry! Mother's vegetable soup was wonderful and often we had soup at night. Her BLTs with homegrown tomatoes were also delicious. In the summertime we often ate such fare and then went back out to play until bedtime.

Mother sometimes made milkshakes for us and were they good! She bought straws in Memphis, and it was a great treat for Sally and me to be able to drink our milkshakes with straws. Straws weren't available in Kenton. She also brought home from Seessels in Memphis such goodies as cream puffs and chocolate eclairs. Man, that was really livin'! She also brought limes and club soda home from Memphis and would make limeades for Sally and me. One of my favorite things in the world was drug store limeades made with carbonated water, something we could not get in Kenton in my early days. George Webb who owned Kenton Drug Company at that time put in a soda fountain but it was not very successful and soon closed.

Back in those days Kenton had concrete sidewalks all over town. Now everybody has to walk in the streets, but we walked on the sidewalks in the old days. We also skated on the sidewalks. It was a little tough when you had to change sides of the street since the streets were gravel but we managed. One of our gang's favorite games was to start skating up on the south end of Maple Heights and then when we got up a good head of steam we would all crouch down, hold to the shoulders of the person in front of you, and form a line or train of skaters for the downhill ride. This would wind up when we got to St. Marys Street where the sidewalk switched from the west to the east side of Maple Heights. Many train wrecks occurred at the intersection of Maple Heights and St. Marys! In the winter when it snowed (and it snowed a lot more then than it does now) we rode our sleds down St. Marys Street. We had to run into the ditch at the bottom of the hill just before reaching Maple Heights in order to avoid any cars that might be coming along. Wonder how many miles we covered in a day's time sledding down that block and pulling our sleds back up to the top? No tellin'!

About this time there was a series of movies with real country talking hillbillies which we Wades thought were hilarious. The most unforgettable conversation, at least to us, was the following with a decidedly slow country twang, "Hey Pa. What, Ma? Get up, ya lazy critter." Mother would come into my bedroom in the morning and our exchange would be, "Hey, boy. What, Ma? Get up, ya lazy critter." I'd laugh so hard that sleep was gone and feet hit the floor with no further prodding. She and Sally had the same waking up regimen. This discovery simplified Mother's morning schedule until the "new" wore off.

There was some sort of ad or commercial when I was a child about "nuxated iron," whatever that meant. Dad would flex his bicep when we were playing around and say, "Nuxated iron did it!" For some reason we all thought this was a scream, and this was our cry when we were "threatening" one another during hijinks.

Most summers we had at least one big picnic in the woodslot on the Brick House farm. Dad always set up an old long wooden table that he had built for such occasions. One time when our Connecticut cousins, the Bevises, were here Jennie Lyde was riding one of Dad's horses in the woodslot and he bucked her off. It scared us all very much, but it didn't hurt her.

One fall Dad and I went to a rodeo at the Gibson County Fair in Trenton. It was a regular rodeo until the bronco event. A cowboy came out of the chute riding a bucking bronco and hanging on for dear life. Though the horse gave the man a very rough ride the man was able to hang on for the required ten seconds. When the whistle blew signifying that ten seconds had elapsed the bronco stopped on a dime, not moving a muscle. The crowd roared with laughter. That rodeo's credibility that night sank like a rock.

I attended Boy Scout meetings on and off for several years. Our scout leader was Joe Ferris Penn. The main attractions about scout meetings for me were the games we played afterwards in the deserted and dark downtown streets of Kenton. We played Kick-the-Can and Tribal Warfare where we wore cloth armbands. Each tribe tried to get the armbands from the other tribesmen, the tribe losing all their bands first being the loser. We met downtown on the second floor of the northeastern building on the main drag across the hall from Dr. Baucom's office. He was the town dentist. Scouting is a great thing — wish I'd taken it more seriously.

One fall our Kenton Boy Scouts troop spent the night at the cabin on the Botts property just south of Union City. The scoutmasters prepared a lardstand of excellent stew. That was one of my all-time favorite meals. The fact that we were mighty hungry most likely added to our enjoyment of that memorable repast.

Back then I listened to the radio a lot at night. Everybody did. We always "watched" the radio as we listened to it. After all, if you'd been there in person you'd be looking at the announcer or performer. CBS had an hour show of Big Band music every night, 20 minutes from the Peabody Skyway or Plantation Roof in Memphis, 20 minutes from the Blue Room in the Roosevelt Hotel in New Orleans, and 20 minutes from the top floor dinner dance club of the Chase Hotel in St. Louis. CBS would cut to Memphis and the announcer always said, "From the Skyway high atop Hotel Peabody in downtown Memphis overlooking Ole Man River, CBS brings you the music of Les Brown and his Band of Renown," or whomever was playing. That program probably was the reason I have ever since loved Big Band music which was still very popular during my college years.

Some of the lyrics to some of the songs of the day were very clever. One went:
So round, so firm, so fully packed,
That's my gal.
So complete from front to back,
That's my pal.
Toasted by the sun
And I'm a son of a gun
If you're gonna have a 5 o'clock shadow
Come on around at one.
You can bet your boots I'd walk a mile
Through the snow
Just to see her toothbrush smile.
Imagine on the radio.

The rest of that song escapes me, but those of us who remember radio commercials from those long ago days will recognize the fact that this song was written using popular ads for cigarettes, razor blades, and toothpaste.

Reid White was a good ole country boy who lived on Dad's farm when I was a child. He worked on the strawberry platform at times and he often sang an old country song. It needs to be sung "real country" and goes like this,

Goodbye my love, it's time to go
I heard th' silver trumpet blow
Twas callin' me home to fight the foe
Goodbye my love, goodbye.

Pat doesn't seem to mind too much when occasionally on the way out the door to work, I sing this song to her. Who's the foe? My competitors, I guess. Life sure would be easier without competitors.

How in the world can I remember the words and music to these songs when the location of important papers or my pen is often a mystery.

One of the fun things to do back then was to attend the Bisbee's Comedians show which always came to town during strawberry season. They set up their tent on the lot across from the railroad platform on the southwest corner of what is now the intersection of Main Street and Carroll Street, and their performances, a different show every night, would run for several days. Kenton's large strawberry acreage and its resultant period of good times may well have been the reason that our little town attracted such an important theatrical troupe! Our favorite of their several-actor company was Toby. We thought that he was the funniest person in the world, and maybe he was.

When we Kenton boys were in our early teens, unbeknownst to our parents of course, we would frequent the hootchie kootchie shows at the Gibson County Fair in Trenton. If we saw any men whom we knew, and we often did, we tried to hide from them among the crowd of men and boys so they wouldn't tell our folks. It never occurred to us that they almost assuredly would never have given away the fact that they were also there!

17

In the olden days Kenton had a very old decrepit fire truck. One fall I had ridden my bicycle down to the gin when the fire alarm went off. Toward the southwest smoke was coming from what looked like it might have been our house. Believe it or not, I passed the fire truck on my bike as we sped west on Taylor Street. The fire was burning a nearby house, not ours. Our good fortune was another family's tragedy.

Mother and Dad gave me a Cushman motorscooter one Christmas. A Cushman was a heavy, blocky scooter that had a top speed of 30 or 35. On December 22, 1948, an employee of Dad's picked it up at Houck Cushman Sales, 114 Union Avenue, Memphis. The price was $382.50. This was a good deal of money at that time which indicates that it was a substantial machine. On July 13, 1949, Paul Litton, an employee of Dad's, took it by Houck for a checkup and lubrication. The charge was $2.72! I rode that Cushman all over town. Sally drove it a time or two but she ran it into a ditch beside what most recently was Wilton and Patsy Roberts' house down Maple Heights from our house, and she never got on it again. It was a good sized vehicle, not particularly easy to handle.

Dad and I, usually with Ferris Penn, our Kenton John Deere dealership manager, often went to the wrestling matches in Union City. They were held in the Armory on West Main Street. The Welch Brothers from Yorkville, who were well known wrestlers in this part of the world, were usually on the card. Though we knew full well that the matches were orchestrated, we still got a kick out of them. As hard as it is to believe, a lot of the fans thought the whole thing was on the up and up. It seems to me that many fans still believe that professional wrestling matches are for real.

John Grisham's excellent book, *A Painted House*, brought back wonderful memories for me. The Arkansas town in his book reminded me in many ways of Kenton with our jam-packed main street crowds on Saturday nights with the stores staying open until midnight or later. My growin' up days in Kenton were wonderful. What I'd give to be able to relive just one of them.

405 Maple Heights

My grandfather, C. R. Wade, and his cousin, E.R. Johnson, developed the Maple Heights area of Kenton. My paternal grandparents built the house in which I grew up at 405 Maple Heights in 1922 or 1923.

After marrying in 1925 Mother and Dad rented an apartment in the house of Cousins Clarence and Fanny Bogle, the big two-story house that still sits on the northwest corner of West Taylor and Flowers Streets in Kenton. I think they then rented the house where the Eddie Jones later lived, just across St. Marys Street from 405 Maple Heights. Some time later Mother and Dad bought Dad's parents' house and lived in it for the rest of their lives. After my grandfather died, my grandmother moved to Memphis and lived with Auntie Moselle, Dad's sister, and Uncle George Tucker for the rest of her life.

There were a good many trees in our yard at 405 Maple Heights, a walnut, several maple trees across the front, and a young volunteer oak (which is now a large oak) in the hedge on the north side of the side yard. A wooden picket fence separated our property from that of the Witherspoons to the east. The old maples in the front yard were cut down, probably in the early 1960s, and oaks and magnolias were planted in their places, and oaks were also planted in the backyard. A few years ago I bought the Witherspoon property, tore down the house, and incorporated it into the backyard of the Wade home, now my office. In 2002 I bought the house and lot just east of the Witherspoon property from Gladys Skinner as well as the lot just east of Gladys' property from Bobby Skinner. We just tore down the house formerly owned by Richard Jenkins (playmates Paul and Peggy Jenkins' father) and later Diane Sanderson's parents, Finis and Edna Finch, and have brought both lots into my 405 Maple Heights property.

In 1994 our old home was completely rebuilt converting it into offices for Will and me and for an assistant, Julie Parker, and a meeting or boardroom. For many years Susie Sturdivant has done bookkeeping, payroll, accounts payable, and other clerical functions for us in an office in the downstairs wing which was built in 1960.

In the 20s, 30s, 40s and 50s our house had a long hall that ran around the corner from the bathroom and Sally's room on the south and then straight on into the kitchen on the north side of the house. This hall was a great place to play. Sometimes we would rig up makeshift basketball goals just above the doors on each end and play basketball with a small ball of some sort. You pretty much had to dribble through, not around, folks. The hall wasn't very wide and it wasn't too easy to finess 'em. Mother kept a clothes hamper on the south end of the hall. Often we'd use the hamper on the south end and create a competitive barrier for the north end, turn off the lights, and throw tennis balls back and forth at each other. We threw as hard as we could throw, and it's a wonder somebody didn't get hurt. But nobody ever did. That hall created many hours of rainy day and winter time fun for those of us in the neighborhood. Back then Mother was very lenient in terms of letting us play rough in the hall — but only in the hall — and she did not worry about grass or shrubs in the yard. She let us have fun. Later she was totally fastidious about the house and yard, but she had what I think was the good sense to give us young people pretty much free rein when it came to having a good time.

All of our bedrooms opened off the hall, Sally's, Mother's and Dad's, and mine, from south to north. The front door opened into the living room. The dining room was north of the living room and the kitchen just north of the dining room. The back porch was behind the kitchen. The sunporch was just south of the living room. Though it wasn't a very big house, it seemed like it was to me.

The attic of our house was a fascinating place to spend time alone when the weather did not allow outdoors play. There's no telling how many hours I spent up there. My favorite thing in the attic was an old wind up Victrola that played very thick records. We had dozens of really neat records of priceless songs. My favorite was *You Can't Fool an Old Horsefly*. It goes like this ...

Oh, you can't fool an old horsefly,
Oh, you can't fool an old horsefly,
Now a bee won't hurt you
When he's buzzing around
But Glory Hallelujah when the bee sits down
He'll sting you 'til the clouds roll by
Oh, you can't fool an old horsefly.

All my records "went missing" when the house was rebuilt in 1994. Uncle George Tucker kept the Victrola working, but it has long since been "on the blink."

I was painfully skinny when growing up. Taking a cue from Charles Atlas and working out with my barbells and dumbbells all one winter enabled me to muscle up and gain ten pounds. I wouldn't mind doing that again from the standpoint of muscling up, but I surely don't need an extra ten pounds! Dad had a punching bag put up in the attic. I punched on that durn thing 'til my arms felt like they would fall off.

Another fun thing about growing up was playing with the toys of that era. One such toy was a football game. The game field was on top of a box with a light bulb inside. The offense had a set of big cards the size of the playing field, and the defense had a similar set. They each had areas allowing the light to come through. The offense showed running or passing plays and the defense had circles denoting defensive players in various spots all around the field. If the play lines ran through a circle, the play was stopped there. If a defensive man was in the dotted line of a pass, it was an interception. This was a game that could be played alone. I also had a baseball game which had a dial that you flipped with a finger. The pointer would tell you what that batter did. Obviously this game could also be played alone, though they both were more fun when you had an honest-to-goodness opponent. These games entertained me for hours on end.

About this same time model plane kits made from heavy paper or light cardboard were often put in cereal boxes. Most of the kits required a penny in the nose of the planes in order to make them air worthy. One time I built one — a model of a World War II fighter — which flew absolutely perfectly. It would loop every which way and always come in for a smooth landing. It finally met its end with a horrendous crash. None of my many other cereal planes were even in the class of this blue and white beauty.

Another one of my all-time favorite toys was a little green play car that moved when its pedals were pumped. It had a steering wheel just like a real car. In a magazine I found miniature replicas of the automobile license plates for all 48 states and cut them out and pasted them on the back of my car. To me this car was the grandest one that had ever been pedaled down the pike. What a shame that it was not kept for my children and grandchildren.

Some of my old toys are still in the attic. A recent trip up there yielded the following that I used to play with: two baseball gloves, two pairs of boxing gloves, a football, my old football helmet, baseball, softball, scout knife, canteen, horseshoes set, old handmade slingshot, hatchet, marbles and steelies, set of drum sticks, pitchin' washers, basketball knee pads, boat paddle, old records, baseball books, autographs including Doak Walker's (Sally got these at Camp Nagawicka, Delafield, Wisconsin. One of the NFL teams trained there.), Boy Scouts handbook, and a miniature UT football player.

Sally and I were mighty lucky to have been able to live and grow up at 405 Maple Heights, a pretty house full of love. Mother and Dad taught Sally and me, by example as well as by teachings, the Christian way. Mother and Dad were Christians. They were kind and generous, honest and ethical, hard working and fair minded, fun loving and dependable, and they were wonderful parents.

Tucson

Because of my asthma we spent three winters in Tucson. Cousin Peter Pelham had bad sinus trouble, and Sally had an allergic rash. So the three of us children, Mother, Pete's Mother (Aunt Zedna), maternal Grandmother Walker, and sometimes maternal Great Grandmother Jennie Smith, around the first of the year would pile into our car and head west. It took us a week to get there and a week to get back. I remember how exciting it was each year when the Tucson skyline finally came into view. Each year we rented a different house.

Dad and Uncle Gordon, Pete's Dad, stayed at home, but one winter Dad came out and stayed about a month with us. He crossed Texas in one day, from Texarkana to El Paso, a distance of 800 miles. In those days, on those roads, that sort of thing was almost unheard of. Dad left our Kenton house unlocked the whole time he was gone. Things have changed, haven't they?

We lived close to a park that year in Tucson, and Jennie took us children there often. One day she gave a Mexican man a dime to catch a horned toad for us. We kept it in a shoebox at our house. That winter we all drove to San Diego where Mother, Sally, Peter, and I caught a train to Los Angeles and Dad and the others drove up to Los Angeles to meet us. Immediately after we arrived in the San Diego train station Peter walked away from the rest of us. Mother was frantic until she found him. Pete couldn't understand why she was concerned. He said he wasn't lost; he knew where he was all the time. In Los Angeles we spent several days with a lady who had moved from Dyersburg to Los Angeles and who was a good friend of Grandmother's. Her name was Miss Annie Vinton. (Interestingly, Pat's Mother, Anna Laura Bishop Thurmond, spent a summer with Miss Annie after Mrs. Thurmond graduated from Dyersburg High School and just before she married Pat's Dad, Robert Clarence (Mike) Thurmond, Jr. — what a coincidence! My Pat remembered the address of Miss Annie's house. Pat and I, Will and Kim Wade, and Rance and Patti Wade Barnes — two of our children and their spouses — were in Los Angeles in August 2002 and found that address. The big old house had been replaced by an apartment building. It was an eery feeling to me to be back at that same location.)

When we got back to Tucson the horned toad, which had been left on our back porch in his shoebox almost filled up with sugar for food for him was gone. I was very upset as that little creature was supposed to have gone back to Kenton with us. Wonder if Mother was less perturbed?

Another year we lived in a modern kind of small house next to a vacant lot which was nothing but one big sandbox. We played outside barefoot a lot of the time. The sand would get so hot that we walked in as many shadows, such as those from light poles, as possible.

One night the landlady came to look things over in the third Tucson house in which we stayed. We children had gotten under the kitchen table which swung out from the wall and which had a leg that folded down to support it, and somehow we had broken the whole thing away from the wall. It just collapsed into a heap. Our Mothers and Grandmother did some fancy footwork in order to keep that lady out of the kitchen. My recollection is that they succeeded and got the table repaired.

Our favorite radio program was *The Lone Ranger* with its marvelous theme song, *The Nutcracker Suite*, which came on late every afternoon. We never missed The Lone Ranger, Tonto, and Silver. Hi Ho Silver - - - Away!

We often had chocolate cake from a bakery which was to this day far and away the best chocolate cake I've ever eaten.

Tucson was great fun and I always felt great out there, but my gradually improving asthmatic condition allowed us to discontinue going after those three years.

School Days in Kenton

The first record of a school in Kenton dates back to 1869, but there was probably some sort of organized schooling in Kenton prior to that time.

A two-story brick building was built in 1883 for Miss Ida Flynn's Kenton Institute which later burned down.

The old two-story building where I attended school was built in 1892. It was torn down in 1948. Construction of a new high school and gymnasium was then begun.

Partially because of my asthma and the trips to Arizona, Mother and Dad kept me out of school until 1940, so I missed three months of school only in the winter of 1941. My elementary school in Kenton was the relatively new east building and then we went to the big old two-story school building in the seventh and eighth grades. At some point prior to my entering school in Kenton the old gymnasium had been torn down in anticipation of building a new one which did not occur for too many years. We practiced basketball outdoors on a dirt, or mud court, and we played all away games. While I was in school the best basketball player we ever had in Kenton was Lavan (Cotton) Perryman. He was also the best player in the county, according to lots of folks. Cotton was a magician with a basketball. The old two-story building did have a big room upstairs in which we played basketball. It only had one basket and though the ceilings were pretty high in this old building, they weren't high enough for basketball so we had to practice with low trajectories. A new high school, middle school, and gymnasium were completed in 1950 on the west side of the elementary school. The new academic wing matched the old east wing. It was great to have a nice new gym with a stage for amateur hours, beauty pageants, womanless beauty revues, minstrels, etc. Later a cafeteria was added to the back of the gymnasium which was located between the two academic buildings.

Kenton School was blessed with good teachers. My first grade teacher was Miss Wilmack Walker with whom I immediately fell in love. My second grade teacher was Miss Myla Smith whose brother, Glen, was Tennessee's second Rhodes Scholar. Mrs. Mary Brewer was my third grade teacher, and Cousin Frances Montgomery, a pure delight, was my fourth grade teacher. Miss Hildrith Smith was my fifth grade teacher, and Mrs. Cordia Zaricor was my sixth grade teacher. Junior high and high school teachers, all excellent, were Miss Adrian Baucom (Myers), Mrs. Gertrude Bingham, Mr. J. V. Dowtin, the principal and boys coach, Miss Ruth Hollomon (Tate), Mrs. Ruby Skiles, Miss Wilda Tilghman (Harris), and Mr. Joe Mac Warren. All these people were good teachers, but two of them, Miss Wilda and Miss Adrian, stand out in my mind as two of the very best teachers I ever had. And there were some mighty good ones at McCallie and UT which were to be my next schools.

The 1950 Obion County High School Tournament christened the new gymnasium. Though the tournaments were always packed, the other gyms in the county, including Union City's, were smaller than our new gym and we set new attendance records with 1,500 folks jamming in for all the games. We went early in the afternoons in order to get good seats. What a spectacle it was! A Final Four could not have been more thrilling for me. The girls' and boys' tournaments were held simultaneously. Back then the girls played a half-court game with three forwards and three guards. They were not allowed to cross the centerline. After a score, the other team got the ball at the center circle.

During the building of the new middle and high school wing we had to go to school in the Presbyterian Church (sadly torn down long ago) which was located just west of the school campus and the

Cumberland Presbyterian and Methodist Churches which were located right across the street from the school.

In 1968 a new junior high school building was built northeast of the old elementary school, and a new modern gymnasium was built later with the use of Kenton Special School District funds. In 1986 Kenton High School closed, and a pall fell over Kenton. Then in 1991 we lost our K-8 school, and for the first time since — at the latest — 1869, Kenton had no school. 1986 may well have been the blackest year, other than wartime, in Kenton's history.

Thanks to the never-ending efforts of the present Kenton Special School District Board, a K-3 school opened in the fall of 2002. This beautiful new school is being operated by the Gibson County School Board. I made a major gift to this cause and am delighted to pay the extra taxes that are required. Maybe this school will be expanded some day to include more grades, but at least our very young children will no longer have to be bused to other towns and locations. Having a school in Kenton again will surely help revitalize our fair little city. It is wonderful to again be bullish about the future of Kenton. Our undying gratitude goes out to our most capable and tenacious school board members, Dr. Mike Farrar, Linda Little, Bill Sanderson, Richard Skiles, and Steven Tate.

We played high school softball, not baseball. Our field was on the northwest part of the campus. The town creek cut across right field. A ball hit over the creek was a ground rule double. By far the best softball player we had during my time in school in Kenton was Virgil Roberts. Virtually every time he batted he hit a ground rule double. If we'd had normal fences just about every ball he hit would have been a home run. He had as pure and good a swing as I have ever seen. He was also a great fielder and had a very strong arm. My opinion has always been that if Virgil had grown up in a situation where he could have played baseball all the time with good coaching that he would have had a legitimate shot at the major leagues.

One day playing softball at school, classmate Bobby Witherington and I ran together chasing a fly ball. Bobby was a big raw-boned boy who had a mighty hard elbow which caught my right eyelid against that bone just above the eye and cut it deeply. It was bandaged, but I did not go to the doctor. It became very infected, and Mother took me to old Dr. Gray who sewed it up.

Another time playing softball somebody threw a ball which hit my right forefinger just wrong. It became terribly infected. Mother took me to Dr. Gray again, and he had to lance it before sewing it up. Back in those days no deadening was done before such procedures. He lanced it from the top side of the nail clear down and around to the center of the end of the finger. This time the results were not very good. The infection finally left, but the end of that finger was left somewhat drawn. I learned how to write with my middle finger, and after the forefinger healed it took a while to get back into the swing of writing properly. It takes very little to get my forefinger sore and irritated. Many years later my strong cousin, William Penn, squeezed my hand so hard that blood oozed out of the scar.

As a sophomore I was Kenton's softball team's starting second baseman. Sometimes the coach played me at third base. The first game we played was against Mason Hall. For some reason their pitcher, who was pretty good and fast, threw me change ups the first four times I came up and each time I managed to hit a line drive single just over the infield. The fifth time he got me on a grounder. So I started off batting 800! Our batting averages weren't recorded, but my hits from that point on were mighty few and far between. One time after college graduation I played in a night softball game of some sort on the school diamond and I hit a home run to left field beyond the lights. William Penn, who was an excellent player and had played for UTM's baseball team, told me that my hit might have been the longest softball he had ever seen hit. That was a great compliment coming from him even though his assessment certainly was more than a little too enthusiastic. At any rate it felt mighty good to trot around those bases.

I was on the basketball squad but very seldom played, and when I did it was late in a game that had already been decided. My best shot was a two-handed set shot, a popular shot of those times, from far out. I would have started my junior year if I had not left Kenton High School.

One summer a bunch of us FFA boys from Kenton High School went to Middle Tennessee to State FFA camp. There were several schools represented, and we spent the week in various sporting competitions with each other. Clarkrange won the week's competition, but Kenton came in a close second. The one event that we swept was pool. We had lots of boys who hung around the poolrooms in town, and we had some real pool sharks, especially Howard Duncan Taylor. That was the only sport in which I did not participate. Mother and Dad would never let me go to poolrooms. Actually poolrooms didn't particularly appeal to me anyway.

The most exciting event in the history of Kenton Schools had to be the 50s high school basketball team that went to the state tournament. This was back in the days before schools were placed in classifications according to enrollment, and the top 16 teams in the state, regardless of school size, went to the state tournament. Mr. Joe Norvell was coach, and the players were Clifton Bryant, Wayne Coday, Sonny Dement, Paul Hicks, Gene Johnson, Billy Sanderson, Paul Taylor, Buddy Viniard, Sonny Watkins, and Dwayne Williams. Kenton's total population was smaller than the enrollment of the next smallest school in the tournament. Before the first tip-off I was told, and read, that Mr. Norvell got up on the playing floor of the Vanderbilt gymnasium with his leather-soled shoes. He was admonished not to do that so he had to spend the rest of the first game down on the floor which was a foot or so lower than the playing surface. Mr. Norvell was an excitable man and during the course of the game he somehow got his hat turned backwards. He wore a business suit and tie and was very proper looking except for his hat. After the first game, which Kenton won in a huge upset, Mr. Norvell went out and bought a pair of white rubber-soled sneakers. The crowd loved it when he came to the gym for the quarterfinal game wearing his white sneakers and crooked hat (he had suddenly become superstitious and pretty much of a ham).

We in Kenton were used to the antics of two of Kenton's staunchest basketball fans, Jack Davis and Walter Cross, but Nashville was fascinated with these two fellows. These old men came early and sat on the front row if at all possible. However, their seats didn't matter much, as they spent most of their time walking, jumping, and prancing on the sidelines, each trying to outdo the other. They razzed the opponents unmercifully while entreating our boys to put forth Herculean efforts. I guarantee they made the difference in more than one game! Some of us watched them almost as much as we watched the games. They were worth the price of admission.

I listened to Kenton's first game against Nashville Bellevue on the front porch of our Pike House at UT. Underdog Kenton came from behind to win. John Ward, later the enormously popular Voice of the Vols, announced the game. He pronounced Sonny Dement's name with the accent on the first syllable which was incorrect. He pronounced Wayne Coday's name with the accent on the last syllable which also was incorrect. Otherwise he did a great job and got me all excited. I decided to go over for the quarterfinal game and talked Brother Dan Johnson into going with me, fully expecting to come back to Knoxville after the game. On the way over we stopped to eat at a favorite restaurant of mine in Sparta and I bought a day old Nashville newspaper. The respected Litkenhous Ratings showed Kenton ranked 16th out of 16, something like 15 points worse than #15. I started to turn around right then and go back to Knoxville. But we went on to Nashville where Kenton took on Knoxville Fulton and won that game also against great odds. We stayed another night to see Kenton play in the semifinal game against two-time state champion Linden to which Kenton lost, thereby putting them in the consolation bracket of the tournament. Dan and I continued to cut classes and stayed over still another night to watch Kenton lose the consolation game by one point to Summertown to place fourth in the state. Entering the state tournament with a record of 13 and 13, Kenton certainly deserved its designation as the tournament's Cinderella team. Kenton was the favorite team of all but the fans of the team we were playing, and the Warriors were the darlings of the media. Kenton's team uniforms were not uniform. The first string's uniforms pretty well matched but that was not the case with the substitutes. This was another thing that endeared Kenton's boys to the people of Nashville. Kenton's Buddy Viniard was selected Most Valuable Player and received the most votes for the All-Tournament Team.

Prior to the 1957 team, the best Kenton had ever done in modern times was a third place finish in a district tournament. We must remember, however, that for many of those years we did not have a gymnasium and our teams had to practice outdoors and play all away games.

Again in 1972 Kenton's basketball team earned a berth in the state tournament under the coaching of Marty Sisco. They gained this distinction by defeating Union City by a single point 42-41, in the regional championship game at McKenzie. As was the case back in 1957, there still were no classifications at this time. Therefore, Kenton once again was playing against schools with enrollments as large or larger than the entire population of the town of Kenton. Kenton took on Boliver in the first round of the state tournament and was defeated. Marty took Kenton to one other state tournament appearance in 1983 and was defeated in the semi-final round by Hampton. As an aside, when Kenton's high school was closed in 1986, Marty was hired at Union City to teach and coach, and while there led Union City's basketball teams to three state tournament championships. One other note about Marty is that his dad, Arthur, worked for Dad for several years, and they lived in the brick house on the Brick House farm a mile north of Kenton. Marty was born in the brick house which is known to be the oldest house in the Kenton area. There is no doubt in my mind but that Marty could have been a successful college coach. He handled boys and game situations brilliantly. He is now a stockbroker.

Back in those days the main, and just about only, cash crops were cotton and strawberries. The majority of students were "country" children whose fathers farmed. The parents needed their children to help them make a living. Our school year started in the middle of the summer, after cotton chopping was pretty much finished. Then we "let out" when cotton picking started, usually the latter part of August to early September. Then we went back to school after almost all the cotton was picked and the bolls pulled, usually around the first of November. We then stayed in school, except for a very short Christmas break, until strawberry season began which normally was around the early part of May. We stayed out while strawberries were picked and cotton planted (these two endeavors coincided) and cotton was chopped. Then another school year would begin in the middle of the summer. Man, it was hot in those classrooms in July and August. Of course, this was before air conditioning. Schools around here continued to let out for cotton picking until the early to mid sixties. By that time, however, strawberries were no longer an important part of the mix so berry season no longer determined any part of our school year.

During elementary school days we Kenton school children used to go to Union City and march in the "Blue Ribbon Parades." All the schools in Obion County would participate. Eligibility to march had something to do with brushing your teeth. One year several of us Kentonians, after the parade, went to the Red Star Drug Store for milkshakes and ice cream sodas. That was my first soda. The Red Star had the best, thickest, tastiest milkshakes in the world. They made their own ice cream. It was a sad day when it closed.

There were 13 good people in our graduating class of 1952. They were: Charles Ashe (class president and a very bright boy who retired from Memphis to Kenton); Jesstine Battles; Patricia Crain (a sweet girl who as a youngster pronounced Dyer, "Die-were"); E. C. Eddings (The best athlete in our class, E. C. retired from a supervisory position with Brown Shoe Company in Trenton to Kenton. E. C. helps us with our strawberries and goes with me to an occasional Tennessee football game, still a true friend); Jere Fowler (class vice-president and close friend and fraternity brother at UT, he was a veterinarian in Memphis who died years ago); Geraldine Goodman (class treasurer); Joyce Holt (a sweet girl and lady who retired from up north to Kenton); Shirley Long (as sweet a girl as ever came down the pike who married Harold Wayne Long); Jimmy Stansberry (a good athlete who pretty much marched to his own drummer; nothing wrong with that); Wanda Tucker (Long) (class secretary and one of my favorite people, she was widowed and later retired to Kenton from Memphis and Mississippi and married Kentonian Jimmy Long); John Wells (retired from Goodyear and retired from Union City to Kenton. John and his sister, Betty, moved from Memphis to Kenton with their Mother, an old Kenton girl, and lived in her homeplace across the street from us. John, Betty, Sally, and I played together every day); Bobby

Witherington (a true southern gentleman who went to UT with me and who became a Church of Christ preacher. Now living in Seffner, Florida); and Elma Wolfe. All thirteen of these people moved away. Five of them, Charles, E. C., Joyce, John, and Wanda came back to Kenton. To me this is a remarkable fact. Kenton ain't no big place, but it sure can tug at your heartstrings. Another member of our class who moved to Dyersburg and graduated there was Vera Dell Davis. Vera Dell always sang in the Amateur Hours, very well in fact.

As a postscript to tales of the school, in late May, 2003, we had a reunion of those who had attended school in Kenton. Almost 400 from coast to coast attended. The reunion was marvelous in every way; I saw folks I hadn't laid eyes on for 55 years. One of those, Jerry Primrose, was a world class competitive cotton picker. He told me that his best day was 928 pounds! He seemed to be most proud of a 31 consecutive day streak of over 600 pounds per day average! Remember my all-time best day was 100 pounds.

"School days, school days, dear old golden rule days. Reading and writing and 'rithmetic. Talk to the tune of a hickory stick." What wonderful times were those innocent and happy school days in Kenton.

Mayo Clinic

We Wades have been going to Mayo Clinic for a long time. My grandmother, Lida Belle Wade, had a kidney removed by one of the original Mayo Brothers. Sally and I went with Mother, Grandmother, Jennie, Aunt Zedna and Peter Pelham to Mayo a couple of times when we were young. The first year I remember being there we stayed at the old Damon Hotel. It was fairly cheap, and in those days that was the main thing we looked for in lodging. Another time we stayed at the Zumbro Hotel which was a medium priced hotel. One of my favorites has always been beef stew, and the Zumbro Cafeteria made great beef stew. The Kahler was the best hotel in town, and probably still is, but we opted for cheaper hostelries.

Mother had extremely high blood pressure when she was in her upper forties, and she had a series of extraordinarily complicated surgeries at Mayo. She had two scars on her back that each must have been eighteen inches long. Dr. Jim Hunt, former Head of Medicine at Mayo who came to Memphis to head up the UT Medical Units, was fascinated to hear about Mother's having had these sympathectomies for high blood pressure. He said that Mayo only did about 300 of them. Of course there's good medicine for high blood pressure now, but that was not the case back then. Mother had several other surgeries at Mayo through the years.

One time soon after I graduated from college Dad was driving Mother to Mayo for some reason when he had a wreck in Davenport, Iowa, resulting in very serious injuries to Dad. I remember Uncle Eugene Wade came to the ballpark down at the Kenton School where I was playing ball that night to tell me about it. Mother hired an ambulance plane to fly them on to Rochester where Dad entered St. Marys Hospital. Instead of having herself seen about, Mother helped nurse Dad back to health. In Davenport they had come to a Y intersection, and Dad and another person drove into the intersection at the same time, slamming the cars together on Dad's driver's side. Dad's entire left side was broken, his collarbone, his shoulder, his shoulder blade, his arm, and several ribs. He came home with his left arm in a wing splint. He recovered nicely, the only visible result being that his shoulder blade lapped over somewhat, leaving a bump on it. Also his left side sagged a little afterwards, but his life was barely affected long term.

When Dad was about 70 years old he became very ill. He first went to Baptist Hospital in Memphis, but they were unable to do anything for him. Mother again chartered a plane and flew him to Rochester. His condition worsened. They didn't know what was wrong with him. At one point Dad said he counted 12 physicians in his room while they mulled over what to do. He was told that if they did exploratory surgery his survival chances would be no better than 50-50. Dad asked his doctor what he recommended, and the doctor said he thought he would hold off another day. They held off surgery day to day, and soon his condition improved so that he finally was well enough to come home. Dad always felt that their conservative approach might well have saved his life. The probable diagnosis was pancreatitis, but that was not a certainty.

Pat, Will, and I went to Mayo in January of 1996 to see if anything could be done about our headaches. While we were there we went through the clinic and received very thorough checkups. We stayed at the Kahler and enjoyed going from place to place through the tunnels that honeycomb downtown Rochester. Will and I were told that we suffer from classic migraines, and Pat was told that she also had migraine headaches, but they are on the opposite end of the spectrum from Will's and mine. The sad news is that very little is known about headaches, though Will and I now use a different kind of medicine that helps a great deal.

Through the years I have recommended Mayo Clinic to a good many folks. Their teamwork approach just makes sense to me. If any of us ever has some unusual malady, my hope is that he or she will go to Mayo in Rochester. In my opinion that's where a fair amount of the world's medical power is located.

Kenton Cumberland Presbyterian Church

The Kenton Cumberland Presbyterian Church was organized in August, 1867, and the present building was completed in 1908. My opinion has always been that our Cumberland Presbyterian original church building is one of the prettiest little churches anywhere. My Grandmother, Lida Belle "Granny Nanny" Wade, designed this Greek Revival structure. My Grandfather gave the land where it sits. He owned "The Opera House" which was located on this property, and he moved it to a lot on the eastern fringe of town where Mr. and Mrs. Arch Taylor lived until they died. In 1952 an annex consisting of seven classrooms, a kitchen, and a fellowship hall was added. An educational annex was added in 1960. Adrian Baucom Myers told me recently that Dad talked to her Mother and probably some others, to see if they thought it would be all right if he bought a plaque in memory of his Mother and Dad and had it mounted on the front wall of the church. Dad was told that it would be perfectly all right and appropriate. So he did. About 20 years ago, it was Sally's and my great pleasure to give two stained glass windows, which my wife Pat designed, to the church in memory of Dad and in honor of Mother who was still living at the time. Mother's is now also marked "in memory of."

Mother often had our ministers and their families for Sunday dinner after church. We sometimes had the visiting preacher for our week's revival as our houseguest. In these cases most of his meals were taken in our home. One year we had a preacher from Sherman, Texas. He challenged the congregation to read verses from the Bible, the more the better. I read a few more each day, and on the final night of the revival I proudly announced that my Bible reading had totaled something over 800 verses that day. That was far and away the most that anybody had read. In the last few years I have read the Bible through twice. The first time was started by my reading several chapters in Genesis in a Gideon Bible while waiting for Pat at her periodontist's office in Memphis. The second reading was in a Bible given to me by Patti and Rance that is organized in such a way as to read it clear through in a year. I opted to read it through in two years.

Three of our ministers, Phillip Dozier (of long ago), John E. Gardner, and John Stammer Smith served as moderators of the General Assembly, the Cumberland Presbyterian Church's top position. Also at various times our Joe Ferris Penn was chosen Superintendent of the Year, Mrs. Karon Howell Teacher of the Year, and Mrs. Creeda Smith Teacher of the Years, not a bad record for our little church.

In my childhood our church was a very strong one, but sadly its membership is smaller now. The Kenton Cumberland Presbyterian Church played a vital role in Sally's and my upbringing.

Family Trips

Our family, Mother, Dad, Sally, usually Grandmother, and I often traveled out west in our automobile during the summers. In the course of our travels we covered almost all the contiguous states. As of this writing I have been in all 50 states with the exception of Maine. We will go to Maine one of these days. Pat and I were in the Canadian Rockies in June 2000, and being at Chateau Lake Louise brought back memories of being there with the above four. It was either at Lake Louise or at Sun Valley when 10 or 11 year old Sally and Dad tripped the light fantastic to the music of their orchestra. On the Canadian Rockies trip we also visited the American northwest, and in the three weeks that we were traveling Dad drove 7,500 miles. We spent a night at a big hotel in downtown Calgary. Grandmother, Sally, and I had seafood cocktails with our dinner in their fine restaurant, and we were all sick the next day. That dining room wasn't so fine after all!

One year when traveling out west we pulled into a filling station in Oregon. The man who was filling our car, obviously having seen our license plate, said, "Y'all from Tennessee?" Mother, "Yes." The filling station attendant asked, "Where from?" Mother answered, "Memphis." He said, "Well I'll be doggone, I'm from Union City." Mother said, "I didn't really think you'd know our town, but we're from Kenton." To which the man replied, "Wellum, I'm actually from Mason Hall." True story. Tis a small world.

On another western trip we ate in a restaurant in a small town. Dad, who always wore a hat, hung it on a hook in this little café and forgot it. When we got home Mother called the mayor of the town and asked him to mail it to Dad. She said he seemed to be a little irritated but he finally agreed to do it. The hat arrived all squashed into a little brown box. It was so wrinkled and bent up that Dad was no longer able to wear it. Mother could be mighty persistent, but sometimes — not often — the other person got the best of her.

One year we headed somewhere toward the east, when I was probably 10 or 12 years old. The first night we spent in an old hotel in Red Boiling Springs, Tennessee. Red Boiling Springs used to be a big vacation destination back when mineral springs were considered to be good for you. There are still two or three hotels left, but at the turn of the century there were probably 15 or 20. The next morning everybody got up and went out on the grounds of the hotel and drank from its spring. The water tasted like rotten eggs and I pleaded with Mother and Dad not to make me drink it, but they insisted. We left and headed northeast, but soon they had to stop and let me out of the car to take care of my nausea.

We continued on to Corbin, Kentucky where we stopped for dinner at a picturesque restaurant that probably was recommended by Duncan Hines. (Mother swore by Duncan Hines' recommendations, and she planned our trips so that, if at all possible, we could sleep and eat in places that he recommended.) I remember vividly the owner of the restaurant who was a real old fashioned looking man with white flowing hair and a white goatee and mustache. In later years this man became Colonel Sanders of Kentucky Fried Chicken fame. Incidentally the Colonel was a Pike! Our family refers to Kentucky Fried Chicken as "Colonel Chicken."

One time we were in Gatlinburg when Sally and I were young, and we went swimming in the Little Pigeon River. After we had been swimming awhile, I noticed a little snake fairly close to us, and upon looking closer, there was a whole nest of little snakes. Needless to say, this wound up our swimming for the day.

One time our family, along with the Gus Pharrs from Dallas, took a trip together up through the Midwest and ended at the source of the Mississippi River at Lake Itasca. My classmates at school could not believe that Sally and I had sat in the middle of the Mississippi River. Some of them may not believe it to this day.

I grew up being an avid fan of the Tennessee Volunteers. Dad took me to a good many Vol games through the years. Back then we played Ole Miss in Memphis every year, and we never missed that game. Every other year UT played Vanderbilt in Nashville, and we never missed that game. In fact Dad claimed, up until his last few years, that he had never missed a UT-Vandy game in Nashville from the time he entered UT in 1916. Once we were sitting in the south horseshoe of the stadium at a game in Knoxville when a beautiful UT cheerleader brought me a miniature football signed by all the Vol players of that season. Somehow they picked me, out of the enormous crowd, to get that football. What a wonderful surprise! That football is still around somewhere. I saw it not too many years ago.

When in Knoxville, Dad always took me by the Pike House. This fact is probably the reason why I ended up being a Pike; more about that later. Tom Henry, who had graduated from McCallie, Bill Taylor, and Charlie Williams were always especially nice to me.

We also saw the Vols basketball team play in Memphis on a few occasions. Once we saw them play in the old auditorium in Memphis when their All-American star, Paul Walther, was on the team. He was a smooth and polished player.

One time in St. Louis Dad took me to see the St. Louis University Billikens play in old Kiel Auditorium. They had a great team at that time, one of the top teams in the country. Their All-American and arguably best college player in America, "Easy" Ed McCauley, reminded me of Walther. Ed was much taller, though.

One summer the Pelhams took me with them to the Gulf Coast on vacation. Unfortunately it rained almost all week and we played a lot of gin rummy. One day, between rains, we went deep-sea fishing. I caught a 15 pound jack crevelle on the 15th of the month. It took several minutes to land him which happened at 15 minutes to the hour, and I was 15 years old at the time. At that precise moment 15 had become my lucky number. Wonder if it still is? Might as well be. Why not?

At one point a little turtle with something painted on its shell was my favorite pet. I treasured my turtle and insisted on taking him on a trip we took out west. After a long hard day of driving we pulled into Kansas City and the Muhlbach, a famous downtown hotel, to spend the night. Dad turned the car over to the doorman to put it in their garage for the night. When we got to our room it suddenly dawned on me that my turtle was nowhere to be found. I was distraught and could just imagine my little turtle lost on the dangerous downtown streets of Kansas City. The next morning when they brought the car to us for our journey on into the West, my turtle was sitting on the passenger side running board. Me and my turtle were mighty happy to be leaving Kansas City in the dust.

Pat's and my family have not traveled as a family unit nearly as much as did Mother's and Dad's family. Seems like we just have so many things going on nowadays that we have very little time when we can all be together. That's not a good thing.

Peter Pelham and Dyersburg

Outside of immediate family my favorite person in the world was my first cousin, Peter Pelham of Dyersburg. Peter was the only child of Gordon and Zedna Pelham, I was an only son, and we were almost like brothers. We visited back and forth a great deal. When he came to Kenton for a week or so I was in Seventh Heaven. And it was great for me to go to Dyersburg to visit him in their home in Latta Woods. Latta Woods really was a woods back then. The Bairds built the first house in Latta Woods, and the Pelhams built the second one. During World War II for hours on end we played a "Junior Commandos" game which consisted primarily of our jumping off of a small dirt cliff to a hump of dirt across a little ditch and a few feet below. This gully area was behind Joanne and Barbara Baird's house. We'd do this over and over again, and on some days we must have jumped 100 times or more. We played with the Baird girls, Tommy Rosser, and Billy Cloar and to a lesser degree Patsy Smith and the younger Scott Rosser. There were many adventurous things to do in the woods including swinging on grape vines and catching small snakes and putting them into fruit jars. I never again touched a snake after we decided the last snake we caught was in fact a young rattlesnake.

On summer Saturday afternoons we'd walk to downtown Dyersburg and go to the Ritz Theater on the square. They always had a double feature, usually westerns, a serial, a cartoon, and previews of coming attractions. We always sat through the whole program twice. We'd get back to Peter's house shortly before dark. Later on the Ritz became a less desirable theater, and we then usually went to the Frances Theater. Long ago there was a third movie theater downtown, the Capitol, but we hardly ever went there. Peter and I used to love the hamburgers at the Silver Castle. They had two diners in Dyersburg, and we would rather have had their hamburgers than to have dined at the Waldorf.

My Aunt Zedna was one of the world's good people. She was sweet and gentle, and everybody loved her. She contracted tuberculosis at a fairly young age and succumbed at age 61. What a loss! Uncle Gordon was one of the four original vice presidents of Mr. Wheeler's Dyersburg Cotton Products, later to be called Dyersburg Fabrics. (The other three were Robert Cloar, Bill Hamer, and Byrl Jernigan.) Uncle Gordon was a bit formal and at times a little hard to figure out. As time went by, though, I became totally comfortable with Uncle Gordon and was always very, very fond of him. Evening meals at the Pelhams were much more formal than were ours in Kenton. We usually ate pretty early, around 6:00, and Uncle Gordon always carved. It seemed like they very often had a roast. Dinnertime in Latta Woods, with its formality, unnerved me considerably. As time went by, however, dinner with the Pelhams became more and more pleasant.

My visits to Dyersburg during those long ago summers were tremendously fun. Latta Woods was full of great friends.

Peter, though only three months older, was always quite a bit taller and bigger than I was. Rocks must have been my equalizer, as I threw them at Peter fairly often. His defense was to twirl himself 'round and 'round, proclaiming that his circular motion made the rocks glance off without hurting him. It must have worked; he never seemed to have suffered any real damage from my rock hurling.

Mother and Aunt Zedna decided Peter and I should wear corduroy knickers in the winter, so we wore them for a lot of years despite the fact that they hung down around our ankles, rather than staying up just below the knees as they were supposed to be worn. We wore long socks, often mighty droopy, which were supposed to cover the elastic bands at the bottom of the knickers. I was the only boy in Kenton who had to wear them, and Pete may also have been Dyersburg's only "knickers boy." We were both mighty relieved when we outgrew those ugly things.

One cold day when we were teenagers Peter and I took a small outboard motorboat across the Mississippi River to hunt ducks from a sandbar. The weather worsened, and the wind picked up. We headed back across the river with the waves getting higher and higher and with the spray hitting and stinging our faces. Getting back to the east bank of the Mississippi was a great relief. We took our lives into our hands that day. We should have stayed on that sandbar and waited for better weather or help before crossing the mighty Mississippi.

Peter's death on January 25, 1976 in the crash of his own plane, leaving five little children, was one of the hardest things I've ever endured. He left a widow, Joy, three daughters, Zedna Kate, Gaye, and Wendy, and two stepsons, Jeff and Jim. Peter was a marvelous person, a true southern gentleman. His death was a great loss to many.

My childhood was greatly enriched by my favorite cousin, William Peter Pelham.

Chapter Two

Life in and Around Kenton

The 1940 census pegged Kenton's population at 892. The 1950 population was also 892. Some people died, some were born, some moved in, some moved out, obviously all in perfect balance. Later on at one point Kenton's population exceeded 1,500, but it has now settled back down to the range of 1,300.

I'm proud of Kenton for many reasons, our White Squirrels being one of them. Kenton has had wild White Squirrels for well over 100 years. There are several theories as to how they got started in Kenton, but nobody really knows for sure just how they chose our fair town to be their home. Kenton, Olney, Illinois, and Marionville, Missouri are the only three towns in the nation that have colonies of these white beauties.

Until 12 or 14 years ago I never remember seeing a squirrel in Kenton other than a White Squirrel. About that time a few gray squirrels started coming into Kenton and crossing with our whites. This greatly disturbed me, but maybe it's not all bad. It's entirely possible that some crossing, as long as the whites are dominant in numbers, might be good for the gene pool. It has always been remarkable to me as to how our White Squirrels have lasted for so many years with the obvious inbreeding that has occurred for all these many decades. Nevertheless, White Squirrels have continued to flourish in Kenton, possibly with some crossing with grays. Kenton might be well served to get some expert advice along this line.

Ten or fifteen years ago a local boy, Terry Stansberry, who was a student at the University of Tennessee at Martin, interested somebody in their Biology Department in the White Squirrels of Kenton. They did two counts, a year apart, and estimated that there were something over 200 White Squirrels in Kenton. Through the years I have occasionally become concerned about their numbers, but somehow they always seem to snap back. They are resilient little creatures. In

2002 some sort of disease wiped out dozens of them, but this scary situation seems to have run its course. However, their numbers now seem to be at a very low ebb. Through the years their primary killers have been cats and cars. Our city government has a law on the books which prohibits cats from roaming the neighborhoods, but this law is winked at by some and to my knowledge has never been enforced. Several times cats have strolled across my office lawn with freshly killed, partially eaten White Squirrels in their mouths. This almost makes me physically ill. White Squirrels are synonymous with Kenton, and I love them both.

I have fairly often come across White Squirrels that have been killed by automobiles. If they are disfigured I bury them. If not, I take them to a taxidermist and keep them or give them to family members. We currently have ten in my Kenton office/homeplace, two in our Union City home, and many in family homes across the nation. My fond hope is that Kenton will have White Squirrels for centuries to come.

Incidentally, white and fox (or red) squirrels do not cross. Their genetics are different. To my knowledge no fox squirrel has set foot in Kenton for at least the past 69 years!

Cousins Charlie Freeman and James Hamilton were heroes to me. Once James told me he'd give me a nickel if I ever killed a bird with my B.B. gun. This proud little fella was finally able to tell James that he had actually killed a bird. When James reached into his pocket, I said, "Oh that's o.k." The vivid memory of sticking my head out our front door as James walked by on the sidewalk seems almost as if it were yesterday.

Charlie has a beautiful voice. He and his wife, Joyce, came up from Tampa to a Cumberland Presbyterian homecoming a few years ago. Charlie sang three songs, one of which, *I Come to the Garden Alone*, he dedicated to Mother's memory. As Charlie mentioned, it was Mother's favorite song. The lump that arose in my throat stayed there for the rest of the service.

With thanks to Dorotha O. Norton, author of the excellent book, *Kenton: Folklore and Fact*, the following excerpts from her book will give the reader a sense of the social activities of Kenton in olden days:

"We went to see the girls in their houses; one night each week we'd invite them to supper at the hotel ... We didn't have dances; that was frowned on ... We'd all go serenading ... hayrides on moonlit nights ... it was wholesome ... there was no unfilled longing in life ... there was the Citizen's Band; it was a brass band and had a band wagon ... we had dinners for our friends ... some clubs ... a needlework club ... the Review Club. There was the Opera House [which my Grandfather, C. R. Wade, owned] where the Cumberland Presbyterian Church is now; it was used for entertainment — school plays and programs, and there was roller skating in part of it ... picnics to Smith's Spring ... going to the depot on Sunday afternoons to "meet the train," mostly to wave at the engineers and brakemen ... a baseball team to brag about [Dad played third base on a good Kenton team]. Knights of Pythias ... Modern Woodmen, and the Masons ... They had dinners and things for the wives sometimes ... One time there was a parade in Kenton; people were doing whatever they were engaged in - there were even women sewing on sewing machines pulled along in the wagons." [*My mother used to make her old ornate foot peddle-powered Singer Sewing Machine sing!*]

Recollections of Troy Bryant *(as told to Tom Wade, Jr.)*

On October 12, 1908 Troy Bryant was born in McNairy County, Tennessee to Mr. and Mrs. Mac Bryant. In November of 1910 Mr. and Mrs. Bryant, Troy, and Troy's seven siblings moved to the Macedonia community east of Kenton.

Troy was the youngest of eight children. His brother, Corbett, was a farmer and was the father of Macedonia's Mary Louise Davis. Troy's son, Theodore, and his wife, Margie, also live in Macedonia as do two of their three children, Teddy and Rebecca. A third child, Lois, lives in Illinois. As of this writing Macedonia is still full of Bryants.

Troy went to school at Macedonia through the fifth grade. A typical lunch that he carried to school in a half gallon bucket would be a hard boiled egg, a piece of meat, a biscuit, and a fried pie *(sounds pretty good to me)*. As was the case with so many farm children back in those days, he had to quit school in order to help his father put in and harvest the crop.

44

In 1912 Mr. Troy's father bought the Wilton Wade home place and they moved there. (*Wilton was my Grandfather's brother and was a big strawberry grower.*) The Bryants, as were most people back in those days, were farmers. Their cash crop was cotton. Cotton was about all there was to grow for money back then. The only livestock they kept were mules, a couple of mares, two milk cows, and enough hogs to kill for their own use. They belonged to a beef club which was headquartered at the nearby Keathley place. Several families who belonged to a beef club would go together and kill a beef every now and then. Troy's father, Mr. Mac Bryant, hung his beef about 20 feet down in a well where it would stay cool and keep. Mrs. Bryant would then cut off whatever they needed each day.

Of course they drank their own milk and churned their own butter. They had a large garden and Mrs. Bryant canned everything under the sun. They had two cellars where they kept sweet and Irish potatoes as well as their canned goods. One way they stored turnips and potatoes was to hill them out in the garden after they were dug. First they put up a ridge of dirt in a circle. Then they lined the ground inside the circle with hay. They stacked their potatoes and turnips on the hay. Then more hay was put on top of them and dirt was put on top of the hay. They dug out potatoes and turnips as needed from the edge of the circle. Then that spot was covered again. These vegetables did not freeze and stayed in perfect condition throughout the winter. Troy says that the children loved to run out into the garden after school and pull up a big onion and eat it along with a piece of middlin' meat. He says that was their idea of some mighty good eatin'.

Just about the only things they had to buy were sugar, salt, and flour. They took corn for crushing to Monroe's Mill which was located on part of what is now our Wade Gin Company lot in Kenton. As payment for the resulting cornmeal, Mr. Monroe took some of the corn that his customers brought in. No money changed hands.

Troy says the winters when he was young were much rougher than what we experience this day and time. He remembers the very severe winter of 1917. He said it had already snowed 18 inches by November 30. It continued to snow and there was a great deal on the ground clear on up to the latter part of January. The Bryant family, and most other people, burned wood. He says it got so rough at one time that people had to cut their shade trees for firewood because the snow was too deep for them to get back into the woods. He says some people would stick a log straight into the fireplace. They kept pushing the log in as it burned until the entire log was burned up. He remembers that during those severe winters, ponds frequently froze over to the extent that they could skate on them for days on end.

Mr. Troy Bryant has seen some truly amazing changes during his 95 years, 93 of which he has spent in the proud and historic country community of Macedonia.

One of Kenton's biggest cotton and strawberry farmers was Mr. Lee Paschall. He was always one of the last to finish his various jobs, especially in getting his cotton out. It was said that one year when his first berry hands got out of the truck, he gave them the following choices: pick strawberries, chop his new strawberry patch, pull bolls from his last year's cotton patch, or chop his new cotton patch. He was our loyal gin customer, and just about every year he was the last man to bring cotton to the gin.

In the early part of the 20th Century Kenton was home to a pretty doggone sophisticated practical joker named Reuben Clark who was the town barber. His downtown neighbors on each side of his barbershop were Joe Potter who ran a shoe shop and Leonard Newbill who owned Kenton's café. Any out-of-town person who entered any of these establishments, especially if he were the "stuffed shirt" type of man, was subject to becoming the "judge" of a badger fight. Clark, by reputation a past riverboat gambler and a man of aristocratic airs, was usually the one to create excitement in the stranger about a badger fight that had been scheduled for an hour or so hence. The stranger was told that Mr. Potter had a dog that had never been defeated by a badger. As the appointed hour drew near, Potter's dog became more and more agitated, barking and straining at his leash as a wooden box containing the badger, with a rope tied to it, was placed in the center of Kenton's main street. Word quickly spread around town and a large number of the local citizenry gathered for the monumental fight between the badger and the dog. The stranger was advised to roll up his pants legs as blood would soon be all over the place. At a signal the

46

judge was to jerk the rope, and he was admonished to quickly run in order to get away from the ensuing bloody battle. Clark would then move out into the middle of the circle of people surrounding the badger while Potter held his little dog's leash as the dog became more and more excited. Clark would then explain the rules of the fight as people placed bets back and forth. The signal was given, the dog was turned loose, and the judge jerked the rope. Out bounced a chamber pot and the dog attacked it in every way possible, shaking it and jerking the slop jar all over the street. The hundreds of locals howled with hilarity while the judge either joined in the merriment or stalked off, promising to never again darken the portals of Kenton. Someone once told me that many years ago there was a homemade sign way down in Mississippi advising people never to go to Kenton, Tennessee. Some "judge" must have painted that sign.

When I was a child there were several blacksmith shops in Kenton including two or three below the railroad. There was one down in the area where Maggie Lancaster, Mother's and Pat's long time loyal maid, lived. My recollection is that it was on the street that runs north and south just west of her house. There was a blacksmith in Kenton at that time named Bates Ridgeway who was known to be an extraordinarily strong man. He died young. Mr. Hollandsworth, my friend Jackie's daddy, also had a blacksmith shop down St. Marys Street from our house.

Fifty-five or sixty years ago, the barbershops in Kenton (and probably everywhere around here) had showers in them. Especially on Saturday men would come in and pay the barber for the shower. He would be issued a towel and some soap, and he would go back into the back room and into one of the shower stalls and take a shower. Obviously many people back then did not have bathrooms in their homes. Also, country folks did not have electricity. Every town had an icehouse and ice trucks which made regular rounds through the country, leaving ice at the farm houses where they would put it into their iceboxes to keep their food cool.

When I was a youngster we had a little saying that went like this, "Shave and a haircut, six bits. Who's the barber? Tom Mix." Don't ask me why we enjoyed this little poem so much, but we did.

In the 30s and 40s the GM&O Railroad had a little passenger train that we affectionately called "The Dinky." One time Mother, Grandmother, and Sally went to St. Louis on The Dinky. Stopping at every little town between Kenton and St. Louis meant that it took them a long, long time to get there. They never again took the train to St. Louis.

There used to be a saying having to do with the railroad in our version of the Tri-Cities, "Dyer Station, Rutherford Switch, and Kenton Jump!" Guess that indicates where we stood in the pecking order, at least in the eyes of Rutherforders and Dyerites. But we Kentonians never subscribed to that assessment of our relative importance.

In the 1960s there was a train wreck on the GM&O right in the middle of Kenton, and the whole train piled onto the depot. It happened on a Sunday, and fortunately nobody was there because it absolutely demolished the depot.

In the old days in Kenton we had two phone systems, the Bell system and the Home system. You either had one or the other (or none). You couldn't call from one to the other. Lots of folks were on "party lines" where several people had the same number and would (supposedly) pick up only for their own ring. For instance, one party would pick up for two rings, another for three rings, and so on. Some folks quietly picked up on just about every ring. It was pretty hard to keep secrets if you were on a party line. If the truth be known, party lines might well have been called "gossip" lines!

Young Eddie Jones from Rutherford began a long career in the telephone business as the night switchboard operator for the Rutherford Home Telephone Company in the early 20s. He set type for the old *Rutherford Register* by day. Back in those days there weren't many calls late at night and small town night operators had the opportunity to do a good bit of sleeping. Eddie switched a lot of calls for a delightful feminine voice from near Yorkville. Over time he became infatuated with that voice and finally asked if he could meet the lady behind the voice. Miss Willie Norman agreed and soon she was the daytime operator for the Rutherford Home phone system.

The Home phone office was located on the second floor of a building on Rutherford's main street. There was a one-story building with a flat roof adjacent to their building, and it so happened that the Cumberland Telephone Company's office was on the second floor of the building next to that building. The Cumberland night operator and Eddie were friends. Sometimes Eddie would cover for his buddy whose company wasn't really doing much business. Eddie and his friend would open their windows and Eddie scurried back and forth across the roof through the night as the rings alternated.

Before long Eddie and Miss Willie got married and moved to Kenton to handle the switchboard here for the Southern Bell Telephone Company. Eddie worked at night and Miss Willie worked in the daytime. Eddie said that their beginning salary in 1925 was $9.00 per month — for both of them! Fortunately for the Jones family, Eddie did sell cars during the daytime for W. W. Ellis Ford Company of Kenton.

Kenton's telephone numbers were single, double, and (a few) triple digits (our number was 18). But who needed numbers? Mother would crank our old phone that hung on the wall and say, "Willie, give me Cuddin' Beulah's" (Hamilton) or, "Eddie, give me Reeves" (Freeman). Sometimes Eddie would say, "Reeves is not at home, Patti;" or "Beulah's on the phone." Dad, being in the cotton business, had several cotton brokers throughout the South. One of his main brokers was his old college fraternity roommate, Pat Apperson, originally from Memphis but then living in Greenville, South Carolina. Dad would pick up the phone and say, "Eddie, I need to talk to Pat." Dad would hang up and Eddie would run Pat down no matter where he was, whether he was in his Greenville office, at home, or at some little cotton mill in Georgia or North Carolina or wherever. Then Eddie would track Dad down, often no easy task itself, and hook up the two men.

In the early days there was no phone on the big railroad platform downtown where strawberries were handled. Bell had a phone booth in their office which was across the street from the platform. During berry season when Dad or Cuddin' Inman (Freeman) or Sam Shatz received a call, Eddie or Miss Willie would send word across the street by their daughter, Mildred (who was out of school for berry pickin') or some other messenger, or step just outside the front door and give 'em a good holler and the "callee" would run across the street and talk with the "caller." People in Kenton who had no phones could also be called. If a messenger were not available, the Jones would locate a policeman, or somebody, to get the person called to the phone office to ring the caller back.

In 1954 our phone service deteriorated dramatically. Dial phones came in, and the Jones retired. We had to know numbers. We had to track down people ourselves. We got lots of "no answers" and busy signals. Prior to '54 Mother seldom rang a number needlessly. Miss Willie would say, "Patti, Yetta's (Shatz) gone to Jackson today" and save Mother the call. Things telephonic would never again be the same. Progress? Didn't seem like it to me.

Our home was right across the street from the Jones family. The Jones had the first television in our neighborhood. We used to go over there at night and watch TV with them. If the head was connected to the body straight on instead of by a neck that stretched "way off to one side," we'd say, "Sure is good tonight, isn't it?" Of course it was always snowing heavily on the TV shows, inside and out. They must have done all their filming in the Arctic, on sets with no roofs.

The Jones were true telephone pioneers in addition to being the most accommodating people in the world. Eddie and Miss Willie are now gone, and we miss them. Their daughter, Mildred, is also gone, having passed away in 2001. Mildred and her also deceased husband, Ray Fox, lived in that same house right across the street from my office/home place. It surely is a pretty house with big rooms and beautiful antiques. Many of my fond memories involve that house.

Several years ago the wife of a Goodyear person who had just moved to Union City took notice of radio station WENK's use of the expression, Ken-Tenn area. She heard this used time and time again, and one day she was talking with another Union City lady and commented that Ken-Tenn did not seem to her to be that big of a town. We would have to agree with her; Kenton really isn't. But in terms of importance I wouldn't disagree with WENK.

Johnny Bogle was one of the most popular citizens Kenton ever had. When he was a teenager he purchased a Model T Ford and painted all over it what I, as a very young boy, thought were hilarious things. The two that I remember were "Henry's First Thought" and up on the hood with an arrow pointing to the radiator cap, "Spit Here." Surely the things that have escaped my memory were just as clever. There was a joint south of Rutherford called Bogota where young folks hung out. Who knows why it was called Bogota? Certainly it didn't look anything like South America. At any rate, many were the afternoons that Johnny would pile a bunch of teenagers into and onto his Model T and they'd chug over to Bogota for an afternoon of dancing and Cokes. Later on when Johnny was married and in the service station business in Kenton he claimed that the tires he sold and the toilet paper in his station restrooms were similar in that they both were puncture proof and skidfree. Johnny always was full of himself, and he may well have been the most popular person ever to live in Kenton. Johnny, who worked for Dad as a car salesman at one time, tragically died at a young age. What a shame and what a loss it was to humanity when he died leaving a lovely young widow, Betty Harper Bogle, and two mighty sweet young children, Beverly and Joe. There were more flowers at his funeral than had ever been seen at Sunnyside Cemetery.

A colorful and successful Kentonian was Mr. Sol Shatz, an immigrant from the "old country" who came to Kenton in the 19th Century as a peddler of some sort, liked what he saw, and settled in Kenton. Mr. Shatz raised a family of five children, all of whom excelled in life. Mr. Shatz was a witty old gentleman whom Dad very much respected. Among other investments, Mr. Shatz was in the cotton gin business. One time when Dad was fairly new in the gin business the cotton market suddenly dived. At that time ginners were buying the cotton they ginned each day. The second day the market opened up the limit down again. Dad decided to drive to Memphis before the market opened the next day to see what he could find out. The market again opened limit down. Mr. Shatz heard that Dad was driving to Memphis for the openings at the Memphis Cotton Exchange and asked if he could ride down with him the next day. Dad was happy to have him go along. They arrived at the cotton exchange just before the market opened. The market again opened limit down. They headed back to Kenton. On the way back home Dad said, "Mr. Shatz, I can't sleep when I'm losing so much money every day. Can you?" Mr. Shatz replied, "Yes, Tom, when the market is going down I sleep like a baby." He hastily added, "But then, if the market is going up I can't sleep." He could afford to lose money, but the excitement of making money exhilerated him so much that he couldn't sleep. Of course, Dad, just starting out, could not afford the losses. However, Dad said that eventually the market recovered sufficiently that he was able to sell all the cotton he had accumulated at a price that enabled him to break even.

One time Shatz Gin caught fire. Dad and his gin crew and everybody else in town hurried to the gin to help in any way they could. Mr. Shatz, who spoke with a somewhat broken accent, came running around the corner of his cotton house just in time to be hit straight on with a heavy spray of water. Mr. Shatz exclaimed, "Vell hell, I'm not on fire!" "Vell hell" was one of his favorite expressions. The Shatz family were pleasant competitors in the gin business, as they had been for my Grandfather in the mercantile and gin businesses.

In addition to Bogota, Rutherford also sported the Davy Crockett Tavern, an out-and-out beer joint. My Grandmother Walker always said it was a disgrace to have such an establishment named for the great Davy Crockett. Speaking of Davy Crockett, longtime customer and friend, Coy Yergin, gave Will and me a beautiful handcrafted clock made from a hand hewn log which he said came from an old log cabin that stood in the vicinity of the Crockett cabin which in later years was moved to Rutherford as a tourist attraction. As we have noted on a brass plaque attached to the clock, it is entirely possible that Davy Crockett may have hewn that log.

Kenton spawned many people who left and achieved great success. As stated earlier Glen Smith, the brother of my second grade teacher, Miss Myla Smith, and Mr. Harry Smith, with whom I served on the Kenton bank board, was Tennessee's second Rhodes Scholar. Another Kenton native who did well was A. J. Ashe, son of Mrs. C. H. Bryant, who was the widow of Dee Ashe. A. J. rose to the presidency of B. F.

52

Goodrich Co., and he later served as a full-time advisor to President Reagan in Washington. Another fine native son who enjoyed tremendous success was Dr. Earl Ramer. He became Professor of Education and Chair of the Department of Continuing and Higher Education with the College of Education at the University of Tennessee at Knoxville. Dr. Ramer served two terms as president of the NCAA (National Collegiate Athletic Association). I bought signs for the north and south city limits of Kenton proclaiming this fact. Dr. Ramer invited me to their home for dinner more than once when I was at UT, and he and his charming wife also had our daughter, Lolly, for dinner when she was an undergraduate. He always maintained his Kenton ties and was largely responsible for a big Kenton High School reunion, all classes, which was held many years ago.

In addition to Earl Ramer the prominent Ramer family of Kenton produced other over-achievers. One of them is Hal R. Ramer who was the founding president of Volunteer State Community College of Gallatin, Tennessee. Dr. Ramer recently retired after 49 years in higher education administration. He served as president of Volunteer State for the first 32 years of its existence. Another brother, Jack, was Employment Coordinator for the Tennessee Department of Veterans Affairs.

Another former Kentonian who became very successful is A. C. (Tom) Boyd. The Boyd family, six boys and one girl, is indeed a remarkable family, as you will surely soon agree. Tom, the second child, who had read the entire encyclopedia by the time he was in the tenth grade, graduated from Kenton High School and decided he wanted to see the world. His first plan was to see South America and his first stop was to be Los Angeles. He left Kenton with $15 and hitchhiked to LA, arriving with $5. He rented a room for $2 or $3 per week and started job hunting. There were plenty of jobs to be had, but none of them would pay him any money for at least five days, and he was getting hungry. After going without food for four days it occurred to him that he could get a quick food fix if he volunteered for the Armed Forces. First he went to an Air Force recruiting office but they required a four-year commitment. He told them he was hungry but not "four years hungry." He went to a Navy recruiting office and found the same time requirement. He went to an Army recruiting office and decided he was "four years hungry" after all. They asked him what he wanted to do. There was an MP poster on the wall, and Tom said, "I want to be one of those." Tom was given some money for food, and he ate so much that he became sick. At any rate he signed up at 1 PM, and at 3 PM they shipped him out to basic training. That fateful decision was to lead to an amazing life story.

Tom became a military policeman. During his time in the service and thereafter Tom met five United States Presidents. As a bodyguard for the U.S. Commander-in-Chief of Europe, General Hodes, Tom sat in on many back room military meetings. He was in the War Room when General (President-to-be) Eisenhower was planning the invasion of Lebanon. At about 2 AM Tom fell asleep in his chair. Eisenhower kicked the chair from beneath Tom and raked him over the coals in no uncertain terms as Tom was scurrying to stand up. Tom's brother, Jim, ran for U. S. Congress as a Republican, and Tom accompanied Jim to D. C. for the Republicans' congressional school for candidates. While there Tom and Jim met President Nixon at a dinner for the candidates. At this same function they met Vice President Ford, destined to succeed Nixon, of course. Tom later talked with President Ford a couple of times on Air Force One. (Tom's brother, Perry, was chief of security for Air Force One, and Tom was assigned to Air Force One on several occasions.) When Perry retired from this prestigious position, Tom met President Reagan at Perry's retirement party. In later years he met former President Carter who boarded a plane and took over First Class, requiring Tom's wife to move back into coach. Tom had highest security clearance and was not required to vacate his seat. When President Carter saw Tom he said, I know who you are. You look just like your brother (Perry, who had been in charge of security for Air Force One during the Carter Administration). Carter then instructed his Secret Service people to bring Tom's wife back to First Class, saying he knew these people and that they were certainly all right.

Another of Tom's brothers, Ricky, is an Obion County school teacher and lives next to our Bruce farm.

Tom Boyd's son, Randy, has also enjoyed extraordinary success. Randy's pet products company, Radio Systems, has experienced an annual growth rate of 50% for a decade. Revenues in 2002 reached $75 million. Radio Systems manufactures such unusual things as radio-controlled fencing and automatic pet feeding systems. Randy predicts that within three to five years his company's sales will reach $250 million. Just another Kenton product. We got the right stuff, folks!

W. G. (Sonny) Dement, Jr. owns a very large road and bridge construction company headquartered in Jackson, Tennessee. Sonny is an unpretentious soul who declined to give me anything specific about his company, but suffice it to say that it is a giant operation. Sonny showed son Will and me a little of his far flung enterprise a few years ago, and we were amazed at what we saw. Sonny's modest ways belie the enormous business successes he has enjoyed. Sonny's and Beth's three older sons work with him in Dement Construction, and their youngest son is a college rodeo star. Their daughter is married and lives with her family in Nashville.

Sonny played on Kenton High School's state-wide fourth place basketball team in 1957. His Dad and my Dad, and later I, served together on Kenton's First State Bank board for many years. (See Chapters 3 and 34 for my Dad's and Sonny's Dad's business associations.)

Adrian Baucom (Myers), born and raised in Kenton, taught school in Kenton for several years during my time in the Kenton school system. Miss Adrian was a mighty good teacher. Her father, Dr. B. R. Baucom, was the local dentist, and his office was above what is now C. W. Sanderson's property on the north side of College Street in downtown Kenton. Mrs. Myers now lives in Springfield, Missouri. In 1999 she shared the following stories with me:

Miss Adrian remembers picking strawberries for Emerson Smith for 2 cents per quart when she was very young. One season she made $3.50 and bought a croquet set which she and her parents and friends enjoyed for years. When she was even younger she earned a dime one day for her picking. When she got home she realized that she had lost her dime and she became distraught. She looked and looked but could not find it. Dr. Baucom told her that he would give her a dime.

Adrian said, "I don't want your dime. I want the one I earned" and continued to cry her heart out.

Many of us will also remember Dan Pierce. Miss Adrian remembers that Mr. Dan was a very clever man. One of his observations was, "I notice that people are a lot like sheep. Those that get sick and linger awhile have a much better chance to get well than those that get sick and die right off." Certainly we'd all have to agree with him on that one!

Dan Pierce doesn't have anything on Miss Adrian. She writes that she's now seeing five gentlemen. WILL POWER comes by every morning and helps her get out of bed. Then she goes to see JOHN. Afterwards, CHARLIE HORSE drops by and takes a lot of her time and attention. When he leaves ARTHUR RITIS shows up. Arthur soon gets bored and takes her around from joint to joint. After a busy day, Adrian is ready to go to bed with BEN GAY. What a life!!!, she exclaims.

She goes on, "The preacher came to call the other day. He said at my age I should be thinking about the hereafter." I told him, "I do that all the time. No matter

where I am — living room, basement, the yard, wherever — I ask myself, 'What am I here after?'" (*I know the feeling!*)

But she says, "Remember that old folks are worth a fortune. They have SILVER in their hair, GOLD in their teeth, STONES in their kidneys, LEAD in their feet, and GAS in their stomachs." (*I guess I don't qualify as "old." So far as I know, I don't have kidney stones.*)

Thanks, Miss Adrian, for bringing some sunshine into our lives. We wish you could get back to Kenton, as fine a little town as God ever created!

Another person from Kenton who went on to great things is Joe Pate. Joe and I were classmates and I was very sad when he transferred to the Rutherford School. Nonetheless I am going to claim him for Kenton. After all, he was here first! Joe, the sister of Mary King of Rutherford, came by to see me a couple of years ago and that was a great treat.

Joe left West Tennessee and went to Oklahoma where he went into radio announcing. Following two years in the Army he worked radio in Missouri and then got into television in New Mexico, then to South Bend, Indiana where he was Sports Director of the CBS Radio and Television stations for 11 years where he annually did play-by-play of more than 100 football and basketball games including Notre Dame basketball. Then he began an 18-year stint as the play-by-play voice of the Purdue Football Radio Network and Purdue Basketball Television Network. For more than 28 years Joe was Media Director at Cranfill and Company and President of Associated Sports Productions in Indianapolis where he administered all radio-television activities and the corporate sponsorship package of the Indiana High School Athletic Association, considered to be the premier such package in the nation.

In 1999 Joe was inducted into the Indiana Basketball Hall of Fame as the 38th recipient of the Silver Medal award given to a person other than a coach or player who is deserving of special recognition for his/her contribution to Indiana high school basketball, a truly great honor considering the prominence of Indiana in the world basketball scheme of things. I knew Joe was an extraordinary boy ... I really did.

Maybe the most famous people ever to come from Kenton are Carl Bell and Jeff Abercrombie, the organizers of the famous rock band, *Fuel.* Carl, the son of Robert and Patsy Bell, grew up right across the road from the entrance to my Bruce farm and my strawberry patches. Jeff grew up about a mile from Carl on Union Grove Road diagonally across from my Brotherton farm. Jeff is the son of Ray Abercrombie and Janice Abercrombie. Carl, who can play just about any instrument, plays lead guitar, and Jeff plays bass. Their singer is from Brownsville, and their drummer is from Pennsylvania, where they lived for some time. Carl has written all their music except for one song which was written by Brett Scallions, their singer. Patsy Bell told me that Carl and Jeff are best friends and that all four members of the band are close friends and get along extremely well. At the present time they live in Los Angeles where they are recording an album.

For some time now *Fuel* has been touring and promoting their albums. Their last tour was with *Aerosmith.* *Fuel* will headline their own next tour. Carl wrote the lead song in the movie, *Daredevil,* and *Fuel* performed it. The sky's the limit for these young men!

Kenton continues to produce extraordinarily successful people.

Further into this book we'll discuss in some detail another enormously successful ex-patriot Kentonian, Hal Bogle.

Chapter Three

Kenton Strawberry History -
the Strawberry Platform

"Doubtless God could have made a better berry, but doubtless God never did." William Butler

Wilton Wade, uncle of Tom Wade, claimed to be the largest strawberry grower in the world. During his peak he had 500 acres, in five different locations of 100 acres each. The locations to the best of my memory of what Dad told me, were Kenton, Union City, Troy, Obion, and Dyersburg. Kenton served as headquarters for Wilton's berry operation. All their strawberries were shipped by rail to northern markets, and supposedly on big days they had as many as 5,000 pickers in the fields! People rode in on horseback and in buggies and wagons from far and wide, pitched tents and camped for the duration of the picking season. Dad said that when he was a youngster, he would get on a row and pick it for two or three days, and then come back to the beginning and start over again. Obviously the rows were very long and full of berries.

(Cousins Frances Wade Caldwell and Ruth Wade Kane have filled me in on the involvement in the strawberry business of their father, William Powell Wade. We readers are indebted to them for the following recollections as well as for information in Chapter 33 concerning these two remarkable cousins and their families.)

Wilton Wade's son, William Powell (W.P.) Wade (Willie to his family and friends, Old Shug to his daughters), partnered with his Dad in the Kenton strawberry operation. This partnership lasted until 1913 when Uncle Wilton (Grandpap to his grandchildren) died. W. P. Wade continued the Kenton area strawberry operation until 1927 at which time he moved to Amory, Mississippi where he went into the strawberry business, also in a very big way. The M&O Railroad, which ran through Amory as well as through Kenton and Union City, encouraged W. P. Wade to move south and grow and encourage others to grow strawberries around Amory so that the railroad would have a steady supply of berries to haul north. This location filled the void between the harvest of berries in Louisiana and in West Tennessee. W. P. Wade grew strawberries at Amory and handled the strawberries for the other area growers until he died in 1937. At that point his wife, Dayle Rodgers Wade, continued his strawberry operation for a time.

Years ago our dear friend, Mary Critchlow, gave Pat and me the following news item having to do with the foregoing enterprising gentlemen, from July 3, 1914 Union City *News Banner:*

"Mr. Wilton Wade and Mr. Will Wade, father and son, the noted successful berry growers of Kenton, were here this week negotiating the securing of 200 or 300 acres of land just on the edge of the city to be planted in strawberries. We understand they want a four-year lease. The Wades are men of broad and liberal ideas and great executive ability. They have specialized on the berry business and understand it thoroughly. Their entrance into this field will be worth hundreds of thousands of dollars to the community. Just what the Wades can and will do will be a revelation to people that have never before witnessed their work. We respectfully suggest that the Business Men's Club get behind this movement and lend all the assistance in its power."

Cousin Ruth's remembrances continue:

"(Cousin) Polly Elder, (Cousin) Evelyn Montgomery, and I went to Dyersburg to work in the sheds there that were supervised by Cousin Charley Montgomery. [*I remember these cousins well.*] We stayed in an old farm house on the property and took Aunt Rachel Gant from Kenton to cook for us and enjoyed it immensely [*Cousin Ruth writes that Aunt Rachel enjoyed delivering a juicy bit of gossip and then would say sweetly "I ain't talkin' 'bout nobody. I'm just talkin' about what I'm talkin' about!"*] ... When Bernard [*her husband*] and I were at the University of Chicago, Daddy (William Powell Wade) would phone me when he was sending carloads there, and I would go early in the mornings to the market (so I could) see how the berries did or did not hold up ... Then I would call

Daddy with my report ... The berries held up very well unless it was a picking after a rain storm or a skipped Sunday (they never picked on Sunday) and even then they were not too bad."

I remember, as a young boy, driving up to St. Louis with Dad occasionally so that he could go to the market very early to check on some of our berries which would arrive that early A.M. From my experience, it is quite obvious that Cousin Ruth's early morning visits were important to her Father.

Cousin Ruth sent me the following article from the Amory newspaper:

"May 1, 1927 — The strawberry crop is large and has proved to be quite profitable this spring. Bill (W. P.) Wade and his partner Oscar Vaughn have in 70 acres and have been shipping a carload a day for the last 14 days. There has been no lack of labor to gather the berries, as many as 600 pickers being seen in the fields of the community at a time. Men, women and children get out early and remain through the morning. They are paid two cents a quart and good wages are made by those who are active and come regularly. A large water tank is placed on a wagon and supplies the crowd with water. The (area) soil is especially adapted to berries, which grow wild all over this section. Mr. Wade and Mr. Vaughn have set out a new patch of 70 acres and next year will have 140 acres of strawberries. Three good crops are picked from one setting."

Cousin Ruth told me that my Dad told her Mother, our Cousin Dayle, that he was most grateful to Cousin Willie for getting him started in berry growing. Cousin Ruth also said that she had found an old letterhead of her Dad's that read, "W. P. Wade, Grower of the Famous Wade Klondyke Strawberries." To a lifelong strawberry man like me (most people think about me in terms of strawberries though they are a fairly small part of what we do) these recollections are darn near priceless.

In 1925 my Dad set out his first patch of berries and from 1925 on, he never failed to set a new patch every single year until he died in 1975 after having set his 51st consecutive new patch! To this day Tom Wade Strawberries still has planted a new patch every year since 1925. This year's patch makes 79 years in a row!

I graduated from UT in 1957 and came back home to Kenton and joined Dad in the berry business. Will graduated from UT in 1994 and joined me in the strawberry business becoming the fifth generation Wade in the strawberry business in Kenton. Dad and I had as many as 50 acres of berries at one time. One day we had 500 pickers. We dropped back to 25 to 30 acres and now I have only ten acres or so. In recent times more money has been lost than made on my berries. We no longer grow them for profit. We grow them because strawberry juice courses through my veins!

Years ago we had a good many patches of strawberries on the Bruce farm. Sometimes it was a chore to try to explain to somebody which patch we wanted him or her to go to for whatever reason. I might say, "Go over to the second patch east of the second irrigation pond," or some such explanation. Misunderstandings often occurred. Finally I hit upon the idea of naming the patches for berry employees. The names were "Modine's Market" (Modine Bradley, our longtime manager of the packing-paying operation); "Dewey's Delicious" (Dewey Bradley, our longtime farm manager who has always helped with the berries); "Voinda's Variety" (Voinda Johnson, Dewey's and Modine's daughter who has worked in berries for us for many years and who does, very well, the job that her Mother formerly did); "J. C.'s Jubilee" (J. C. Reed, our longtime employee who looks after the berries almost year round); "Shorty's Shortcake" (Herbert "Shorty" Hill, the retired longtime employee who worked with J. C. when we had a larger acreage); "Treva's Table" (Treva Adams who worked for many years in the packsheds and was one of the harvest managers); and "James Jam" (James Turner who worked for us for a good many years in various capacities). This system worked wonders. No longer did we have trouble communicating among ourselves as to which patch we meant. Also we had signs painted pointing to the various patches which was a great help during harvest. Apparently none of these loyal helpers minded their names being used in such a way!

Kenton always was a large strawberry point. Probably there was more concentrated acreage in the small area around Kenton than there was around any other town in Tennessee. Humboldt shipped more berries than any other town. Portland shipped the second most.

Kenton ranked third in shipments, but these other towns drew from much wider territories than did Kenton. Almost every farmer in the Kenton area had some strawberries. There were strawberry buyers in every little town around here back in the heyday of the business.

In 1942, at eight years of age, I began to work at the strawberry platform labeling crates. We had beautiful "Kenton Brand" labels which were glossy and which we thought were the prettiest ones around, but the fairly heavy, slick paper made it difficult to keep the corners from curling up. Consequently, we labelers had to brush hard. It took a lot of paste and a lot of brushing to keep the corners down. A labeling crew consisted of two or three of us boys. If we were real busy, three worked best — one to slap on the paste, one to stick on the label, and one to brush it down. Sometimes two of us handled it — one to apply the paste and the other to stick on the label and brush it down. If the paster brushed on the paste too fast and recklessly (which happened often), paste could get on some of the berries. We were constantly admonished not to do this, but when the bosses were out of earshot we reckoned that all this did was make it easier for those Yankee ladies (all berries were shipped north) to make their shortcakes. After all our white paste looked pretty much like shortcake makins'! Back in those days we packed in 24-quart Dyer Box wooden crates. My starting wage was 15 cents per hour and within a few years when we were big enough to "tote" crates, they raised us to 25 cents per hour. On good weeks we labelers made as much as $10.00! Of course, nobody worked on Sundays back then. We started work in early to mid morning and on big days worked 'til 10 or 11 or even midnight. We mixed up our paste in lardstands at the hydrant in the alley beside Shatz Produce which was directly across the street from the berry platform. Then we poured the paste into gallon buckets and brushed it on the crates with a paintbrush. We took pride in getting our pants, which we usually wore for a full week, saturated with paste. One of the boys — I'm pretty sure it was Tommy Hamilton — claimed that he stood his pants in the corner of his bedroom at night and "jumped into" them in the morning.

Lots of boys rotated through the labeling crews, but three others of the regulars I remember especially fondly were Jackie Glisson, Freddy

Jordan, and Bobby Keathley. One night late after a string of long, hard days, Jackie decided he'd had enough and dropped his brush, crawled off the platform and headed home. Dad saw him walking away and hollered at him to come on back. Jack said, "But Mr. Tom, I'm <u>soooo</u> tired." Dad talked him into coming back, but soon when Dad was on the other end of the platform, Jack disappeared into the night heading in the direction of home. From that point on, just about every time Dad saw Jack he'd say, "Jack, are you still <u>soooo</u> tired?"

Bob Keathley didn't label on Saturdays. On Saturdays during strawberry season there was lots of money floating around Kenton's main street, and Bob could make far more than 15 cents an hour shining shoes in his Daddy's barbershop. Then in the shank of the evening he moved his popcorn popper out onto the sidewalk. No tellin' how many thousands of bags of 5 cent popcorn Bob sold. I can hear him now – "Red hot popcorn – butter on top – makes yo' lips go flippedy flop!" Take it from me, Bob has been a moneymaker all his life! He's still making money, and plenty of it. As we boys got older and bigger we "toted crates" and got a full quarter an hour! Some of the "big boys" who had graduated from labelin' to totin' were Johnny Bogle, Charlie Freeman, James Hamilton and Joe Lane. The dean of the toters was Carthel McNeely. Nobody ever told him to come to work; he just "showed up" when the first crate showed up. As he got older sometimes he'd hold back a little to avoid that dreaded "bottom" crate. One of Carthel's favorite expressions was, "Good morning, Mrs. Worts!" I never did understand what he meant by that. Mr. Jim Buchanan (Jim Buck we called him) was another old toter I remember fondly.

Johnny Bogle and T. C. Karnes graduated to driving one of Dad's Diamond T trucks on nightly runs to St. Louis. Sometimes when they were late in the morning getting back home, we accused them of stopping at the Black Hawk (a dance club, or glorified beer joint) in Chester, Illinois.

E. C. Eddings picked berries in the mornings for Mr. Russell Henderson. Around noon he'd hitch a ride into town on one of Mr. Russell's big truckloads of berries and work the rest of the day and into the night "totin." E. C. retired from his "real job" a few years ago, moved back to Kenton, and he now helps us with our berries. Often what goes around comes around. Others who brought in big loads (which we boys kinda hated to see comin') were Willie George Dement, Luther Neil, Lee Paschall, Les Ross, Paul White from Obion, and Dad.

Notwithstanding an occasional "pastey" berry, many good lessons were learned by many young folks on the platform.

Dad was the manager for the Kenton Berry Growers Association. It was a loose affiliation of growers, and the farmers of the area met once each year and always re-elected Dad. It was understood that I.W. Freeman, Dad's cousin-in-law, would participate as an equal partner in the operation with him and the two of them for many years bought and sold berries on a margin basis. During World War II there was a ceiling price on many items, including strawberries. I remember one year the strawberry ceiling price was $8.80 per crate, and it did not matter what the grade was; you simply got $8.80 a crate. In other words, if the government inspectors called them "Unclassified" or "U.S. No. 1," they still brought $8.80 a crate. Needless to say, during these years of scarcity due to World War II there was very little incentive for farmers to fill quarts very full or to do a very good job of picking out the bad berries. This was an anomoly, though, and times later on became much harder for the strawberry growers insofar as grades were concerned. During the War when there was a guaranteed commission allowed for the handlers of berries, Sam Shatz, who had been a produce man all his life and had followed the harvests up and down the Mississippi River Valley, came to Dad and Cousin Inman and asked them if he could sell Kenton berries on a commission. The government allowed this "middle man" an extra commission, so allowing Mr. Shatz to sell the berries would cost nobody any money, except for the eventual consumer, of course. Therefore, they asked Mr. Shatz to come into the operation to sell the berries. He stayed on after this time for a good many years. The three of them, Dad, Mr. Freeman, and Mr. Shatz had a very good relationship, and it was a pleasant business albeit a pretty hectic one at times.

One year on "Big Monday" we received 12,000 24 quart crates (36,000 of today's flats!). It took us until the middle of Tuesday afternoon to get rid of all those berries. They were beginning to look pretty sick by the time they were all moved out from Kenton.

Back in those early days the majority of the berries were shipped by rail. The icehouse across the street from the big old railroad platform did a booming business in icing down and pre-cooling the cars. The way this was done was that the ice was put into ice vats on both ends of the boxcars, and big fans were then set into the cars to blow against the ice. The doors were closed for some period of time, and when they were opened and the fans moved to other cars for pre-cooling, the cars were very cool. The hot berries were then put into the cars where the cool air cooled the berries down, and they traveled in very good shape. On long shipments to Philadelphia, New York, and Boston, for example, they had to stop along the way and add new ice to the cars.

55 to 58 years ago we began to ship berries to distant markets by refrigerated truck, and soon the railroad cars were totally phased out. The last carload of berries we shipped was involved in a wreck between Kenton and Philadelphia and the total load was lost. Most likely the railroad company paid for this load of strawberries.

We continued to run the Kenton Berry Growers Association until about 35 years ago and the number of growers, because of the scarcity of labor in the area, decreased to the point where there just was not enough volume for us to handle their berries anymore. Willie George Dement, the largest Kenton area berry grower at the time, partnered with Dad in the handling of Kenton berries for one year toward the end of our strawberry handling days. The last year Dad was in business we lost $5 on the total year's handle of customers' berries. From that point we just raised and sold our own berries.

Many of our school friends went out into the berry fields early in the morning and picked for 2 cents a quart, later 5 cents a quart, which held for many years, and then some of them would come to the berry platform after they quit picking and spent the rest of the afternoon and night working on the platform for hourly wages. They could make more money picking in the mornings, and after the picking was finished for the day, they supplemented their income by working on the platform. Dad and Cousin Inman worked between 25 and 35 boys and men on busy days.

Mr. Roy Carroll managed the Shatz Produce Company, owned by Mr. Abe Shatz, directly across the street from the strawberry platform. Mr. Roy kidded us boys who worked on the platform unmercifully but good-naturedly. One of his favorite questions to us was "How old would you be if you were right fat?" We never knew the answer. Who would? This went on for years. Finally I got up the nerve to ask him to please, please tell me the answer. He said, "Well, Tommy, you'd be Old Fatty." The answer seemed so dumb! But it made sense. We could stand more of this kind of humor nowadays. Fairly often I ask youngsters this question. Never yet has a one of them given me what Mr. Carroll perceived to be the correct answer.

All the capped berries were handled by processors. We picked berries with the caps on them for the fresh market as long as the quality was good enough. Once the quality dropped to a point that they would no longer sell well in the fresh market, the berries were capped in the fields by the pickers at a higher rate of pay and then carried to the processing plants where they were washed, cleaned, and frozen. They were used for all sorts of purposes such as preserves, jams, ice cream, and toppings.

At one point there were two strawberry processing factories in Kenton. One of them was in Tilghman Chevrolet's old garage on the highway. It was run by Stokely (later Stokely Van Camp) of East Tennessee, and one of the young Stokely men was here one season. Also the old tomato-canning factory, which Dad and I. W. Freeman owned and which later then belonged to Dad alone, was used for strawberry canning. We used to go down there at night to watch the men and women working on the assembly line where they were cleaning strawberries and sugaring them in big lardstands. This probably was during World War II. There were several other processors in this area. At one time there were two or three processors in Humboldt, Breyer Ice Cream Co. in Newbern, one in Tiptonville owned by the Craddocks, and one in Paducah, Kentucky. Incidentally, Thurmond Lumber Co. (my Pat's family's business) built the plant for Breyer in Newbern. Breyer liked the plant so much that they asked the Thurmonds to go to Missouri and build another one for them, but Mike Thurmond (my father-in-law) told me that they declined.

Believe it or not I can remember seeing trucks and wagons loaded with strawberries lined up for the better part of a mile in every direction out of Kenton. They lined up far beyond our house on Maple Heights.

During the War strawberry growers around here sometimes cleared as much as $1,000 per acre of strawberries — on land that probably was worth no more than $100 per acre!

Needless to say, strawberries paid for lots of farms around Kenton.

Chapter Four

Memphis and the Peabody

Memphis is almost like a second home to me. We went to Memphis often "for the day." Dad, being in the cotton gin business, took samples to Memphis to shop them up and down Front Street which was the center of world cotton trade in those days. Now we trade cotton electronically, but back then we used samples cut from the bales which the buyers picked up and looked at and from which they pulled the staple (the length of the fiber). Samples are still used by brokers, shippers, and mills but not by ginners. The samples would be placed on heavy paper on a long table and then the samples, enclosed in the paper, would be wound into large rolls which would then be tied with twine. Usually Mother and Sally, and often Grandmother and Great Grandmother Jennie who would be picked up in Dyersburg, and I went along with Dad. He always parked at the same little parking lot on Front Street where he tipped the attendant, a nice black man, a dime. Dad and I would then start making the rounds of the brokerage offices while the ladies headed for the shops and department stores of Main Street. Usually Dad and I would spend a little time in the Cotton Exchange Building checking the market. Later on when my age permitted it I'd go by myself to the movies at Loew's Palace, Loew's State, the Paramount, or the Malco. They were all ornate, first class theaters, and it was a thrill for me to go to the movie in a fine theater. The Memphis theaters had the first air conditioning in West Tennessee. They advertised with big banners that they were cooled by "refrigeration." Sure enough, it was a great feeling to walk into one of those air-conditioned palaces on a hot, sultry day like only Memphis can suffer. I remember one time seeing Army's great All-American fullback, Doc Blanchard, at the Malco in conjunction with a movie about the National Champion Army team he played on with Glenn Davis, their All-American tailback. What a thrill!

We usually ate at Britling's Cafeteria, a good restaurant on Union Avenue between Front and Main. Often I had spaghetti and chocolate pie. Yum, yum! When we separated in the morning, arrangements were made to meet at a specific time late in the afternoon in order to start our three-hour trip home. In the very early days we met at the Gayoso Hotel but then we switched to the Peabody, the "South's Grand Hotel." In 1935 David Lewis Cohn wrote that the Delta begins in the lobby of the Peabody Hotel. He was correct, and it still does. Just take a look in the Peabody lobby on Friday night of the annual Southern Cotton Ginners Association Farm and Gin Show and Convention, and you'll have to agree. The ducks still come out at 11 AM and go back upstairs at 5 PM every day. Tourists and guests crowd the lobby at those times every day year 'round.

Over time it got harder and harder to park the car near the back entrance of the Peabody, and Mother came up with the bright idea of taking two or three 16-quart crates of our strawberries down to the Peabody doormen each year during strawberry season. From that point on they would let her park her car there any time she wanted to. Mother could be a wheeler-dealer when she set her mind to it!

We often had lunch in the Peabody in their lovely dining room which was off the east side of the lobby (now the location of the Peabody's acclaimed restaurant, Chez Philippe). In the old days the Peabody always had a big name "big" band which played in this room for the luncheon crowd and then on top of the hotel in the Skyway for dinner and dancing. In the summertime, weather permitting, the band played on the Peabody's Plantation Roof. (See Chapter 1 for CBS' broadcasts of the Peabody's bands.) One time we were all having lunch in the Peabody dining room, and I requested the real low down bluesy song, *Night Train*, which had been made famous by the internationally known band which was playing, Buddy Morrow. I was real young, and the band got a big kick out of my requesting *Night Train* which was certainly not the airy luncheon type music they had been playing. But they played it, and I loved it. They could sure play it. Boom Boomp, Boom Boomp, Boom Boomp, Boom Boomp, Boom Boomp — the beat is coursing through me as I write.

Pat and I became engaged at the Peabody (see Chapter 14), and Sally was a Maid of Cotton finalist at the contest held at the Peabody (see Chapter 24). My nose was broken at the Peabody (Chapter 13). There are several other references to the Peabody in this book.

We Wades have spent many, many nights in the Peabody. We have attended scores of conventions of the Southern Cotton Ginners Association always staying at the Peabody. I have attended three Pi Kappa Alpha conventions at The Peabody as well as many other weekend PiKA meetings there.

Annie Laurie (Lolly) Wade was born in the Baptist Hospital in Memphis on July 18, 1963. Pat, Sally, and I went to Memphis for Pat's weekly checkup with her obstetrician. Lolly was already several weeks (supposedly) past due. After the checkup the three of us went to see *Cleopatra* starring Elizabeth Taylor at the Crosstown Theater in Memphis. It was a very long movie, and after it was over Pat said she thought maybe we should spend the night in Memphis. We checked into The Peabody. Pat woke me at midnight, and we headed for the Baptist Hospital. Annie Laurie Wade (Lolly) was born about noon that day.

The Peabody has played an important part in the lives of my family. We were greatly saddened when it went downhill and closed for those few years. But when the Peabody came back, grander than ever thanks to the Belz family, we were ecstatic! It's still a thrill every time we walk through their doors.

Chapter Five

St. Louis and the Cardinals

The Cardinals have always been the favorite team for most folks around here. Their long-ago great radio announcer, Harry Caray, made the games come alive in a way that just almost automatically made you a Cardinal fan. No telling how many hours I listened to Harry Caray. They had some great teams back in the 40s and 50s with legends such as Stan Musial (my all time hero), Enos Slaughter, Red Schoendienst, Marty Marion, Whitey Kurowski, Howie Pollett, Harry Brecheen, Terry Moore, and other greats. Their big rival was the Brooklyn Dodgers. Cousin James Hamilton was a Dodgers fan. I never could understand that. Jack Barton was a Yankees fan. I never could understand that either, but at least they were in a different league and "we" never had to play them except in the World Series, which happened fairly often.

The most magical moment of my young life was the first time I walked into Sportsman's Park with Dad. I thought I had died and gone to heaven! From that point on, undoubtedly because it was so important to me, we went to several games almost every summer for a long time.

Dad and I went to see the first game and Mother and I the last game of the 1946 World Series against the Boston Red Sox. We were sitting down the left field line in the first game when Boston's slugger, Rudy York, won the game with a home run into the left field bleachers in the 10th inning. We were sitting high up behind first base when St. Louis won the seventh and deciding game in this series. It was the most memorable game I ever attended. In the bottom of the eighth Enos Slaughter scored from first on a legitimate single by Terry Moore. Enos just kept on running. Harry Brecheen shut down the Red Sox in the top of the ninth for his third win of the Series. The Cardinals won 2-1. We rode back downtown on the streetcar (we always rode them) after the seventh game and saw tons of confetti in the streets from a ticker tape celebration. Mother, Dad, Will and I have seen several other World Series games during our treks to St. Louis, but these two games are my most memorable.

Dad and I went to a couple of World Series games in the 60s. We saw some in the interim, the particulars of which escape me. Will and I saw the fifth game of the 1985 World Series in a great box behind home plate about six rows back (Continental Grain's box, they gave me the tickets). We could see right in the Kansas City Royals' dugout and saw George Brett when he slid down the dugout steps trying to catch a ball. Our seat was only about 15 seats from Mr. August Busch and eight seats from Cardinal football great and NFL announcer Dan Dierdorf. Mr. Busch did not stay for the entire game, or at least he did not stay in his box for the whole game.

Enos Slaughter used to come to Dyersburg to hunt with a man who lived right across the street from my Aunts Ethel and Mary Gee Walker. Enos passed away during the summer of 2002.

Many years ago Houston was a farm club of the Cardinals. They were in the AA Texas League. The Cardinals always played Houston in an exhibition game or two each spring. One year when St. Louis was in Houston for their game, a cotton gin machinery salesman whom Dad knew well was staying in the Cardinals hotel. The salesman was trying to sell Dad a lint cleaner, and he knew that I was a big Cardinals fan. He got the following signatures on a baseball and gave it to me the next time he was in Kenton: Stan Musial, Enos Slaughter, Marty Marion, Howard Pollett, Terry Moore, Nippy Jones, Del Wilbur, Del Rice, Johnny Beasley, Fred Schmidt, Joff Cross, Al Papay, and Butch Yatkeman (Property Man).

The salesman sold Dad the lint cleaner! The ball is in our home in Union City and is one of my most cherished possessions. (See Chapter 9 for the story of my Stan Musial autographed picture.)

One of my other autographed baseballs is one of pretty well all the players of the Union City Greyhounds of the Class D Kitty League. The only names still legible are Richard Coffman, Ed Knepp, and Bob Ofinger. Another of my baseballs was autographed by Virgil Trucks, a Detroit Tigers pitcher, who lived in Birmingham. Laura and Jack Barton got it for me one time when they were at a party in Birmingham at Laura's cousin's. Virgil Trucks was there and gave them the autograph.

One time we were in St. Louis when the Cardinals were out of town, so Dad and I took in a St. Louis Browns game. The crowd was small, and there was one old lady sitting behind home plate who ranted and raved like no fan we had ever heard. My recollection is that the attendance of only a little over 200 set a modern day major league record for smallest attendance. St. Louis was a Cardinals town. And a National League town.

Going to St. Louis was a great thrill. Most of the time Mother and Dad, Sally, Grandmother, and sometimes Jennie would go. The ladies and Sally would shop and Dad and I went to the games which were almost always daytime games. We always stayed at the Statler, a big good downtown hotel. We ate there and often at The Whip, a neat diner across the street. Another of my favorite places was the really good dining room on the top floor of Famous Barr, a big downtown department store which is still there, though it's not nearly as viable as it was in the 40s and 50s. Other big downtown department stores were Stix, Bayer, and Fuller and Scruggs, Vandervoort, and Barney. Sadly the part of town where the Statler building (it's been closed for a long time) is located is mostly boarded up and run down. In the summer of 1999 some of our family and employees went up for some Cardinal games and stayed at the Mayfair Hotel (across the street from the Statler) which was a fancy hotel in its day and is still nice. We were told that Marriott was considering refurbishing and adding to the old Statler and creating a fancy property. It would be great if they would.

In those days, as was the case with all big cities, St. Louis had some beautiful and ornate movie theaters downtown. Dad and I went to the movies quite often. Again, as age permitted, I'd go by myself. One of my favorites was an all-time classic which was showing in St. Louis, *Rhapsody in Blue* which was about the life of George Gershwin. This may have been my first exposure to really good music. At least this was the first time I had paid any attention to music other than popular music and country music. One of the things that amazed me most about St. Louis was that we could stand on a downtown street and look in any direction and see tall buildings almost all the way to the horizon. Wow!

The trip to St. Louis was an interesting one. Often we stopped in Bardwell, Kentucky at a good restaurant constructed of rock, which was run by two sisters. They had the world's best country ham sandwiches which were simply country ham on plain light bread. Man, they were goooood! From Cairo we headed up Highway 3 which ran through Chester and such colorful old towns as Columbia and Red Bud, Illinois and on to East St. Louis where we crossed the Mississippi River bridge into downtown St. Louis. (Incidentally one year during World War II the Cardinals had spring training in Cairo.)

How exciting it was to be in what had been, once upon a time, the nation's fourth largest city, behind New York, Chicago, and Philadelphia. Our family still enjoys St. Louis and the Cardinals immensely. Interstate 55 from Cape Girardeau enables us to get there in three and a half hours or so. Wouldn't it be wonderful if my son and five grandsons could know the same magic experienced by this little boy on that long ago first trip to Sportsman's Park! I'm afraid, however, that television has removed lots of magic from the world.

Our family continues to go to St. Louis for Cardinal games almost every other year. Though downtown St. Louis is not as vibrant as it was 55 to 60 years ago, the Arch and other amenities make our grandchildren, our children, and us happy to be in the great midwestern city of St. Louis.

Chapter Six

Camp Hy-Lake

When we were eleven Peter Pelham and I went to Camp Hy-Lake located between Sparta and McMinnville, Tennessee. We stayed eight weeks each summer and continued to go for four years. I was not a happy camper the first part of our first year. Second thoughts came rushing at me just as we turned off the highway and into the woods leading over to camp. Homesickness hit me like a heavyweight fighter's punch to the midsection. Adding insult to injury was the fact that the cool night air bothered my asthma. For awhile they required me to sleep in the Coverdales' (the owners) house. Then they tacked canvas sheets onto my bottom bunk in my screened cabin, and I slept, or tried to sleep in this claustrophobic situation. Another thing they did for my asthma was to have me drink a glass of goat's milk at the end of every meal. That stuff tasted awful and it was most embarrassing to have to go to the kitchen and get it three times every day. Thankfully they cut that out after awhile. All it did was upset my stomach. Toward the end of the first summer, though, Hy-Lake was becoming more and more fun. I was a Navajo and Pete was a Comanche. We were always sorry that we weren't in the same tribe, but once you were one or the other, you were branded for life. Guess I'm still a Navajo. The two tribes played all sorts of sports against each other all summer. The different age groups played against their peers. At the end of the summer all the wins were totaled and a champion was declared. The Comanches won three years and we Navajos won once. Some of the competitions were baseball, softball, basketball, volleyball, riflery, horseshoes, tennis, badminton, swimming, diving, water polo, dodge ball, and tribal warfare. We swam in the Caney Fork River. A dam a few miles below the camp formed a man-made lake, and the camp was located on this lake. One year there was a drought, and the lake was considerably lower than normal. We swam in a "crib," which was a slatted wooden swimming pool floating in the lake on barrels.

Toward the end of my fourth year, when I was fourteen, they suggested that they might give me a position as a junior counselor the next year. After a good deal of soul searching I decided not to go back for a fifth year. My last three years were pure fun, and homesickness never again reared its ugly head.

The first day we arrived at Hy-Lake, the first person Dad saw was an old college friend and fraternity brother, Frank Davenport from McMinnville whom he had not seen for many years. Often when Mother and Dad visited me at Camp Hy-Lake they would stay with the Davenports in their lovely McMinnville home. From Hy-Lake days until Frank's death, he and Dad were again close friends and they saw each other often. They were both active in ΠKA activities at the University of Tennessee from then on, especially after I pledged ΠKA. The Davenports had one child, a sweet daughter named Livy Deering. Livy Deering was a good friend of Mary Ellen Coverdale, the charming daughter of the owners of the camp. Livy Deering spent a good deal of time at Hy-Lake because of this friendship. Frank's widow, Edna Davenport, died in 2001. She was almost 100 years old.

We had cabin and personal inspection on Sundays. The first visit from our parents during our first summer at camp was a momentous occasion. They arrived relatively early on a Sunday morning while we were still cleaning the cabins. There was a bucket of water in the front door of our cabin, and somebody was in the process of mopping the floor. Uncle Gordon Pelham came down the hill toward our cabin, and Peter Pelham was so excited to see his Dad that he ran and jumped over the bucket, knocking it over, and literally sailed into Uncle Gordon's arms, almost knocking him over.

One of my fondest memories of Camp Hy-Lake was eating Sunday dinner with Mother, Dad, Sally, and Grandmother in the old Sudberry Hotel in McMinnville. It was a marvelous place to eat, and people came from far and near for their elegant Sunday dinners. Genteel black men in white coats waited tables, and the food was served family style with a genuine Southern flourish. The Sudberry may have been Tennessee's finest restaurant. The food tasted just like Mother's.

Charles Dismukes from Union City also attended Hy-Lake. One summer weekend Mr. and Mrs. Dismukes went over with Mother and Dad and Sally, who was about ten years old, to pay us a visit. They went to see our close friends, the Davenports in McMinnville. The Davenports lived back off a highway and their yard dipped down into a fairly deep depression. For some reason Mr. Dismukes, a rather distinguished man, decided to drive the car as they were leaving the Davenport's house. Mr. Dismukes needed to back up in order to turn around and head out of the Davenport's driveway. He backed up close to the precipice and then shifted into low. He killed the engine and the car edged back closer to the cliff. He did this several times, to the point that the car was just about to back off down that very steep hill. The last time it happened, Sally, who had become visibly agitated, jumped up off her seat and yelled, "Lemme outta here, Mr. Dusmicks!" This was one of our family's all-time favorite stories. Any time one of us wanted out of any place or situation, one was liable to hear, "Lemme outta here, Mr. Dusmicks!"

Another local camper was Jimmy White from Obion, now of Union City. Jim and his family lived next door to Pat and me in Union City for years. We do all our fuel business with their family's Reynolds Brothers and their Kenton outlet. Jim and I serve together on the board of First State Bank and the executive committee of Community First Bancshares.

Each summer we campers would paddle canoes downstream in the Caney Fork River to a small cave up on a hill beside the lake. The name of this cave is Screaming Cat Cave. Major Coverdale was a great storyteller. The first time I went to the cave, just before we were to bed down, he told us the legend of Screaming Cat. Screaming Cat was a peaceful Indian with a squaw and two papooses. When the White Man was settling that part of Tennessee some renegades caught Screaming Cat's family in their wigwam while Screaming Cat was away hunting for food. They killed and scalped the three innocents. Screaming Cat came back to his wigwam to find the horribly mutilated bodies of his beloved Squaw and children. He screamed and screamed so loudly that his piercing cry could be heard for miles around. He became a madman and sought vengeance against the White Man. He was able to track the renegades to Screaming Cat Cave where they had camped for a night. They were sound asleep when he attacked them. He silenced them, one by one, with his powerful hand while he sliced their throats from ear to ear. When he had finished his bloody work, four scalped white men lay dead, the blood having drained from their bodies. IIIIIEEEEEEEAAAAIIIIEEEE!! Major Coverdale quickly and loudly screamed. I don't think any of us campers slept a wink that night. From that point forward the little cave on the Caney Fork has been known as Screaming Cat Cave.

Screaming Cat, with four scalps hanging from his waist, marauded throughout South Middle Tennessee for years to come, killing white people. When his distinctive scream IIIIIEEEEEEEAAAAAIIIIEEEE was heard through the countryside, the settlers knew that another white person had been heinously killed and scalped. My skin is crawling this minute.

One football weekend when Will was about ten or eleven years old, he and his young friend, now Dr. Tim Ragsdale, went with me to a football game in Knoxville. As we were driving on Interstate 40 I told them the story of Screaming Cat. They became so engrossed that they stood in the back floorboard, literally hanging over the front seat. It just so happened that we were right beside the Kingston Steam Plant when I let go with a blood curdling scream. Both boys jumped so high that their heads simultaneously hit the ceiling of the car. Never since have I seen the Kingston plant's giant smokestacks without thinking about Will and Tim and Screaming Cat.

One year at Hy-Lake we went on an overnight camping trip to Fall Creek Falls State Park. The most memorable thing about the trip was the Hy-Lake stew which was prepared by the counselors in a lardstand. As was to be the case with our Kenton Boy Scouts overnight stay at the Botts cabin, they put everything under the sun in that stew. We ate it with light bread, and that Hy-Lake stew stands out in my memory as quite possibly the best meal of my entire life.

One of the things I remember most fondly about Hy-Lake was Reveille in the mornings and Taps at "lights out" at night. We had a good bugler. Reveille was very upbeat, and Taps was very soothing. One morning, earlier than usual, we were awakened by an unworldly screeching noise, the likes of which none of us had never heard. Turns out a dingbat young camper had swiped the bugle from our regular bugler and had decided that he would do us campers a favor and wake us up with his own rendition of Reveille. Needless to say, that never happened again. That boy was always a space cadet.

These were four memorable summers, summers in which Pete and I grew up a lot.

As a youngster Sally also went to camp. Hers was Camp Nagawicka in Delafield, Wisconsin. She rode the train up and back from Memphis with several Memphis girls who also attended Nagawicka. The first year when she came home she told Mother that her best friend at camp was a girl from Memphis, Jean Sanders. Mother said, "Sally, she's your cousin." Sally and Jean have remained close all their lives. (Pat and I were at Jean's house the night we got engaged.)

Every unit at Nagawicka had their own song. I've forgotten the name of the unit to which Sally belonged, but I'll never forget the words to one unit's song. It was sung to the tune of Irish Washerwoman and went like this:

Oooh Pat says he, what says he, tell me the truth, says he
Which of the units is best for me, says he
Oh says he, that is easy for me, says he
Nothing is in it but Gamma for me.
Oooh Gamma, Gamma, Gamma, Gamma
I am so happy that I am a
Gamma, Gamma, Gamma, Gamma
You can't imagine how happy I am.

Isn't it amazing how one can remember such insignificant things and then sometimes forget very important things?

Chapter Seven

Horned Herefords

Shortly before Dad graduated from UT he discussed his future with his primary Animal Husbandry professor. Dad told this gentleman that he thought he would establish a Shorthorn herd. His professor asked, "Tom, do you want to sell your cattle?" to which Dad replied, "Yes, of course." The professor said, "I think you might want to consider Herefords, then. They are a much more popular breed, and there would be many more prospective buyers for you than you would have with a Shorthorn herd." Dad took his sage professor's advice and never regretted it. He loved his Horned Herefords, Mother said almost as much as he loved his family. Nevertheless, she, like Cousin Fanny Bogle with Cousin Clarence, did not allow Dad to track manure into her house, even though it was "registered!"

I often went with Dad on Hereford trips. We went together several times to the Wyoming Hereford Ranch outside Cheyenne. My favorite western hotel was the Plains Hotel in Cheyenne which was decorated western style and had real Indians as bellmen. All the furniture was western, and everything about it was authentic Old West. Dad bought several bulls and heifers from WHR through the years. Mr. Lazear, the manager of WHR and one of the nation's most respected cattlemen, was always very nice to Dad. One time he and Mrs. Lazear invited us to have lunch with them in their home on the ranch. That was a great thrill. Their sales back in those days, and this dates back into the 40s, were averaging $8,000-$9,000 per animal. One time we bought a bull at WHR, and he was delivered to Kenton by railroad car. The railroads had some sort of arrangement where they would stop and feed and water livestock periodically, and the bull arrived in good shape. Another time Dad bought five heifers and a bull, and he sent some of his farmhands out there to get them. The fellows thoroughly enjoyed that long trip out West. Another time we were at WHR in the winter when the snow was deeper than we realized. Dad drove our car for a distance on the road leading to the headquarters. The snow was deep enough that we could not see the road. Dad just pretty much followed the line of light poles which were beside the road. Finally we ran into a drift and snow packed underneath the car to the extent that we could get no traction. At this point we could not see any buildings over the hill we were approaching, and I wondered if we were going to expire in the Wyoming snow. We got out and started walking, following those telephone poles, toward the ranch headquarters. Finally we came across a hill and saw the headquarters buildings. They sent a tractor out to tow us in. We followed our tracks back out after Dad transacted his business.

We often went to big cattle shows such as the granddaddy of them all, the National Western in Denver, where in later years Dad and I met and shook hands with John Wayne who, with another man, had one of Herefordom's top herds of that time. This was an enormous thrill. My main recollection of John Wayne was that his were the biggest hands I had ever seen. We also went on several occasions to the American Royal Livestock Show in Kansas City, the Fort Worth Fat Stock Show, and the International Livestock Exposition in Chicago.

In addition to shows, we also attended a good many sales around the country and we also visited several of the big Hereford operations looking for private treaty purchases of bulls, cows, and heifers. My most memorable Hereford sale was one year when we went to the Bridwell Ranch sale which was held on the ranch at Windthorst, Texas, a little town near Wichita Falls where we stayed. At that time their bloodlines were as popular as any in America. As was usually the case in those days, the sale was held in a tent. Senator (at the time) Lyndon Baines Johnson just happened to sit directly in front of me on the bleachers. He was then majority leader of the Senate. The bleachers were so close together and so crowded that my legs were constantly touching the small of his back. LBJ bought three fairly high priced bulls, and we bought the last one to sell and paid $3,000 for him which was far below the average price paid by the buyers that day. He was a bull that we picked out as one that we really liked and felt might be in our price range, so we were happy. Hereford breeder P. H. White, Jr. of Dyersburg and Sheriff Cocke of Somerville, another

Hereford breeder, were with us on that trip. We had a great deal of confidence in P. H.'s judgment, and he liked this young bull. P. H.'s father was an old friend of Dad's and a fellow Horned Hereford breeder. Both father and son were known around Dyersburg as P. W. Old Mr. P. W. had died several years before our trip to the Bridwell Ranch. In later years young P. H. was on the board of directors of the American Hereford Association from which he rose to the presidency of the A.H.A. Incidentally, Dad's framed A.H.A. membership certificate which hangs in my office happened to have been signed by the A.H.A. president of that time, J.S. Bridwell! I have many fond memories of traveling with Dad on his Hereford travels. Back then we never flew. We drove everywhere.

One Christmas Pat painted a big Hereford sign including a painting of a bull for Dad. This may have been his all-time favorite gift. This beautiful and impressive sign was displayed in one of the lots in front of the big white barn from that point on until his herd was finally dispersed in 1977. The next Christmas Mother bought a cattle weather vane for the barn, and Pat painted the bull on the weather vane with Hereford markings. This gift ranked right up there with the sign.

Dad always had Holstein cows to use as nurse cows for his show calves. This was common practice until registered cattle breeders finally realized that the mother cows should be bred to give abundant milk themselves. About the time we quit using our Holsteins for this purpose, other European beef breeds came into vogue. We decided to try our luck with Simmentals, a big Swiss breed. Buying good registered Simmentals was very expensive, so we decided to breed our Holsteins artificially to some of the breed's top bulls. The Simmental Association allowed us to register the resulting half breeds, three quarter breeds, etc. After you got to a certain point, 15/16s as I recall, the animal would be considered a full bred Simmental. We were hearing exciting reports of the prices these cattle were bringing at sales. One day a cattleman who had just been at a very successful Simmental sale in Lexington, Kentucky came by to look at our cattle. Dad had a half breed with a three quarter bull calf at her side. She had been bred back to a well known bull. That man offered Dad $7,500 for the cow and calf. I couldn't believe it when Dad declined to sell them. He simply said, "If they are worth that much to him, they're worth that much to me." Soon after that the bubble burst, and our part Simmentals were worth no more than beef price.

I often called daughter Lolly, Patti and daughter Patti, Lolly (still do). Later it got to a point where I would often catch myself in midstream and call them Lapatti and Palolly. We used two famous bulls in our artificial Simmental breeding program, and we named the female offspring from one bull Palolly 1, Palolly 2, etc., and the females from the other bull, Lapatti 1, Lapatti 2, etc. If the bubble hadn't burst, Lolly and Patti might have become renowned in the annals of Simmentaldom.

Dad loved his cattle. I liked them but not enough to continue the cattle business which wasn't really making any appreciable money. After selling out in 1977 I bought a dozer and commenced to take out fences, trees, and ditches, replacing them with terraces and retention dams, and our farms became total row crop operations.

Chapter Eight

World War II and Other Tragedies

When the Japanese bombed Pearl Harbor on that fateful Sunday morning of December 7, 1941, I was at home in Kenton. My faint recollection is of sitting with Mother and Dad and it seems to me, other members of our family later that day while listening to the accounts of the bombing on our big old Atwater Kent radio. I seem to remember that it was hard for me to understand the gravity of the situation. Because of the effect it obviously was having on the grown folks, I knew it was really bad.

I was working at my desk in the house in Kenton when JFK was assassinated on November 22, 1963. I watched developments unfold on the television out in the sunporch. Many years later I learned that old fraternity brother, David Stewart of Gallatin, was doing his residency in surgery at Parkland Hospital in Dallas and was on duty when the President and the others wounded in the attack were brought in. David actually worked on Governor Connally who survived. Two days later he was on duty again when Lee Harvey Oswald was brought in, and David was one of several who worked on him, this time without success.

Pat and I were at home in Union City on September 11, 2001, when New York and Washington were attacked by terrorists. I was about to leave for work when Van Walton, the contractor for our house expansion, came in and told us to turn on the television. We did and learned of the attack. About 30 minutes later I left for an important bank meeting but did not have my mind on the business at hand. After an hour we took a break and found out that the Pentagon had also been hit, and a couple of other places in Washington were rumored to have been hit by bombs (the latter part turned out to be false). I simply had to go home where we watched TV nonstop until almost 3 PM when I did go back for another bank meeting.

Back to World War II, the only time I ever saw my Dad cry was one day when he came home and told Mother in the kitchen where she was preparing a meal that my first cousin, Charlie Wade, was missing in action and presumed dead. He was the navigator of a bomber which, with three other bombers, was on a raid in the Pacific. His and two of the other bombers were shot down by Jap Zeroes over the Pacific. All were lost. After the war Uncle Eugene and Aunt Floye, Charlie's parents, went down to Louisiana to visit a crewman from the bomber that survived the mission to get that man's story of what had happened. He told them that he saw Charlie's plane as it spiralled downward and that he saw one man get to the open door of the plane but that man was thrown back into the plane which then crashed into the sea. It's a shame that Uncle Eugene and Aunt Floye ever went to Louisiana.

From the files of the *Union City Daily Messenger* this article appeared:

"Mr. and Mrs. Eugene Wade of Union City were to participate in military ceremonies 10 A.M. Saturday at Dyersburg Air Base. They will receive the Air Medal and Purple Heart, which will be awarded posthumously to their son, Lt. Charles R. Wade, 23, the navigator of a Liberator bomber which was shot down over Shortland Harbor near Bougainville Island Feburary 13, 1943."

Prior to the above the *Daily Messenger* reported:

"Among those from Obion County who have earned citations in the armed forces are: Charles R. Wade, decorated for bravery in the Battle of Wake Island."

January, 1995, *Union City Daily Messenger*:

"The War Then — 50 Years Ago, column reported, Hope that 2nd Lt. Charles R. Wade, nephew of Tom Wade of Kenton and son of former Kenton residents Mr. and Mrs. W. Eugene Wade, may have escaped the crash of a bomber on which he served as navigator in the Pacific, has been practically given up."

Tommy Tilghman who lived up the street on St. Marys in Kenton had a Great Dane, a beautiful dog. Whenever they came our way — they seemed always to be together — I would meet them at the north or south side of our sidewalk and ask Tommy if he would please let me ride his dog to the other end of our walk. He always let me do it. We were all heartbroken when Kenton received the news, as was too often the case with Kenton boys, that Tommy had been killed in the South Pacific in World War II. In later years while standing beside his grave in Sunnyside Cemetery after a funeral, someone, Miss Karon Howell I believe it was, told me that Tommy had been a sniper on one of those infamous South Pacific islands and when they found his body at the base of a tree they also found the bodies of several Japanese soldiers whom he had obviously killed. What a kind and handsome young man he was. He was one of my heroes. Other Kenton area boys killed in World War II were Robert Allen, Roland Bryant, James Craft, Bishop Dillard, James Foster, Neil Gordon, James Long, Grady Reed, L. J. Smithson, Fred Tilghman, Ray Tilghman, and William Todd. Kenton did far more than its share for world peace.

At age nine or ten I began to read the news of the previous day's war action in *The Commercial Appeal*. My favorite cartoonist was Pulitzer Prize winner, Bill Mauldin. His two G.I.s, Willie and Joe, were loved by the nation and by me. One of my vivid memories was reading the paper at Grandmother's house in Dyersburg during summer vacation. I would read about the war as we had breakfast on their screened-in back porch where we often ate. They had a cook who made wonderful fluffy biscuits. Even at that tender age, seven or eight biscuits with sorghum molasses along with eggs and sausage was this skinny little fellow's usual breakfast. My goodness, I almost ate my weight every morning!

From what I have seen, heard, and read, during World War II the people of the United States of America pulled together for the common cause in an unprecedented way.

Chapter Nine

McCallie School

Primarily because Kenton High School did not offer some courses which we felt would be helpful for my college career, Mother, Dad, and I decided it would be in my best interest to attend a private boarding school. Leaving Kenton was a very hard decision on my part — I had always been very happy in the Kenton school system — but fairly late the summer after my sophomore year, Dad, Peter Pelham, and I headed east to look at schools. First we went to Battle Ground Academy in Franklin, Tennessee which was owned by the Coverdales, the family that also owned Pelham's and my old Camp Hy-Lake. I liked BGA and knew the boys who attended both BGA and Hy-Lake. Then we went to Castle Heights Military Academy from which Dad had graduated in 1916. CHMA was a beautiful school which was also an enticing possibility. From there we went further east to Sewanee Military Academy, another beautiful school. Our last stop was The McCallie School, another military academy, in Chattanooga. Dad was pulling for Heights, and Pelham, who had entered McCallie the previous year, very much wanted me to join him on Missionary Ridge, McCallie's historic home. Pelham and I were mighty close and I liked what I saw at McCallie. It so happened that the boarding department had been filled up but a vacancy had just occurred. The boy who had canceled had recently been in a train wreck with his father who had been killed. The McCallie folks told us that the father threw himself across his son to protect him and the man died. They told Dad that they would have to drop me back to the sophomore class since my Kenton School was such a small one. Dad told them that my grades were good and that I would go to one of the other three schools unless McCallie would take me into their junior class. They agreed to give me an entrance exam which I easily passed, and McCallie was destined to be my home-away-from-home. It was a wonderful decision. McCallie was, and still is, a marvelous school in every way, in academics, in sports, in the caliber of the student body, and in terms of morality and Christianity as taught there. We had an honor system that was remarkable, and every boy had to take a semester of Old Testament and a semester of New Testament. The McCallies were Presbyterians, and they were devout. I wound up as a top ten student. In my senior year my fellow classmates elected me to the second semester Student Council from our dorm, defeating the very popular Jim Daughdrill who went on to become a Presbyterian minister of some very large churches and then to be president of Rhodes College in Memphis. That was my main claim to fame! The council elected me to be its secretary.

Maybe the thing that I'm most proud of at McCallie was the organization of what came to be known in the annals of McCallie School as "The Infamous Midnight Raid on Jarnigan Hall." The idea was mine, and Wayne Miller and I planned it. Wayne had attended McCallie's first summer camp for boarders in 1946 and had lived in Jarnigan so he knew all about the rooms, stairs, and hallways. We lived on the second floor of South Hutchison Hall which was on the south edge of the campus. Several of us met after midnight in Malcolm Colditz's room on the first floor of our dorm and we crawled out his window. We picked up trash cans from a stack of them at Founders Home and carried them over to Lockett Lodge where we filled them with water. We then crept across the parade ground and onto McCallie Avenue and stealthily entered Jarnigan Hall which faced McCallie Avenue which was on the north side of campus. Each of us entered the room of the boy to whom he was assigned. Wayne held the front door open and upon a whispered OK from the top and the bottom of the stairs, he clapped his hands once, loudly and sharply, and "all water broke loose" as we simultaneously threw the contents of our trash cans on every single resident of Jarnigan Hall. We hit the front door and ran as fast as we could, this time on the McCallie Avenue side of the hedge which separated the parade ground from the street. We headed south down Kyle Street and returned the cans to Founders Home. By the time we got back in our beds, lights were on all over campus. Every boy in Jarnigan Hall was literally soaked, and nobody ever knew who did it. Years later at a reunion I told Major Burns, the longtime beloved head of the boarding school, who done it!

Some of those involved, besides Wayne and me, were Malcolm Colditz, Bob Greer, John Hoff, Bill (Monk) McDonald, Bill Monin, and Peter Pelham, all but Wayne later becoming my PiKA brothers at the University of Tennessee.

I have always been a rabid college sports fan and used to watch college football point spreads pretty closely. At McCallie I started laying off bets on games with some of the boys and won more often than not. Some Saturdays my winnings would approach $1.00! At any rate the word got out that some of us cadets were gambling on the games, and the Headmasters told the student body in no uncertain terms to "cease and desist." That wound up my McCallie betting.

Ted Turner was an eighth grader during my senior year at McCallie. One Christmas Billy Parker, destined to be a PiKA brother of mine at UT, and a classmate, Peter Stewart, drove down to Savannah, Georgia to spend the holidays with Peter's mother. Ted's mother also lived in Savannah and she called Billy's mother to ask if Ted could ride down with them. This was fine with Mrs. Parker, but I'm not so sure how Billy felt about it. You see, Ted was considered by us older fellows as something of a "worry wart." At any rate the three of them headed south. Ted rode in the back seat, constantly interrupting Billy and Peter in the front seat. In every case, Ted had a better story or he knew more than they (reckon Ted really did know more than Billy and Peter?). He constantly popped bubblegum and made a general nuisance of himself. Late in the day they stopped for gas at a filling station in a little town in Georgia. After filling up, Billy gave Ted two nickels and told him to go inside and get Cokes for Peter and him. He told Ted to get one for himself, too (Ted later became better in numbers!). As soon as Ted stepped inside they drove off and left him. They drove down the highway a bit and stopped and stretched and loafed for about 15 minutes. Then they went back to get Ted and found him standing out front with two warm Cokes and a worried, forlorn look on his young face. Billy said Ted did not utter another word for the rest of the trip. Ted recently gave McCallie $25 million. Wonder if he's mentioned Billy and Peter in his will?

McCallie was a military school 'way back when Ted was in Peter Pelham's squad (our close friend, John Hoff, was also in Pete's squad). While drilling, Ted usually wore his cap sideways, his tie undone, his shirt unbuttoned, his shoes unpolished, and was almost always out of step. Pelham always lovingly(?) called him "Dog Boy." "Hey, Dog Boy, get yo a _ _ in step!"

The competition in sports at McCallie was too great for me to do much athletically. At the end of my sophomore year in Kenton the underclassmen played the graduating seniors in a basketball game before the student body, and I was our leading scorer with 20 points as we won handily. The boys at McCallie, however, were just too big and tall and good for me to compete. For instance our senior year football team was undefeated and had twelve — count 'em — twelve boys who went on to play major college football at Tennessee, Vanderbilt, Georgia Tech, Alabama, Auburn, and South Carolina. Some of these boys played basketball, and three of our basketball players played on a previous state championship team at old Knoxville High School which had been disbanded when they built new East and West High Schools in Knoxville. (The discontinuation of Knoxville High was the reason why Tom Ayres and Kyle Testerman, great McCallie athletes, came to McCallie. Kyle went on to become Mayor of Knoxville, and Tom played football for the Vols.) Though I was somewhat frustrated athletically, McCallie served me extraordinarily well in every other way.

The school spirit at McCallie was absolutely amazing. Our cheering at sports events could be heard on the other side of Missionary Ridge! The top honorary at McCallie was called Keo Kio. One of our cheers went like this:

Keo Kio, sis boom see
Me O My O, rah rah ree
Zippedy zappedy, zee zum zee
McCallie, McCallie, Mc-call-ie.

Mother mailed the *Tri-City Reporter* to me each week. The boys in the dorm got a kick out of our little paper (which I still read and enjoy every week). They thought it funny that almost every report of any kind of meeting indicated that they had good attendance. They also couldn't get over the extensive coverage of what seemed to them to be pretty insignificant events. One afternoon Wayne Miller came into my room and noticed the new *Tri-City Reporter* on my bed and announced to all of us present, "Did y'all see the headlines? Farmer Jones' pig house burns down, with good attendance." His Dad, Loye Miller, was long-time editor-in-chief of *The Knoxville News Sentinel.* Maybe that's the reason why Wayne paid so much attention to the news from Kenton, Rutherford, and Dyer.

While we were at McCallie Billy Graham held a crusade at the baseball stadium where the Chattanooga Lookouts played. Many, if not all of us McCallie boys attended one night. Dr. Graham is truly a powerful Man of God.

After vacations Hoff, Pelham, and I sometimes went back to Chattanooga on the *Tennessean,* a Southern Railroad passenger train that we boarded at the Buntyn Station in Memphis. There were always sizable groups of Virginia school girls also returning to the east, and these trips were great fun. Our sleeper car would be dropped off in Chattanooga, and we'd get up at 7AM and take a taxi to campus. On one of those trips the famous athlete, Jim Thorpe, was being treated to dinner by a prosperous looking man. Mr. Thorpe kindly gave me his autograph. It has long since been misplaced; maybe it'll turn up some day. Mr. Thorpe, who was most gracious to me, did not appear to be prosperous.

In the summer of 1952 Wayne and his brother Mike Miller came over from Knoxville to Memphis on the bus where I met them and brought them up to Kenton where we then met Jim Curlin from Marion, Arkansas, and John Hoff and Peter Pelham from Dyersburg at our house. The next morning we drove up to St. Louis to see some Cardinal games. We stayed at my family's usual place, the Statler Hotel. Wayne, Jim, and I had just graduated from McCallie, and Pelham, Hoff, and Mike were rising seniors there. One night in St. Louis we had dinner at Stan Musial and Biggy's Restaurant. As luck would have it, Stan was at the restaurant that night and came over to our table where he talked with the six of us while holding Curlin's shoulder. Then he autographed pictures for each of us. My autographed picture hangs in my office. After Stan moved on to another table Curlin said, "I will never again wash this shoulder!" This experience was one of the great thrills of our young lives. As mentioned earlier, Wayne and Mike Miller were the sons of *Knoxville News-Sentinel* editor-in-chief, Loye Miller, and Mrs. Miller. Mr. and Mrs. Miller were delightful people who were to become good friends of our family. They invited me for several meals with them in their lovely home on Rose Avenue in Knoxville while I was a student at UT.

The great education received at McCallie made it possible for me to do well at the University of Tennessee without studying almost constantly as I had done at McCallie. I made some of the best friends of my life at McCallie. In fact, most of my best buddies at McCallie were a year behind me and at the beginning of my sophomore year the following McCallie buddies followed me into PiKA at UT: Malcolm Colditz and Bob Greer of Knoxville; John Hoff from Dyersburg; Bill (Monk) McDonald from Oneida, Tennessee; Bill Monin (who was my roommate at McCallie, who became my roommate in the Pike House, and with whom I went to Antarctica in January/February 2001) from Bowling Green, Kentucky; Billy Parker from Chattanooga; and Cousin Peter Pelham. We eight had a marvelous time together in school, and all of us except Pelham, who is deceased, and Parker, who marches to his own drummer, still have a great time together in our Pike Super Group doings (more about that later).

As a postscript to this chapter my 50th class reunion at McCallie was held on October 11 and 12, 2002. I have attended just about all our class reunions, but this one topped them all. The following great friends were in Chattanooga: Richard Abercrombie, Tom Ayres, Bob Bridgman, Buddy Browder, Burton Brown, Sam Campbell, Charles Claunch, Jim Daughdrill, Cecil Davis, Jim Ensign, Joe Estes, Bill Ewin, Lewis Fowler, Bill Garrett, Toy Gregory, Charlie Gulley, Charlie Huff, Jay Levine, Ron Levy, Ed Loughlin, Wayne Miller, Scrappy Moore, George Morris, Paul Morris, George Muse, Tom Pankey, Nate Parks, Lentz Reynolds, Gene Robbins, Carter Smith, Kyle Testerman, Buddy Wellman, Stan Worlen, and myself, 34 in all. 25 of the 89 boys in our class are deceased. So more than half of the surviving members of McCallie's Class of 1952 were there. What a great bunch of guys we are!

Chapter Ten

UT and ZETA Chapter of Pi Kappa Alpha

In the fall of 1952 I entered the University of Tennessee in Knoxville and was as green as the freshman beanie they made us wear for the first week we were on campus. Freshman registration in the old gym was a nightmare. Hunter Partee from Trenton, an old Camp Hy-Lake buddy, and I had the same advisor. We sidled up to him and told him we wanted to major in how to run a cotton gin. Hunter's Father, Willis Partee, like Dad, was a cotton ginner. Our advisor thought we were kidding; we were dead serious.

I was in a Melrose Hall suite with Watkins Ewell and Billy Davis from Dyersburg. Watkins, like me, was a Pi Kappa Alpha legacy. His Dad had gone to Washington & Lee, and my Dad had gone to Tennessee, and Watkins and I went through rush together. All the Dyersburg boys were ATOs and Billy quickly decided he would pledge there, but Watkins and I continued to look at several fraternities closely. The ATOs "hot boxed" us which didn't work with me, but it apparently worked with Watkins, as he also went ATO. McCallie friends rushed me for Kappa Sig, and Union City friends and other West Tennesseans rushed me for SAE. The Pikes rushed me very hard. I narrowed it down to PiKA and SAE but just couldn't make up my mind. Finally pledging day came, and I called Dad three times that day. The third time he said, "Tom, I think you should pledge SAE." It was obvious how much he wanted me to be a Pike and when he said this, it was like a light bulb went off in my head, and I said, "Dad, I'm going Pike."

I went to the Pike house early the evening of fraternity-pledging-decision day. After all the new pledges were welcomed and the initial indoctrination was accomplished, all pledges, actives, and a few holdover pledges went to Highlands Grill which was the students' favorite spot to dance and drink beer. As I recall the Kappa Sigs had the upstairs, the Sigma Chis the back room downstairs, and we had the main downstairs party room with the dance floor and jukebox.

As a freshman I was painfully shy, especially with girls. During my first quarter our Pike S.M.C. (president), Bill Taylor, asked me to go with him to a Sunday sorority tea. I stewed and stewed about it and finally just didn't show up. Bill raised Cain with me about not being there as he wanted to "push" me on campus. Never until now has he heard the truth about why I was a no-show. In any event our pledge party turned out to be a major turning point in my life as far as my shyness was concerned. This party was the genesis of the process which moved me beyond this unfortunate part of my personality.

The previous summer a bunch of us Kenton boys somehow bought some beer in Union City and went out in the country to drink it. I drank half a beer and threw the rest away. It tasted terrible to me. However, at our pledge party my Big Brother-to-be, Charlie Williams, bought me two beers and gave me two cigarettes, the first cigarettes ever to have touched my mouth. (Charlie did me no favor in terms of the cigarettes. Starting that night I smoked for about 18 years except for a 15 months hiatus. I quit hundreds of times, but by about 10 AM or so the irresistible urge conquered my good intentions. I finally quit in late 1969 or early 1970 by telling myself that tomorrow might be different but that I would not smoke today. This day-at-a-time approach worked for me. It was tough, but my opinion has always been that emphysema would have gotten to me long before now had I not quit smoking. Now it is most unpleasant to me to be around smoke. It's totally amazing to me that this terrible addiction ever took hold of me. My allergist at Oklahoma Allergy Clinic in Oklahoma City, Dr. George Bozalis, in our first interview asked me if I smoked. I said, "Yes, sir." He replied, "You can't afford to smoke." That's all he said. I am an asthmatic and knew that he was absolutely right. Soon after that advice I quit once and for all.)

After the pledge party broke up, Charlie took several of us to the G&H Restaurant (a favorite restaurant on what is now known as The Strip, Cumberland Avenue), and he bought me a greasy hamburger. Afterwards Charlie dropped me off at Melrose Hall. After undressing and getting into bed a terrible urge hit me, causing me to jump up and run to the bathroom where I became violently ill. Undoubtedly it was the combination of beer and cigarettes and the greasy burger. Now I knew why so many students referred to the G&H as the "Gag and Heave." Nevertheless I ate lots of meals at the G&H during my time in Knoxville. Many years later while eating at the G&H prior to a football game, the proprietor, Tony, greeted me as Tom. It was surprising that he remembered my name. But he should've, in years past he'd welcomed me into his eating establishment many, many times.

Our pledge class elected Roger Bradley as our president, and he was a good one. Roger was a veteran, a Marine, when he entered UT. He was much more "advanced" than I, and he and I never ran around together. After our reunion group started in 1985, Roger and I began to draw closer and closer, and now he's one of my dearest friends. Many of us have drawn closer than we ever were in college.

We pledges were required to go to football games early in order to stake out a good section of seats for the actives and their dates. In 1952 the student section went to the 50-yard line in the southeast quadrant of Shields-Watkins Field. Our goal was to get there early enough so that the chapter officers could sit smack on the 50. They often did. Our biggest games were Kentucky and Georgia Tech, at that time a member of the Southeastern Conference. During my years in college we beat Alabama like a drum, and we didn't play Florida often. They are now, of course, our two biggest rivals.

I never looked back about my fraternity decision and never regretted it. PiKA was not as strong as it appeared to be, but we had a nucleus of six in our pledge class who were to turn the fraternity around on a dime (more about the six of us later). I was named rush chairman at the end of my freshman year, and we had a great pledge class in the fall of 1953. Going into the fall of '53 we had no Memphis or West Tennessee boys and no McCallie boys. That fall we pledged six other McCallie boys — Malcolm Colditz, Bob Greer, Bill McDonald, Bill Monin, Billy Parker, Peter Pelham — and soon thereafter we had a total of 15 Memphis and West Tennessee boys including a good ole Baylor boy, Bruce Dunlap from Ridgely, Tennessee. In 1954 we pledged an eighth McCallie boy, John Hoff. At the end of my sophomore year my brothers elected me president of the chapter, a position held for two terms.

One of the many good things about fraternities is the Big Brother — Little Brother system. Charlie was a great Big Brother for me, and Ernie Bacon and Ed Person were great Little Brothers for me. I will always have a unique good feeling for these three fine men.

I have been blessed with good friends all of my life. I had many good buddies when I was growing up in Kenton and have many very good friends now in Union City and Kenton and other places. Ever since my teenage years I have considered four boys as my all-time best friends. The first best friend dates back to our earliest childhood. He was my first cousin, my summer camp cabinmate, fellow McCallie boy, collegemate, and fraternity brother, and my close confidant until his tragic death in an airplane crash at much too early an age, in 1976, Peter Pelham. Another was John Hoff from Dyersburg. John and I were also McCallie schoolmates, college and fraternity brothers, Yellowstone Park workers together, roommates on an extensive trip to Europe in 1956, and close friends ever since. Another was Bill Monin, now of Louisville, Kentucky, also McCallie School roommate, college and fraternity brother, and roommate, and also great friends ever since. The fourth was Bill Upchurch from Memphis, later of Huntsville, Alabama, college and fraternity brother and roommate, and dear friends right up until his death from cancer in 1994.

In my case those four fellows were extraordinarily important to me during my formative early years and high school and college years. They have always seemed to me to be my very best friends. We were all in each other's weddings, we were fraternity brothers, and we were, at one time or another, roommates. What a great bunch of guys! How sad that half of them died young. I miss those two very much, and I look forward eagerly to the times spent with the other two. These men have made my life far better than it would have been had they not been my friends.

As for those six of us mentioned in my pledge class, four of us, including Frank Grace, Gene McGowan, Dave McSween, and yours truly, were Scarabbeans, were included in Who's Who Among Students in American Universities and Colleges, and were ODKs.

Remarkably all four of us served as chapter president. We had a student body vice-president (Grace), a defeated student body presidential candidate (me), a senior class president (McSween), an editor-in-chief of *The Orange & White*, the student newspaper, (Grace), and the president of ODK (McGowan). We held dozens of other campus positions. I was campus Pep-Coordinator and charter president of Adawayhi, the campus school spirit organization; chairman of the Election Commission; a member of the All Students Club (ASC) Executive Council; and vice president of the Vol Pep Club, the forerunner of Adawayhi. I was vice president of the Society for the Advancement of Management and treasurer of the Marketing-Retailing Club; chairman of the Awards Committee for All-Sing; served on the Awards Committee for Carnicus; and was chairman of the Line of March Committee of Aloha Oe, the graduation ceremony. In the fraternity I was selected as the Most Outstanding Pledge Initiate, and later on was chosen as Zeta's Man of the Year.

Zeta Chapter of Pi Kappa Alpha became very strong at the University of Tennessee. Our brilliant artist, Bob Seyfried, led us to three homecoming lawn decoration championships when this was the only homecoming competition. Then they switched to floats and we won the first float competition, again when it was the only competition. Under the leadership of Jack Thomas, a brother who had his own dance band, we sang our way to three second place finishes in All-Sing during my time at UT. Under the direction of Buster Pellettieri, Jim Gray, Bill Grafton, and later Bob Smith, we finished second three times in Carnicus. We were the perennial bridesmaids in those two events, but we represented Zeta Chapter extraordinarily well nonetheless.

During my time at Zeta somebody had the bright idea to buy an old fire truck and use it to ferry us around campus. We bought an antique truck from the Clinton, Tennessee Fire Department. Some of the fellows went up there, got it running, paid for it, and headed to Knoxville. As Bill Upchurch, George Bishop, and some of the other brothers drove it across the Clinch Street Bridge, they turned on the siren which still worked well. We brothers who were at the house ran out onto the front yard, and we then heard a second siren. A police car followed our old fire truck right up to the curb in front of the Pike House. Unbeknownst to us, other than on vehicles of the Knoxville police and fire departments and on ambulances, sirens in Knoxville were illegal. We begged our way out of a fine and removed the siren. One of the main purposes for the fire truck was to pick up our dates and ourselves at Ellis and Ernest Drug Store (E&E) where we usually met our lunch dates. E&E was considered the "corner" of the campus. Our fire truck brought lots of attention to PiKA at UT, and our idea was picked up by dozens of other chapters across the nation and soon was a Pi Kappa Alpha tradition coast to coast.

Another thing we started during my years at Zeta Chapter was the Pi Kappa Alpha Calendar Girl contest and calendar. Each sorority — there were twelve at the time — picked a pretty girl to be their calendar girl. We had pictures made of all the girls which were sent to some Hollywood celebrity who picked a winner. The winner then became the Pike Calendar Girl. She was announced at a party, and in addition to appearing on "her month," the winning calendar girl's picture graced the front cover of the calendar. We paid for them by selling ads. Frankly I was dubious about this project, but it turned out to be very successful. The calendar idea likewise was picked up by many other Pike chapters around the country. My Pat was AOPi Calendar Girl in 1961 and again as Miss March, 1962, representing Alpha Omicron Pi. What a beautiful girl Pat was and is.

I sang in All-Sing each year and sang and danced in Carnicus each year. Some interesting things happened to me in Carnicus. I was a chorus member in a skit we did on *Tarzan and Jane*. Buster Pellettieri staged this show and decided to use black lights and phosphorescent stripes on us natives which would glow bright gold in the black light when the other lights were turned off. At dress rehearsal we tried out the paint and black lights for the first time. We were painted up, the black lights were turned on, and all other lights turned off. There were several dozen Carnicus committee members and workers on the floor of the gym, which doubled back then as the school auditorium, and a sudden, great peal of laughter erupted from the floor. Nobody on stage had a clue as to what was so funny. Well, it turned out that I had inadvertently touched my fly and that spot was glowing brightly.

The next year we did a skit on Dean of Students Ralph Dunford going to Las Vegas in hopes of winning enough money to keep UT, which was having real budgetary problems at that time, afloat. Bob Smith was directing and had not settled on a brother to be Dean Dunford. One night at rehearsal he pulled me aside and said, "Wade, you're going to be Dunford." I retorted, "Man, there's no way I would do that." He said, "You've got to. We simply don't have anybody else for the part." Being very shy insofar as public speaking outside the chapter was concerned, the idea of dancing and singing solos in front of 5,000 people was more than daunting. Bob persisted and finally I retorted, "The only way I'll do it is if you will agree to let me hit the sauce, to the extent necessary, prior to going on stage." Reluctantly Bob agreed, with the admonition not to overdo it. So we had a deal. Sure enough the afternoon before the Saturday night performance, the other lead and I hit the fraternity's downstairs bar and proceeded to "get ready." Well, to my way of thinking, things went just about as well as they possibly could have gone. We thought for sure we had won, but once again we came in a very close second. Incidentally Ralphie, Ralphie Dunford, Dean from Tennessee (to the tune of "Davy, Davy Crockett"), who had motored west in a Model T, did hit it big and was chauffeured back to Knoxville in a Cadillac limousine.

My third year in Carnicus brought on a new problem. Our talented writers had all graduated. Well, I agreed to write a skit and proceeded with the help of Robert E. (Pete — now Bob) Palmer IV of Memphis, to write *Smokey Joe's Café*, a skit named for the theme song of our play. This song was a moderately popular song of the time and went on to be the title of a smash Broadway hit which has run for years. Well, anyway, I had a lead and my name was Acey Boy or Ace. Bill (Luke) Weller was Smokey Joe, the proprietor of the beer joint named for himself. Luke had also been my co-lead the previous year. The final lead was Flo Freely, played by the wonderful dancer, Gary Davis. Flo was Joe's girlfriend, and Ace came into Smokey Joe's Café, took a liking to Flo and started flirting and dancing with her, a turn of events which greatly irked Smokey Joe. At one point Joe asked Ace about his intentions. Ace, "I is takin' Flo to Florida." Joe, "Florida?" Ace, "Yeah, I is goin' to Tampa with uh." The final scene was a big dance among the three of us and in the finale Joe "rams his knife in Ace's gut and jerks his innards out." As I fall to the floor the chorus continues, "And now he lies upon the flo at Smokey Joe's Café, because he wooed this two-bit chick (the censors wouldn't let us say 'ho') at Smokey Joe's Café. Too bad he ever came in here, too bad he did not know no fear, he never should have drunk his beer, at Smokey Joe's Café." We thought we should have won, but we again came in a close second for the third year in a row. Once again Bill, Gary, and I made the same sort of preparations in the bar before that evening's finals, but this time I might have gone just a wee bit too far. At least Acey Boy's sense of invincibility was not manifested quite as strongly as it had been with Ralphie Dunford's.

This is an excerpt taken from Zeta minutes dated February 15, 1960: "Brother (David) Broyles moved that we do not give East Tennessee State our 'Smokey Joe' skit." (When our chapter at East Tennessee State was installed into Pi Kappa Alpha I was head of Zeta's initiation team and initiated half of the new brothers, the other half being initiated by the team from our chapter at Virginia Tech. I am complimented by the fact that they wanted to perform my skit and am disappointed that Zeta did not see fit to pass it on, especially in light of my history with that chapter. My 2002 reading of these minutes is the first I have ever known of this request.)

We Pikes had lots of great parties, both in the chapter house and at rented venues. The biggest party each year was our Dream Girl Ball at which time our new Dream Girl was announced. Normally this party was a weekend bash in Gatlinburg. Knoxville was a dry town, and on big party weekends we'd send some of the brothers up to Gate City or Abingdon, Virginia, or both, depending on how much liquor was ordered for the brothers. Virginia's ABC (Alcoholic Beverage Control) stores were much cheaper than Knoxville's bootleggers, but they had a limit as to how much one person could buy. For this reason the cars were loaded with six brothers, each of whom would buy all the law allowed at each store visited. Sometimes they would have to go to the second town in order to fill all the brothers' orders.

Knoxville did have dozens of bootleggers. More often than not deliveries to the fraternity house were made by motorcyclists dressed in black leather. Their choices of brands were limited, and prices were sky high. Echo Springs was the bourbon of choice — not our choice but the bootlegger's choice. One of Knoxville's top bootleggers passed out business cards which were imprinted simply with a phone number and "Knoxville's Finest Interior Decorators."

UT's dance board was called Nahheeyayli (many campus organizations had Indian names). In order to publicize these well attended events the members, all male, wore an outlandish getup of long red underwear, a feathered headdress, and other silly things for a week leading up to the fall and spring dance weekends. A typical weekend would include a Friday night dance, a Saturday afternoon concert, and Saturday night dance. All events were held in the old gym which is currently being renovated. We had big name bands such as Ralph Marterie, Ralph Flanagan (Brother Ray Stone, a great trumpet player, left school to play with Marterie and Flanagan), Les Elgart, Larry Elgart, and other equally fine swing and dance bands. Nahheeyayli weekends were enormous fun. As an aside UTK was recently named the nation's Number One Party School. I think that designation is long overdue!

Often I returned from home to Knoxville on Sunday nights. About 50 miles from Knoxville my car radio would begin to pick up one of my favorite radio shows, *The Mull Singing Convention of the Air*. The show consisted of gospel music sung by Reverend and Mrs. Mull. The show's opening was priceless, "This is the Reverend (said by him in his deep voice) and Mrs. J. Bazzel Mull (said by her in her high kinda squeaky voice) bringing you the Mull Singing Convention of the 'Ur'" (said by him). Yep, he pronounced air, "ur." They could really sing.

We took old Highway 70 to Knoxville. During my years at UT Interstate 40 was started. As sections were completed we would switch over to the new interstate and then back to Highway 70 when the new sections ended. It was interesting to follow the progress of this monumental project. A couple of years ago I took much of 70 on the way home from Knoxville. It was a beautiful and nostalgic autumn drive.

One year Brother Leroy Smith and I volunteered to run track in the fraternity intramural track meet. They assigned me to the mile run.

I'd never run a mile, but it looked pretty easy to me. They lined us up on the old track at Shields-Watkins Field (now Neyland Stadium), and I took off like a bat out of you-know-where. I streaked by the west stands far ahead of the pack. My friends shouted encouragement and I zipped into the first of what was to be several turns, spurred on by the groundswell of noise following me. As I entered the east straightaway my legs and wind rapidly played down. By the time I reached the north turn I was walking, which I did right on out to my car where I became deathly ill. Guess my friends still wonder what happened to the "Kenton Flash!"

Leroy decided to run barefooted on the cinder track. He finished his shorter race, but his feet looked like hamburger meat when he returned to the Pike house from the UT infirmary. Leroy always had an abundance of spunk. Maybe not always an abundance of judgment, but plenty of spunk.

While at UT I was heavily involved in school spirit organizations. I was a member of the Vol Pep Club and was then appointed school Pep Coordinator. The Pep Club was involved with cheerleaders, pep rallies, and football field decorations. The president of the club appointed me chairman of the stadium decoration committee during my sophomore year. We did such things as wrap the goalposts and write slogans on the fence surrounding the field in crepe paper. I had a hard time getting people to get up early enough on Saturday mornings to get the job done, so I invited some students to the Pike bar early on those mornings to get them "warmed up." Then we would meet on the fifty yard line periodically in order to "spur them on." The "encouragment" was disbursed from my big, bulky overcoat. To finish out the group I persuaded Molly Conyers, a Chi Omega from Dyersburg who was an old friend, to join us. Molly had no problem recruiting Pike pledge Bill McDonald who had a crush on her. We now had a good committee and the rest of the season went smoothly.

We also had a Beaver Club which was in charge of card tricks at football games. The All-Students Club decided to combine the two organizations into what we called Adawayhi which was then responsible for all school spirit affairs. While I was involved in these school spirit activities we decided on a blue tick hound dog for a Vol mascot. A new Tennessee tradition, Smokey, was born.

In later years they also outfitted a student as a hound dog to act as a mascot for football and basketball. The uniform chosen was very poor. In fact one couldn't tell whether he was supposed to be a dog, or a rabbit, or a rat. Dr. Boling appointed me to the UTK Athletics Board in the mid 80s, and we worked with a firm to come up with a better human mascot uniform. The result was excellent, so good in fact that the "new Smokey" has twice been chosen the best human mascot in the nation.

The students lost interest in the football game card tricks a few years prior to the time I was involved in such things. The Beaver Club members, now members of Adawayhi, decided to try the card tricks again. We spent countless hours and thousands of dollars and got everything all set up for that season's first game on Shields-Watkins Field. The cards and printed instructions were put underneath the seats. Everyone was to raise his or her cards on signals from the leaders standing on the cheerleading ramp. On the first signal virtually every card section student sailed their cards off into the wild blue yonder. It's a wonder no one was decapitated. Thusly, the card tricks met an ignominious end at the University of Tennessee. That was a sad day for dozens of us students who had worked hard to bring back a tradition which we fans had enjoyed for years throughout the thirties and forties.

In 2003 the Tennessee Spirit Squads, the cheer team, the dance team, and Smokey collectively were judged the best overall program in the nation, not the first time that has happened. Makes me proud.

For some unknown reason the block bordered by White and Clinch and 15th and 16th Streets in Knoxville had long since been excavated and was nothing more than a great big hole. We students called it the Rose Hole. Each year after a big rain we Pikes would have an intrafraternity football game in the mud. Our clothes would get so muddy that they would never regain their former color. White clothes would be gray. It was great fun. During my sophomore or junior year a Masonic Lodge was built on the southwest corner of the property, and Byerly's Cafeteria moved into the back of this building after they had to vacate their location on Cumberland Avenue in order to make way for the new UT Student Center. The UT Foundation, of which I am a director, is currently working with an Atlanta firm in developing and building an 800 bed dormitory for UT in the Rose Hole.

Hunter Partee, who later asked me to serve as a groomsman in his wedding, and I had a marketing class together. We had a class project whereby one person would call on another in order to sell him something. Hunter's Dad, who was a ginner, sent us some cotton samples. We opened the roll of samples and inserted notes chronologically at the folds of the samples so we did not have to memorize anything. He played the part of the seller and I was Bill Hamer, cotton buyer for Dyersburg Cotton Products. We made an "A." We were both nervous so Hunter came to the Pike house early — it was an 8 o'clock class — and we had a couple of snorts of vodka beforehand to loosen us up. Credit the vodka with the "As!"

During my sophomore year I went with some fraternity brothers from Bristol to a Saturday tea dance at Sullins College, a girls school in Bristol. It was a pretty spring day. Coming into town I had bought a pint of bourbon and had suavely put it in an inside pouch of the top of my Plymouth convertible. At intermission some of the girls and we Pikes took a spin around town. Since it was such a nice day and having forgotten the bourbon, I put the top down. As the top was folding back the bottle suddenly burst with a loud pop showering us all with bourbon and glass. The girls lost all interest in us. For a long time thereafter, glass sifted down into the back seat, and every time the sun came out the car smelled like a distillery.

Spike Jones, who had a Dixieland band which featured lots of bells, whistles, and horns, was one of my favorite bands early in my career at UT. We used to eat at a restaurant out on Kingston Pike, Dixieland, which had a good jukebox. Spike had a number on the jukebox and one night I played it something like ten straight times. It soon became obvious that nobody else in the establishment was anywhere near as enamored with Spike's music as was I.

One winter while at UT I went up to The University of Virginia to visit my Lake County friend, Ed Willingham who was a student at UVa. We had a great time due in no small part to the fact that Louis

Armstrong was playing the party weekend called Mid-Winters. Seeing Satchmo in person was a treat.

At Christmas, 1955, Dad, a Chrysler-Plymouth dealer in Union City, gave me a new Plymouth convertible, briar rose and black, to replace my yellow '54 Plymouth convertible. Back in those days they had you take out the "breaking-in oil" at 500 miles and replace it with regular oil. Upon getting back to Knoxville after Christmas it was time to change the oil. As had always been the case, I took my car to Paul Campbell Gulf on Cumberland for this purpose. The new car had a brand new kind of transmission with push buttons. The service attendant had never before seen them and assumed that the wheels would be locked if the Drive button were pushed. Well, it didn't work that way. To lock the wheels you had to put it in "P" for park. Anyway, he pushed "D" and raised the car on their hydraulic lift. About the time it got to the top it began to roll forward. Sure enough it rolled off the front of the lift and nose-dived into the concrete floor, doing all sorts of damage to the front end of the car. I was heartsick. As soon as we talked with Paul about his insurance my fraternity brother and very close friend, Bill Upchurch from Memphis, and I repaired (across the street and up a block or so) to the Roman Room, a cheaply decorated Romanesque bar and grill, and drank a beer or two. Soon the ball started rolling to getting the RM3, as my sister was later to call my car, repaired.

One Thanksgiving Frank Grace, a brother from Providence, Rhode Island, and I drove to Kenton for the holiday. We decided to leave Kenton Saturday afternoon in time to catch Papa John Gordy and his band at his club in Nashville. Papa John, father of Vol captain, All-SEC and Detroit Lions All-Pro tackle, John Gordy, Jr., had a great Dixieland band. His club was near downtown in a dark area. Frank's and my clothes were hanging above the back seat. While we were partying some low-life thief cut the convertible top over the passenger seat, opened the door, and cleaned us out. This was especially tough on Frank, as these were probably his best clothes. Our insurance probably covered a good bit of his loss.

I didn't get around to repairing the top for a good while. In the meantime at night a piece of plastic was placed on the top over the hole, and when it rained the plastic would pooch down with the weight of the water. The plastic was removed each morning. One morning after a big rain I forgot the plastic. One of the brothers rode with me to 8 o'clock classes. We were running late, as usual, and I made the corner of Clinch and 13th Street on two wheels. Guess what happened? The entire contents of the <u>big</u> pooch emptied into the lap of my rider. Tom Wade wasn't on his Hit Parade for a good while after that.

Speaking of Frank Grace, he was the Pike representative for a Knoxville bookie who sold football pools on the UT campus. These sheets listed about 25 or 30 games with point spreads. The sheets cost $1.00 each. The bettor picked ten winners against the spreads. One Saturday almost everybody was a winner, and the bookie skipped town. My uncollected bet would have paid me $50. Frank was most embarrassed, but he obviously had no responsibility. Campus gamblers lost no telling how many thousands of dollars. My McCallie betting had been much more successful than my UT gambling career. At least the cadets gave me the nickels and dimes that they owed me.

Pete Henly, Hoff, Bill McDonald, Monin, and I took the RM3 to Washington, D.C. for a long weekend one winter. The patch had been repaired. We spent the first night in the bar on couches in the Pike House at Washington & Lee. Then, after very little sleep, we drove on to Charlottesville where we picked up Zeta's Dave McSween's twin brother, Bill, a member of PiKA's Alpha Chapter at the University of Virginia, and we all went to Carroll's Tea Room (which did not sell tea) and spent a couple of very happy hours drinking beer and singing Pike songs to the excellent accompaniment of Bill, who plays the piano by ear, very well. After this interlude it was on to Washington where we stayed at Pete Henly's mother's apartment in D.C. Sally was a student at Holton Arms at that time and she got us dates with great looking girls. Two of the girls were Sally's and my close friend, Lew White from Osceola, Arkansas, who was to go to Europe with us in 1956, and our cousin Ann Alexander of Paragould, Arkansas, whose mother was a Montgomery from Kenton. We took them to a fancy jazz nightclub, Casino Royal. The great jazz band, Louie Jourdan, was playing. We had many drinks and danced until it was time to get the girls back to their dorm. Our very professional waiter brought our bill and it was enormous, at least for us. We all divvied up the money as best we could, left Hoff to make final settlement, and headed for the exit. Soon Hoff came running down the stairs out the door. We asked him why the hurry? He said, "I only had 33 cents for his tip. Move out!" This evening may have been the only time Hoff failed to get up on stage and sing *Kansas City* with the band. He could sing it!

On Sunday morning we all went to the Presbyterian Church in Washington which Sally attended. President and Mrs. Eisenhower also attended there. After church we stood outside and watched the Eisenhowers get into their car and pull off followed closely by a real old-fashioned looking car (Untouchables — looking) carrying their Secret Service men, some of whom were on the running boards.

The weather turned bad on the way home. We drove all night to make classes that Monday, and it was some kinda cold in that back seat. That rag-top never did have a great heater and the back seat, in addition to not getting much heat from the front, was plum breezy.

The next school year Bill McSween transferred to UT. The first morning he was at our fraternity house he and twin brother David were in the bathroom shaving side by side. Charlie Milam, who had been to a pretty good party the night before and who did not even know that Bill existed, came into the bathroom, saw what he saw, didn't believe it, said nothing, turned around, went back to bed, and slept it off.

Sally ended up with the RM3 at UNC Chapel Hill. She and some Pike buddies of hers gave it this dubious name. They thought the "briar rose" color, which I liked a lot, was more than a little bit gaudy. TR3s (British Triumphs) were popular at the time.

The RM3 brought fraternity brother Tim Sullivan of New York home with me for a weekend. Tim grew up in Glens Falls, New York and in Manhattan and has lived on East 80th Street in New York City almost since graduation from UT. When we drove by downtown Kenton Tim said, "Tom, this is certainly a nice little shopping center." To which I replied, "Shopping center the dickens, this is it!"

Reed Mabe, a Pike from Memphis and a great guy, came up with a greeting that was a real Mabeism. He would shake your hand and say, "Congratulations, salutations, and valedictorians!" Reed was a fire engine redhead and was a distinctive looking fellow, and I told Sally all about him. One late night in Memphis Sally and her date went into a Toddle House for a bite to eat. Sally saw Reed and, believe it or not, figured out who he was and went up to him and exclaimed, "Congratulations, salutations, and valedictorians!" Well, as you can imagine, Reed, who had never laid eyes on Sally, could have been knocked over with a feather.

During my years at Tennessee we played Alabama and Auburn in Birmingham on alternate years, and I went to the Birmingham game every year. One year a Pike alumnus drove several of us Pike undergrads, Jerry Robinson from Nashville being one of them, to Birmingham. We had reservations as we usually did at the Tutwiler Hotel downtown. As we pulled up to the curb in front of the hotel there were some press folks there and I remarked to the others, "The press is here to interview ME." They laughed, of course. Well, I got out of the car first and sure enough the reporter and photographer came right up to me and started asking me questions about tomorrow's game. The previous year Auburn had beaten Tennessee badly, and when I predicted a Tennessee win they wondered what in the world caused me to make such a rash prediction. "Because of a sophomore tailback named Johnny Majors," I said. In those days freshmen could not play varsity sports, and this was to be Johnny's first game as a Volunteer. After my little interview they asked me to go into the hotel and get Tennessee and Auburn couples for a photograph. I agreed and went into a bar that opened out to the sidewalk as well as into the lobby of the Tutwiler and immediately saw and enlisted an Auburn couple but saw no Vol couples. I did see a popular and pretty little blond from UT, Smut Smith, and asked her if she would join me for the photo. She agreed and the four of us went out onto the sidewalk where the photographer took a picture of us. Well, believe it or not, the next morning *The Birmingham News* had a very large full color picture right on the top of the front page of the four of us waving our pennants and shakers. By George, the press <u>was</u> there to interview ME!

The next day at Birmingham's Legion Field the Majors-led Volunteers annihilated Auburn by four touchdowns or so. Many years later I was to go to New York for Johnny's induction into the College Football Hall of Fame.

The most memorable football game of my college career was the 1956 Georgia Tech game in Atlanta. Both teams were undefeated, Tech was ranked second, and we were only a spot or two below them. Tickets were non-existent. A Buick dealer traded a new car for four on the fifty. Fraternity brother Dave McSween dressed as a janitor with a mop and bucket and simply walked in. Fraternity brother Leroy Smith was with a group of 100 or so who pushed down a fence and stampeded in. Other brothers were equally as resourceful. I actually had a ticket — a good one. It was a game never to be forgotten. We won the game, 6-0. The smartest plays I ever saw were called by Johnny Majors, our All-American tailback and runnerup to Heisman Trophy winner Paul Hornung. We had the ball, first down, on our ten yard line. Johnny faked a quick kick and ran ten yards to our 20. First down, Tennessee. Johnny then quick kicked almost 70 yards. During this game second string tailback, fraternity brother Bobby Gordon, booted the ball 76 yards from deep punt formation. This was Tennessee football at its greatest. This game was selected as the best college game of the year and a few years later the Associated Press picked it as the second greatest game of all time. Our team ended the regular season undefeated and ranked Number Two in the nation.

When I was president of PiKA at Tennessee early one evening several of us went out to Highlands, our favorite beer-jukebox spot. Some rough high school boys came in spoiling for a fight. Sure enough a fight broke out. Trying to prove my leadership ability, I stepped in between a college boy and a high school boy and tried to reason with them. Lo and behold the high school boy with no warning suddenly hit me in the stomach with a real haymaker which doubled me over with pain. That was my last attempt at breaking up fights.

In 1954 I was Zeta delegate to the PiKA convention at the Peabody Hotel in Memphis. We had a great time. I remember the house detective telling Pelham to GO TO BED — which he did posthaste! Another great memory of that convention occurred after the Dream Girl Ball held in the big ballroom on the mezzanine floor. A bunch of us started throwing coins from the mezzanine into the famous fountain in the lobby. Hoff went down to the lobby, calmly took off his shoes and socks, rolled up his tuxedo pants, and started wading around in the fountain, picking up coins, putting them in his pocket, and singing, *Three Coins in the Fountain*. Some of the others in Memphis were Sally, our cousin, Jean Sanders, Shirley Hendren (UT Chi Omega from Dyersburg and Zeta Dream Girl), and Layton Smith, a member of our Upsilon Chapter at Auburn and my McCallie roommate before Monin. At this convention immortal PiKA Robert Adger Smythe and Zeta's (and the Fraternity's) first Dream Girl, "Miss Johnnie" Johnston, met for the first and last time.

On my 21st birthday I had a date with Molly Conyers. She lived in a rooming house up Clinch or White or one of those streets near the Pike House. Unbeknownst to me, pledges Spud Hale and Gene Lyons, both big men, were just inside Molly's front door and were hidden on each side. As I walked in the door they simply lifted me and carried me backwards to my car and stuffed me down into the back floorboard. They blindfolded me and drove me to a place that later was determined to have been the back side of the ag campus where they stuck me in with another active who had been abducted by some other pledges and then headed for parts unknown. Probably about an hour and a half later they stopped the car, took us out and took off our blindfolds. Though it was a cloudy night and pitch black dark it was obvious that we were somewhere in the mountains. Charlie Marshall and I headed down the mountain. We walked for hours, at times with critters walking off the road to the side of us through the leaves. We figured they were bears. At any rate we finally arrived at Fontana Dam. Luckily it was near their middle-of-the-night shift changing time, and we soon caught a ride with a guard into Maryville. I called roomie Bill Upchurch and asked him to come get us. (Spud and Gene had been kind enough to take my car back to the fraternity house. Wasn't that nice of them?) Dawn was breaking as we pulled up to good ole 1305 West Clinch (the Pike House). It had never looked better. For several days after that we unmercifully paddled Spud and Gene. (Spud left school and received a good-sized bonus to sign as a pitcher/outfielder with the Los Angeles Dodgers. His first year was with the Union City Greyhounds in the Kitty League. His next year was with Reno, after which time he came back to his Dad's Yorkville farm.) Spud was initiated into PiKappa Alpha at our 2000 reunion as a Special

Dispensation initiate. Gene was initiated into Pi Kappa Alpha at our 1995 reunion. PiKA gained two true gentlemen, goat rides notwithstanding.

My 21st birthday was not at all what had been planned, and goat riding is not in my all-time list of favorite things to do. But I wouldn't take a pretty penny for having had the experience. Every fraternity man should experience a goat ride. They were meant for pledges, but they worked just as well for actives. The harmless things that we did hurt nobody and an argument could be made that they actually helped build character. The problem is that some hazing is extreme, and with the world having become a much less innocent place there is no doubt but that the Greek world is better off with no hazing at all.

Surely nobody ever enjoyed a college/fraternity experience more than I did.

After a wonderful college career I graduated in March of 1957 and immediately went to work for Zeta, Inc., Zeta's house corporation, and organized and managed a campaign to raise funds for a new house for Zeta chapter.

Chapter Eleven

Yellowstone and the Jimmy Wade Story

In the summer of 1954 John Hoff and I drove to Yellowstone Park where we had jobs obtained through our congressman, Jere Cooper. We took my 1954 yellow Plymouth convertible with a Continental kit. (A Continental kit was an extension of the back bumper which allowed the spare tire, which was enclosed in a round chrome holder, to be outside the trunk. My car had wire wheels, and despite a rubber liner that fit between the wires and the inner tubes, the wires somehow often got to the tubes causing one flat after another. One night on Highway 70 between Knoxville and West Tennessee, with several Pikes and dates along, we had a flat. We changed to the spare and drove a few hundred yards and had another flat. We were near a motel and walked there to telephone for assistance.)

On our first leg of the trip to our summer jobs between home and St. Louis we hit a torrential downpour. Water literally poured onto Hoff and me from between the windshield and the top. The floorboard filled with water which we bailed out when the rain stopped. We persevered and drove on to Columbia, Missouri where in the late afternoon we went by the Pike House at the University of Missouri. They were a great bunch of guys and some of them invited us to go with them to a local student pub hangout. We partied with them until about midnight when we decided it was time for us to hit the road and continue westward, so we bid the brothers adieu. About halfway from Columbia to Kansas City we ran out of gas. It was a limited access highway. We coasted to a stop in the emergency lane and decided to get some sleep. I slept in the front seat and Hoff in the back seat. At about daybreak I got out and hitched a ride to the nearest service station and brought some gas back to the car. We then filled up and continued our journey to Wyoming.

Yellowstone was a blast. Hoff worked in the cafeteria on one side of the Yellowstone River, and I was a yardman-scrubber at Canyon Lodge on the other side of the river. Congressman Jere Cooper from Dyersburg, who was chairman of the House Ways and Means Committee at the time, got Hoff his job in Yellowstone a year or so in advance. At the last minute Mother and Dad, good friends of Jere's (more about that later), called him and he got me what amounted to an even better job than John had. This was simply the luck of the draw. We workers were employed by Yellowstone Park Company (YPC). My job was to work with two cabin maids in cleaning a section of cabins. I took out clean linens and picked up dirty linens in a 2-wheeled pushcart and cleaned out the stoves and replaced kindling wood and "dope" (a mixture of sawdust and kerosene which was used by the "dudes" — our word for the tourists — to start fires in their wood burning stoves). About a third of my cabins had linoleum floors which had to be mopped with some sort of oil. The rest were wooden floors which the cabin maids swept. The wooden floor cabins were far and away my favorites! My least pleasant duty was emptying and cleaning the chamber pots each morning. The cabins did not have running water, and communal bathrooms and showers were located in each section of cabins. Our instructions were to take the pots to those bathrooms and pour the contents into the toilets and then clean them with the supplies which were furnished. Sometimes when they weren't too bad, some of us yardman scrubbers would just walk back into the woods and sling the "leavings" into the bushes. This illegal practice was known as "shooting ducks." Some of my compatriots picked out spots pretty far back in the woods and slung in the same place for weeks, if not months. They prided themselves on turning the trees into great hanging gardens of toilet paper. These hanging beauties were referred to as "duck feathers."

My chores were usually finished by noon (unfortunately Hoff's hours were longer than mine). Often in the afternoons some of us would go somewhere in my car. On our one day a week off we would usually go to a more distant place like Jackson Hole which we all loved. Back then Jackson Hole had casinos on the square and just off the square. Two that I remember are the Million Dollar Cowboy Bar and the Silver Dollar Bar. The Cowboy Bar is a rustic lounge with saddles used as bar stools. The Silver Dollar's bar is encrusted with silver dollars. Pat and I were in Jackson a few years ago and those bars are still there and look great. Their casinos, however, closed years ago. We saw several well known movie stars in one of the casinos in '54. They were in Jackson Hole on location for a movie, and they were well "into their cups."

Another distant trip was to Red Lodge, Montana where we ate in a restaurant known for all types of game such as bear, moose, elk, and venison. All of it was good. Other places closer by that we frequented were West Yellowstone, Montana and Gardiner, Montana. Gardiner was a town of about 600 with probably ten saloons. We usually went to Bloody Mary's. Mary was an old hag who played an upright piano and sang risque songs. She had a wooden cat with a big mouth on the top of the piano with a sign that read, "Feed Me." We threw coins into the cat's mouth when she played songs we particularly liked. One night two cowboys sitting together at the bar had a big argument and invited each other out the back door into the alley to settle their differences. A while later they staggered back in the front door all beat up and bloody with their arms around each other's shoulders and sat back down at the bar, as happy as larks.

There was a lounge in West Yellowstone that had a great pianist, much better than Miss Mary, who probably weighed 350 pounds. His best song began, "Sarah, Sarah, sitting in a shoeshine shop" and continued with many similar verses. We thought he was a scream. He was a good entertainer.

When we arrived at Yellowstone in early June, snow was up to the eaves of the buildings. Our elevation was about 8,000 feet. On July 4 it snowed a little. We workers celebrated July 4th in fine fashion. Each dorm, especially the girls' dorms, had fancy hors d'oeuvres and we drank our version of "purple passion" and other such drinks. We had a July 4th parade. A boy from Alabama (now a physician whom Pat and I saw in a restaurant in Gulf Shores, Alabama about 25 years ago) and I paraded with a smoking (with dry ice) chamber pot slung between us on a tree limb which rested on our shoulders. We celebrated Christmas on July 25. The dorms and the lodge were decorated with

Christmas trees and all the usual Christmas decorations. It was just another excuse to have a good time with parties at all the dorms. I don't recall exchanging gifts, but we may have. My recollection is that the cafeteria served turkey and dressing and all the trimmings. If they didn't, they shoulda!

These celebrations were traditions at Canyon Lodge that had been going on for years. It was widely felt that Canyon Lodge was the premier place in Yellowstone Park at which to work. We surely thought so. Several of the workers had been coming to the lodge for years. A few had even reached early middle age. At least they appeared that old to me.

Good ole Hoff usually had to walk from his location to Canyon Lodge, which was about a mile across the Yellowstone River Bridge. All the girls were at the Lodge so he was a regular visitor and was just like one of the Canyon Lodge bunch. He cooked up a story about being a country singer who had appeared on the Grand Ole Opry.

Just like Hoff backed up my football story (an account of which follows), I backed up his music story. He could sing pretty good, though he never seemed to sing very many verses of a song. My guess was that he actually didn't know any complete songs. At any rate we were the unchallenged celebrities of 1954!

One of my best friends at Canyon Lodge was Alabamian Bert Nettles. Bert is now an attorney in Alabama. He, like fraternity brother Luther Hodges, Jr., a Tau Chapter (North Carolina) Pike whom I met at the '56 Pike convention in Mexico City and with whom I have stayed in touch through the years, switched political parties and became Republican nominees for U.S. Senate races from Alabama and North Carolina. Also, like Luther, Bert lost. I think it's interesting that two good friends of mine had the same unique experiences. (Luther was the son of the governor of North Carolina who was later Secretary of Commerce in the Johnson Administration. Luther, Jr. had a successful career with North Carolina National Bank, now Bank of America and then went on to become C.E.O. of a Washington, D.C. bank.) Bert, originally from Monroeville, Alabama, the home of famous writers Truman Capote and Harper Lee, now lives in Mobile, and Luther now lives in Phoenix. Bert came to Pat's and my wedding.

At about the time I entered UT the Volunteer football team had just recently had an All-SEC tailback (the Vols ran the Single Wing) by the name of Jimmy Wade. One day I was sitting in the dorm talking with another YPC worker who had played freshmen football at the University of Minnesota. He probably weighed 250 pounds which was real big back then. Out of the clear blue he asked, "Do you play football at Tennessee?" I answered, "I did." He asked, "What did you play?" "Tailback," I replied. He said, "You're pretty small to have played major college football." I probably weighed 150 or so then and countered, "All tailbacks at Tennessee have been pretty small," probably adding something like, "They don't care about your size; they just want you to be quick and fast and to be able to pass and punt well." How fortunate that we didn't have a football! At any rate the word spread around Yellowstone about the little fellow who formerly had been an All-SEC tailback at Tennessee. Your writer has never before or since felt so important.

Two of my friends at Canyon Lodge were students at Hampden-Sydney, the fine small Virginia college. That fall they came down to Knoxville on a football weekend. I alerted the fraternity brothers to my deception and asked them to go along with me. We all went to the game on Saturday and Shields-Watkins Field (the stadium itself is now called Neyland Stadium) was jampacked with fans. The two boys were snowed out of their minds. They asked me lots of questions about football during the course of the game and I answered them to the best of my knowledge, which as you can imagine really wasn't all that great. They left Knoxville the next day none the wiser.

About three years later, after my graduation from UT, I was standing out on the walk in front of our automobile agency in Union City and much to my surprise one of those Hampden-Sydney boys, John Sharp, came driving by. I hollered, "Hey John!" John braked his car and was just as surprised to see me. He was in Union City for a few months during the installation of the refrigeration unit of the new Reelfoot Packing Company plant which was destined to be, for awhile at least, the world's most up-to-date packing plant. John was the refrigeration engineer for the job. I invited him to come to dinner with Mother and Dad and me at home in Kenton. During the course of the evening he quizzed me considerably about my being in Kenton and Union City since Jimmy Wade was from Lynchburg, Virginia. I told him that when Tennessee was recruiting me the athletic department set Dad up in the automobile business in Union City. He asked why I was now called Tom instead of Jimmy. I told him that my full name was James Thomas Wade and though I had always been known as Tom in Virginia the Knoxville news media, picking up on my first name, started calling me Jimmy which had stuck. I did my best to explain all these inconsistencies, but my perception was that old John left our home that night with great doubts about my veracity.

One final twist to the story. Years later I was in the bar at Deane Hill Country Club in Knoxville and met Jimmy Wade for the first time. I told him this story, and he really got a kick out of it. Sadly, Jimmy recently died. He was one of Tennessee's all-time great tailbacks.

When Hoff and I came home from Yellowstone we brought a carload to the South. We dropped off a girl whom Hoff had dated some, in Denver, and we spent the first night in her family's home. Then we headed home the next day with all the rest of those of us who were headed to Dyersburg and Kenton and points further south. We left Denver about mid morning and Hoff and I soon decided it would be great if we could get back home in time to go to the Supper Club that next night, Saturday night. So we drove all night long and did arrive in West Tennessee in time to make Jackson's Supper Club. The Supper Club was not an impressive place by any means, but it was pretty big and had a terrific black band. The band leader's name was Snowball Davis. There was a smaller, rougher looking black club just before you got to the Supper Club (which incidentally did not serve any food at all). Hoff and I decided we would peel off into the real rough dive first and watch the expressions on the faces of our Yellowstone friends. Sure enough, they looked shocked — and scared. We laughed uncontrollably and whipped on around and headed for the Supper Club. Their expressions weren't much different when they saw the real thing. It didn't take long though for our buddies to see why we liked the Supper Club so much.

We had a great contingent from the Southeastern Conference at Canyon Lodge. Two of us from Tennessee, six (all girls) from Vanderbilt, five from Alabama, and four from Florida. The Vanderbilt girls had a Canyon Lodge reunion in Nashville and Franklin that Christmas, and 35 or so of us from all over the eastern and southern United States from Miami to Minneapolis attended. What a blast!

A year or so after we worked at Yellowstone our lodge was torn down and a new Canyon Lodge was built on the other side of the Yellowstone River. Pat and I were in Yellowstone on a trip three or four years ago and we went to the site of the old lodge. I never could figure out just exactly where everything had been which was very disappointing to me.

Even though my total wages were only about $200 for the entire time we were there, that summer in Yellowstone Park was a highlight of my life. How wonderful it is to be young and to have no responsibility other than to try to figure out how to have a good time.

Chapter Twelve

1956 Trip to Europe

In the summer of 1956 Sally, Pelham, Hoff, Sally's roommate
from Bennett Junior College (a girls finishing school at
Millbrook, NY) Flo Pittman from Memphis, Lew White (Sally's
classmate at Holton Arms, a girls prep school in Washington, D.C.),
Molly Conyers from Dyersburg, and several others we either knew or
knew of, went to Europe on a seven week trip. Hoff and I roomed
together. There were 38 of us on the trip which was composed of
college age folks. Mother and Dad and Grandmother drove Sally,
Pelham, and me to New York where we met the rest of the people.
Our group spent the night before departure in the old Gotham Hotel
which is now the Peninsula. The next day we boarded the *Queen Mary*
in New York Harbor. All of our own group went First Class. The total
cost of the trip for Sally and me was $5,000 which was a bunch of
money in 1956. When Dad protested that it was mighty extravagant to
send us first class, which added a good deal to the cost, Mother said, "I
have $5,000." Dad said, "How come?" Mother then proceeded to tell
him that over the years she had taken clothes out for approval, most
from Memphis, and paid for them with a check on Dad. Then if she
decided she didn't want them after all, she would return them for cash
refunds which she put into a secret bank account for some such
purpose. Though Dad was probably somewhat miffed with Mother for
her subterfuge, he must have been relieved not to have to foot the bill.
At least not with new money!

Our five days over on the *Queen Mary* were wonderful in every way.
The food and service were truly outstanding. Drinks in the
Observation Lounge, our favorite watering hole, were 25 cents. Sally's
favorite during her time in Europe was Dubonnet on the Rocks.
About half of the participants went Tourist or Cabin Class. Pretty
soon several of them figured out ways to get into First Class. The

waiters and bartenders got so used to seeing them that they were never questioned.

Our first stop was Paris after arriving at Le Harve, France. My McCallie buddies, Wayne and Mike Miller from Knoxville, were also in Europe and met us at our hotel in Paris soon after we arrived. Wayne had just graduated from Princeton, and Mike was a rising senior at UT. Wayne spoke French and they suggested we go out to a sidewalk café on the Champs d' Elyssee which we did. When we got there Wayne explained to us that the little cracker things in the center of the table were counted and we would pay for what we ate. Hoff ordered a "Taum Caw-Leens." Well, everybody but Hoff ate a bunch of the crackers. Our trip was totally dutch, and everybody paid his or her own way. Somehow when we got our bills Hoff got charged for all the crackers, a not inconsiderable sum. When Wayne finally made Hoff understand that he had been billed for all the crackers, an incensed Hoff jumped up, looked the rather distinguished waiter in the eye, pointed at the now empty center of the table and said very excitedly and loudly, "Me no eata these! Me no eata these!" Hoff's long suit obviously was not the French language, but he got his point across and the rest of us divvied up the price of the crackers.

While in Paris our leader, Mrs. Brown, offered us an optional nightclub tour of the city. Everybody went. We had dinner and champagne at The Lido, the famous nightclub, then champagne at Folies Bergere, another world famous nightclub, and we ended the night at another famous nightclub, the cave-like Scheherezade which had a 21 piece Russian violin orchestra. The place was almost deserted, as it was about 3 AM when the 38 of us traipsed in. As you can imagine, they were happy to see such a large crowd at such a late hour and the orchestra broke into *God Bless America*. We were all pretty well into our cups at this point, and Hoff grabbed the right arm of the orchestra leader, hung on for dear life, and sang for all he was worth. Watching that poor man trying to play his violin, struggling to move his arm, was a sight to see.

Later in the trip when we checked into our big old ornate hotel in Nice in the middle of the afternoon after a pretty much sleepless night on a train, I decided to take a nap. Hoff went to the bathroom and then could not figure out how to flush the toilet. He pulled a cord hanging from high up on the bathroom wall. The toilet did not flush but almost immediately a maid burst into the room and ran straight into the bathroom. I heard a commotion and watched as she beat a hasty retreat. Hoff swears that when she saw him she said, "Uhmm, nice!" I didn't hear that, but Hoff was always known to be a very truthful person.

In Heidelberg, Germany we went to a famous beer hall which had lots of graffiti on the walls. We sat in a back room and Pelham tipped our waitress to turn her back as he carved a very large PiKA above the door leading back out into the main room. I've often wondered if this carving is still there. It may well be.

In Cologne we stayed in a fine hotel across from the famous cathedral. While we were there Konrad Adenhaur, Germany's world famous Chancellor, walked right by me on the way to a state dinner.

In Weisbaden we stayed in a hotel considered by some to be the best in Germany. Hoff and I had a very large room, just above the hotel entrance, and we decided to throw a champagne party for our group. The party got a little out of hand and one or two of the boys (not me, of course) sprinkled a little champagne on some guests entering the hotel. The hotel detective quickly came up to our room and closed down the festivities.

In Rome we all went to an opera at the Caracalla Baths, a famous antiquity. About halfway through the opera, Sally and I, not appreciating opera — our first — decided to leave. We caught a horse and buggy back to our hotel. The smell from the horse gave me a first class attack of asthma which I handled with my atomizer upon reaching the hotel. Leaving that beautiful opera was not Sally's and my finest hour.

In Florence we stayed in the Excelsior Hotel (Pat and I stayed there in '93). A Caldwell boy from Humboldt, a Vanderbilt student who had our itinerary, met us in the bar of the Excelsior. Another boy whom we met in that bar was Ed Goldstone, a Hollywood boy who was traveling in Europe with his family. His dad was a famous movie producer. Ed took a liking to Sally, but she had no interest whatsoever in Ed. Every time another member of our tour would arrive in the bar

Hoff would go to great lengths to introduce him or her to Ed "Gallstone." Ed would immediately counter "Goldstone." This occurred several times during the evening. Ed got our itinerary and called Sally several times over the next few days trying to arrange to meet her. She still had no interest in Mr. Gallstone — uh, Goldstone. In later years I read a great deal about Ed Goldstone who became a very big Hollywood producer in his own right. He was married to some pretty famous women including the actress and dancer who was also married to Frank Sinatra at one time, Juliet Prowse.

Also in the Excelsior bar Sally and Flo met a couple of slick young men who claimed to be counts, whatever counts are. Somehow these two men convinced the girls to go with them to the villa of one of them up in the mountains near Florence. Sally said she and Flo "kept moving" around the villa and soon persuaded the "counts" to take them back to our hotel.

Another hotel in which Pat and I had stayed in 1993 and which our 1956 tour also stayed in was the Danielli in Venice. In '56 we referred to it as the Royal Danielli. I remember in '56 that Hoff's and my room faced a small back canal. Pat's and my room faced the Grand Canal and had a nice balcony overlooking Venice, quite an improvement.

Also in Italy, in Sorrento, Hoff and I had a room in the famous Grand Hotel Excelsior Vittorio. We had a fabulous ornate room which had a balcony from which you could see the hotel gardens in one direction and the Bay of Naples in the other direction. There was an impressive hand painted mural on the ceiling. We were told that Enrico Caruso came to this hotel each year and that this was the room he always stayed in. Ole Hoff and I were impressed, to say the least. Pat and I explored this hotel in 1993, though we did not stay in Sorrento. A pizza we college folks had on our Sorrento hotel terrace which overlooked the lights of Naples across the bay and Mount Vesuvius to the right, was the best we all decided that we had ever had. Maybe the atmosphere affected our taste buds. I do know for sure that the worst pizza we had ever had was at lunch in a Naples hotel prior to our arriving in Sorrento. It was virtually tasteless.

In Switzerland we stayed at the Palace Hotel in Lucerne where Pat and I stayed on a UT trip 15 or 20 years ago. We also spent a night in Interlachen and took the train up to the top of the world famous Jungfrau. Because of the spectacular scenery most of our travel in Switzerland was by bus.

When we got to Bergen, Norway, Hoff left the group and spent a day with his Norwegian relatives. Afterwards I asked him about his cousins. He remembered very little about the day which was spent primarily in toasting each other. Hoff's middle name is Haaken, and he is descended from Norwegian royalty. There have been King Haakens in Norway's history. From that point on we referred to John as King Haaken.

In Copenhagen we spent an evening at the fascinating Tivoli Gardens. Another interesting thing we did was to go to the Carlsberg Brewery. After our tour of the brewery they took us into a large room with long tables and all their brands of beer and soft drinks in bunches on the tables. Free beer! I happened to sit down with a Pittsburgh boy from a school up east who quickly established the fact that his family had a summer home outside Knoxville on one of the TVA lakes. We got to be good buddies and he and his pal hung around with us for the rest of our time in Copenhagen. When I got back to UT that fall, my roomie, Bill Monin, who was in school at UT that summer, told me that he had met a great guy from Pittsburgh and that he (Bill) had spent a lot of time with him and his family that summer doing a lot of water skiing. Immediately I realized that he was talking about my Copenhagen friend's younger brother. It's a small world after all!

Our last stop was London which we all loved. We saw two or three shows. After seeing *Romanoff and Juliet*, starring Peter Ustinov, several of us went to the famous Ivy for a late supper. Jack Benny was in Europe that summer filming a series of TV shows for the next fall and winter. Well, by George, Jack Benny came walking by our table. Another fellow and I said, "That's Jack Benny." The others said, "No way." On his way back by our table one of the girls said, "Mr. Benny?" He stopped and said, "Yeees." Everybody was flabbergasted. This other fellow then said, "These girls would like to have your autograph," to which he replied, "All right. Do you have a pen and something to write on?" We scrambled around and got a pen and paper from a waiter and Mr. Benny proceeded to sign autographs. We boys were too proud to ask for autographs. Or too dumb? He was with a beautiful young lady.

Other countries we visited were Scotland, Sweden, Monaco, Luxembourg, and Belgium where all the girls bought lace in Brussels.

After five and a half weeks on the continent we took the boat train from London to Southampton where we boarded the *Queen Elizabeth*, again first class, bound for New York. Except for the bus in Switzerland we traveled by train to the many countries we visited, and the *Queen Elizabeth* was a welcome and luxurious change of pace. We again had a marvelous crossing. Our 1956 trip to Europe was an unforgettable and wonderful experience in every respect.

When we arrived in New York Bernard Baruch and I tried to go through the same small shipboard door at the same time. I jumped back in deference to him. In addition to being a famous and distinguished person, he was a very big man.

We had planned to spend the night in New York and fly home the following day. However, our gang was able to move our flight up a day, so we flew to Memphis that night. Despite the fact that we had experienced a once-in-a-lifetime journey, we were all ready to get home.

Chapter Thirteen

Life After College and Before Marriage to Pat

During my college years and for a few years afterwards, the Supper Club south of Jackson was the favorite hangout for UT students from West Tennessee. While home on vacations from college and after graduation I went down there many Saturday nights and would always see lots of West Tennessee friends from UT. It was like a little homecoming every Saturday night.

One Saturday night during the time of our regular Supper Club forays, Hoff and Pelham didn't have dates but came on over from Dyersburg anyway and joined some of us who did have dates. Hoff reminded me that they were pretty much snookered when they got there and didn't slow down a bit when they got to Jackson. But they did make it on back to Dyersburg late that night where they were pulled over by the police. Pelham was driving and the officer questioned him and suggested that Hoff drive. The officer asked Pelham if Hoff had been drinking and Peter said, "Oh no, he never drinks." At that, Hoff, most insulted, rared up in his seat and said, "I have been known to have one!" Nevertheless, the officer insisted that Hoff drive. So Pelham got out of the car and started around the back of the car while Hoff slid over to the driver's side. Before Pelham could get clear around, Hoff pulled off. Pelham started running, trying to catch the car. The car was right up against a high curb, too high for the passenger door to open, so when Pelham was finally able to get Hoff to stop he couldn't open the door. Pelham told Hoff to pull up some more which he did several times, but each time Pelham still could not get the door open. Eventually Hoff got to an intersection and when Pelham was finally able to get in the car, Hoff said some big time yelling took place between the two of them. All this time the officers were watching and, Hoff suspected, shaking their heads. Hoff then drove down College Hill and up in front of the Methodist Church with the police car right behind them. Then Hoff says he just flat ran the stop sign there and headed on up Troy Avenue toward home. The terrible twosome was mighty fortunate to have been stopped by such understanding policemen.

After graduation from The University of Tennessee I soon took on the position of PiKA's District President for the chapters in Tennessee, Kentucky, and some of Arkansas. During this time a group of boys who had formed a local fraternity at UTM and who desired to affiliate with a national fraternity contacted me. UTM had only 1,000 students at that time and, everything considered, we decided to pass. The group became a chapter of another national fraternity. Soon thereafter I got a call from my distant cousin, William Penn of Kenton, who was a member of another local. I went over to meet with them and was most impressed. I called National and told them that despite UTM's size my opinion was that we should pursue these boys. We did and they became one of Pi Kappa Alpha's good chapters. I became their first house corporation president, helped them acquire their first house, and enjoyed helping them during rush for several years. One of their early men was current UTM Chancellor, Nick Dunagan. Epsilon Sigma, PiKA's UTM chapter, has graduated many outstanding men through the years. Another of the great Epsilon Sigma and UT alumni is David (Gruder) Graham who grew up in Union City and has long lived in Nashville. Gruder almost single-handedly made a new house for Epsilon Sigma possible. He is one of those people who will not take "no" for an answer. He went to UTM on and off for nine years, and when he graduated he hosted a champagne reception at the Pike house which was attended by 200 or so people. He has served as a Regional President for PiKA and is presently a member of the UT National Alumni Board of Governors. As I always say in introducing him to Pike and UT alumni, "Gruder is the world's greatest alumnus." Certainly he's the best alumnus I have ever known. Helping to bring that fine local into PiKA is one of my life's foremost accomplishments.

For years after World War II even little towns had glass enclosed airplane spotting booths on top of buildings. Kenton had a booth downtown atop one of our two story buildings. The authorities asked citizens to take turns being the "spotter," something I enjoyed doing occasionally. We were to report any planes we saw to some central location. Obviously America was paranoid about Russia during those Cold War days.

For a couple of years right out of UT I was a member of the Union City Jaycees. The highlights of those two Jaycee years were a state convention in Memphis where we elected Jackson's Bob Conger as Tennessee State President, and a national convention in St. Louis where we elected Bob as National President of the United States Jaycees. In St. Louis the Tennessee delegation stayed at a hotel out near the Chase Park Plaza Hotel. Late one night Oliver Gilliam of Union City somehow got hold of a frilly pair of ladies shorty pajamas and a little matching nightcap. All of a sudden Oliver came running out of the shadows, ran up on the diving board of the hotel pool, and jumped in with an enormous splash. Jack Daniels Distillery gave the Tennessee delegation a large number of Black Label Jack Daniels miniatures which we took out into the middle of the wide street that runs in front of Kiel Auditorium where we stopped St. Louisians on their way home from downtown work and presented them with these mementoes. We made lots of friends for Tennessee that late afternoon, and had lots of fun doing it.

One spring Sally called from North Carolina and invited me to join a bunch of her Chapel Hill buddies for spring break week in Daytona Beach. Sounded good to me. I called Bill Cloar from Dyersburg who was enrolled at Georgia Tech. He invited me to spend the night with him in Atlanta but said he could not go to Daytona. After the drive down from Kenton we went out to a favorite restaurant of Tech students. The Notre Dame Glee Club was just behind a partition from us and they sang and sang, beautifully. It was a festive evening, and Cloar decided he could after all cut the week's classes, so he and I headed south the next day. One of the North Carolina boys in our small group was Doug Moe, a great college basketball player at the time who went on to be a great NBA player and a respected NBA coach. One morning early I drove my Edsel on the beach at 100 miles per hour. All in all, we had a ball.

The next year Sally called again with the news that a bunch of them were going to Nassau for spring break. I called fraternity brother and close friend Bruce Dunlap from Ridgely and we took off for Tampa where we met the Tarheels and boarded a flight for Nassau. We called the stewardesses "nurses" which they didn't think was very funny. The Chamber of Commerce had a tray of rum drinks for us when we arrived at the Nassau airport which set the tone for the week. Another great time was had by all.

While working in Union City in the automobile and John Deere businesses and after we had given up our Edsel franchise (more about that in Chapter 34), I bought a 1954 Corvette. It was a beautiful white car with red interior. Though the car was very "clean," it wasn't perfect mechanically. I sold it to a young Union City boy named Jackson for $1,250. It had cost me about $1,100. Dad then got in touch with a former Kenton new car dealer who was then a Chicago used car dealer and asked him to locate a used Corvette for me. Mr. Fairdean Doherty found a 1957 light green and white Corvette and sold it to me for $2,700. Mother and Grandmother flew to Chicago and drove this car back to Kenton. I drove that great automobile for years.

Our automobile and John Deere agencies did considerable business with the small loan department of the Old & Third National Bank. Bill Harrison, later to work in our Union City bank, and Mr. Donald Kerr ran that department. Mr. Kerr took me to Rotary several times as did my Uncle Eugene Wade. Though I was invited to join Rotary it never happened, and soon I began to work full time in Kenton. Mr. Donald and his brother, Mr. Walker Kerr who was president of the Old & Third, were originally from Kenton. The Kerrs were one of Kenton's most prominent families.

Tennessee used to play Alabama and Auburn in alternate years in Birmingham. One fall I decided at the last minute to catch the Birmingham game and called fraternity friend, Spud Hale from Yorkville, to see if he wanted to go. He parked his cotton picker and we took off. We had a room at the Tutwiler Hotel and spent some time in one of the Tutwiler bars. We met some gullible appearing folks in the bar, and I introduced myself as Johnny Fortune and Spud introduced himself as Spud Danger. We were quite a pair. Those people probably still remember those two jokers with catchy names.

Mother, Dad, and I attended the 1960 Pike convention in Miami Beach where Dad was elected to the PiKA Supreme Council. His office was National Secretary. The fraternity had an optional cruise to Nassau after the convention. The three of us enjoyed the cruise, but the ship was a far cry from the *Queen Mary* and the *Queen Elizabeth*! My recent Pi Kappa Alpha Order of West Range fellow inductee, John Hein from Huntington Beach, California, told me at the 2002 Pike Convention in Palm Springs that he remembered a cocktail party a group of us, including Mother and Dad, had aboard the ship. So do I.

In those days we had what PiKA called Leadership Academies prior to national conventions. Since I was a District President, the fraternity asked me to attend the Academy in Lakeland, Florida just prior to the Miami convention. PiKA has a chapter there at what was then known as Florida Southern. My Kenton cousin, Charlie Freeman, had been a member of that chapter, and my pledge brother, David McSween, and his wife, Mary Homer, have lived in Lakeland for many years where David was treasurer of Florida Title. My main memory of the Academy is that a group of us ate at McDonald's, my first ever of what was to become hundreds, if not thousands, of visits to McDonald's.

Cotton Carnival used to be a really big deal in Memphis. Its reputation was that it was the second largest festival celebration type event in the nation, next to Mardi Gras. Cotton Carnival had many secret societies which had numerous parties and big time parades with enormous floats, marching bands, etc. I never did belong to a secret society but had friends in several of them, primarily Osiris. My society friends often invited me to their parties. One year I was there for several days during Carnival and went to three or four parties a day, usually a brunch at somebody's house, a late luncheon/party at some other house, and dinner at somebody else's house, followed by a dance and party at a secret society's party room, usually a hotel ballroom. Those few days just about wore me down to a nubbin! But what a great time we had.

One year during Carnival a bunch of us West Tennessee Association of Bachelors fellows (see below) rented a room on the west side of the Peabody in order to see a parade come down Second Street. A drunk boy who knew somebody in the room — there were lots of us boys and girls there — staggered into the room and was very offensive and vulgar. I invited him out in the hall to try to calm him down. He persisted and without even thinking about it — I never did anything like this before or since — I knocked him to the floor. Immediately realizing the folly of my ways I commenced to try to smooth it over. He got up and came at me with his arms swinging like windmills. For some strange reason I got tickled and started laughing while he was hitting me in the back, but one time he got a good lick on my nose obviously breaking it. Blood was squirting everywhere. My Pike roommate, Bill Upchurch from Memphis, grabbed the boy and he and some others got him calmed down. My nose has been a little crooked ever since.

I belonged to Yuletide Revelers, a Memphis party club of young single men. We usually had two parties a year, the big one being a formal dinner dance at the Peabody's Skyway. Sally had lots of Memphis friends from camp, prep school, and college, and primarily through her and her Memphis friends I was included in a good many social events in Memphis, Carnival and Revelers parties as well as other events at the Hunt & Polo Club, the Memphis Country Club, and the University Club. Memphis was a fun city for a little country boy back in those days of yore.

Two or three years after college a group of seven of us decided to organize a Bachelors Club. Pelham, Hoff, Bill Cloar, and David Lanier, all from Dyersburg, and Bruce Dunlap and Frank Hardison from Ridgely, and I were the founders. All but Cloar and Lanier were Pikes from Tennessee. The whole thing was cooked up in the bar of the Dyersburg Country Club. I was a member of Revelers of Memphis and suggested to the others that we could do the same type thing up here in the country. So we organized and I was elected president of what we called the West Tennessee Association of Bachelors, WTAB for short. We used a Shakespearean quote for our motto and Pelham, a good artist, designed a great logo with a top hat, cane, and gloves. Our intention was to have a big formal party each winter during the Christmas season and an informal party each summer at Reelfoot Lake or some such place. We recruited members from all over West Tennessee, and WTAB took off. The second big formal party that we had at the Dyersburg Country Club was a doozy. About 75 couples came and we took in about $1,500.00. We could hardly believe that we could gather together that much money at one time, but we did. We had Piano Red, a famous black singer-piano player, and his band from Atlanta. We paid him $500.00 which was a princely sum at the time. Piano Red had several big records such as *Rockin' with Red, You Got the Right String Baby but the Wrong Yo Yo,* and other national hits. Man, could you ever jitterbug to Red's music! In my opinion he had the greatest beat of his day. What a party we had! I wrote a skit to the tunes and lyrics of *My Fair Lady* which about ten of us performed at intermission, and it was a big hit. Of course, by that point in the evening the bachelors and dates weren't too discriminating.

Somehow the word got out in Atlanta on Sunday after the party that Piano Red and his band had been killed in a car wreck between Dyersburg and Atlanta. Since the arrangements were all mine I felt totally responsible and spent several anxious hours before finding out that there had been no such accident. What an enormous relief.

We also had parties at Reelfoot Lake, at the New Southern Hotel in Jackson, and at the Holiday Inn in Jackson, all of which were very successful.

After Pat and I got engaged the remaining directors elected Dunlap as president of the club. Pretty soon he and Sallye Conyers became engaged, and the West Tennessee Association of Bachelors died a natural death as all of us founders, one by one, got married off!

My carefree bachelor days were drawing to a close.

Chapter Fourteen

Pat

Patricia Lee Thurmond was born in Dyersburg on August 24, 1941 to Mr. and Mrs. Robert Clarence Thurmond, Jr. (Mike and Anna Laura). Their first child, Pat, came home to Parkview Street in Dyersburg where she was the apple of her parents' eyes.

Pat's father, an only child, was a lumberman, her grandfather, Clarence Thurmond, was a lumberman, and her great-grandfather Thurmond was a lumberman. Her great-grandfather came to Tennessee to work for the Mingle Corp., a giant timber operation. Mingle owned tens of thousands of acres of land in the Mississippi River bottoms, and this is why the Thurmonds settled in the Dyersburg area. Bob, Pat's brother, carried on the family lumber and building supplies business, so there have been four consecutive generations of Thurmonds in the lumber business in Dyer County.

Pat's Mother was Anna Laura Bishop Thurmond. Her parents were Mr. and Mrs. O. P. Bishop. Anna Laura Bishop was one of six children. Her sisters were Mary Bishop Johnson of Dyersburg and Janie Bishop McCreary of St. Petersburg. Her brothers were Billy Bishop, a deceased Dyersburg veterinarian, James Bishop, a retired automobile dealer of West Point, Mississippi, now living in Memphis, and Calvin Bishop, a retired Memphis OB/GYN.

When Pat was born, her grandmother, Mrs. Clarence Thurmond, wanted to make sure Pat was not mixed up with somebody else's baby so she had the bottom of Pat's feet painted with purple medicine. The first thing that Mike, Pat's father, looked for when she was born was crooked little fingers. Sure enough that trait was inherited by Pat and her brother, Bob, from their daddy.

When Pat was old enough to leave the house her doting grandmother, Mrs. Clarence Thurmond, Bududa (with the emphasis on the first syllable) to her two grandchildren (Pat and Bob), picked Pat up every morning and took Pat around with her on her daily rounds.

They went to Latimer's Drug Store on the square in Dyersburg every day. While Bududa drank a Coke and smoked a cigarette, Pat always went behind the pharmacy counter where the pharmacist gave her a malted milk ball. Then Pat went next door to Schlesinger's ladies shop and often Mr. Schlesinger let her pick out some costume jewelry for herself. From there she went next door to the hardware store where Pat enjoyed looking at their stuffed wildcat every day. Then she and Bududa walked next door to Piggly Wiggly and picked up the groceries for which Bududa had earlier called. Thus went Pat's and Bududa's morning routine.

When she was very young Pat liked to sit in the driveway of their home on Parkview Street and play with rocks. She loved putting them in her mouth, and Bududa would sit on an old wooden kitchen chair and take a wet cloth and wipe off the rocks so that when Pat put one in her mouth it was clean. Pat never told me exactly how this transpired, but undoubtedly Mrs. Thurmond was very careful that Pat didn't swallow any of those little rocks. At least I hope she was. However, come to think about it, at times I have noticed Pat "rattling on" a bit.

Bududa spent almost as much time with Pat as did Pat's Mother. Pat suspects that as a young child "Bududa" was as close to the pronunciation of "Grandmother" as she could manage. Younger brother Bob just picked up Pat's name for old Mrs. Thurmond. Bududa and Mr. Clarence (Pat's paternal grandfather) lived on Sampson Avenue.

Pat called her maternal grandparents Momee and Daddy Bishop. They lived on East Court Street about two or three blocks from Dyersburg's square.

Parkview Street where Pat and Bob grew up was across the street from the municipal golf course, now Dyersburg State Community College. When Pat was young there was a little store, Little Store as it was cleverly named, just south of Dyersburg's municipal pool, Okeena Pool, which is still there. Pat, usually with some of her Parkview friends which included the Jenkins children, the Locklear girls, Bobby and Marianne Burks, and others, would often walk around the west side of the golf course next to the highway to the Little Store where Pat usually opted for a popsicle. One time Pat and her close friend, Tippy

Moody, were left at home together for a short time. Mrs. Thurmond returned home to find that Pat and Tippy had crawled out a second story window onto the roof of their house where they were walking around in some of Mrs. Thurmond's high heel shoes.

The Thurmonds and Moodys spent a lot of time at the Dyersburg Country Club. Their mothers played bridge and their fathers, usually after a round of golf, played poker. Pat and Tippy loved to play in the cloak room and would occasionally even get to check somebody's coat. When nobody but the bartender was in the bar, they enjoyed dancing on the tables. Pat hasn't changed much.

The Parkview gang had a great time together. Notwithstanding a little mischief at times, it was a wonderful place to grow up.

Pat's Mother was very careful about what her children ate especially in terms of sweets. One time she took Pat to Memphis and to reward her for something good that she had done Mrs. Thurmond took her to the soda fountain in the drug store in the Peabody Hotel and bought her a banana split, something for which Pat had always longed. It came and looked wonderful. Pat took her first bite of a banana split and was visibly disappointed. Mrs. Thurmond couldn't believe it, so she tasted it and immediately understood Pat's reaction to the much anticipated treat; the whipped cream was sour! To this day Pat has never eaten a banana split.

Pat has always been a voracious reader. She saved her money as a little girl, and one time she and two or three of her Dyersburg friends dressed up and took the bus to Memphis. This was their first "big girl" experience. Pat went straight to the book department in Goldsmith's on Main Street. After weighing all the exciting possiblilites, with the money she had saved she purchased *The Complete Works of Shakespeare*. Then when she was about thirteen years old a bond of hers matured, and with that money she bought a set of *The World Book Encyclopedia*. It cost just over one hundred dollars. This beautiful set of books is now in the library in our home. She has long spent most of her "free" time on her artistic projects, so for many years most of her reading has been done while we're traveling — or at football games! As will be mentioned in Chapter 20 having to do with our travels, Pat read twenty books during our three weeks trip to Tahiti. 'Nuff said!

Pat

From Parkview the Thurmonds moved to Latta Woods. Pat spent her teenage years and part of her twentieth year (her age when we married) in their lovely Latta Woods home. Their house included a large room with a fireplace downstairs. This great room for entertaining soon became a gathering place for Pat and her fun-loving crowd of young folks. They did lots of dancing down there. *Rags to Riches* was a popular song back then. When it first came out Pat bought the record and entertained a group that night. They played it time and time again. Finally, hearing no music Mr. Thurmond came downstairs and asked Pat, "Is the party over?" Pat answered, "Yes." He asked, "Has everyone gone?" Pat again answered, "Yes." He then proceeded over to the record player, removed *Rags to Riches*, and calmly broke it into tiny pieces.

Mr. Thurmond was an amateur tournament golfer who once won a seniors tourney in Mississippi. He had a total of seven holes-in-one. Mrs. Thurmond was also a very good golfer with one hole-in-one to her credit. (Mr. Thurmond taught Will how to swing the club, and Will is a very good golfer who enjoys playing with his friends here and with some old fraternity brothers and other friends once a year on a long spring weekend in Destin.)

Pat always had horses and loved to ride them. She had a horse named Terry that learned to untie rope knots. Pat's and Bob's horses were kept on Thurmond property that joined their Latta Woods home. Pat, Bob, and Mr. Thurmond quickly learned that Terry's gate had to be fastened in some way other than with a knotted rope. Pat and her friends took long rides together sometimes all the way to the Mississippi River. One time they stopped at an old abandoned shack. For some unknown reason Pat took a flying leap into this old house only to discover to her horror that it was writhing with snakes. She leapt back out of that snakepit, jumped on Terry, and raced away, not into the sunset but to the east and the safety of good old Dyersburg.

Pat attended Jennie Walker Elementary School and graduated from Dyersburg High School in 1959. Some of her Dyersburg school friends with whom she remains close are Tippy Moody Roach, Elizabeth Magee Taylor, Carolyn Harrington Brewer, and Eleanor Rice Dean.

Pat and her high school friends often ate lunch at The Hut where they usually had Dyersburgers and Cokes.

The first time I asked Pat for a date was at the Dyersburg Country Club Christmas Open House in December, 1958. I sat at a table with her as we ate cookies and drank punch and asked her for a date that night, probably four or five hours later. She declined later telling me that it was not proper to ask for a date for the same day. I knew this but didn't necessarily subscribe to that theory. A year later at the same table and the same function I again asked her for a date for that night. This time she accepted. Pat was a freshman at Lindenwood College in St. Charles, Missouri, just west of St. Louis, and was 18 years old. I was 26. On one of our first dates I arrived to pick Pat up in my Corvette with the top down. After pulling into the Thurmond driveway I somehow felt a presence, turned around and was startled to see their Great Dane, Susie, looking down into the car at me. What a shock! It was probably on our first or second date that I arrived to pick Pat up, and Mrs. Thurmond asked me where we were going to go. I told her that we would go to the country club, which was our gang's hangout. We did go to the country club and down into the bar and nobody was there. We asked the long-time bartender, Jack, where everybody was, and he said that they had all gone to David Lanier's cabin on Reelfoot Lake. I asked Pat if she would like to go and she said, "Sure." So we did. There were several couples there and Lanier went around the room turning lights off and some of the girls pretty much followed him around the room turning them back on. Everything was on the up and up, but when I picked up Pat for another date a night or two later Mrs. Thurmond met me at the front door as mad as a wet hen. She said, and I paraphrase but with the same exact gist, "Tom, what do you mean by taking Pat to an unchaperoned party after you had told me that you two were going to the country club? After all, Pat is only 18 years old!" I tried to explain to her about how it had transpired and how the gathering was completely innocent. But she let me know in no uncertain terms that we were never again to go anywhere other than where we said we would go. She had already let me know on our first date that Pat was never to be home later than 11 o'clock. You'd better believe that from that point on we always went where we were supposed to go and Pat was home no later, ever, than 11 o'clock.

After one year at Lindenwood Pat transferred to UT. Though I had been driving to Knoxville fairly often since graduation, I now went considerably more often than had theretofore been the case! I immediately took Pat to the Pike house and introduced her around, quietly mentioning to the brothers that it seemed to me that it would be better if she dated at the Pike house rather than elsewhere. Early on I introduced her to a Pike who had been president of the chapter at Martin prior to transferring to Knoxville. I told him, Bill Murphy from Memphis, that it would be good if he would date her some. It appeared to me that Bill might have been a little smitten with Pat when he enthusiastically said, "You mean it?" And I said, "Yes." Not too long after that it became obvious to me that they were dating more than I really preferred. Pretty soon Pat and I were dating more seriously, and she and Bill drifted apart.

During Pat's junior year at UT she and her good friend, Dyersburg next-door-neighbor and AOPi sister Elizabeth Magee, flew over to Memphis for a Tennessee-Ole Miss football game weekend. Elizabeth had a date with my fraternity brother and close friend, Bruce Dunlap, and Pat and I had a date. On that Friday night we went to a party at my cousin Jean Sanders' home in Memphis. Their's was a beautiful home on Shady Grove Road, just north of today's Embassy Suites Hotel in East Memphis. We went to the game on Saturday and partied at the Peabody Saturday night, spending some time at a UT SAE party off the mezzanine. After the party I spontaneously and unrehearsed said to Pat, "Will you marry me?" Her reply was, "O.K." Somehow I always figured a proposal and acceptance would be a little more flowery, but our verbal exchange worked.

Pretty soon Thanksgiving rolled around and Pat was coming home for the holiday. We thought that this would be the weekend for us to tell Pat's parents of our intentions. Actually, unbeknownst to me, Pat had told her parents about our intentions and they invited me to join them for Thanksgiving dinner. The whole family and I were there. I was real nervous about asking Mr. Thurmond for Pat's hand, so Mother gave me two of her phenobarbitals which I took just before knocking on the Thurmonds' front door. After dinner Mr. Thurmond and I went down into their downstairs room. I just could not get up my nerve to ask Mr. Thurmond for Pat's hand. Finally at about 2 o'clock or so Mr. Thurmond went upstairs and told Mrs. Thurmond and Pat, they later told me, that I had changed my mind and that he was going to play golf. So he did. After playing 18 holes he came back home, and after fidgeting for those hours I finally got up the nerve to pop the question. He immediately consented and was I relieved! Pat also seemed to be relieved.

At a later date Mr. Thurmond told me that for some reason boys always considered him to be a virtual tiger. Little did he know that I was one of those boys. Mr. Thurmond was a very strict but very loving father. One of his pet peeves was for Pat not to be ready when a boy came to pick her up for a date. After getting to know him it was my opinion that Mr. Thurmond simply didn't want to be bothered with trying to entertain some nincompoop of a boy, me included, while Pat preened. He solved this dilemma one time when a boy came to get Pat to take her to a big party. As usual Pat was not ready at the appointed time so Mr. Thurmond told the boy, "Pat has decided not to go," and he dismissed the boy. Pat was never again late for a date. Of course, I came into the equation later and for a long time was amazed that Pat was always waiting for me at the appointed hour. Then she told me the above story.

Pat was fortunate to be able to accompany Mel and Betty Schlesinger Sembler on one of their Schlesinger's ladies shop market trips to New York to buy her trousseau. For many years the Semblers have lived in Florida where Mel has been extraordinarily successful in real estate development. Mel is currently United States Ambassador to Italy. A few years ago he was U. S. Ambassador to Australia.

When Pat and I got engaged the big thing was to have the picture of the bride-to-be and the wedding announcement in *The Memphis Commercial Appeal*. The first page of the society section of the paper was filled with large pictures of the girls. Often engaged couples tried to keep the engagement secret from those other than family, and the girl would not wear her engagement ring until after the announcment came out in the paper. We successfully kept our plans secret. There was a party at the Dyersburg Country Club the Saturday night before Pat's announcement. Pat still was required to be home at 11 PM. After taking Pat home, as was my custom I went back to the party. Jack Davis, a teenager at the time, somehow got word from somebody who had seen an early edition of *The Commercial* about Pat's and my engagement. Jack, who was dressed to the nines in a three piece suit, came up to me and said, and these were his exact words which I have always remembered, "Tom, allow me to be among the very first to extend to you my heartiest congratulations." Man, was I impressed! Jack was always and continues to be one of my favorite people. He spent several fall seasons working out of our Kenton offices buying cotton for a broker in Harlingen, Texas, Jack's long-time home. Jack and his brother, Eddie, have remained some of our best friends over the years. They recently lost their 94 year old Mother.

Three weeks before the wedding I broke my foot in the Thurmond's downstairs room. (There's a lot of history in that room!) I had been carrying a log for the fire in one hand held over my shoulder when the log slid forward and nose-dived down onto the top of my foot breaking it. The Campbell Clinic doctor told me that it would not damage my foot to remove the cast before the wedding but that it would be painful at times. Eddie Davis took me to Memphis two days before the wedding, and the cast was removed.

Pat and I were married at the Dyersburg First Methodist Church on March 31, 1962. I was mighty nervous waiting in a room off to the side of the altar with Dad, my Best Man, and the preacher, Henry (Hank) Russell. That wait is one of my most vivid memories. Mr. Thurmond gave Pat away. Sally was Pat's Matron of Honor. Her bridesmaids were Betty Cutchin, Frances Dorris, Carolyn Harrington, Mary Louis King, Elizabeth Magee, and Tippy Moody. The flower girls were her first cousin, Pam McCreary, and her second cousin, Mary Helen McDaniel, daughter of Pat's first cousin, Frances Ann Johnson McDaniel Gwin. My groomsmen were Eddie Davis, Bruce Dunlap, John Hoff, Mike Miller, Wayne Miller, Bill Monin, Peter Pelham, Bill Reed, Bob Thurmond, and Bill Upchurch. The reception was held at the Dyersburg Country Club and was a big affair. Mrs. Thurmond had arranged for a champagne fountain which was a big hit. Mr.

Thurmond had hidden my car in Halls where he and Mrs. Thurmond had lived for a few years after they first were married. After the reception Mr. Thurmond drove us to Halls, and Pat and I got away without any trailing of cans or soaping up of the car windows. We spent our first night at the Chisca Plaza in Memphis.

We had gone to great lengths to keep the Chisca Plaza a secret. Our next day flight to San Francisco was booked on American Airlines. We were to leave Memphis for San Francisco the next afternoon, but unbeknownst to us a strike against American began the next day. Our friend, Elaine Horton from Memphis, was a Memphis American Airlines ticket agent. She called just about every hotel in Memphis before she finally reached us to give us the bad news. Elaine arranged for us to fly on another airline, and she and her family, who were dear friends of my family, had Pat and me out to their house late that afternoon. They invited lots of mutual friends in. About all I remember of the time at the Hortons house was Elaine's playing the harp, which she did very well.

We finally got out of Memphis that evening and flew to Dallas where we had a long walk, probably a mile or longer, for a connecting flight to Los Angeles. My foot started hurting bad! Finally I stopped and called my Campbell Clinic doctor at home who said something like, "It'll be all right. I told you it would hurt."

From Dallas we flew to Los Angeles where we spent the better part of our second night in the airport. We then flew up to San Francisco, arriving at daybreak, and checked into the Mark Hopkins Hotel. My cousin, Estelle Norvell, was living in San Francisco at that time and we joined her that evening for a night on the town visiting such places as the Purple Onion and North Beach where we saw Mose Allison at a neat nightclub. The next day we received word that the Matson Line, a cruise ship company plying the waters between the West Coast and Hawaii, had gone out on strike. We were to take their *Lurline* from San Francisco to Honolulu, a five-day voyage. We went to Matson's office on Union Square and got a refund of the fare. I called The Royal Hawaiian, our Honolulu hotel, to see if they could take us five days early. Fortunately they could, and we flew over the next morning and checked into this grand hotel.

Pat

The Royal was THE place to be. At 5 AM Honolulu time on our first morning in Hawaii the phone rang. It was a collect call from my Louisville party friend, Chips Johnston. Many of the gang were still in the Dyersburg Holiday Inn, our wedding weekend headquarters hotel, and apparently the party had been going on pretty much non-stop since the end of the reception. We had a good conversation with several of our buddies who had stayed over for a couple of extra days.

Charlton Heston and his family were staying at the Royal Hawaiian while he was filming the movie, *Diamond Head.* A year or two prior to this time he had the lead role in the epic movie, *Ten Commandments.* One day Pat had been down to the beach and I was in the room. She came running into the room all excited and out of breath and said, "Guess who I was just on the beach elevator with?" "Tell me who," I said. She stammered, "Uh, Uh, Uh, MOSES!" (More about Charleton Heston later).

We had a terrific room with a big screened balcony near a corner. The famous *Tonight* host, Jack Paar, and his family had a room just around the corner from us and on our same floor. We could look from our balcony directly at their balcony where they spent most of their time. Another famous movie star, Richard Egan, and his wife were also in the Royal. One afternoon I had a drink next to him at the beach bar. The two of us talked quite a bit, and he could not have been nicer. His wife and Pat had their hair done side by side in the hotel salon one day, and Pat said that she also was very cordial and pleasant.

One night after we had gone to bed all hell broke loose in the room adjacent to ours. It got so loud that I got up, put on my robe, and went downstairs to the lobby to complain. After being shown into the night manager's office and voicing my complaint he said, "Oh, that's Mr. Sinatra. He's having a party in his room for local disc jockeys. Honolulu is the first stop on his around-the-world tour promoting his new album." I said, "Oh, that's o.k." Finally the party broke up and we got to sleep. The next morning as we walked by his room his door was ajar. We peeked back into his room and Frank Sinatra was having breakfast in bed and the head of his bed was against the same wall as

149

was our headboard. We had slept literally inches from Frankie. What a thrill!

The first day we hit Waikiki Beach my foot hurt like the dickens. I went back upstairs and put on my heavy cordovan shoes and from that point on clodhoppers were the order of my days on the beach. Wonder if any of those fancy folks thought I was a redneck?

While we were on the beach one day Pat got real hot and we went up to the beach bar to get a drink and cool off. Pat didn't drink and still doesn't except for a glass of wine at a party or if we go out to eat with friends. Pat saw a drink that looked good and she asked the bartender what it was. He said, "a banana cow." Pat said, "I'll have one." He mixed it for her and, as she does with water or Diet Cokes, she drank it right down and asked for another. The bartender obliged and Pat drank that one right down. She wanted another and the bartender asked if she were sure. She allowed as to how she was sure. Well she drank that one right down and we headed for a grassy area just off the beach where she lay down on a beach recliner and went right to sleep. She slept very soundly so I decided to go to a movie across Kalakaua Avenue. After the three-hour movie, *Trial at Nuremburg*, Pat was still asleep. She finally woke up and was no worse for the wear. Later we found out that a banana cow consisted of a shot of rum, a shot of vodka or gin, maybe something else, and fruit juices. Pat has never since drunk more than a glass of wine at a time, and she goes weeks or months at a time without drinking anything alcoholic at all. Her alcohol intake in that five minutes or so would be roughly equal to her current annual intake.

There was a neat lounge, Don the Beachcomber's, right across Kalakaua Avenue from the Royal Hawaiian. Most afternoons and sometimes at night there was a great trio, Nat Nichols, playing. He was a fine pianist. We thought they were very good and were surprised that we never again heard from them. Maybe we had stars in our eyes. This bar had a minah bird in a cage where he could see the sidewalk, but it was virtually impossible to see the bird. The bamboo building was right on the sidewalk. When good looking girls walked by, the bird would whistle the way you whistle for pretty girls, and it gave them fits trying to figure out who had whistled. Also, the bird would ask, "What's the cat say?" After a rather long pause he would say, "Meow."

One night Pat and I went to a luau at the hotel. We sat with some folks from Iowa. One of the Iowa men asked Pat and me if we knew how poi, which we had just been served, got its name. Of course we didn't, so he said, "When Captain Cook discovered the Hawaiian Islands the first people his sailors saw were some good looking topless Hawaiian lasses doing the hula in their grass skirts. One of the crewmen said, 'Oh Poi, Oh Poi'." Sounded like a good explanation to me. Still does.

One of the places we frequented in Honolulu was the Tapa Room in the Hilton Hawaiian Village. The Tapa Room was the hangout of some of the detectives in the very popular TV show of the time, *Hawaii Five O.*

King Kamehameha is famous in the annals of Hawaiian history. While Pat and I were there we saw his name plastered everywhere. We pronounced it "Ca (like car without the r) -Me-Ha-Me-Ha" with the emphasis on the first and third syllables. Years later we heard it pronounced correctly, "Caa-May-Ah-May-Ah" with emphasis on the second and fourth syllables. How embarrassing to think about how country we sounded when talking about King Kamehameha. But we is country!

While we were in Hawaii Elvis Presley came over. He was to be brought from the airport to the Hilton Hawaiian Village by helicopter. Pat and I went over to see him and lined up with several hundreds of others on the path he was to take from the chopper pad to the hotel. Sure enough, he walked right by us.

Actually John Hoff and I had met Elvis a few years earlier when he was still a virtual unknown. At that point he had done only one record of significance, *Blue Moon of Kentucky*, which had sold about 200,000 copies. Elvis was singing at a popular nightclub out on the edge of Memphis. It was a big place beside a lake. Elvis was alternating with another act so that there was continuous music for dancing. During his breaks he sat at a table in this big room, and at one point Hoff and I sat down with him. My recollection is that he was not real talkative but was pleasant and cordial. Later when Hoff was a student at

Memphis State he got to know Elvis during a Cotton Carnival. One time when Natalie Wood was in Memphis dating Elvis, they came by the Memphis State campus on Elvis' motorcycle when Hoff and some of his friends happened to be on the sidewalk, and Hoff says Elvis waved at him and hollered, "Hey, John!" John says he was a BMOC from then on. After Elvis became famous he was booked on the *Ed Sullivan Show* for his first television appearance. Several of us had dates that night and all of us went to Hoff's house to watch Elvis for the first time. He sang *Heartbreak Hotel*, my all-time favorite Elvis song. It was a thrill for all of us.

Pat and I have never been back to Hawaii. Maybe we'll do that soon — and spend some time at the Royal Hawaiian. I hope so.

Mrs. Thurmond died in 1997, and Mr. Thurmond died in 1999. They were exemplary parents-in-law.

Chapter Fifteen

Our Early Married Years

Pat and I spent our first married year in a duplex apartment in Kenton which we rented from Pete Tilghman. (We always bought cars from Pete and continue to patronize Tilghman Chevrolet of Kenton and his sons, young Pete (P. T.) and Ben. Their service is excellent and, of course, totally convenient.) One of our first mornings after setting up housekeeping Pat decided to make waffles for me with a waffle iron that had been given to us as a wedding present. Unbeknownst to me she set out to make the waffles early that morning. That evening I learned "the rest of the story." The waffles kept sticking to the waffle iron as she continued to try time after time. She went up to Mother's house a couple of times during the day for additional instructions. She worked on making waffles until early afternoon, and every time she tried to take them out they just fell to pieces. Finally in great consternation she repaired to our back yard with the waffle iron and a claw hammer and proceeded to beat the iron with the hammer until the iron was unrecognizable. Pat has never since attempted to make a waffle. When we happen to be eating breakfast somewhere other than in our home waffles are often my breakfast of choice.

Soon after the waffle episode we invited Bruce and Sallye Dunlap from Ridgely to come over to the duplex for dinner. Our kitchen was very small, and Pat had to improvise as to where she would put things until they could be placed on the kitchen table where we ate. She made a scrumptious looking chocolate pie and could not find a surface for it, so she placed it on the floor. In her running around the kitchen doing last minute things she stepped right in the middle of that wonderful pie. The Dunlaps had to do without dessert that evening.

A week or so later the first day of strawberry season arrived. The night before I told Pat that we would have to get up very early the next morning. She said, "Have to? You mean get to!" Pat has always been an early riser. She gets up every morning at 4:00 AM or slightly afterwards. Four AM has become the time for my nightly trip to the bathroom after which time Pat arises and charges into the day as I drift back to sleep. Our neighbors in the duplex were George and Patricia Hurt, and we were fortunate to have had such nice neighbors.

Pat enrolled at UTM that first winter and took a full load. Having babies slowed her down, but she continued to attend UTM on and off, including night classes, for a good many years. She changed her major from Education to History, and despite the fact that she probably has enough hours to graduate she doesn't have all the right ones. Pat made an A in every UTM class she took, and she always had the highest GPA in all these classes. During her involvement with UTM, Pat and some other Union City and area AOPi alumnae organized what is now an excellent AOPi chapter at UTM.

After spending our first year of marriage in Kenton, in March, 1963, Pat and I bought a two story colonial house on Reelfoot Avenue in Union City from Martha Avery. We thought it was a beautiful house, and it sat on a 2.6 acre lot. I left Kenton and moved to Union City with great trepidation. Everything considered it really has turned out to be a good decision. I go to Kenton six days, often seven days, every week, and my plan is to do this from now on. Working in my refurbished and rearranged office in my old Kenton home is a delight. Business and farm responsibilities and volunteer work keep me busy. So does writing this book! It would never do for me to hang around our Union City home. That would drive Pat and me both crazy.

Our Reelfoot Avenue house had wings on each side, the east wing being a garage and the west wing being a full two-bedroom apartment complete with a kitchen. We were on a tight budget and decided to rent the apartment. We had some mighty colorful renters who came and went rapidly. Early on I decided to keep a record of this activity for posterity. So posterity, here she comes!

Our first renters were Alice and Jim Zimmerman who rented it for about three months, June to September, 1963. This fun-loving couple had some very active parties.

Ruth Butts from Fulton taught school in Union City one year. She moved in during October and stayed until June, 1964. She hosted several school parties and was a very nice quiet girl. She was with us for eight months, and we hated to see her go.

Next came a newly married Rutherford couple who moved in on July 4 with her children. They only stayed five weeks and moved back to Rutherford. He played a guitar too loud and drove too fast around the driveway.

Late in August, Patsy and Jack McWhirter from Rives moved in with their seven-months old daughter. They stayed four months.

At that point Wysetta (Wy) and Richard Lattus moved in with their daughter, Allison, three years old. A week later Richard went off for his final two years in the Navy. Wy and Allison stayed through the first week in February.

Ray Ferguson and his fiancee, Mary Ann Bethel, retained the apartment beginning the second week in February, 1965. They were married on March 27th and moved in immediately after their honeymoon. They both worked at the hospital and were delightful renters. They were our last renters. Sadly, Mary Ann died of cancer in 1986 leaving Ray with three teenagers.

So ends the rental saga at what we lovingly called "Wade Oaks."

On our first anniversary right after we moved in, on Sunday morning, March 31, 1963, Pat surprised me with a champagne breakfast with eggs benedict, my favorite, on the screen porch between our downstairs bedroom and the garage. It was a beautiful early spring morning and our star magnolia was blooming. I'll never forget that breakfast. It's certainly been downhill, breakfast-wise, ever since.

During our first year on Reelfoot Avenue I bought a John Deere riding mower from our Union City dealership and mowed the yard. It took the better part of a day to mow it. We had a long-time mechanic at the John Deere place, Bill Cooley, who had a teenaged son named Marion. The second summer I worked out a deal with Marion to sell the mower to him and gave him $7.50 credit on his note each time he mowed that 2.6 acre yard. He paid for his mower this way. And then he gave up the yard! Certainly couldn't blame him.

Migraines have been a problem for me pretty much all my life. One Sunday morning about 2 AM the worst headache, by far, to ever hit me woke me up. It was excruciating, and we were afraid that something really bad might be happening. Pat called Dr. Jack Gray in Kenton. Dr. Jack came to Wade Oaks in the middle of the night, checked me over, and gave me a shot. This is the kind of doctor he was. His Dad, old Dr. Gray, also the quintessential country doctor, routinely made house calls even in the middle of the night. When Kenton lost Dr. Jack, it lost the last of a family institution which had made our little town a much better place than it would have been had not the Grays been a part of our Kenton community.

One time Pat's brother, Bob, and his buddy, Paul Yarbro, also of Dyersburg, came over to spend a Saturday night with us. They went out partying and came in late. We had locked the doors and both Pat and I were very soundly asleep when they started trying to get in. When we finally woke up in pretty much of a stupor it didn't register with us that it was Bob and Paul, so I called the police. Needless to say it was most embarrassing to have called the law on my brother-in-law and his friend!

Some time later a commotion of some sort woke me up, and it appeared to me that a strange man was standing in the yard. I again called the police, and once again they came tearing up the driveway, lights flashing and siren screaming. It turned out that our "trespasser" was a small tree that we had just set out. From that point on I had virtually no credibility with Union City's finest.

Wade Oaks had a driveway that came off Edwards Street, circled around the back and west side of the house, and continued out to Reelfoot Avenue. One afternoon I came home from work and parked my Corvette behind the house as was my every day custom. Pat's Chevrolet was parked in front of my car which was usually the case. Pat needed to go someplace and she went out and got into her car. For some strange reason she put the car in reverse and backed rapidly into my Corvette knocking out the whole fiberglass front end. I sold it to a Milan body shop for $500. In later years 1957 Corvettes became the most popular of all collector Corvettes. How unfortunate that I didn't have it repaired and stored for my children and grandchildren. But we needed the $500!

In 1964 Pat and I left right after strawberry season for Las Vegas and a visit with Sally and her husband, Pitt Tomlinson. We took the money Pat had made selling food and Cokes to the pickers, $250 in all, and headed West. We drove out to the Grand Canyon and spent a night there, and then it was on to Vegas. Sally and Pitt had an apartment on Sahara Avenue, three or four blocks off the Strip, and we stayed with them. We saw lots of shows and had a great time. One day at one of the big casinos we saw a Lounge Show which featured four people of whom we had heard. One of them was Frank Sinatra, Jr. Back then you could see a great Lounge Show for the cheap price of a drink, and sometimes even that was waived. Downtown you could get a big shrimp cocktail for 50 cents and an enormous breakfast for less than a dollar. Things surely have changed in Las Vegas. After a week of fun we headed back East spending one night with my cousins, the Pharrs, in Dallas. When we got home, our daughter, Lolly, who was about eleven months old, did not remember us. Tears flowed down Pat's face. She never again left one of our children when they were young enough that they might not remember her upon her return. Nonetheless, it was a fun and carefree trip, at least for me.

One winter while we lived on Reelfoot Avenue during a very deep snow a funny looking little dog came up to our house. She was very shy and skittish and obviously very hungry. We fed her, and before long she was ours. She constantly wagged her tail rapidly, and we called her Happy. She lived with us until she became so fond of the Morrisettes (Charles and Margaret) across Edwards Street from us that we finally just gave her to them. Happy was a sweet little dog. While we had her she had pups, and we were successful in giving all of them away.

Later we had a German Shepherd puppy, and we never did name her. Most of the time we called her "No Name." One time when Mother was visiting in our home on Reelfoot Avenue, out of the clear blue No Name took a flying leap and jumped into Mother's lap. Mother never was very fond of dogs in the first place, and this unexpected occurrence did nothing to change her lifelong dislike of hounds of all types.

One spring Pat decided that she would plant a vegetable garden. She went to Obion Farmers Co-op and told the man that she would like to have a corn seed. He said, "How's that?" She repeated that she would like to have a corn seed. He said, "You don't like corn much, do you?" She said, "Yes, we like corn a lot." Pat had never thought about corn very much but reckons that she thought it might grow on some kind of a big bush that branched out and produced many ears of corn. The man finally convinced Pat that she would need more than one grain of corn, so she bought several. For the life of me I cannot remember how that garden turned out. My guess is that it did not reduce our grocery bill by very much.

One time Pat and I were in Memphis at a party and ran into a girl I knew and admired, Dudley Weaver. Pat and I thought Dudley would be a good match for our close friend from Roellen (Dyersburg), Eddie Davis. We asked Dudley if she would consider coming up and spending a weekend with us at Wade Oaks and dating Eddie. She agreed, as did Eddie. So Dudley came to Union City and Eddie came over and met Dudley and they seemed to have a good time together. Later on we found out that they actually hadn't gotten along too well after all. As we heard the story, Eddie went to Memphis about six months later and decided to give her a call. He did, and the rest is history. They have two extraordinary children, a boy and a girl, grandchildren, a lovely home outside Dyersburg, and have had a wonderful marriage. Pat and I are very proud of having gotten them together. Eddie has always been a mighty good friend. He buys our "Mr. Ed" brand feed for his horses. If his horses could talk, surely they would emulate their master after a good bait of Mr. Ed's and a full stomach and proclaim, "I'm sufficiently sophosophied."

One Saturday night Pat and I went to a neat party at the Dyersburg Country Club at which a local very talented person had drawn and painted lifesize pictures of movie characters, one of which was Baby Jane from the movie, *Whatever Happened to Baby Jane?* His Baby Jane was a hefty young lady with a bright red dress with white polkadots. After the party was well underway I worked out a deal with a buddy to snatch Baby Jane and hand her out the window of the parlor of the club to me. So far as we knew, nobody was the wiser until this gentleman started gathering up his really good characters to take them home. Through the grapevine we heard that the artist was very much upset about the loss of Baby Jane, so I decided to add insult to injury. I bought plain postcards and cut out words and letters from magazines and newspapers and pasted them on the cards (much like ransom notes) that read, "Whatever happened to Baby Jane?" and signed them, "The Phantom." I then sent these cards to friends all over the nation with instructions as to when to mail them back to Dyersburg. Over a period of time he received these cards with postmarks from Los Angeles to New York and from Houston to Chicago. He must have kept all this to himself, as we have never since heard a word about any of this.

We had a room in our basement which we called "Bottom o' the Oaks." I read all of Ian Fleming's James Bond books for the most part in this room. Pat painted some murals on the walls, and often when we had parties we invited guests to add to our art. Oliver and Ollie Gilliam, Fred and Patsy Roberts, and Gordon and Sandra Silvey, all frustrated artists, contributed their considerable talents. The room wound up being one big "work" of art. When the house was moved (more about that to follow) these murals were exposed to the world, and it was a most unusual sight to see these painted walls beneath ground level with nothing above or around them. The house was moved in three sections, and it was an amazing thing to see.

We sold Wade Oaks really well — at least we thought we did — to The Old & Third National Bank in 1968 for what was to us a big profit. However, a few months later the Marshall Estate sold 25 acres or so in the pasture next to us for as much per acre as we received for our property, and our property included a beautiful big house and was a corner lot. The Marshall acreage soon became a shopping center which is now the Obion Square Shopping Center. Of course the bank had no use for the house, but it was a lovely, substantial building. The bank offered the house to me if we would move it off the lot. After much deliberation we declined. Leon and Hattie Lou Brown accepted the bank's offer and had it moved to Stonewall Drive, the street on which we now live. It's still a pretty house, but to me it was even more impressive all stretched out 'way back on that big lot. Sam and Chris Sinclair now own it and live there. The Chamber of Commerce must have been impressed with it, as they featured it in a long ago marketing piece for Union City.

We loved Wade Oaks and the big yard with its big oak trees. I set out some more oak trees while we lived there. The sizeable oak just to the east of the present driveway from Reelfoot Avenue up to what is now The Commercial Bank was one of mine. That tree, which was dug on our farm, was bent double our first winter at Wade Oaks by an ice storm. Several trips out from the house with hot water which was poured on the tree until the ice was melted enabled the tree to straighten up. Today it is a beautiful tree.

Pat and I left lots of wonderful memories when we moved from Wade Oaks to Sherwood Hills.

We rented a house on Lady Marion Drive in Sherwood Hills from Dan and Grace Gary. There were 17 children on this short street. The girls loved it — Will was not yet born. The first morning after we moved in, a Sunday morning, I was sitting in the breakfast room in my robe eating and reading *The Commercial Appeal*. Somehow I felt a presence and looked down to my left. Standing there quietly looking up at me was two year old Scott Denaburg. That was a proper initiation into Sherwood.

After two and a half years in Sherwood Hills we moved into a new house on Stonewall Street in the Pleasant Valley area of Union City.

Life in Union City was very good indeed.

Chapter Sixteen

The Children — The Early Years

As a youngster I often wondered if I would find a wife and if so would we have children? As I grew older and started to date I figured marriage might be in the cards for me but still wondered if children might be part of the equation. Within a few months after marriage Pat became pregnant. This news gave me a sensation of amazement never before experienced. Pat went to an obstetrician in Memphis, Dr. Louie Henry. Mother had given birth to all three of her children in Memphis, and we must have thought that Memphis was the birthing place! As mentioned in Chapter 4, Pat, sister Sally, and I had gone to Memphis on July 17, 1963, for Pat's regular doctor's appointment. We went to a movie afterwards, and as we were leaving the theater Pat suggested that maybe we should spend the night in Memphis. She sensed that our first child might soon make its appearance. As was my family's custom we checked into the Peabody. At midnight Pat woke me, and we got up and rushed to Baptist Hospital. Annie Laurie (Lolly) Wade was born at about noon on July 18, 1963. Lolly's grandparents, Tom and Patti Wade and Anna Laura Thurmond, and Lolly's great aunt, Mary Johnson, came that morning. After Lolly was put into the nursery her grandparents and I along with Dr. Henry went to the nursery to see Lolly (At this point she was still called Annie Laurie and the "Lolly" came a few months later.) I simply could not contain my amazement at the birth of our new baby. Finally Dr. Henry said to me, "What did you expect?" A good question to be sure. Lolly's other Grandfather, Mike Thurmond, saw his first grandchild the next day.

For me Lolly's birth was almost like an out-of-body experience. (For Pat it really was an out-of-body experience, wasn't it?) Similar feelings repeated themselves when Patti and Will were born. As my old pal Chips Johnston would have said, life is an "amazing phenomenon."

Patti was born on August 12, 1967 in the Obion County Hospital in Union City. Dr. Bill Carpenter delivered her. We were still living in Wade Oaks on Reelfoot Avenue, and I remember calling the Thurmonds from there to tell them that we had another little girl. Mother and Dad were at the hospital. We named our new daughter Patti for Mother and little Patti, and Katherine for Sally (Sarah Katherine Wade Tomlinson). Patti was a delight except for the first three months or so when she slept in the daytime and stayed awake all night just about every night. I finally told Pat that something had to give. Being up much of the night and working hard all day was a tough combination. (Harvest began a few weeks after Patti was born, and that involved long, hard hours.) Somehow we got through it, and soon all that lost sleep was forgotten. As Patti learned to walk she followed me everywhere, even into the bathroom. I had to start locking the bathroom after slipping in when she wasn't looking.

Will was born on October 15, 1971. He also was born at the Obion County General Hospital in Union City, at about eight o'clock on a very dark, blustery, and stormy morning. My recollection is that Mother and Dad were at the hospital. The delivering obstetrician, Dr. Robert (Bobby) Young, a good friend and PiKA brother, came out and told me that we had a healthy halfback. (The last part was wrong; Will was a high school offensive guard and defensive linebacker.) I could not have been more excited and pleased. We did want a boy this time, but if he had been another girl that also would have been great. I called the Thurmonds and then Delbert Orr, our longtime weigher and check writer at Wade Gin — 40 years on this job, in fact — and told him to go to Newmon's Store in downtown Kenton and buy two boxes of the best cigars they had and start passing them out to customers, employees, and friends. As it turned out Bobby Seals of Yorkville probably got most of the cigars at the gin. This became quite a joke, as Bobby, the principal of Yorkville High School, was a witty person anyway and constantly smoked cigars. It didn't take us long to name our son Thomas Wilton Wade III. Will was a delight from day one.

Pat and I now had three beautiful children, all were healthy, and everything was right with the world.

Pat had been a Methodist in Dyersburg, and my church, and our church for the first year of our marriage was the Kenton Cumberland Presbyterian Church. After moving to Union City we looked at churches for awhile and started attending St. James Episcopal Church which we liked very much. Soon Pat joined, but I held back for awhile, all the time going to church with Pat. After two or three years I also joined St. James. The church was small, and our children weren't getting a Sunday School experience. They began to go to Sunday School at Union City's First United Methodist Church with some of their friends. Before too long Patti and soon afterward, Will, joined the church. Lolly's friends had all joined the church before Lolly began going to Sunday School with them, and Lolly made no church decision for a few years. Finally Pat and I asked Lolly if she would join the Methodist Church if we would join with her, on a Sunday night when it would be less of a production. She immediately agreed, and in a short time all five of us were a church family together.

Lolly was christened at the Kenton Cumberland Presbyterian Church, and Patti and Will were christened at Union City's St. James Episcopal Church.

Our children had some neat sayings. Here are some of them that I remember.

Thomas Wilton (Will) Wade III called himself "Nottis Weekum Way Durd."

Lolly called lightning "lighting," popsicles "sicklepops," and Mentholatum "lemonlatum."

Instead of saying "once upon a time," Lolly said, "sonse a wanna tine."

Lolly's possession saying was "That's mine's," not an unreasonable way of making that point.

When Lolly was young, instead of saying "no such" she would say "nutch," as in "nutch thing." Sounds logical to me. Lolly had a real way with words. She would have been a good linguist.

Patti called Will Austin Nailling, "Miz Austin." She heard us talk about going to the home of our friend, Fritz Hansen, saying, "We're going to Fritz's house." So she called him, "Fritzie."

When Lolly was little and I used to tell her stories about the past, my usual preface was, "When I was a little boy." So, when she started telling stories when she was little she began them with, "When I was a little boy."

One time when Will was real young on our first trip to a city with him along, we spent a night in a Holiday Inn in Nashville. He was really excited by the elevator. We finally figured out what he meant when he said, "Momma, punch the doeybell. Let's ride the alligator."

Will called the Olympia Restaurant the "Nimponee."

Lolly referred to clothes in the singular as "clo," and would say, "give me that clo for my doll."

Lolly always referred to colors fitting instead of matching and insisted on calling the dining room the living room.

One time Lolly called Pat out of the house saying, "Momma, there's a sneak in my sandbox." Not understanding, Pat went out to discover that sure enough there was a small snake in Lolly's sandbox where she had been playing.

When Lolly was a little thing Pat and I called her "Miss Madame," obviously because we thought it was a neat thing to call a cute little girl.

Patti one time in hearing us refer to some "hippies," as we called bearded long-haired boys in the 60s, said, "I don't see any hippimopatuses." Notice her mispronunciation of hippopotamus. When Patti was little, she did not like rice. She still doesn't. One time she felt the little hairs on her legs and said to Pat, "The whiskers on my brains feel like rice." Pat figured out that she thought the hair (whiskers) on her brains (veins, or legs) felt like rice. And she did not like the way the whiskers – or rice – felt.

One Christmas holiday season Pat baked some cookies for some folks. She sent Patti who was real young over to our across-the-street neighbors, the Armstrongs, Red and Miss Ruby. Since Mrs. Armstrong was known as Miss Ruby, Patti thought Red should be called Mr. Ruby, which she pronounced, "Mr. Wuby." She went to their back door and knocked. Red came to the door; Miss Ruby was just behind him and heard the conversation. When Patti handed Red the cookies he reached in his pocket and held out some money for Patti who exclaimed, "No, Mr. Wuby, they're a Cwismas pwesent."

When Lolly was little we used to sit upstairs in our house on Reelfoot Avenue and watch the trucks. Every time an eighteen wheeler would roar by, she would excitedly say, "Cruck!"

Shortly after Patti's birth it became evident to Pat and me that Lolly was growing more and more jealous of Patti. I sat Lolly down in a private place in our house and told her that we loved her so much that we were very concerned that we would not be able to love the new baby enough when it was born. Immediately after Patti came into the world, however, it became obvious to Pat and me that God had expanded our capacity for love so much that we loved Lolly just as much as we ever did and we also loved Patti just as much as we loved Lolly. Lolly's demeanor changed as we talked. After that little conversation Lolly never again seemed to be at all jealous of Patti. Today they remain best friends.

Pat used to dress the girls in matching long dresses when they were about two and six years old and for a few years afterwards. This prejudiced father sure thought they were a mighty cute twosome.

When Annie Laurie was little and into absolutely everything on a constant basis, I called her Annihilation Laurie. Once Lolly, thinking she was being helpful, washed her hair in the dog bowl. Pat pretended that it was helpful but gently suggested that it would be better if she let her (Mom) wash her hair in the future. One time we checked into the Hyatt Regency Hotel in Atlanta. It is a large hotel with an open lobby that is over 20 stories high. The glass elevators were lit up with lights much like rides at the fair. As soon as we walked into the lobby, Lolly asked me to buy her a ticket so she could ride on that elevator.

When Patti was a little bitty girl she went with me to one of my offices one day, and a customer said to me, "You certainly do have a fine looking little boy, Tom." Before I could open my mouth Patti chimed in, "I not a boy. I a gull." Ever since then little girls are gulls to me.

At age six or seven Patti began to have some allergy problems, and she went with me to the Oklahoma Allergy Clinic in Oklahoma City. We went to Memphis and boarded an early flight, Patti's first time on a plane, to fly to Oklahoma City. I will never forget the expression on Patti's face. She got up in the seat and her little legs stuck straight out.

Her eyes were as big as saucers when the plane started taxiing down the runway, but she thoroughly enjoyed the flight. Patti didn't think too highly of those allergy tests where they stick your skin with all those little needles.

When Will was about 6 or 8 years old, our family went on a four day Caribbean cruise with the David Critchlow family. The big old *Leonardo de Vinci* had a casino where you had to be 18 to play. All the children had played the slots some, but about the second day they stopped all the children from playing. Will had to stand on a stool to reach the slots and when the casino manager mentioned the fact that Will was too young to play, Will replied, "I am 18; I'm just small for my age." The man got such a kick out of Will's rejoinder that he let him, and only him, continue playing until Will ran out of money. On this same trip our family played Bingo every night. Of course, there was a crowd of us (11 in all) but we won time and time again, maybe as many as 8 or 10 times.

When Lolly was little, she was crazy about a dog that some friends of ours had. This dog was a male English bulldog, and his name was Chauncey. Our friend, James Hall Shaw from Ridgely, gave us a female Great Dane, and Lolly wanted very much to name her Chauncey. We reluctantly went along with her wishes, but it was not too long until Chauncey seemed like the right name to us, too. She was a perfect dog, a wonderful, gentle pet that was greatly loved by the five of us.

When Will was a little boy he fell in the backyard and cut the back of his leg badly which required eight stitches. Dr. Bob Clendenin was in the emergency room and sewed it up. Everybody there was real nice to Will and complimented him on his bravery. As he and I left and were going down the hall to the front door of the hospital, holding hands, Will said, "Daddy, that was fun!"

Lolly and her Union City friend, Heather Cultra, went to Camp Monterey located just outside Monterey, Tennessee on Lake Monterey. Lolly went back for a second summer, and then the following summer she spent at Camp Nakanawa near Crossville, Tennessee. At Nakanawa she met her cousin from Dallas, Margaret Coleman. The two girls, not knowing they were cousins until later, became good friends and Margaret came to Union City afterwards and spent a week with us. It seemed to me that Lolly and Margaret spent the whole week primping and washing their hair. Sally and Margaret's mother, Pat Nelson Coleman, not only are cousins but they also became good friends when they were together at Bennett Junior College, a girls' finishing school in Millbrook, New York. Margaret now lives in McKinney, Texas, a suburb of Dallas with her husband and three children. Pat and Jack Coleman still live in Dallas and have two children in addition to Margaret. It's quite a coincidence that these four cousins from two widely separated families got together in similar ways.

Patti also went to Nakanawa one summer. She was the most homesick little girl we ever saw. I could certainly understand what she was going through, as my first year at Camp Hy-Lake had been a mighty homesick time for me.

Over the course of a few years I bought Pat a fair amount of jewelry at H. Stern in St. Thomas (H. Stern is an internationally known South American-based jewelry concern). Patti had paid close attention. We promised Patti that we would buy her a little ring the summer when our family spent several weeks in St. Thomas. We went down town one of those days for the express purpose of following through on our promise. Pat, Patti, and I started at some mid-price jewelry stores, but Patti just couldn't find a ring to suit her in our price range. When we finally got to H. Stern her eyes began to sparkle as only Patti's can sparkle. She quickly found a ring to her liking. (In later years Pat and I became disenchanted with Stern.)

All five of us went to Williamsburg the summer of '83 and then on to Washington. Sally and her family lived in Williamsburg. When we first got there, before getting in touch with Sally, we went to a nice restaurant on the main street in the commercial area. We ordered onion soup. Will was eleven. He tried to grind some peppercorns into his soup. The top was barely on, and it came off and almost all the peppercorns fell into Will's soup. The peppercorns filled the bowl to overflowing, and Will was terribly embarrassed. Pat swapped bowls with him. The waiter, before noticing the pepper, asked Pat if she was finished with her soup. She said yes and we and the waiter got tickled and stayed that way for a good while. The next morning he was the person who read the *Declaration of Independence* in the mock ceremony depicting July 4, 1776. We were on the front row. He had a hard time keeping a straight face. So did we. A day or two later in a tavern where we were having dinner Will thought the salt bowl was the sugar bowl and spooned a generous amount of salt into his iced tea.

Pat and I could not have had finer children than our Lolly, Patti, and Will. Pat did a great job with them in every respect. My long, hard hours at work precluded my being able to be deeply involved with their upbringing. Pat deserves virtually all the credit for the wonderful way in which all three of them have turned out.

The Children Grow Up
Lolly

Annie Laurie (Lolly) was part of an extraordinary class in the Union City Schools system. Her old friends remain close friends. She was a cheerleader and a flag girl in Union City's award winning band and was in the main stream of Union City's young people's social doings. She played on the Union City tennis team and graduated with excellent grades.

She entered UT and pledged AOPi, her Mother's UT sorority, for which she eventually served as Executive Vice President. She roomed with Laura Hansen from Union City who served as AOPi President. Later Lolly roomed with Ann Stephens, the daughter of revered UT Political Science professor, Dr. Otis Stephens, who is blind. Dr. Stephens is a remarkable man having won several awards as one of the top professors at The University of Tennessee.

While at UT Lolly sang in AOPi's All-Sing entries and sang and danced in their Carnicus productions. During this period of time AOPi won something like 10 or 12 consecutive Carnicus titles. Lolly was Union City's Lady of the Realm in the 1982 Memphis Cotton Carnival. We attended some of her parties and enjoyed being with several of our old Memphis friends.

One summer she and some of her AOPi friends worked at Canyon Lodge in Yellowstone Park. As best I could figure she left for Yellowstone 30 years to the day from the date I left to work at Canyon

Lodge (6/8/54 and 6/8/84). She had a great time that summer again rooming with Ann Stephens.

With some of her many close UT friends Lolly spent two or three spring holidays in Key West, a destination for which her siblings would later opt. Her younger sister and brother always looked up to Lolly and often followed her lead. Lolly set a good example for them, and their lives have been enriched by Lolly's leadership.

After an excellent career both in academics and extracurricular activities she graduated from UT with High Honors, a 3.42 GPA in Marketing, in December of 1985 and went right to work for Dillard's in their Little Rock corporate offices. Later she managed the children's clothing department for them at their North Little Rock mall store. After three years with Dillard's she accepted an offer to open and manage Kirkland's first Arkansas store at the Park Plaza Mall in Little Rock. This was one of the many Kirkland's stores owned by Robert Kirkland of Union City and his first cousin, Carl Kirkland, of Jackson. In 1988 Lolly's new Little Rock Kirkland's store doubled its budget for the first two months of operation and was the gift store chain's leading store that year in either sales or profits, and, if my memory serves me correctly, was second in the other category. My opinion, naturally unbiased, is that Lolly is a natural born businesswoman!

Lolly lived in Little Rock for four years and enjoyed it immensely. She had some very attractive roommates and friends and was sorry to have to leave them behind when she and Don Bearden married and moved to Shreveport, Louisiana.

Patti

Patti also had a good class in school. She was challenged by her big sister and also made very good grades. She was a cheerleader and head majorette in the band. Patti won Union City's 8th Grade Spelling Bee. For weeks prior to the contest Pat and I gave out words to her. Patti has always been the kind of person who usually got what she set out to get. She ran for Student Body President of Union City High School when she was a sophomore. Her theme was Peppermint Patti, a Charley Brown cartoon character, and she used peppermint stripes on all her literature. She lost to a junior but gained valuable insight into how to run a campaign. Patti ran for and was elected Senior Class President and later was selected Miss Union City in the only beauty pageant she ever entered. She also was voted by her class, "Most Likely to Succeed."

Patti was the best strawberry Pick-Your-Own employee we ever had. One year when she was about 16 we had a late strawberry crop and school was out for summer vacation in time for her to work the whole season. When nobody or hardly anybody was picking for themselves she would go out into the patch with her money box and pick berries which she sold at her packshed at our pre-picked price. In effect her salary cost me virtually nothing because of this conscientiousness on her part. In addition Patti was terrific with her customer relations. She really enjoyed working, but on the early morning of the 21st consecutive day that she had worked, as we left the house she asked, "Daddy, do people sometimes get tired of going to work every day?" To which I replied, "Yep, they sure do." (A year or two later Norma Hobbs was our PYO lady, and she was great at it. She and Patti were equally outstanding.)

Patti followed her big sister into AOPi at UT and set her cap for the presidency of the chapter. On my advice she let some key girls know early on about her aspiration. In her junior year she was elected AOPi President. Prior to that, she was AOPi's all-time youngest vice president. She had a very successful extracurricular career culminating in the presidency of the top honorary on campus. Patti roomed with Carol Stephens, Ann's little sister. Like big sister, like little sister! Patti graduated with an excellent GPA, her major being Communications. AOPi National talked to Patti about taking a job as a chapter consultant, but she had other plans. As you will soon see!

Patti also worked at Canyon Lodge (again like big sister, like little sister) in Yellowstone Park the summer between her sophomore and junior years at UT. She worked on the cafeteria line dishing out food. She said they had lots of Japanese "dudes." She quickly learned that when they wanted rice they ordered lice and when they wanted corn they ordered mice (maize). Another summer Patti worked for Unisys in Atlanta, rooming with Patricia Drerup, now Patricia Drerup Cotter, daughter of our dear friends, Jack and Peggy Drerup of Union City.

Patti paid me a great compliment when she once said that my life reminded her of Jimmy Stewart's life in the movie that all of us Wades love, *It's a Wonderful Life*, in which the difference this man's life made in his small hometown is chronicled. Patti is giving me far too much credit.

After a remarkable career at UT Patti graduated in December, 1989, three days before her marriage to Rance Barnes.

Will

Will also had a great class in the Union City Schools. He was always class president and his close friend, Clint Joiner, was vice president. Will decided to go to my old alma mater, McCallie School in Chattanooga, for his sophomore year where he had the highest GPA of any sophomore boarder. After a great experience he decided to come back home for his last two years of high school where he again excelled but was Vice President while Clint was President of the Junior Class. The next year Clint was President of the Senior Class, their close friend, Jason Cameron, was President of the Student Body, and Will was Student Body Vice President. Will played football all the way through school and, unfortunately, hurt both knees, one requiring arthroscopic surgery in Chattanooga and the other being an ACL tear requiring reconstructive surgery at Campbell Clinic in Memphis.

While at McCallie Will took a spring break trip with a group of other boys who wanted to see some Ivy League schools. The group flew to Boston and boarded a bus which took them to Harvard, Yale, Princeton, Brown, Penn, Dartmouth, Georgetown, Johns Hopkins, and Tufts. These prestigious schools rolled out the red carpet for the boys, as the academic reputation of McCallie had preceded them. I wanted Will to go wherever he wanted to go but was mighty happy that he decided on the University of Tennessee. It has always been a little joke with us that my children could go to college anywhere they wanted to go, but if they wanted me to pay for it they would have to go to UT. Obviously this was a facetious statement but my three children surely made me happy when they followed all us Wades to Knoxville.

Will graduated from Union City High School with a strong GPA and entered UT.

Will, like his sisters, had a remarkable career at UT. He pledged PiKA and was elected President of his pledge class of 32, all 32 of whom made their grades the first semester and were initiated. This sort of thing is virtually unheard of. Will was twice Vice President of his very strong Pi Kappa Alpha Chapter at UT. Will served on the Interfraternity Council Judicial Board and was the IFC Panhellenic Director. He was a member of the Student Government Association, Golden Key Society, Phi Kappa Phi, and Beta Gamma Sigma honoraries, and he was also a member of UT's top honorary. During his junior year Will was selected Outstanding Junior Greek. Interestingly, that same year a Kenton AGR, David Grant, was selected Outstanding Sophomore Greek. You might stretch the truth just a tad and say that Kenton, population 1,300 (892 during my young life in Kenton), furnished two of the four top Greeks at The University of Tennessee that year. A pretty amazing fact.

In addition to all his fraternity and campus duties, Will applied himself to his studies and graduated Summa Cum Laude in 1994 with a 3.90 average in Finance. If he had had a few more liberal arts credits he would have been Phi Beta Kappa.

While a student at Tennessee and following in the footsteps of his Grandfather Wade, who was a member of the Pi Kappa Alpha Supreme Council from 1960 to 1962, Will was elected one of two North American undergraduate members of The Pi Kappa Alpha Supreme Council. *Horizons*, a PiKA publication for alumni, printed the following article written by Will in 1993:

"Thomas W. Wade, III (Zeta 1991). A charter member of the Educational Foundation's Phi Phi Kappa Alpha Club, Will Wade is a junior at the University of Tennessee where he is majoring in finance. Thanks to Pi Kappa Alpha, I have enjoyed many leadership opportunities at Zeta Chapter and on campus and I have developed lasting friendships. Upon graduating from the University of Tennessee in May of 1994, I will have the social and intellectual skills necessary to succeed in the business world and my fraternity experience will have a lot to do with that. Certainly I should not, and will not, put PiKA out of my mind after graduation. As a young alumnus trying to establish a career and a family, I may not be able to devote a great deal of time to the

Fraternity. But I fully intend to contribute what I can financially to the Pi Kappa Alpha Educational Foundation, as well as to Zeta Chapter, on a regular basis. Our great Fraternity exists only through the efforts of alumni like you and undergraduates like me. But we must always remember that the future of Pi Kappa Alpha rests with the men who follow us in the chapters. It is our inherent duty to ensure that PiKA continues to exist and flourish so that the sharpest and brightest young men will have the opportunity to take part in our brotherhood for decades to come. Please keep Pi Kappa Alpha in mind whenever you make charitable contributions and never forget, 'Once a Pike, Always a Pike!'"

Will met AOPi Kim Oglesby of Knoxville, and he never dated another girl. It was love at first sight. He had always thought he would work one summer at Yellowstone as had his Dad and both sisters. But when the logical summer arrived he decided to partner with one of his closest friends, Chris Kirkland of Union City, and formed a company, Dogwood Detailing, to wash cars in Knoxville. They washed a few cars, but Will was near Kim, and that's all that mattered.

At the end of his senior year, Will and his fraternity brother and close friend, John Pryor, went to Europe on a young people's tour. Before he left Will went to Mednikow in Memphis and bought a ring for Kim. He wanted her to have it before he left the country.

After returning from Europe Will started working with me.

The Children Get Married
and Set Up Housekeeping

On December 16, 1989, Lolly and Patti married William Donald (Don, or Donny) Bearden, Jr. and Rance Deslonde Barnes, respectively, in a double wedding. On a weekend home from Knoxville where Patti was a senior, she and Rance, whom she had been dating for a while, were at our house when Rance, the son of Nicky and Jennifer Barnes of Obion County, came into the kitchen where I was alone and asked for Patti's hand in marriage. You could've knocked me over with a feather. I was shocked but immediately agreed. Lolly was in Union City that weekend with her beau, Donny. Could it have been possible that Patti's and Rance's engagement gave them ideas? At any rate three weeks later Lolly and Don, the son of Don Bearden Sr. and Nancy and Mike Udouj of Fort Smith, Arkansas, came back to Union City from Little Rock where Lolly was managing a Kirkland's store (Don was terminal manager for ABF Freight Lines in Hot Springs), and Don popped the question. This possibility had occurred to me so I was not quite as shocked this time and also quickly agreed that Lolly could marry Don.

The four lovebirds decided to have a double wedding. The girls worked out lists and Pat worked on arrangements. Since neither of the girls lived in Union City it fell on Pat to do most of what was done. It was a monumental job, and Pat said afterwards that she never would have agreed to a double wedding if she'd known what all it was going to entail. Pat sought advice from experts in multiple weddings and discovered that we could do pretty much whatever we wanted to do. It was decided that each girl would send invitations to each person she wanted to invite. This meant that most people received two invitations, but some received only one. Each bride had her own bridesmaids and each groom had his own groomsmen. When all of us who were in the weddings were standing up front, we numbered 34. I brought Lolly, the older, in first. Then I went back to our First Methodist Church vestibule and picked up Patti. Some of Lolly's friends, not knowing it was a double wedding, could not figure out why I left the church. They were shocked when I came back in with Patti. Some of Patti's friends, when I came in first with Lolly, thought they had stumbled into the wrong wedding. Patti married a Baptist. Lolly married a Catholic. They were married by our Methodist minister, John Archer. Union City's Catholic priest was in the congregation which sufficed for their church.

The reception was at the Moose Club. Instant Replay, our extraordinary big band of the time, played. It was a big, boisterous party which I think everyone enjoyed immensely. As is usually the case with AOPis, they did their patented circle singing and passing of champagne bottles. Then the Beardens left for Cancun, and the Barnes left for a Caribbean cruise. Pat and I had gained two wonderful sons-in-law.

This was my toast to my prospective sons-in-law on the occasion of the rehearsal party at the Union City Country Club the night before the wedding.

<u>Ode to Rance and Donny</u>

On the first day of their engagements your true loves gave to me a bill for wedding dresses in which to marry thee

On the second day of their engagements your true loves gave to me a bill for garters to wear above their knee

On the third day of their engagements your true loves gave to me a bill for wedding veils, golly gee, I wanted to flee

On the fourth day of their engagements your true loves gave to me a bill for invitations for friends and family

On the fifth day of their engagements your true loves gave to me a bill for candles to light their ways romantically

On the sixth day of their engagements your true loves gave to me a bill for their trousseaus to wear across the sea

On the seventh day of their engagements your true loves gave to me a bill for enough flowers to fill the sanctuary

On the eighth day of their engagements your true loves gave to me a bill for the reception; I could hardly believe the fee

On the ninth day of their engagements your true loves gave to me a bill for a cake; is there nothing about a wedding that's free?

On all the days of their engagements your true loves gave to me bills in total enough to break the treasury.

On this last day of their engagements your true loves give to me the knowledge that tomorrow they'll be on your salary

If there were any more days of their engagements, your father-in-law-to-be in all probability, would beg for mercy, or skip the country

On the first day of their marriages your true loves will give to me two more fine sons to add to our family tree.

Will and Kim, the daughter of Eddie and Judy Oglesby of Knoxville, married on July 8, 1995 at the Cedar Springs Presbyterian Church in Knoxville. I was best man, as Dad had been for me. They had a big, beautiful wedding and a gala reception with a band and much dancing at Fox Den Country Club in Knoxville, after which they left for their honeymoon on Maui. Pat and I gained a perfect daughter-in-law. And she is an AOPi! The four girls — Kim, Pat, Lolly, and Patti — are all sorority sisters. This has been fun for them.

Pat and I entertained the night before the wedding after the rehearsal at L'Orangerie, a wonderful restaurant in Knoxville. A large crowd was invited. The food was excellent, and the many toasts and videos were marvelous. Even I seemed to do a decent job as toastmaster of the evening's activities.

We had 'em all married. Pat and I could not be happier with their choices. Our sons-in-law and daughter-in-law, like our children, are extraordinarily good people, devout Christians, dedicated spouses, and exemplary parents.

After their honeymoon in Cancun, Donny and Lolly moved to Shreveport. Don grew up in Tulsa and in Fort Smith, Arkansas and is a graduate of the University of Arkansas where he was a Lambda Chi Alpha. He was starting quarterback on his Tulsa high school football team.

Lolly was successful in the mortgage loan business in Shreveport prior to her leaving that company in order to be a full-time mom. She and Don are operating their own business, a Heavenly Ham franchise store in Shreveport. Honey Baked has just bought out Heavenly Ham, so their signage will probably eventually change. Though Lolly is still a full-time mom, she spends some time at their store.

Don left a position as a pharmaceutical salesman with Watson Pharmaceuticals after having been a terminal manager in Hot Springs and then in national sales in Shreveport with ABF Freightlines. After that and prior to his pharmaceutical career, he was in national sales with U.S.A. Truck, another major truck line.

Lolly and Don have two beautiful daughters, Meg and Ellen, and have a lovely home on a beautiful street in a substantial part of midtown Shreveport, a delightful old southern city.

After their honeymoon Caribbean cruise, Patti and Rance, who is also a UT graduate, moved into an apartment in Antioch, just outside Nashville, and Rance continued his work as an electrical engineer with Bridgestone Tire Company in Lavergne. Rance graduated from Obion County Central High School where he played safety and was a backup running back on the football team. Patti went to work for MCA in

Nashville. Among their many clients whom Patti came to know, Reba McEntire was probably the most famous. Later Patti went to work for Steve Buckingham, a major Nashville producer of country music for CBS Records, later to become Sony Music. Steve's artists included Dolly Parton, Ricky Van Shelton, Ricky Skaggs, Sweethearts of the Rodeo, and Mike Reid. Mary Chapin Carpenter was not one of Steve Buckingham's clients, but Patti picked her up at the Nashville airport on her first visit to Nashville. Carpenter was on their CBS (later to become Sony) label. Dolly Parton and Patti became good buddies. In fact, when Patti was pregnant with young Rance, Dolly felt her stomach and said, "Patti, I have a knack for this. You're gonna have a little girl." Well, young Rance, she doesn't have all that much "knack for that" after all, does she? After Rance Deslonde Barnes, Jr. was born, Patti left that fun and exciting job for good. Their next two sons, Walker and Thomas, were born in Union City.

Big Rance had always wanted to farm, and I gave him that opportunity. So in January, 1997 Rance resigned from Bridgestone. The Barnes family bought a house on Wedgewood Drive in Union City and moved home to Obion County. Rance became a full-time farmer, farming more and more of my land each year. Rance farms about 2,500 acres of cotton, corn, soybeams, wheat, and milo (in descending order of acreage planted to each). He is already considered to be one of the best farmers of this area, and he is, by far, Obion County's largest cotton farmer.

After their Maui honeymoon Will and Kim, also a UT graduate who grew up in Farragut on the west side of Knoxville and who graduated from Farragut High School, moved into a house they had bought on Howard Street in Union City. Kim served as a substitute teacher for the Union City School System for one year and then became a first grade teacher for the Union City system for two years, resigning prior to having their first child. Will and Kim lived on Howard Street until 2000 when they bought, renovated, and moved into a lovely house on Oaklawn Street in Union City where they live with their two sons, Wilton and John.

Will is a natural born businessman with a real knack for numbers. He does a great job for our family.

Chapter Seventeen

Pat's and My Middle and Recent Years

In addition to our many Kenton friends, Pat and I also have many good friends in Union City (Chapter 36). After all, we have now lived in Union City for 40 years. Two of our three children and five of our seven grandchildren live within four blocks of us which obviously adds a great deal to the quality of our lives. Many a pleasant evening is spent in Graham Park watching our grandsons play ball. Considering their ages, from two to twelve, we can look forward to that fun activity for a long time to come. We just wish we could watch our Shreveport granddaughters play ball also. But that's an eight hour drive away.

My 40s may well have been the best ten years of my life. I had a great wife, three great children, good health, a lovely home, and a successful business. All the things I had always hoped, and in some cases prayed for had come true. It was a heady feeling. Life was good. It still is.

For many years I have sponsored Kenton's Junior Babe Ruth baseball team. Years ago I promised to take them to St. Louis to see the Cardinals play if they won their league championship. Seems like they won every year! One year we went for a weekend which included Mike Shannon's, a good restaurant, for dinner Saturday night before the game. They just about ate me out of house and home! Mike, the Cardinal radio announcer and one-time Cardinal all-star third baseman, gave autographs to all the boys. Great memories were created that weekend.

Our somewhat strange string of pets continued with a beagle named Louise Kirkland. Louise Kirkland, a dear friend of ours, gave the pup to us so we named the dog for her. At any rate Louise (the dog, not the friend) was a weird animal, nothing at all like her namesake! Pat decided the beagle needed another home, and an arrangement was worked out with one of the families on one of our farms to take her. The problem was that we couldn't catch her. One day Pat caught Louise asleep in her doghouse and quickly nailed a board over the dog house door. We took her to the farm, doghouse and all, and Louise had a new family in a familiar home.

Pat and I never liked cats much. One summer day I came home from work and Pat was painting in the garage, something she often did when the weather was good. Pat was leaning over her work, and this beautiful calico cat was on Pat's back, peering over her shoulder, watching Pat paint. Naturally I thought Pat had lost her mind. As it turned out this cat, without a collar but obviously well fed and healthy, had strolled into the garage. Pat had tried to run it off but finally gave up and had actually grown, during the course of the day, to kind of like the cat. We decided to keep her, and we named her for the calico cat in the Broadway show, *Cats*, Jenny Any Dots, just plain Jenny for short. A year or so later Jenny had four very cute kittens. After they were weaned we decided to try to give them away. Pat advertised "Adorable Kittens to give away" in *The Messenger* Want Ads with no luck. Then Pat had the bright idea to advertise them, "Adorable Kittens to give away. GOOD MOUSERS." They probably had never seen a mouse, but the phone rang off the hook with people wanting them. Not only did we give away the four the next day, but a stray kitten had moved in with our four, and it was also given away. We could have given away a dozen. We then had Jenny neutered and she lived to a ripe old age finally dying about three years ago.

About 25 years ago I went on a trip to Los Angeles to see Tennessee play either UCLA or Southern Cal and spent some time with my old fraternity brother from Nashville, Charles W. (Buster) Pellettieri who had gone to L.A. after graduation from UT to make his fortune in the movie business. Buster had a neat bachelor's pad on Benedict Canyon Drive in Beverly Hills. He had a very good-looking girlfriend who was an assistant to some legitimate movie mogul. Our group was staying at the Beverly Hilton Hotel in Beverly Hills. On Sunday afternoon Buster and his girlfriend, wearing the briefest bikini I'd ever seen, picked me up in his Cadillac convertible with a bottle of champagne iced down. This was vintage Buster! They took me to visit another fraternity brother, Bill Grafton, and his English wife who lived in Santa Monica while Buster and his girlfriend went on out to Santa

181

Monica Beach. Buster suggested that I move to L.A. and join him in the movie business. It was tempting. He and I had worked together on Carnicus skits at UT, and we both thought we were ready for the big time. Actually Buster did go on to have some success. He co-wrote, co-directed, and co-produced a movie, *Race With the Devil*, starring Peter Fonda, Loretta Swit, and Warren Oates, from which he told me he netted $900,000. (When I told this story to fraternity brother Howard Hurt in Knoxville, he laughed and said, "Tom, Buster just called me last week to ask me for a $50 loan." Buster must have exaggerated. It wouldn't have been the first time.) Pat and I did see *Race With the Devil* at the Capitol Theater in Union City and enjoyed it. Buster had bit parts in a couple of other movies which we saw, but he never had a major role. He barely hung on and died an early and lonely death.

In 1981 somebody told me during strawberry season that Willard Scott, the weatherman on the NBC *Today Show*, had talked about the Strawberry Festival that was taking place in Humboldt, Tennessee, and that he wished somebody from way down there in West Tennessee would send him some strawberries. I decided to give it a shot and sent four beautiful quarts of berries to Memphis to be air freighted to New York in time for the next day's show. Good ole Willard showed the berries to their national audience and said that they came from "good ole Tom Wade from down there in West Tennessee." Several old friends called and wrote to tell me that they had seen my berries on the *Today Show*. Sally called to say that she was doing her exercises in front of her television set while watching *Today*, and that as soon as Willard remarked that they came "from West Tennessee from good ole" she just knew he was going to say, "Tom Wade." What a thrill for all of us! Unfortunately I was too busy at the berry patch to see the show, but Pat did.

One of the best experiences that our family ever had was going to Los Angeles with the Union City High School Band, band boosters, parents, and brothers and sisters of the band members in December 1984/January1985. About 350 people from Union City took two Delta flights to L.A. We stayed in a good Marriott Hotel in Newport Beach right across from an exclusive large shopping mall and in downtown Newport Beach, a delightful city. We had a wonderful time in every regard. The children were extremely well behaved and were very popular with everybody out there. Patti was the head majorette of the band and both NBC and CBS zoomed in on her as the Union City Band came into their filming area. (Right after we returned to Union City, a talent agent from New York who had seen Patti in the parade called us and asked if he could come talk with us about representing her with modeling agencies. We declined. He called again. We again declined. We've often wondered what might have happened if we had pursued this possible opportunity. It's probably good that we didn't. Patti has had a great life, and undoubtedly she wouldn't have changed a thing about it.) Almost everybody in West Tennessee saw the band and saw Patti. A friend made wonderful videos of both filmings for us which we have greatly enjoyed. One of the great thrills of our lives was being in the viewing stand with a large number of other Union City relatives of band members and seeing the Union City band come into view out from behind a Volvo dealership on the Colorado Avenue parade route in Pasadena. There were many tears rolling down mothers' cheeks at that instant. The band had already marched for several miles and they were worn out, but when they saw us and we started cheering they perked up and played enthusiastically and stepped lively. Another big thrill was when our band marched along with one other high school band which was in the Rose Parade (there were only seven high school bands in the Rose Parade) as well as the McDonald's High School All-American Band in Disneyland one day. The band also went to the famous Los Angeles Farmers Market and to Universal Studios. Another day the band went to the San Diego Zoo. We rented a car that day and all of us except for Patti toured Los Angeles and Beverly Hills rather than going down to San Diego. (Rance and Patti and Will and Pat and I did go to the San Diego Zoo when we were there for a Beltwide Cotton Conference in San Diego a few years ago. On that trip we stayed part of the time at the world famous del Coronado Hotel. Kim missed this trip as she had to stay home to teach first grade.)

Some time ago I wrote a Tom Wade Strawberries song to the same tune as my Freeman & Wade Chrysler-Plymouth jingle (Chapter 34).

A remarkable young banjo player from Gleason, Mike Snider, played and sang this radio ad which was a big hit. Mike later became famous as one of the world's top banjo players and for a good many years has been a mainstay on the Grand Ole Opry. We paid him $25 for his services!

Later I contracted with the nationally known country humorist, Cotton Ivy, who lived in Union City for a pretty good while, to do strawberry spots for me. My patch sales, both pre-picked and pick-your-own, set all time records that year.

Our friends, Newell and Bettye Graham, have a large wine cellar and are wine connoisseurs. One year Newell called and said that Bettye at the last minute was not going to be able to go to a tasting in Chicago and that everything was paid for and he wondered if I would like to go. My quick answer was an emphatic "Yes!" This tasting was put on by the Chicago Wine Company, one of the nation's top importers, at the downtown Ritz Carlton where we stayed. We had ten kinds of wine and fine food and stayed in a hostelry that has often been picked as America's top hotel. It was a most interesting experience, though I surely was glad that Newell volunteered to drive all the way home the next day.

The world was enraptured with our putting men on the moon. The morning after the landing was covered on the TV screens of the world one of our long-time employees in all seriousness said to me, "Tommy, they sure were lucky it was a full moon last night, weren't they?" To which I replied, "Yep, they sure were." Another Kentonian, Forrest Crockett, never did believe it happened. He went to his grave thinking the whole thing was orchestrated by a conspiracy of the government and Hollywood. Wonder if Mr. Forrest was right?

Pat and I went to a new sandwich shop in Memphis for lunch. Pat usually eats salads in restaurants, especially at lunch, so she asked if she could get a salad and was told that they did not have salads. She and the waiter wrangled around awhile, good naturedly, so finally she said, "Bring me a ham sandwich with lettuce and tomato. Hold the ham and hold the bread." He brought her a lettuce and tomato salad. Pat has always been pretty quick.

Pat and I hosted a big money raising reception for Congressman John Tanner and his lovely wife, Betty Ann, early on in his congressional career. At the time more money was raised for John than had ever before been raised for a politician in Obion County. John and I are distant cousins on Mother's side going back to my Great, Great, Great, Great Grandfather and Grandmother White who are buried in a little family plot west of Union City just off the Lake Highway.

Jay Galloway, "Auctioneer Coon Hunter," according to the sign painted on the back of his pickup truck, held an auction to sell the deceased Miss Yetta's and Mr. Sam Shatz's belongings at their lifelong Kenton home. Pat, Mary Nell Butler, and I attended the sale. Nobody puts on a more fun sale than does Jay. Miss Yetta had some fine oriental rugs, and a rug dealer and I bid them up to far higher numbers than any of the auction group expected (I only bought one small rug). After the last one was sold Jay said to his wife, Sue, who was helping at the sale, "Honey, run out to the house and gather up all the rugs you can find. And hurry back!" Later in the sale he sold Miss Yetta's mink stole for a good price and he said about the buyers, "Folks, can't you just see 'em now. They'll go to a fine party, she'll be wearing her stole and holding his arm as they prance in, and everybody'll say, lookee there, lookee there, they've got it all!" The three of us could hardly bid for laughing at Jay's antics. The world needs more Jay Galloways.

Pat and Will and I have been at the Governor's Mansion in Nashville on several occasions during the McWherter and Sundquist Administrations. We have met some pretty famous folks during those pleasant interludes, one of whom was the very personable Hubert Humphrey III.

As of this writing my golf game is absolutely pitiful, probably because I haven't averaged much over 18 holes a year for the past 20 or 25 years. Fairly soon after Pat and I moved to Union City I was fortunate to become involved in a regular Sunday game with Jere Doss, Oliver Gilliam, and Fred Roberts. Jere and I played Oliver and Freddie and it was a fairly even match. We had a great time together, and it was plum' sad to have to leave the 19th hole at Poplar Meadows on Sunday afternoons. After a very few years Freddie moved to Memphis and somehow the magic was gone. I played with Jere and Oliver and others for a while and then kind of drifted away from the game. Jere, Oliver, and Freddie remain to this day three of my favorite people, though we no longer see them often. We need to rectify that!

When I was playing most Sundays during good weather and occasionally on other days my usual score was in the mid to high 80s and low 90s on the Poplar Meadows course. One time I had some Dyersburg friends over to play. John Hoff, Milton Magee, and William Anderson were in the group. That day I shot a 79, one of only two times I ever in my life broke 80. My approach shot on No. 17 hit the pond, but it skipped across. A good approach and putt salvaged a par. For all Hoff, Magee, and Anderson knew, that was my usual game. To this day they must think I'm a crackerjack golfer. Hope they don't read this book!

The last time I played was during a weekend in Ponte Vedra Beach about four years ago with fraternity brother Bill Taylor and a couple of his friends from Chattanooga and North Carolina. Bill and Kitty Taylor had three couples of us down for a long weekend. We had a great time but my golf was atrocious. After playing the first three holes of the first day fairly well, I started hitting water, traps, and out of bounds and finally got to a point that when my ball landed in hazards, I'd just pick up. It was most embarrassing. Maybe I should take the two golf lessons that Will and Kim gave me four years ago. Probably the logical thing to do is to give up the game for good.

While on the subject of golf, in addition to the Chapter 11 Jimmy Wade story, another little white lie that was great fun occurred at the only Masters Tournament I ever attended. This was the Masters in the mid-60s that was won by Jack Nicklaus in an 18-hole playoff on Monday. Jack, Gay Brewer, and Tommy Aaron had tied on Sunday. (I only saw Nicklaus play three times — the Masters, the U.S. Open at Pebble Beach, and a Memphis Open. He won all three!) Lolly was real young and a little under the weather and Pat did not go. Sally and Pitt came up from Florida and I met them, and we stayed with Sally's old North Carolina Chi Omega roommate, Fran Merry Simpkins, and her husband, Bryan Simpkins. The Simpkins were society folks in Augusta so we were invited to some nice local parties and met a lot of sharp local people. One young man we met was a scratch golfer – he might have played college golf – and he and I hit it off. Taking a cue from Yellowstone days, I told him that I also was a scratch golfer who had considered turning pro. Embellishing the story had Dad offering to back me on the P.G.A. tour but that I had decided to go into the family business instead. He was very impressed. We went together to the Saturday and Sunday sessions. After awhile he started asking me some questions about golf, such things as, "Why do they not allow you to touch the sand with your club in the traps?" I answered his queries to the best of my limited knowledge, but he seemed to become more and more suspicious before the weekend was over. At any rate he apparently had no interest in accompanying me to the Monday playoff.

Lying is, of course, an abomination. It's something I do not practice. Though my rule certainly was bent those two times, it didn't seem to really hurt anybody. And those little white lies sure did wonders for my feelings of self worth.

Johnny Majors, All American tailback and runnerup for the Heisman Trophy and later Tennessee head coach and I were not close friends at UT but we were friends and had stayed in touch to a degree through the years. So when he was elected to the College Football Hall of Fame in 1987 it was a logical time to do what I had always wanted to do, go to New York in early December for the College Football Hall of Fame festivities. I decided to go and went up four days early and saw four Broadway shows. Pat and Patti then came up for four additional days, and we took in four more shows. The entire time was spent in the Waldorf Astoria which was a delightful experience. On the night before the induction we Tennesseans were invited by The University of Tennessee Athletics Department for a cocktail party in honor of Johnny. Then I went to the black tie reception and banquet the next night. On Friday and Saturday nights I met many famous football people which was a great thrill. There were about 70 Tennessee folks there which was by far the largest contingent. After the banquet a picture was taken of our group. I was out in the crowd collecting autographs and missed the call for the photo. Later UT sent me a copy of the group photo. Taking a cue from another man who had a similar experience (Kenton's Joe Penn of the famous Centre College "Praying

Colonels" football team that upset Harvard in the early 20th Century and who missed his team picture), I put on a tuxedo and had Union City photographer, Jill Emmons, make a photo of me. She then sent it to a studio which superimposed my picture on the right side of the third row of the group picture. Though my picture looks like some kind of gray ghost haunting the group from over there in the corner, I really was there in the flesh!

Johnny invited me to join a small group of his close friends for some nightclub hopping after the banquet. Stockton Adkins from Union City (twice Jacobs Trophy winner given to the best blocker in the Southeastern Conference and a great Tennessee blocking back); Tommy Bronson (that Volunteer team's terrific fullback); Barry Switzer (famous Oklahoma coach and later coach of the Dallas Cowboys); Mack Dove (close friend of Johnny's and good friend of mine and owner of the very large trucking firm, AAA Cooper based in Dothan, Alabama); Larry Lacewell (head coach at Arkansas State and later long time assistant coach of the Cowboys); and other teammates Bob Gleaves and Bill Wise, and I joined Johnny for a celebratory tour. We hit three great clubs and were out until the wee hours of the morning. At the third spot, P. J. Clarke's which was only a few blocks from the Waldorf, Mack and I decided we had had enough fun for one night and walked back to the hotel. Those eight days were unforgettable.

On December 10, 1996 John Michels, Zeta PiKA and Volunteer All-American guard, NFL and Canadian League player and coach, and offensive line coach for the Minnesota Vikings for 27 years, was inducted into the College Football Hall of Fame. Pat and I took our children and their spouses to New York and Sally and both Pitts came up from Bethesda. In addition to John, Rance, Will, and me, Zeta Pike Roger Bradley, my old pledge class president and close friend, and slightly older Zeta Pikes and longtime UT Athletics Department executives Bob Davis and Gus Manning, went to New York for John's induction. John had graduated the spring before I entered UT in the fall of 1952 so I did not know him until he became involved with the Super Group after he and his lovely wife, Ann, retired to Gatlinburg. John and I have become good buddies, and his Hall of Fame induction was a perfect opportunity for our family to have a marvelous time together. We invited the Michels and their extended family and Roger and his lady friend, Peggy Makepeace, to join us Wades, Barnes, Beardens, and Tomlinsons for lunch at "21." This was a festive affair which the club manager had kindly planned for me. We ate in the downstairs room which has an enormous collection of "things" hanging from the ceiling. I later sent the manager a small cotton bale, and he wrote to tell me that it was hanging up there with all that other stuff. All of us except the Tomlinsons were invited to UT's party for John. We seven Zeta Pikes got together for photos. The next night I took Will, Don, Rance, and Julian Bach, noted literary agent from New York (see Chapter 37) to the Hall of Fame cocktail party and banquet. Our family also saw two Broadway shows and Radio City Music Hall's Christmas production. Those four days may have been the most exciting experience of our family lives.

Pat and I have been to New York many times. As a child, with Mother, I saw *"Guys and Dolls"* and *"The Pajama Game"* at the famous Blackstone Theatre in Chicago which whetted my appetite for Broadway shows. Pat and I, often with our children, have seen many New York shows and have also enjoyed its restaurants, shopping, and museums immensely. New York is my favorite city in the world.

Pat's and my life together has become richer as time has gone by. As our children have grown older they have become even more fun to be with. All three of ours have been absolute joys from days one, and they and their spouses and our grandchildren have made life for Pat and me a continuing delightful journey. The Lord has blessed my family and me in many ways. It has been and continues to be a wonderful life.

Pat's Talent

Pat started painting soon after we married, portraits in oil to begin with. From there she went on to work in many mediums, and as far as I am concerned she can do just about anything she sets her mind to. Our friends, Robert and Carl Kirkland, started a chain of gift shops, Kirkland's, that developed into a very large operation. A few years later they decided that they might as well be in the wholesale end of the business as well, and Robert developed a wholesale gift import business, CBK Ltd., in Union City. (A few years ago Robert bought out Carl's interest in CBK, which Robert recently sold. Some years ago Robert and Carl sold controlling interest in Kirkland's. CBK also grew into a large operation with, the last I heard, 150 sales people nationally who work exclusively for CBK, several hundred people in their headquarters operation in Union City, a beautiful suite of offices, and a 400,000 square foot warehouse building.) Early on Pat did some design work for CBK. They had their goods produced in the Far East and in other underdeveloped countries for the most part. Pat would create designs, and Bob would take them and other ideas on his two annual trips abroad and work out deals with those people to produce the gift items which would then be imported into the United States. One late afternoon Bob came to Pat and told her that for some particular reason he needed some designs for his trip to the Orient on which he was to embark early the next morning. Pat worked all night long and painted some designs which Bob liked. These designs went on little lamp shades which were very popular then. Pat was working on a commission. Well, by George, they sold millions of them. Though they were very cheap, Pat still realized a good deal of money out of them, much more than we ever thought she would earn from CBK. For three years Pat made good money with CBK and she had several years leading up to her big break and several afterwards in which she did pretty darn well. For the first couple of years that she worked on CBK projects she made very little money. In fact I told her that she was probably foolish to spend so much time for so little money. But she and CBK persevered, and they both cashed in mighty well, Pat, of course, in a much lesser way.

Pat has not done anything for CBK for a few years now, but she has continued her art endeavors and still turns out beautiful paintings, carvings, murals, faux finishes, furniture, quilts, and sculptures in wood. Several of her watercolors and oil paintings hang in our house and in the homes of our children. In addition many of her paintings have been sold. Several of her faux finish works also grace our home. Examples are Pat's great grandfather's cast iron fireplace which she marbleized, an antique table the top of which she marbleized, a chest which she refinished with several types of faux wood finishes, and waste baskets with faux tortoiseshell finishes. She and our friend, Paul (Pete) Tate, have made numerous wooden book tables which Pat has finished and painted to look like stacks of books. Our children and we have several of them in our homes, and Pat has sold a good many of them. Two of Pat's murals cover walls in Will's old upstairs bedroom and in one of our downstairs bathrooms. In addition she painted a mural in Patti's house. She also has painted several murals for others for fees as well as having painted and donated murals for Union City Schools and our First Methodist Church. She recently carved an eight foot tall Indian in a totem pole-type way as well as three miniature totem poles and several large wooden bowls. She has made many quilts and painted dozens of pieces of furniture (for others as well as for ourselves).

Pat's artistic endeavor of which I'm most proud involved her very complicated quilting of two large fabric paintings by my cousin, Estelle (Fire) Norvell Cruxent, and her husband, Jorge Cruxent. I bought one of these paintings at a show of the Cruxents' works at Pat's alma mater, Lindenwood College outside St. Louis, fifteen years ago and gave it to Pat that Christmas. She decided to quilt it. She devised a big quilting frame which she hung in the wide double door entrance into our family room and went to work. Literally tens of thousands of stitches and months later, Pat had turned the Cruxent painting which was on loose hanging muslin into a three-dimensional masterpiece. When it was finally finished and stretched we knew we had something extraordinary. The completion of this monumental effort was bittersweet for Pat. She was happy to have finished it but missed having this quilting project to work on. I called and asked the Cruxents if they still had the other painting. They did, and I bought it and gave it to Pat the next Christmas. She repeated the first process, and these two marvelous pieces now hang side by side reaching almost to the vaulted ceiling of our family room. The shadows created by her quilting and by lights shining on them from above and below create stunning works of art. An interesting sidelight to this story is that our bank was organized in that big room while the second painting was hanging in that doorway. We organizers had to dodge around the painting for most of the six months during which time the new bank came to fruition.

I have paid the income taxes on her income from her work, and Pat Wade of Union City, her company, is now worth a pretty piece of change. Even more important are the extraordinary works of art she will leave for her family and future descendants to enjoy for centuries to come.

Pat, a kind, compassionate, talented lady, will leave this world a better place than she found it.

Chapter Eighteen

Grandchildren

Rance Deslonde Barnes, Jr. was born to Rance, Sr. and Patti Katherine Wade Barnes at West Side Hospital in Nashville on May 13, 1991. Little Rance weighed in at a not-too-little 9 pounds 2 ounces. Big Rance's parents, Nicky and Jennifer Barnes, and Pat and I arrived shortly after Little Rance entered the world.

Magdalene Ann (Meg) Bearden was born to William Donald (Don, or Donny) Bearden, Jr. and Annie Laurie (Lolly) Wade Bearden at Schumpert Hospital in Shreveport on May 28, 1992. Meg weighed 8 pounds 15 ounces. Meg was named for her paternal grandmother's mother.

Walker Lee Barnes was born to Rance and Patti at Centennial Medical Center, formerly West Side Hospital, on December 9, 1994. Walker weighed 8 pounds 14 ounces. Nicky and Jennifer and Pat and I were in Nashville to welcome Walker into the world. Walker was named for my Mother's maiden name.

Patricia Ellen (Ellen) Bearden was born to Don and Lolly at Schumpert Hospital on June 18, 1995. Ellen weighed 9 pounds 8 ounces and is very proud of the fact that she was the biggest baby to be born in our family as well as to Don's three sisters. Ellen was named for Pat (Moma Pat).

Thomas Nicholas Barnes was born to Rance and Patti at Union City's Baptist Memorial Hospital on January 14, 1999. Thomas weighed 8 pounds 10 ounces. The Barnes and we Wades were at the hospital to welcome Thomas to the clan. Thomas was named for Nicky (Papa Nicky) and me (Papa Tom).

Thomas Wilton (Wilton) Wade IV was born to Thomas Wilton (Will) Wade III and Kimberly Michelle (Kim) Oglesby Wade at Union City Baptist Memorial Hospital on October 21, 1999. Wilton weighed 7 pounds 3 ounces. Pat, Patti and I were at the hospital when Wilton came into the world. Kim's parents, Eddie and Judy Oglesby, came the next day.

John Raymond Wade was born to Will and Kim at the Union City hospital on April 6, 2001. John weighed 6 pounds 7 ounces. Again, Pat, Patti and I were present to welcome the newest member of our growing family. The Oglesbys came the next day. John is a family name on both sides of the family. Raymond is for Kim's paternal grandfather and her Dad.

How wonderful for Pat and me to have seven grandchildren! Will and Kim opted not to know the sex of their impending arrivals as did Patti and Rance with their first and last child. Lolly and Don knew in advance that their two children would be girls. We're prejudiced, of course, but we do know for a fact that all seven of them are extraordinary! After reading the following, you're bound to agree.

Little Rance was fascinated with shoestrings at eight months of age and would "test" things for hours by dangling a baby shoe up and down to see how the string would curl on different surfaces. He called Uncle Micah Barnes, "Boggy," and Lolly, "Nonny." He got a ukulele for his second birthday which began a love affair for guitars that lasted for several years during which time he was hardly ever without his latest guitar. He was also fascinated with weedeaters and would play at weedeating for hours on end. He is presently in the sixth grade in Union City Elementary School. Rance plays soccer and basketball and is a good left handed baseball player. He has made all his All-Star teams and played his natural position at first base each time except for the 2002 season when he played centerfield. Rance is also a good pitcher with a beautiful delivery and is rapidly becoming more and more effective. Rance is also a good hunter. He mainly hunts ducks and deer. In 2002 he killed one deer with a bow and arrow, one with his uncle Genie Barnes' muzzleloader, and two with his deer rifle. Rance is a good student, belongs to the prestigious LEAP honor society, and has been Student of the Month on several occasions. In August of 2001 Rance made his public profession of faith, and in September he was baptized at the Barnes' Reelfoot Baptist Church.

Meg received a purple babydoll as an infant, and she still sleeps with "Purple Babe." She was christened at St. Scholastica Church in

New Blaine, Arkansas, her Dad's family's church, in Granddaddy Mike's christening gown. At age one she visited my strawberry patch and picked and ate all the berries she could cram into her mouth. Red juice all over her! By age 10 months she loved Barney. At age 1-1/2 she could identify all the videos by their labels. When visiting Granddaddy Mike in Dyersburg she always wanted "tunny" (candy). Meg tested extraordinarily well in the Gateway program for academically gifted children at three years of age. She attended preschool at Broadmoor Methodist Day School and at A. C. Steere Gateway School, and she attended South Highlands Magnet, for several years Shreveport's number one ranked elementary school in Louisiana. She is now in the sixth grade at Caddo Middle Magnet School. Meg enjoys and is proficient in softball, soccer, swimming, golf, and art, and she was fifth grade Team Leader for South Highlands' Running Club. Meg recently designed a tile mosaic which was then created by the fifth grade and was their gift to South Highlands and hangs permanently in that award-winning school. She was assistant director of the fifth grade play (their drama teacher was director) and spent a great deal of each school day performing her duties, requiring her to keep up with her demanding school work on her own time. Last but not least, she loves to scare the Bearden's Great Dane, Pepper, with their stuffed Kenton White Squirrel!

Walker was always an outgoing and personable young fellow. When his "berber" Rance went to school, Walker cried and cried. Despite this fact a day or two after Walker arrived at home big brother Rance asked Patti when she was going to take him back to the hospital. When he started preschool he wore a backpack, like his big brother did. He wore cowboy boots every day and changed clothes several times a day — to Superman, or to Batman, or to whatever else he could find in his closet. Walker liked everything to do with farming — tractors, planters, "pray" coupes. Like big brother, Walker had a long attention span — coloring, Nintendo, TV, etc. He called his Mother's freckles, "sprinkles" and wondered who put them on her face. Once the family went to the Gulf Coast, and after ten hours of driving he asked if they had gotten to (our) country club yet. Then he asked if they had been through Mexico. But he never complained for a minute.

Walker kept his distance from baby brother Thomas for months one time after Thomas spit up on Walker's head. Can't say that I blame him. Walker is presently in the third grade at Union City Elementary School, and his teachers have all been impressed with his kindness and intelligence. Some of their comments: Could be valedictorian ... no telling what he can accomplish ... reading at 4th grade level in 1st grade ... auto skills tested 8th to 9th grade at end of 1st grade ... could be an astronaut. Walker enjoys Cub Scouts and has said that he wants to go to West Point. He enjoys reading about World War II and the Civil War. He plays baseball and soccer and enjoys hunting. He has been the catcher for his baseball team and has improved his catching and hitting with each game. When Walker was five years old he told his parents that he was a born again Christian.

Ellen's first trip was at age three weeks, 1600 miles round trip from Shreveport to Knoxville to Uncle Will's and Aunt Kim's wedding. She also was christened at St. Scholastica Church in New Blaine, Arkansas, in Granddaddy Mike's christening gown. She first smiled at four weeks, and she hasn't stopped yet! She has a captivating smile. Once when Ellen was very young and very upset big sister Meg said to Lolly, "Will you please find somebody to stop my baby's crying!" Ellen first called Meg "Ooh Ooh," because Meg used to crow like a rooster (cock-a-doodle-do) to announce to all that she was "up and at 'em." Ellen called Santa Claus "Ho Ho." Makes perfect sense. She danced before she walked. At seven months old she would sit in the floor with a musical toy and twist to the music. She plays softball and soccer and is a gifted cheerleader. Her Mother says that she does approximately 300 cartwheels through the house every day. Ellen wants to be a babysitter and competitive cheerleader when she grows up. She has always loved playing with dolls. She also likes to serve breakfast in bed to family members who sleep later than she does. Ellen has always had a very nurturing personality. Like her big sister she attended preschool at Broadmoor Methodist Day School. And like Meg, she achieved the very high testing standards required for acceptance into South Highlands Magnet Elementary School where she is presently in the third grade. Ellen recently was the seventh girl selected to participate in a cheerleading squad of 30. This squad is primarily a competitive group which will enter competitions in Dallas, Houston, Shreveport, and other cities. Taking a cue from her big sister, Ellen's oil and pastel drawing of a parrot was chosen to appear in the Shreveport telephone directory.

Thomas has also been a precocious child. He was saying "Moma" and "Dada" at six months old. Early on he enjoyed taking things out (like pots and pans) and then putting them right back in. At age 1-1/2 he fell into a display rack at The Dollar Tree and cut his forehead badly. Dr. John Clendenin sewed it up. When he was almost two years old he jumped off his bed and broke his leg. He has a high tolerance for pain and hobbled around on it for two days without complaining before Patti had it x-rayed. Sure enough it was broken, and a cast was put on it. Daniel Boone was "Danny Boom," thanks was "ranks," water was "wah wah," and stickers were "tickers." He wondered why Frosty had that carrot on his nose. So do I. One Christmas Patti strung cranberries, nuts, and popcorn on a string for tree decorations. Thomas asked her if he could string the rest of his bologna and cheese sandwich on that string. Like his brothers when they were little, Thomas likes to wear costumes, Superman being his favorite. He came to our house one day wearing his Superman cape. As he got out of the car he flung the cape to the ground exclaiming, "I'm not gonna fly any more today!" Pat offered him a cracker. He said, "No thank you, Moma Pat. I am crackerful!" Patti explained that she had just given Thomas several crackers. Thomas' favorite outfit now is anything camouflage and rubber or cowboy boots. His preschool teachers have gotten a kick out of him, and he is obviously very bright. He loves being around the carpenters at our house project, especially the contractor, Van Walton. At just over three years old, Van took him in his truck on an errand. Thomas asked Van, "Do you have a Mother and Daddy?" Van replied that he did and that his Mother lived in Mississippi and that his Daddy had died and gone to heaven. Thomas asked, "Was he saved?" Van replied that he was, and then Thomas asked, "Was he baptized?" Van replied that he had been. From the mouths of babes ...

Wilton is the sixth in a line of very intelligent Wade grandchildren! He has obviously been very bright from a very young age. He has always hated to see his Dad go to work in the mornings. As time has gone by he has developed a routine. He gives Will a hug, a kiss on his nose, a kiss on his cheek, a High Five, and says, "Have a good day, Daddy! See you for suppers." Wilton loves his dogs, Chauncey and Chief. He wears a bright red St. Louis Cardinals baseball cap (the only one he will wear) and loves to swim in their pool and jump on a "trampotrine." Some of Wilton's expressions: When John was very young, Wilton told John, "Dat moma, dat moma, dat moma," as if to introduce John to their Mother. For "No, thank you," he said, "No, please." He called Thomas, "Bodnus." He called Moma Pat, "P Pat." He loves ketchup and asks for it, "tetchup peas." Pat told him how smart he was, and he ran to Will, exclaiming, "I smart, Daddy." After being given a chocolate sucker, he said, "Um, I like dat sucker pie." When staying in a downtown Shreveport hotel he looked out the window and said, "It big outside, Mommy." At Christmas time coming home from church at night Will took a circuitous route to look at Christmas lights, and Wilton said, "I'm having a hard time." Kim asked him why, and he said, "I'm havin' a hard time finin' my house." Wilton enjoys singing Christmas carols and likes his old blue jeans instead of new stiff ones. He sings "Joy to the World, for soft blue jeans." After a trip to the Dairy Queen he said, "Mom I sure like shnakes" — long pause — "I mean lizards." Kim said, "Do you mean blizzards?" Wilton, "Yea, yea." Will and Kim say the Lord's Prayer with each of their boys. Wilton is quick to remind them that it is time to do "Our Father." Just like all seven of our grandchildren, Wilton is receiving a Christian upbringing. He enjoys his preschooling as well as his times at our First Methodist Church.

John has a head full of red hair. He and Wilton are inseparable, though they are different in some ways. John's vocabulary is coming right along, but for a pretty good while his talking consisted primarily of grunting and pointing. As Will said, John was very much like "a finely tuned birddog." Until not too long ago, John got a kick out of dropping his food from his high chair to the floor. Kim got him better trained in that regard. John loves to play outside and with the dogs and is pretty doggoned tough. Wilton is pretty much of a cuddler, but John is all action. He is moving constantly, though he must have his "blue blanky" with him at all times. John, like his big brother, is usually very happy and very adept at the art of laughing. He also enjoys preschool and the activities at our church. At John's six months checkup the nurse gave him a shot. He cried for a few seconds and then smiled at the nurse. At another checkup with Dr. John Clendenin he smiled at Dr. John the whole time. John is just naturally a happy little boy who smiles almost constantly. If Wilton is not with John, John is looking for Wilton. Oftentimes when music is playing in the house, John will grab his Mother by the finger and dance with her. Once when Wilton was riding on P Pat's knee, John ran up to her and said, "Do me," his first two-word utterance. John is a veritable bundle of energy. John noticed how his Daddy put on deodorant and he began to stick the capped deodorant underneath his shirt in the general vicinity of his armpits. One day Pat was changing John and a penny rolled out of his diaper. John had noticed his Dad putting change into his pockets, and he decided to carry change in his pants, too!

Pat and I are inordinately proud of and adore each of our grandchildren. Can you blame us?

Chapter Nineteen

2022 Stonewall

After two and a half years in Union City's Sherwood Hills Pat and I started building a house at 2022 Stonewall Street (later changed to Drive) in Union City. I had bought a lot on Wedgewood Drive from Red Armstrong, and we decided to swap it back to Red for two lots on Stonewall. The lots cost $3,750 each, so I had $7,500 in our two lots. At the time I bought the lots from Red he offered to sell me the 40 acres just south and west of our property for $40,000. I thought it would have been a good buy, but I simply didn't have $40,000. At that time Stonewall deadended at Red's house (now Al and Laura Oliver's) and our property. In later years that property was developed, first by an extension of Stonewall by Red and a couple of years ago by the opening up of the property just west of Stonewall and south of the Oliver house, by Al. Each lot in that new subdivision is now bringing about as much as the whole thing would have cost me in 1970.

Our house was begun and finished in 1970. It contained four bedrooms, three baths, entrance hall, living room, dining room, breakfast room, kitchen, utility room, family room, and library. Ronnie Hunt of Kenton and Danny Corley of Rutherford built it, and a Memphis architect designed it.

In 1974 we decided to add a south wing which consisted of our present sunporch, a bathroom, and our big family room. Will Austin Nailling built it, and he and Pat designed what turned out to be a lovely addition.

Then in 1984 we decided to add to our house again. The designs of Gil Humphrey from Memphis with Pat's ideas and help improved the house greatly with several additions and changes. Robert Taylor from South Fulton was the contractor. We converted the garage into a back hall, and Will's bedroom and bathroom. We added a new three-car garage with a storage room and usable attic. We added a gallery that ran from the utility room behind the kitchen to the family room and opened up the middle part of the house to this back gallery. We built a studio and sewing annex for Pat on the back side of the family room and converted part of a closet to an anteroom of the south bathroom with a bathtub with jets. Pat painted an art deco type mural on the walls surrounding the tub.

But, alas, we weren't through. In late March of 2001 we started another expansion. Millard and Stevens of Memphis, who were the architects for Robert and Jenny Kirkland's home, are our architects. (A quick side note, John and Blanche Millard took Pat and me to lunch one day when we were in Memphis. In our conversation my cousin, Jean Sanders, was mentioned. Blanche allowed as to how Jean had been her little sister in Tri Delt at Vanderbilt. Jean has popped up several times in this book. She was an important part of the early lives of Sally and me.) Van Walton, formerly of Memphis and Union City and now of Martin, is the contractor. Van built the Kirkland house as well as Cybill Shepherd's Memphis home. On the northern edge of our house we have added a "keeping room" which includes a new kitchen, sitting area, and fireplace. To the front, or west, of this room is a hall that runs from the main house and divides the keeping room and a family dining room which lies west of the keeping room. Behind the keeping room is an extension of the existing back hall and a powder room. The garage has been reduced from a three car to a two car with the bay nearest the house becoming more of a working area for Pat's summer use. Some of the interior walls of the original house were moved to accommodate a larger dining room than we formerly had. Our old television room has become an extension of a new entrance hall.

The extension to the south side of the house is a master bedroom suite for Pat and me. In addition to the bedroom there is a sitting room and a conservatory off the sitting room. (Our English-built conservatory was made by Amdega. The crew that assembled it consisted of two men from Indiana and one from Wisconsin. Coincidentally the same men built conservatories for our friends and acquaintances, the Jim Haslams of Knoxville and the Billy Dunavants of Memphis. Jim is the owner of Pilot Oil, and Billy owns the world's largest cotton firm. We Wades are 'way out of our league!) The bathroom area includes a whirlpool tub for Pat and a shower for me. The extension also includes a sound proofed exercise room for Pat's treadmill. And we just keep on adding closets, pantries, and storage rooms!

The outside of the house is dramatically changed. Most of the brick was removed and replaced, and has been painted. A considerable amount of limestone was used on the house and in the landscaping. The windows were changed, many to doors, and the architecture which had been kind of French will be more French.

Gil Humphrey of Memphis will again be involved, this time with drapes and some furniture. Gil recently completed Bob and Ann Cameron's fabulous new home which happens to be across the street from Will and Kim's house. The Cameron house certainly did not detract from Will and Kim's neighborhood!

We have never regretted building on Stonewall. The location is great, as are the neighbors. It's even better situated now since Patti and Rance, Rance, Jr., Walker, and Thomas and Will and Kim, Wilton and John are only three and five blocks away. However, when we started thinking about expanding we looked all over the area for a lot. We liked George Botts' property south toward Kenton, but he did not want to sell us as much property as we wanted. I did not want to be any further from Kenton than we already are, and this limited us a great deal. We knew it would have been better business to sell our house and build a new one from scratch. After much looking and soul searching we finally decided to add to what we had despite the fact that our one acre was too small for what we are building. Nevertheless, the location is perfect for us. Another good thing is that when Lolly and Donny and Meg and Ellen come from Shreveport to visit, the whole family is very close together.

2022 Stonewall has been a great house in which to live, raise children, and entertain. The new house will have those same attributes, substituting the word "grandchildren" for "children!"

About 25 years ago we took the children to Gulf Shores for spring break. We returned home to find that our home had been burglarized. We discovered that having one's home violated is a very traumatic experience. The burglars stole a coin collection, a small amount of jewelry that had been left in the house, our sterling silver tea service which had belonged to Pat's Grandmother, and about half of our sterling flatware. The reason they left some of the flatware was obvious to us. Some of our outside lights were on when we returned, and they had been turned on from the inside of my upstairs closet. One of the burglars had gone into my closet and flipped those switches thinking they turned on the closet light. When the others realized the outside lights had come on, they thought the "jig was up" and they quickly hit the road. They had loaded my shotgun and placed it on a chair at the front door which was left slightly ajar. We shuddered to think about what might very well have happened if we had come home and surprised them in the act of the burglary. It was later determined that the gang was comprised of four St. Louis men who had committed a series of robberies and burglaries from New Orleans all the way up to St. Louis. Nothing was ever proved, but one of the men was arrested in St. Louis a short time later and remarked to the arresting officer that the Union City burglary had not netted them $25,000, the reported loss. Of course, he later denied having made such a remark. Another of the four men was killed in the perpetration of a robbery within a week of ours.

We were told that the burglars probably would have burned our house and any possible evidence if they had not been scared off. Needless to say, after the fact we put in a sophisticated burglary and fire alarm system, and we also always have a "house sitter" when we are away.

Pat has wonderful taste, and in my humble opinion our house and its contents are mighty pretty. In addition to our Steinway Baby Grand piano, Sally also gave Mother's beautiful old massive sideboard to us. Therein lies a story. Cousin Lydabeth Tucker Nordman was to get Grandmother Wade's dining room furniture when she married. In the meantime Auntie Moselle had let Mother and Dad use it. Lydie married and got the furniture, Mother soon found another table that suited her, but for the life of her she could not find a sideboard that she liked. Somehow they heard about a severely damaged sideboard that some antique dealer in Middle Tennessee owned. We all drove out into the country somewhere over there and found this beat up sideboard in which Mother was not at all interested. Dad, who was fed up with all their fruitless sideboard-hunting trips, said, "Patti, I'm going to buy it." Sure enough he paid the man $100 for it and bargained with him to rebuild and refinish it. The result was astonishing. The back was beautifully reeded, the cherrywood was lovely, and the mahogany was extraordinary. The sideboard was one of Mother's and Dad's most cherished possessions. It is now one of our most cherished possessions.

After it had been in our home for several years, Sally needed Mother's dining room table. She also took a small table which had come from Grandmother Walker who had told me when I was a child that it had been in her family for over 100 years. We liked both tables very much and decided to try to get duplicates made before the moving people picked them up to take them to Sally. Pat arranged for Mr. Red Bond of Dyersburg, a noted furniture maker, to come over and measure and photograph the tables and then to duplicate them. He did a wonderful job, and we cherish our two beautiful replicas.

Our house is full of paintings. In Chapter 33 the fact is mentioned that we have seventeen paintings and drawings by my cousin, Estelle (Fire) Norvell Cruxent and her husband, Jorge, and in Chapter 17 I related the story of the two large Cruxent paintings on fabric which Pat quilted and which now hang in our big room.

We have several other paintings possibly worthy of note. One spring holiday we took the children to Sarasota where we met Bob and Jenny Kirkland and two of their children, Macy and Christopher, who have always been good friends of our children. While there we visited a good art gallery on St. Armond's Key. We particularly liked some paintings by a California artist named Lindbergh. I made an offer on two of them, but the gallery owner would not consider taking the much reduced price that was offered. After a few weeks, the owner called me and told me that he and Mr. Lindbergh had had a falling out and that he would let me have the two paintings at my price. This Mr. Lindbergh has become very well known in California.

Once we were in San Francisco and called the Chamber of Commerce and asked them for the name of a reputable art gallery which handled paintings at modest prices. They told us about The Poor Man's Art Gallery; certainly sounded good to me so off we went. We liked a small painting by a man who will remain nameless. The gallery owner told us that the artist was an inmate at San Quentin who consigned paintings to him and that the owner had not heard from the artist in a good while. This was the last of the artist's paintings that the gallery owner had, and he sold it to us at a reduced price. Imagine our surprise when years later we saw an article in *American Artist* about this painter who had hit the big time in California art. A few years later we were at a fine gallery on Rodeo Drive in Beverly Hills and asked an employee of the gallery if he knew of this man. He said that he certainly did know him and that he was a very popular California artist. We've been lucky a couple of times.

Another time a bunch of us Union City folks went up to St. Louis for some Cardinal games. Rather than go to a hot Sunday double header, all the girls decided to go to a monastery an hour or so out of St. Louis in hopes that they could buy some art from a monk named Brother Matthew who was a very well known artist throughout the Midwest. Pat found one she liked very much. It was a painting on wood of the folk singer of long ago, Rosie O'Day. She was able to buy it — for a ridiculously modest amount. It is one of our most valued possessions. Our friend, Mark Shatz, brought a salesman from out of town to our house just to see it one time.

For several years Dyersburg State Community College had a young art teacher named John Wilkinson. John was also an excellent watercolorist. We bought a painting from him entitled "The Blind Man." It is, without question, a marvelous watercolor. A year or two after we bought it he asked if we would loan it to him so that he could show it at the 1977 Southeastern Watercolor Society Show which was to be held that year in Nashville. We agreed and it won the Memphis Watercolor Society Award. We almost bought another one from John which he later exhibited in the American Watercolor Society Show in New York. That painting finished very high in the national show. Too bad we didn't have the money to buy that one, too.

There was an oil painting by the internationally known Memphis painter, Paul Penzner, in the Laurelwood Gallery in Memphis which I badly wanted. The lady at Laurelwood had deacidified and refurbished a large number of old Wade and Walker family photographs for me, and I was in this good gallery many times. Finally I bit the bullet and bought his oil painting of the Apostle Philip. Mr. Penzner is a PiKA. We have enjoyed this painting enormously.

Another good painting we own is Bruce Graham's "Waitin' for a Ride." Pat and I were on a western trip with Tauck Tours in 1995 when we spent a night at the U Cross Dude Ranch on the South Dakota-Wyoming border. Bruce managed the ranch. We were smitten with his paintings and should have bought two others he had on display in the ranch shop. A couple of years later Bruce won "The People's Choice Award" at the annual Buffalo Bill Art Show & Sale at the fabulous Buffalo Bill Historical Center western art museum in Cody, Wyoming. His paintings are now handled by major western art galleries.

On this same Tauck trip we bought a limited edition Austin Barton sculpture, "Attitude Adjustment," a cowboy riding a bucking bronco, from The Legacy Galleries. We also bought two limited edition sculptures by Anita Pauwel, "Taking the High Ground," two rams butting heads, and "Shadow Dancing," a rearing horse, at the Buffalo Trail Gallery. Both galleries were on the square in Jackson Hole, Wyoming.

A sleeper oil painting we have is one I bought for Pat at a New Orleans gallery. "Rue le Pic Window" by Yavai is hung over a lamp and the light shining from underneath the painting makes the painting almost literally come to life.

In our sun porch we have a collection of Haitian paintings. Pat and I bought some in and around Port au Prince on our first Caribbean cruise with the David Critchlows and Milton Hamiltons. We liked these paintings so much that we asked Sally to buy some more for us on a cruise that she and her family took shortly afterwards. Sally also bought some really good ones for us. Each of our three children took Caribbean cruises which we gave them for high school graduation, and each of them bought us a Haitian painting to add to our collection. We treasure them all.

Russian art fascinated me during my 1991 trip to Russia. While there I bought several Russian lacquer boxes, one of which is extraordinary. A couple of years ago I purchased as a Christmas gift for Pat a wonderful third quarter 19th Century Russian icon from Tillman's Antiques, a very good store in Hot Springs.

From Frances Klein Antique and Estate Jewelry on Rodeo Drive in Beverly Hills I bought a Faberge bell push, workmaster Wigstrom, for Pat. Later at A La Vieille Russie in New York I bought a Faberge match box for Pat. She keeps both of them in our bank lockbox!

On my 1999 trip to China I bought a life size terracotta army soldier, a General, at a great shop of local artisans in Xian. Even though I felt that the chances of it arriving in perfect condition were slim, it turned out to be carefully packed, and not a blemish was to be found when it was uncrated. It stands majestically in a corner of our gallery. We love having it.

One time when Pat and I were in New York we went by Christie's new (at the time) location in Rockefeller Center and looked at items that they were going to be selling in an auction to be held in a few days. We bought their catalog, picked out some things that we very much liked, and made arrangements to bid by telephone. I bid on several items but only bought one. It was described in their catalog as follows: An Italian parcel-gilt walnut figure of Saint Justina of Padua, possibly Siena, late 15th Century. We have very much enjoyed this wooden sculpture.

Our house is full of Pat's creations. She marbleized the false cast iron fireplace in our sun porch which came from her Great Grandfather's house in Dyersburg. She also used some etched glass panes from his old house in the sun porch. Pat bought an old table at an auction at Henry, Tennessee, refinished the legs and base and marbleized the top. It is beautiful. She did various other faux finishes on furniture, some of which was old and some of which she built. I'm especially proud of some miniature totem poles that she carved from tree limbs. Her stacks of books tables are marvelous as are her decorated trunks, some old and some which she built. Most of her paintings hang in our children's homes, but some of them hang at 2022 Stonewall. Her mola panels are among our neatest hangings.

Pat has made 2022 Stonewall a great home in which to live. I have a wonderful and talented wife.

Chapter Twenty

Travels

Pat and I have been very fortunate to see a good bit of the world. Through the years we have been to New York a good many times, Florence and Rome three or four times, London several times, Paris two or three times, and Los Angeles several times. I believe these would be our favorite major cities though there were many smaller ones that we also immensely enjoyed. My personal favorites of these cities, in descending order, would probably be New York, London, Florence and Rome, Los Angeles, and Paris. Pat's might be different.

In this chapter I will describe some of our trips that we considered to be particularly interesting.

Peter Pelham, William Penn, and I went to a Kentucky Derby one time between graduation from college and marriage. We spent a night in Bowling Green on the way up. The next morning we saw the first astronaut, John Glenn, on America's first manned flight into space. He did not orbit the earth; he was shot up into space and then after a flight of a few hundreds (or thousands) of miles, the spacecraft and Glenn were brought back down safely into the sea. In Louisville my good friend, Chips Johnston, arranged to have me invited to some really fancy private Derby parties in people's homes. Somehow Pelham had gotten me a blind date with a girl whose father was Kentucky Commissioner of Transportation. We had excellent box seats for the races. Around noon a couple of Kentucky Highway Patrolmen obviously were heading to our box with sacks of some sort. Having come from very "dry" circumstances, Pelham, Penn, and I got busy "hiding" our mint julips from the officers who were only bringing us box lunches of fried chicken. We felt kind of silly about hiding our drinks. After the Derby my date and I went to the Derby penthouse party for dignitaries.

What fun it was to meet and shake hands with Don Ameche and Bill Dana, "Jose Jimenez" of Steve Allen's *Tonight Show* fame. I talked with Bill Dana a long time, and the two of us really hit it off. He told me where he was staying, and I called him later that night from one of those fancy parties mentioned above and asked him to join us, which he did not do. It was a wonderfully fun weekend.

My second and last Derby was with Pat, George and Edith Botts, Jack and Peggy Drerup, Robert and Jenny Kirkland, and Barry and Lois White. We sat in Fulton's Fred Homra's box and had dinner with the Homras and some of their friends at a private club that evening. It was a fun weekend.

Possibly my favorite of all of Pat's and my trips was a UT trip in 1979 to Egypt which started in Cairo where we stayed in the Nile Hilton, directly across the street from the magnificent Cairo Museum which we enjoyed immensely. The Nile Hilton was a great hotel, and we could see the Pyramids of Giza from our room. While we were there two or three very elaborate weddings took place. The brides and grooms were from other middle eastern countries where such affairs would not have been allowed. Somehow Pat got invited to some of the festivities of one of the weddings.

Charlton Heston was a guest of the hotel. We watched him play tennis and then we had a drink in the hotel bar at a table next to his. (Remember, on our honeymoon we had been in the Royal Hawaiian Hotel when he and his family were also there.) One day we went to the Giza Pyramids, the Sphinx, and on to Memphis.

We had lunch that day at the famous Giza Mena House. That night we went to the magnificent Light and Sound Show at the Pyramids and Sphinx. Then we flew to Aswan. When we got off the plane and onto the tarmac it was as if we had walked into an oven. The heat was stiffling to me, but Pat loved it. The hotter the better for her. Not for me! We spent a little time in the Aswan hotel made famous by Agatha Christie's *Death on the Nile*. (Its tiny bar contained a bottle of Black Label Jack Daniels Tennessee Sippin' Whiskey. Don't believe we've ever been anywhere that didn't have Jack Daniels.) I then flew down to the almost unbelievable Abu Simbel monument. Pat elected not to go. We then boarded our riverboat which took us to Kom Ombo, Idfu, Isna, and finally to Luxor. This may have been the worst boat we ever sailed on. The rooms were tiny and uncomfortable, and the food was barely edible. But what a wonderful time we had. UT and Washington University (St. Louis) alumni filled the boat. Those Yankees were delightful. One of them played the piano in the lounge, and we sang songs every night during "tini time." The last night aboard they had a big spread of "funny food" and concocted drinks of dubious origin. An East Tennessee alumnus (whose name is best left unmentioned) must have eaten and drunk too much. He and his wife repaired to their cabin. He went to the bathroom and didn't come out for a good while. His wife checked on him to find that he was sitting on the toilet and had passed out and fallen forward. His head was resting on the opposite wall of the impossibly tiny bathroom. The bathrooms were the kind where the shower sprayed all over it. The Luxor Temple and especially the 100 acre Temple of Karnak were magnificent. Karnak may have been the most amazing man-made thing we've ever seen. We went to the extraordinarily beautiful Light and Sound Show at Karnak one evening. Pat and I were also absolutely in awe of the Valley of the Kings, where we visited King Tut's Tomb, and the Valley of the Queens. We had lunch one day in a Luxor hotel at a table next to (yep, you guessed it) Charlton Heston. Pat and Charlton, obviously recognizing one another, nodded. We were sorry to leave our old friends and new friends, both UT and Washington U., when we flew back to America. John Sheridan was our outstanding UT staff person.

In 1980 Pat and Martha (Lawrence) Rippy took our Patti and Will, and Martha's Bill and Peter Lawrence to St. Thomas for a month. Martha had been making tennis and golf skirts, and Pat had been painting them appropriately for some time. They had been very successful at this endeavor and, having noted that St. Thomas was a great place for tourist shopping, they felt that their most attractive skirts would sell like hotcakes in this idyllic place. Somehow Martha slipped her sewing machine onto the plane, and the six of them departed for what they thought would be a profitable and fun vacation. They rented a three bedroom condo in The Anchorage, a very nice and well located facility out in Red Hook. The first day down there Pat went into town and began what came to be a two day quest to obtain an "itinerant vendor's license." The red tape and bureaucracy were horrendous, but she finally prevailed. She later thought that things would have gone much more smoothly if she had greased some palms. They printed up some signs, "Skirts for Sail," and set up shop downtown on a vacant lot near where the cruise ship passengers disembarked. They noticed that the locals seemed very unhappy to see these strangers competing with them for "sails," and business was very slow. Pat called me that night and filled me in on how things were going. My immediate advice was to pack up the sewing machine, fold up the skirts, put away the paints, and enjoy the rest of their time down there. Which they did. Lolly had not wanted to leave the good times of her teenage crowd's summer for a full four weeks, but she agreed to go down with me for the final two weeks of our family's time down there. Lolly moved in with the Wades and Lawrences and I checked into the neat Lime Tree Hotel. We all had a marvelous time during what turned out to be a delightful vacation.

In 1981 Pat and I took Will and Patti to Bermuda. Lolly was at UT at the time and unable to go with us. We stayed at the impressive Southampton Princess. A few years ago Pat and I went back to Bermuda for a Tennessee Bankers Association convention. We went with the Critchlows, George and Edith Botts, and Jack and Peggy Drerup. One day Mary and I played golf at our hotel's golf course. Dan and Jean Weber were there, but they were staying at the convention headquarters which was the beautiful Princess Hotel downtown. We all were taken by Gatlinburg banker friends of Dan's to dinner at a marvelous restaurant there. It was a festive evening and one of the highlights of the trip.

Maybe our second favorite trip was a 1982 UT picture-taking trip to Kenya with the Critchlows. At a first-night cocktail party by the pool of our Nairobe Intercontinental Hotel we met a delightful older couple from Knoxville, Stewart and Hope McCroskey. The six of us hit it off real well and arranged to be in the same van for the duration of the trip. Stewart had been a Pike at Tennessee, president of the Knoxville Rotary Club, and owner of a printing company, and this was their third trip to Africa. We soon discovered that he loved Thompson Gazelles (Tommies) and despised Gnus (Wildebeests). (Gnus really aren't very pretty to look at.) Abercrombie and Kent was the tour provider, and the excellent driver of our van was named Charles. At Mount Kenya Safari Club (William Holden's famous lodge) we played golf, had an enormous cedar fire in our lodge fireplace, had a bathtub you walked down into, and looked out our front windows at the snow topped Mount Kenya. After leaving Mount Kenya we drove to Aberdare Country Club, the site of the last Mau Mau uprising in 1962, for lunch. Then it was on to The Ark that evening. The Ark is a hotel in the shape of Noah's Ark with very small rooms and communal baths. It sits beside a watering hole and salt lick frequented by many kinds of animals. If you like, they will buzz you on the buzzers in the rooms during the night to see animals. One buzz for elephants, two for rhinos, etc. Though the accommodations were spartan, the experience was fascinating. From there we went to Keekorok Lodge where we woke in the middle of the night and looked out at literally dozens of zebras grazing on the front lawn. At Kichwa Timbo tented camp at the base of the western escarpment of the Great Rift Valley, we saw hundreds of animals of all kinds in their daily afternoon procession heading back to their watering holes. We had dinner one night by an enormous campfire. Porters with flashlights took us back to our tents after dark, as wild animals were very abundant in that area. Continuously burning fires heated the water for our bathrooms, and, unfortunately, smoke filled our tent both nights we were there. My allergies and terrible beds that sagged very low prevented me from any appreciable sleep for our two nights there. We then returned to Nairobi for a night where we celebrated Mary's birthday at Bobby's Bistro, a most unusual restaurant. Then we headed to Amboseli National Park and Serena Lodge where the back picture window of our room looked out at Mount Kilimanjaro, the highest mountain in Africa. In Amboseli we saw an injured antelope of some kind with its mate, we presumed, running alongside it, one of the injured animal's legs flopping straight out to the side, obviously completely disjointed from its body. The two animals were running back and forth beside a line of trees, up and down, up and down, frantically. It was one of the most poignant things we had ever seen. Our driver, Charles, said that the antelope wouldn't be alive much longer. Pat and I often talk about this heart-rending experience. Serena Lodge was a most impressive structure designed to resemble a Masai village. We saw large numbers of Masai people in the Masai Mara, Kenya's great wildlife plain. From Amboseli we went by Mzima Springs where we saw many hippos. We had lunch that day at Kalaguni Lodge, and then it was on to Taita Hills in Tsavo West National Park. Taita Hills was a beautiful hotel in the middle of nowhere. Pat enjoyed riding a camel during our time there. Then we drove to Salt Lick, a fascinating hotel beside another salt lick. Our rooms were thatched roof huts sitting high up on poles, high enough that even elephants could walk underneath us. A great fire was burning many miles away. The people at the hotel said that it was a poacher's fire that had been burning for several days. We saw large numbers of animals there. In addition to the animals already mentioned at one place or another, we saw giraffes, gazelles, cape buffalo, monkeys, baboons, lions, impalas, topi, cheetahs, dik-diks, and a rare gazelle, the name of which escapes me.

From Salt Lick we drove to Mombasa on the Indian Ocean. After a pleasant day at the beautiful Nyali Beach Hotel we caught a late night flight to London. In London we stayed at the excellent Carlton Tower Hotel. Then it was time to head home. This trip was a wonderful one made even better by the fact that our outstanding tour leader was Ted Lutz from Amsterdam who had been our guide on a previous UT trip, a Caribbean cruise. The Critchlows and we saw the McCroskeys several times later. Stewart died a few years ago. John Sheridan and John Chrisp were our UT staffers. We called them John the Large (Sheridan) and John the Small (Chrisp), though John Chrisp was also a pretty fair sized man.

Many of my photos were ridiculous, so poor in fact that Pat made a separate album of them. On our drive up to Mt. Kenya Safari Club we crossed the Equator. Somehow I took two identical pictures of the back of Mary's head as she sat in the seat in front of me. One Pat entitled, "Mary, crossing the equator — northbound." The other she entitled, "Mary, crossing the equator — southbound." Other photos chronicled a "green glob" that followed us around London. Pat's album is priceless.

For a few years Union City had a scuba diving club which involved 100 or so families at one time or another. Pat and I were never divers, but Will enjoyed it thoroughly and several of his friends were also divers. Bill Simrell was the "diving" force behind all this. In 1986 Pat and I took Will and Patti on the club's annual trip, this time to Cozumel where we stayed at Le Ceiba Beach Hotel. The Simrells, the Critchlows, the Rob Joyners, and many other friends of ours went. We had a very nice and relaxing time.

In the summer of 1986, Patti and Will joined Pat and me on the Southern Cotton Ginners Association tour of the San Joaquin Valley of California. We joined a group of other Mid-South ginners and their wives and children in San Francisco for a day or two. Then we boarded a bus for the Monterey Peninsula and Carmel, after which we headed for the valley, enjoying stops in the Redwood Forest, at several farms and gins, and at Bakersfield and Fresno, winding up in Los Angeles. We checked into our Beverly Wilshire Hotel on Wilshire Boulevard at the foot of Rodeo Drive. Our hotel was marvelous, and we had a great time in Los Angeles as well as on the tour. We saw *Cats* at the Shubert Theater in Century City and hired a limousine one day to show us the sights and then to take us to the Beverly Hills Hotel, one of Pat's and my favorite hotels. Believe it or not, our limo broke down, and we walked a few blocks to the hotel. The children got a kick out of seeing it, and this little misadventure did not detract at all from what was a fine trip.

Union City also had a large number of skiers. One spring break Pat, Will and I accompanied Bob and Jenny Kirkland and two of their children, Macy and Christopher, to Vail in the Colorado Rockies for a week's skiing vacation. Bob's first cousin and partner, Carl Kirkland, and his wife, Alice, and their children, Miles and Brooks, were also there. One night we all met David and Tommie Faye James and their children, Lee Ann and young David, for dinner. Though Pat and I passed on the skiing, a fine time was had by all.

In the 80s the Critchlows, the Drerups, and we booked an American Express tour to Spain, Portugal, and Morocco. We flew to Madrid, where we had dinner at the world famous Casa de Botin. While in Madrid we made a trip out to Escurial Monastery and took in the world famous Prado Museum. Then we boarded our bus and headed for the amazing city of Toledo. Continuing across La Mancha we stopped in Granada where we saw "The Beautiful Alhambra." The Alhambra is never called anything but The Beautiful Alhambra. Then we crossed into Portugal where we spent two nights in Lisbon. Then it was back to Torremolinos on the Costa del Sol and then to a ferry in Algeciras that would take us to Morocco. The ferry trip took us across what is almost the mouth of the Mediterranean and within sight of the Rock of Gibraltar. Our first night in Morocco was spent in Tangier. Then we went to Rabat, the capital city. We visited King Hussein's palace where we saw the Secretary-General to the United Nations, Kurt Waldheim, walking by himself up to the palace. We then headed across country toward Marrakech. Fez, with its enormous and forbidding medina, was a fascinating old city. While we were in the medina a funeral procession came rushing by. The body, shrouded in white linens with a red spot placed over the deceased's face, was held high above the crowd of 100 or so men who were rapidly moving the corpse around to all the places in the medina that their deceased friend had frequented. We quickly moved to the side, or this entourage would have run over us. We were cautioned not to take photographs. One inconsiderate tourist did take a picture, and we thought the funerary procession might attack him. If looks could've killed, he would have been one dead ugly American. Meknes was another interesting city, and then Marrakech, near the High Atlas Mountains, was our favorite city of the whole trip. We arrived in Marrakech late one afternoon and went directly to a vantage point overlooking the famous market square, Djemaa el Fna, to watch the activities as the day drew to a close. The most memorable thing we saw was a snake charmer entertaining a customer who, after the performance was over, walked away without tipping the man who immediately ran after the slacker, brandishing his cobra. The tourist almost tore out his pockets, grabbing for money to appease the snake charmer. All ended well. The Critchlows and we went into the medina to look for rugs. Our Marrakech guide took us to a good rug shop. After much tea and a little beer we decided against a purchase and went back to our hotel. The rug merchants followed us back and persuaded us to allow them to again show us two rugs we liked. They spread them out on the Critchlow's tiny balcony and they and we each bought one. Ours has been in our entrance hall ever since. Then it was on to Casablanca and then home to the states after another fine reasonably priced trip led by a marvelous guide, Humberto Borges of Lisbon, with whom we stayed in touch for several years.

In 1987 Pat and I took Will on a tour of New England in late August, early September. Will had decided to go to McCallie, Union City High School had started, and this was a good way to bridge the gap between Union City's school schedule and McCallie's later starting schedule. We flew to Boston where we spent a night or two and then boarded a bus for Intrav's trip up into Vermont and New Hampshire. On the way we saw Sturbridge Village in Sturbridge, Massachusetts. We spent a night at the famous Woodstock Inn in Woodstock, Vermont where Will and I played a round of golf. We saw the beautiful campus of Dartmouth College and had lunch one day at the Deerfield Inn in Deerfield, New Hampshire. While there we took a look at Deerfield Academy, a fine private school. Then we boarded our Clipper Cruise Line ship and headed for Cape Cod with stops at Martha's Vineyard, Nantucket, Providence, Rhode Island, and Newport where we visited some of Newport's famous old mansions, the most impressive of which was Cornelius Vanderbilt's massive and ornate "The Breakers." On the ship we met a man from Texas who looked us up after having noticed on the passenger list that we were from Union City. He had trained to be a pilot at Embry-Riddle Field, the air base at Union City, during World War II. While in Union City his "adopted parents" were Union City's popular Cecil and Bess Moss. That fall he sent Pat a marvelous bunch of turkey feathers for her art work. She had told him that she would love to have some but didn't know how to get them. He said he hunted turkey often and would send her some. And he did. Another interesting thing that happened was that a lady with the alumni/development office of the University of Texas (they had a group, including our new-found friend, of Texas alumni aboard) looked exactly like sister Sally. The similarity was uncanny. The Texas lady was shorter than Sally, but their faces looked like twins. Unbeknownst to this lady, I took a couple of photos of her and sent them to Sally with a letter. Sally wrote back asking me where I had taken those pictures of her.

It was a very nice trip, and Will entered McCallie energized and ready to go.

In 1988 while Lolly was living and working in Little Rock, Pat and I took her on a one week trip to Ocho Rios, Jamaica. We stayed in the very nice Plantation Inn. Our hotel had a reciprocal agreement with some other good hotels, and we had a fancy lunch one day at the well-known Jamaica Inn and dinner one night at the Sans Sonci Hotel.

In 1988 I took Will with the Union City dive club to the Cayman Islands. We stayed on Grand Cayman at the Hyatt Regency, a very nice hotel. Pat did not go on that trip. Will's roommate from McCallie, John Brackin of Greenwood, Mississippi, went along with us. Also Will's close friends, Clint Joiner and Chris Kirkland, were with the group. The Hyatt became famous a few years later, as many scenes of the movie version of John Grisham's book, *The Firm*, with Tom Cruise and Gene Hackman, were filmed there. This was another pleasant trip. (As a side note, Julie Critchlow Gresham gave me an autographed copy of *The Firm*. I wrote John Grisham telling him how much I enjoyed his book and remarking on the fact that I was very familiar with the locales in the book, Memphis, the Gulf Coast, the Caymans, and the Cayman Hyatt Regency. I promptly received a cordial handwritten letter from Mr. Grisham.)

The Union City Dive Club enjoyed tremendous success for a few years, and then it unfortunately faded into oblivion.

One of our most fun trips was with the Critchlows and Frank and Betty Caldwell (Frank is Mary's brother) to London to see part of the 1988 Wimbledon tennis tournament. In London we stayed in the Londoner Hotel and took the train out to Wimbledon for several days of exciting tennis action including matches on Centre Court and on the Number One Court. While we were there the commodity markets moved 'way up, and I spent part of my vacation on a Wimbledon phone with First State Bank president, Dan Weber, arranging for loans from several banks to make margin calls. Everything worked out, thanks to a mighty fine banker. After Wimbledon we rented a car and made a three day tour of southern England. We stayed in a neat little hotel in Brighton which had a marvelous restaurant. In one of the towns we visited somehow we ended up driving our rented car on city streets in a bicycle race. Frank eluded the police. Among other places we enjoyed were Salisbury, Portsmouth, Southampton, and the lovely city and awesome Cathedral of Canterbury. Stonehenge was also an amazing sight. The last afternoon we pulled up to our hotel in some quaint village. There were fire trucks everywhere, and water was running out of the lobby as Critchlow and I stepped over the fire hoses and waded up to the front desk to register. We told the clerk that we had reservations, and she said, "But gentlemen, the hotel is on fire." We found another hotel and flew home the next day from Gatwick after a memorable holiday.

By far the worst trip we ever took was a rather long February trip to Tahiti. David and Mary Critchlow and Pat and I were under the impression that Tahiti was an absolute paradise. Barry and Lois White went one year, and the next year Robert and Jenny Kirkland went. Both men told us that Tahiti was indeed a paradise. When Jenny told Pat to take a lot of books we should have had second thoughts, but we like to read so off we went. We arrived in Tahiti and Papeete about 2 AM in a torrential downpour. On the way to our hotel I commented on the rain to the cab driver who said, "This is our rainy season." One could almost have heard four hearts sinking.

After two nights in a nice hotel on the island of Tahiti we took a ferry to Huahine. Pat's and my room on the ferry was so tiny that we had to walk on our luggage to get into our bunk beds. My top bunk was no more than 18 inches from the ceiling. We landed at the Huahine dock where we were supposed to have been met. But we weren't, so we traipsed through a grove of trees to our hotel, dragging all our luggage. It wasn't easy, but it wasn't far, thank goodness. Our hotel, which had grass huts for rooms, was all right, and we did have a very large walk-down-into bathroom and shower. It rained almost all the time we were there —four days I believe — and we started what turned out to be a reading marathon.

The ferry ride was so bad that we were able to convince Pat, who does not like to fly especially on small planes, to fly to our next destination which was Raiatea. This was the Whites' favorite island. It wasn't ours. We had rooms that were grass huts out over the ocean. As one can imagine they were very humid. At night the rodents played

221

in the grass around, over, and underneath us. It was like Raiatea's own percussion band. At one point David went after a sound on a high ledge and almost threw his hand into a giant rattrap. He could have lost fingers. It rained the whole five days that we were there. One day Mary and Pat sat at the bar and played charades. One of the charades that was quickly solved was "Raiatea sucks!" That same day they noticed a lizard playing around the bar. The bar had a machine with mai tai mix. After each mai tai the bartender mixed, the lizard would slip over and suck up the drop of the mix that was left hanging underneath the spigot and then he would scurry back out of sight. That must have been one happy lizard. The girls were not drinking those mai tais, but surely that could have been left unsaid.

From there we flew to Bora Bora which is a beautiful island. We checked into Hotel Bora Bora. It was also comprised of glorified grass huts. We got there after dark, and the only rooms they had for us were two suites that were very, very nice. We thought we had died and gone to heaven, until the next day when they told us that our previously reserved rooms were now available. The main hotel was very pretty, and the food was the best we had experienced, so despite the continuing rain it was more pleasant than the last two hotels had been. The famous Bloody Mary's was within walking distance of the hotel. It was a large restaurant/bar that had grass walls and ceiling and the sand of the beach was its floor. We were having their signature drinks when we began noticing mice and rats running all over the ceiling beams. In fact we noticed mice on the grill eating the dried grease. It must have been at that moment that Pat stopped eating and drinking anything but bottled water which was not always available.

From Bora Bora we flew to Moorea, our last island. It is also a beautiful island with spectacular mountains. Once again we were in grass huts. This time we had to stay off the beaches because they were invaded by millions of sand fleas. However, it didn't really matter because the rains continued to fall. For a week during our stay we were just outside the perimeter of a typhoon, and the hotels had their windows taped for high winds and downpours. We stayed on Moorea for five days. Two days before we were to leave for home we were having dinner in a restaurant when Pat suddenly, quietly slipped underneath the table. She was out cold. We were scared to death. The management told us where the island's only doctor lived. We carried Pat out to our rented jeep. A nice American at the next table told us that he would lead us to the doctor's home. We took off in a Tahitian downpour behind this good Samaritan, Pat's head in Mary's lap in the back seat. I asked Mary time and time again, "Is she still breathing?" We arrived at the doctor's home. Pat revived after a few minutes, and after a few minutes more we headed back to our flea stricken quarters. The next morning we went to the doctor's office, and he gave Pat some more medicine. As it turned out, this French doctor was the only doctor on Moorea, and he left later that day for six weeks in France. We shuddered to think what might have happened had he already been gone. It was after this episode that we realized that Pat had pretty much been faking eating and drinking very little ever since Bloody Mary's. What a nightmare!

It rained 19 of the 21 days we were in paradise, most days buckets of rain. Pat read twenty books on our trip. She is a very fast reader, but even I read ten books. Including James Michener's *Texas*, a 1,200 pager! The Islands of Tahiti are lovely to look at, but I would advise anyone contemplating going to avoid its rainy season like the plague.

In 1990 Pat and I took Will, Lolly, my first cousin, Lydabeth Tucker Nordman, and Patti's mother-in-law, Jennifer Barnes, on a two weeks trip to England, Scotland, and Wales. Patti had to cancel shortly before departure due to having gotten an exciting job with a well-known producer of country music, Steve Buckingham, and at the last minute we were able to substitute Jennifer for Patti. It was a budget American Airlines trip, but an excellent tour guide made it a fine trip. We started in London where we saw two plays, one of which, *Buddy*, a musical show of Buddy Holly's life, was pure rollicking fun. The other show, *Run for Your Wife*, was also good. We loved England and the delightful towns of Oxford, Chester, York, Avon, Bath, and Durham. We spent only part of one day in Wales which is a colorful country. In Scotland we visited Glasgow, Inverness, and St. Andrews where it was a thrill to see the Olde Course. We greatly enjoyed Loch Lomond and Loch Ness where we searched for but did not find the Loch Ness Monster. We wound up Scotland with two nights in Edinburgh, a city we all enjoyed immensely. One day our group toured the Edraduer (scotch) Distillary which was located in an area of Scotland where there are several single malt scotch distillaries. It was obvious that the distillary had not been operated in some time. After the tour we all gathered in a large room and were given drams of "Edraduer" Scotch to drink. Since nobody else in our own group was drinking, it became my duty to drink all six of our drams. Good blended scotches, rather than single malts, are my favorite, but the scotch we were served was most pleasant. I sauntered over to the tour leader and indicated to him that this blended scotch lover had truly enjoyed his single malt. He whispered, "Keep it to yourself, but you were given some of Bells finest blended scotch." My taste buds were certainly vindicated! We returned to London for a night and then home.

In July, 1991, I took a Travcoa trip to Russia without Pat. She did not want to go to Russia!

There were only eight other tourists on the trip, a delightful couple from New York, David and Esther Dicker; a man from Florida; a lady from Manhattan; two ladies from Chicago; and two ladies from California, all very nice people. We were ably led by Clayton (Clay) Nicol, our tour leader from Manhattan. (Pat and I met David and Esther for dinner one night a year or so later in New York. Clay was out of town.)

We flew from New York to Vienna and on to Leningrad (now St. Petersburg, of course) where we checked into our good hotel, Hotel Astoria. During the World War II seige of Leningrad, Hitler, anticipating the taking of the city, planned a victory celebration at the Astoria. These aborted plans and the guest list were found in Berlin after the war. The view from my room was of a beautiful park and the extraordinarily beautiful St. Isaac's Cathedral. Leningrad is on the Baltic Sea and is so far north that they have very little darkness in the summer. Of course, in the winter they have very few hours of light. When we were there, rationing had been in effect for a few months. There were long lines for everything from vodka to meat to bread to vegetables to gasoline. They swapped or sold ration coupons that they did not want or need. The black market was winked at, and people sold everything one can think of on the streets at higher-than-government prices. There were three exchange rates, and tourists pay much more than do the citizens. The Summer Palace, Hermitage Palace and Museum, the Armory, and Palace Square are all truly world class. In the Catherine The Great Park, I bought a very good still life from a "struggling artist." It is a pleasant addition to our dining room. St. Petersburg is undeniably one of the world's most beautiful and historic cities. From Leningrad we flew Aeroflot to Moscow. The flight was smooth on takeoff and landing, but the plane vibrated and rattled greatly on the runways. The plane was dirty and almost ragged inside, and when pressure was applied to the back of my seat it fell into the lap of the Russian man sitting behind me. I sat straight up, not touching the back of my seat, for the entire flight. Actually the engines sounded very smooth.

In Moscow we boarded a bus to tour The Golden Ring, seeing the sights in Vladimir and Suzdal, the ancient religious center of Russia. We spent two days on this excursion and two nights in Suzdal in a charming former convent compound which had been converted to a hotel. Suzdal is known to be THE place to buy authentic Russian lacquer boxes at reasonable prices. I bought several boxes, one of which borders on being museum quality.

From there we drove back to Moscow and checked into the barely adequate Hotel Intourist which was on the main street of Moscow, Gorky Street, and which overlooked Red Square. Red Square is bordered by Gum Department Store, gigantic but threadbare, St. Basil's Cathedral, and the Kremlin with Lenin's Tomb. The Kremlin itself with all its buildings and history was also most impressive. Rossia Hotel, to which I had to go to exchange dollars to rubles, was the largest (though most plain) hotel in the world. While in Moscow we very much enjoyed a Georgian folkloric show at a beautiful concert hall as well as a performance at the marvelous Moscow Circus. Our final dinner at the Commercial Men's Club was festive, and we also had a good meal at the Georgian restaurant, The Aragby. At The Aragby and at our hotel in St. Petersburg I bought a total of seven very good tins of caviar which I later enjoyed immensely. It was illegal to take more than two tins out of the country, but I did not know this until we got to the Moscow airport to come home. Fortunately I was able to get them through. I paid $5 to $10 each for these good sized tins of excellent caviar.

Some observations of Russia and the USSR at the time. There were 14 republics other than Russia in the USSR. Our guides felt that some republics such as Lithuania, Latvia, Estonia and others would eventually be allowed to break apart from the USSR (we all know what has happened since). They said that these republics were poor and had no natural resources and would have a hard time going it alone (they are). They added that Siberia (population 20,000,000) which is a part of Russia had almost all of the USSR's resources. Changes had come fast in the previous two years with Gorbachev's Glasnost (openness) and Perestroika (reorganizing and restructuring). Our guides were frank to say that thousands and thousands of people were tortured and executed in KGB headquarters (across from the Bolshoi Theatre in Moscow) during Stalin's time. Stalin demolished Russia's and Moscow's largest (and third largest in the world) cathedral (Russian Orthodox, as were all the cathedrals we saw) in 1931. It had been the focal point of Moscow. The gigantic block-size basement is now a year around heated swimming pool.

Our tour guide, Nadia, told us that doctors and engineers earned 400 to 500 rubles (officially $14 to $18) per month. Rents had not been raised since 1928. (The government owned all the housing in the cities.) Dachas (pronounced dachurs) are houses in the country which are individually owned. About one-half of Muscovites own dachas.

I had a great deal of trouble with my back during the trip and often had to sit down on a little folding chair I had wisely taken along. In group pictures they always sat me in front of the rest of the group which would stand behind me. One day while walking back from Red Square through the tunnel that connected the Square to Gorky Street I sat down to rest for a minute and to take a picture of two very cute little girls singing for tips with their Dad who played the harmonica when this old Russian lady dressed in peasant-type garb stopped and really blessed me out for some reason. A Russian man beside me was obviously embarrassed and said something to me in Russian while circling his finger at his temple to indicate that she was "touched in the head." I thanked him, stood up, and headed on toward the hotel. A little further down the tunnel this same woman was barking at a poor old beggar woman who appeared to be blind. I felt sorry for the old beggar, but at least I felt a little better about myself. Undoubtedly the kind gentleman had the rude woman properly pegged. As a postscript to this story a short time after getting back home I had back surgery. During my convalescense many hours were spent at the televison set watching the fall of the Soviet Union which began right after our trip. On a TV show I saw the two little girls and their Dad in that same tunnel. They were as charming on national TV as I remembered their having been in the flesh.

Pat's and my Danube River trip had preceded the falling apart of the Eastern Europe Communist bloc by only a few weeks, so we barely missed two enormously important historical events. Sure glad we did!

Our guide in Vladamir-Suzdal was named Svetlana. She was nice and a good guide, but she really got riled when the subject of the movie, Dr. *Zhivago*, came up, saying it was ridiculous and nothing at all like old Russia had been. Needless to say, that subject never again was raised.

Natasha, our Moscow (Mockba as it is written in Russian) guide, was outstanding. Our tour-long guide Nadia, was good and sweet, but Natasha was my favorite of all our guides. I did send peanut butter, chocolates, and dried fruit to Nadia and her family. She wrote a nice "thank you" letter.

Christianity seemed to be coming back rapidly in 1991. We met and talked with several people from America who were there on mission trips of one kind or another. During intermission at the folkloric show in Moscow I met two physicians who were there with a Billy Graham Crusade. They were with Graham's World Medical Mission, an adjunct of his crusades. One of the men was a neurosurgeon. When I told him about my back troubles he told me in no uncertain terms, "You get out of this country before you let anybody cut on you." Two weeks later I went under the knife for very successful surgery performed by Semmes-Murphy's noted surgeon, Dr. Morris Ray.

We were told some interesting facts about Moscow and Russia. Moscow was founded in 1147, had 2 million visitors per day, and had

650,000 university students in Moscow alone. (I wondered if these "facts" were entirely correct.) Most city children attend summer camps. Russian applause is mostly staccato. All icons (we have one in our home) were painted by monks, and they actually are supposed to hang in churches.

Possibly our third favorite trip, an entirely different one, was a Travcoa trip to Italy in 1993. There were only twelve of us plus our tour leader, Richard Prince from Santa Barbara, on the trip. Our favorite people were Jim and Ilene Roper of Los Angeles and George and Barbara Butler of Philadelphia. Jim was a prosperous attorney originally from South Carolina, and George was the recently retired chairman and CEO of one of the largest Philadelphia banks. This was a luxurious trip, and we stayed in fine hotels and ate in great restaurants. We started in Rome where we stayed in the LeGrand Hotel and had dinner in the beautiful Piazza Navona. Then we went to Florence and the Excelsior Hotel. From there we drove (we had a full-sized bus for the few of us) to Siena and stayed at the Park Hotel Siena. The next stop was Capri and the world class Grand Hotel Quisisana. From there we headed to the Amalfi Coast and the Le Sirenuse Hotel in Positano, maybe the most beautiful hotel and town that we have ever seen. We wound up in Venice and stayed in the Danieli where our room overlooked the Grand Canal. Interestingly I had stayed at the Excelsior in Florence and the Danieli in 1956. We spent part of one day in Sorrento where I located Caruso's favorite room in the Grand Hotel Excelsior Vittorio, the room where John Hoff and I spent two nights in 1956. Two of the interesting places we saw were Pompeii and the monastery atop Monte Cassino, the site of a bloody World War II battle. Maybe our favorite small town was San Gimignano where I secretly bought Pat some ceramic platters for Christmas. Usually on our trips I have been able to buy gifts for Pat without her knowledge. At least she has paid lip service to not having known! Richard Prince took us to many wonderful restaurants for lunches and dinners. Pat and I were, without question, in the lap of luxury. We have stayed in touch with some of the people with whom we shared this marvelous trip. (In the summer of 2002 Richard made arrangements for Pat and me, Patti and Rance, and Kim and Will for an excellent trip to Los Angeles, Santa Barbara (Richard's home), and winding up in Palm Springs for the 2002 PiKA convention. It was a fun trip which included two nights in L'Ermitage in Beverly Hills, two nights in Santa Barbara and a trip into that area's wine country of Solvang and Los Olivos, two more nights in Los Angeles, and the great PiKA convention in Palm Springs.)

In 1995 Pat and I took a very good Tauck trip to the West. We flew to Rapid City, South Dakota and spent the night in a fine old downtown hotel and met the other folks. From there we went to Mount Rushmore, a beautiful and impressive monument. Then it was on to the Ucross Guest Ranch on the South Dakota-Wyoming border. We spent one night there and enjoyed a cowboy singer-guitar player who played and sang on the large porch that evening after dinner. We bought an excellent painting from the ranch manager, Bruce Graham, who has since become a very well known western artist.

Then it was back on the bus and on to Cody where we very much enjoyed the Buffalo Bill Historical Center, an outstanding museum of western art and artifacts. While in Cody we had lunch at the old Irma Hotel, once owned by Buffalo Bill and named for his daughter. The Irma's hand carved enormous bar which was given to Buffalo Bill by England's Queen Victoria was truly extraordinary. The gift was valued at $100,000, a princely sum indeed a century ago.

We continued on our bus to Yellowstone Park where we spent the night in the beautiful very large all-wood Lake Yellowstone Hotel. When John Hoff and I worked in Yellowstone Park in 1954 we referred to this location in the park simply as "Lake." Some of our UT and Dyersburg friends worked there and at Fishing Bridge in 1954, two of those friends being Milton Magee, Jr. and David Lanier. Then our bus took us to Old Faithful where we stayed at the magnificent Old Faithful Inn for another night.

The next day we drove down to the Tetons and checked into the famous and lovely Jackson Lake Lodge for two nights. Pat and I spent those two days in Jackson, or Jackson Hole as it's more popularly known. Jackson Hole is a great town. It was fun to go back to the Million Dollar Cowboy Bar and the Silver Dollar Bar in the old Wort Hotel, places Hoff and I frequented in 1954.

From there we drove to Salt Lake City where we toured the Mormon Church's buildings and grounds and drove out to the amazingly huge Kennecott Copper Mine. Over the years this whole mountain has been taken down and is now a giant crater in the ground where $1,500,000 trucks on enormous Goodyear tires haul the ore to the surface. I took a picture of Pat beside a tire that they had on display and sent it to Jimmy Cagle, the PR man at Union City's Goodyear plant. Jimmy put the picture and a story about the tire in their company newspaper. While in Salt Lake City we also drove up to the famous Snowbird Ski Resort. Then it was back to Tennessee after another great trip. Our experiences with Tauck have been outstanding. Their trips are worth the money.

Pat and I have spent five Caribbean vacations with Robert and Jenny Kirkland. In 1994 we went with them to Cap Juluca on Anguilla. Cap Juluca is a world class resort. The facilities are luxurious and the beach is one of the world's greatest. Later we spent time with them during two winters at Coco Point, an exclusive resort on Barbuda. This is the type place that brings people (mostly from up East in the case of Coco Point) back on the same dates year after year. It's almost like a reunion each year. We met many interesting people at Coco Point. We also spent two winter vacations in 2000 and 2001 with the Kirklands on the French island of St. Barths. We stayed in the good Filao Beach Hotel and enjoyed the excellent restaurants and general ambiance of probably the Caribbean's most exclusive island.

In June, 1998, Pat and I went with UT to Provence, staying for seven days in Aix, after spending three days and nights in Vence, just north of Nice, in the marvelous le Chateau du Domaine St. Martin, with Robert and Jenny Kirkland. While in Vence we visited the picturesque hilltop towns of St. Paul, Gordes, and Roussilou. Then we drove through Monte Carlo and on to Aix in time to meet the UT group. We enjoyed Aix immensely. Our hotel, the Grand Hotel Roi Rene, was within a short walk of the Cours Mirabeau, their wonderful tree-lined boulevard of sidewalk cafes and shops. Former UT Pike fraternity brother, Dick Kidwell, and his wife, Barbara, also a good friend from UT, from Murfreesboro were with us. We also enjoyed David and Janis Fite of Jackson, and I took the eight of us, including

Robert and Jenny, to dinner our last night in Aix at the famous café on Cours Mirabeau, Lex Deux Garcons. One day Pat and I walked the considerable distance to the studio of the famous artist, Paul Cezanne. While in Aix we took day trips to Arles, St. Remy (of Vincent Van Gogh fame), Les Baux, Avignon, Cassis, and the Pont du Gard Roman aqueduct. All of the towns and cities were fascinating. Our UT staffer was our good friend Jack Williams, who is also head of UT Development. Jack handled the arrangements admirably, and it was a terrific trip.

By the luck of the draw we were in Aix on the one Sunday each month when they have an artists market on the Cours Mirabeau which is closed to traffic that day. There were many excellent works of art of every imaginable type. We came home with some watercolor note cards, very good original art, and a neat collage. I have often wished we had bought all the note cards those people had. They were very reasonably priced and were all really good. Aix is one of our all-time favorite cities; we want to go back there some day.

The next year, our old and good friends, Marty and Rich Hopkins, were our staffers on another UT trip. We spent seven days and nights in Cortona, a picturesque medieval hillside town with Etruscan roots, in the Tuscany section of Italy. Cortona overlooks a beautiful valley. Our unairconditioned hotel San Luca in Cortona was probably the best one in town, and it did have a beautiful view from all the rooms as well as from the public rooms. However, the rooms were tiny (though we did have a nice little balcony) and the bathrooms were tiny and just plain ridiculous. The top of the toilet would not stay up as it was jammed too far back into a corner. The shower was a folding arrangement, and if you did not have the sides folded out and placed perfectly, you got water all over the bathroom. I never did figure it out, and the whole bathroom was soaked after each of my showers. Our bed almost filled up our room, but we had a lovely view of a great Tuscan valley from our balcony and it cooled off enough at night for us to be able to sleep fairly well.

One day Pat and I walked the loop up and around the mountain above Cortona, up to Frances Mayes' house and on up to a cathedral which housed the relic — her entire body in this case — of St.

Margherita, and then back down to Cortona. Seeing Frances Mayes' house was exciting after having read so much about it in her excellent book, *Under the Tuscan Sun.*

The last night they had a little program where everybody gave their impressions of the excellent trip. My interpretation of taking a shower was one of the hits of the night.

Our day trips to Montepulciano, Perugia, Assisi, Siena, and to one of our very most favorite cities in the world, Florence, were all interesting and fun. Tuscany and its towns are great places to visit.

About half of us spent three extra days in Rome. We again saw St. Peters, to me the world's most magnificent edifice, and the Vatican, the Colosseum, the Roman Forum, the Fountain of Trevi, and the Borghese Gallery. Rome is, again to me, the world's greatest sightseeing city.

Though our fellow passengers were a really good group of people, we especially enjoyed Dr. John and Donna Crenshaw from Pine Bluff, Arkansas; Myers and Ann Nora Parsons from Murfreesboro; Dr. Jimmy and Barbara Trentham of Martin; and Bill and Noel Wade of Pasadena, California. John Crenshaw, Tom's brother, was from Humboldt, and Donna was from South Fulton. We had been with Myers and Ann Nora Parsons on a couple of UT trips some years ago, and I talked with them at a football game in Knoxville and convinced them to go to Italy. Jimmy Trentham is a retired professor from UTM. Bill Wade is the retired chairman and CEO of Atlantic Richfield (ARCO), an oil company which was then in the process of selling out to BP and Amoco for $28.5 billion. We enjoyed all four of these couples very much.

One day John and Donna and Pat and I heard that Placido Domingo was opening that evening at the opera, and we were able to get four of the very last tickets at the world famous Rome Opera House. The opera house was not air conditioned, but we enjoyed the performance immensely. (Will, Pat, and I saw Placido Domingo along with Luciano Pavarotti, and Jose Carrera, The Three Tenors, in concert in Chicago in December of 2000. My friends from my China trip, Philip and Ana Pappas, had us for dinner in their lovely home, and we all went together to the spectacular concert.) Another night the Bill

Wades, the Crenshaws, and we had dinner in the restaurant on top of the Hassler Hotel, directly above the Spanish Steps. Pat and I had done this in 1993 on our Travcoa trip, and the nighttime view of Rome is breathtaking. Another night the six of us had dinner in Piazza Navonna, another repeat from our earlier trip to Rome. Our hotel on the famous Via Veneto, the Ambasciatori, was excellent. This was another extremely good UT trip.

Another neat trip we took to Europe in 1998 was with First State Bank and its tour leaders, Maudie and Scotty McCullar, and lots of local folks including the entire Drerup family and Laura Joyce Barton, Jessie Elder, and Ann Mitchell from Kenton, and Mim Hightower from Atlanta. We took Lydabeth again, and she enjoyed being with her old friend, Laura Joyce, and the other ladies. We flew to Zurich and drove to Lucerne where we stayed in the lovely Grand National Hotel.

Our rooms were luxurious. After two days there and a trip up to the top of Mount Pilatus we drove through the mountains, stopping at Berne and Innsbruck, to Zermatt which sits just below the Matterhorn. It was a sight to behold. Two days there and then we took the train, *The Glacier Express*, to St. Moritz where we spent the night. From there we drove to Salzburg, Austria, a beautiful city which we all enjoyed very much. One lunch there in a famous restaurant was memorable. Their dessert, an Austrian specialty, a three-peaked meringue concoction, was wonderful. I ate all mine and some of the ladies' leftovers. Pure delight! We saw a fun *Sound of Music* show one evening. It was in Salzburg that we received word that our dear friend and many times travel companion, Mary Critchlow, had died. The rest of the trip was much less festive. Next we drove to Munich where we spent part of the day. I went by myself to a famous beer hall which was fun. Munich is the home of our friend, Christiane Monin. We spent the night in a lovely hotel in Garmisch, a well known German ski resort. This reasonably priced trip was well worth the money.

Pat and I took another excellent Tauck trip to New Mexico in 1998. We started out at El Paso's ornate old hotel, the Camino Real Paso del Norte. The first day we went down to Juarez for a few hours and then boarded the bus for Carlsbad Caverns, an amazing sight. (When I was very young Mother and Dad on a long ago western trip left Sally and me with a baby sitter while they went down into the caverns. My recollection is that this was a bad experience for me. We had mashed potatoes and peas for lunch, and the lady made us lie down for a nap which Sally and I did not want to do. We wanted to go see the caverns!) Then we spent some time in the White Sands National Monument. From there we went through Ruidoso on the way to Mescalero where we spent two nights in a nice Indian casino hotel. From there we went to Santa Fe where we spent two nights. Santa Fe is one of Pat's and my favorite cities. We stayed at the very nice Hilton, but next time we would like to stay at the lovely Inn of the Anasazi. From there we went up to Taos, another great place for art. Then we saw Bandelier National Monument, an ancient home of Indian cliff dwellers, and Los Alamos of atomic bomb fame. Our last stop was Albuquerque where we spent our last night. While there we went out to Old Albuquerque where we found far and away the best iron shop we've ever discovered, and we bought several great things such as lamps and sculptures which we enjoy having in our home. As has been the case with each of our Tauck trips, the people were wonderful. Milton and Elenor Hans of New York and Pat and I spent a great deal of time together. A year or so after the trip we had Elenor for dinner in New York. Milton was busy and could not join us. Our trip tour leader, a lady named Lolly, was perfect. She knew New Mexico very well, and she dressed the part of a western lady. New Mexico is a most interesting state, and we enjoyed the trip immensely.

In August, 1999 I went to China without Pat who simply did not want to go to China. It was a Pacific Bestour and was an excellent trip with a terrific tour manager.

The flight arrived in Beijing, after a stopover in Tokyo, on the evening of August 17. Our hotel was the five-star China World Hotel which was a fabulous facility. One night while we were there, there was a very large reception in the hotel for the prime minister of another Asian country (cannot remember which country). Beijing's population is 12 million. They always count the county population in the city's population, and Beijing is a large county. Beijing is the capital and cultural center of China, and there were many beautiful tall buildings and hundreds of buildings in progress. As is the case in all cities in

China, there are enormous contrasts with housing ranging from one room hovels to expensive apartments in high-rises. One sees very few single-family dwellings in Chinese cities.

Couples are limited to one child. If a husband or wife is an only child, that couple will be allowed two children. If a lady is divorced with one child and remarries, she can have one more child. Sometimes a clerk of records can assist people with payment under the table to have more than one child. Sometimes if a first child is a girl, that baby is disposed of by putting her up for adoption (under the table) or otherwise disposing of her. Farmers are allowed two children. The first son always stays on the farm. If farmers and their wives have two girls, they often take the second baby to the nearest city and leave it for someone to find and take to an orphanage. There were several adopted Chinese babies on the plane back to America. Men retire at 55 and women at 50. If they are professionals their retirement ages are 60 and 55. One reason the government encourages early retirement is that there is a great deal of unemployment. What was once a totally planned economy is now a market economy. If people are caught with one kilo of heroin, they are executed. One-half kilo of heroin is punished by three years in prison.

On August 20 we flew to Xian where we stayed at the Shangri-La Golden Flower Hotel. There were no five-star hotels in Xian, and this was one of the two four-star hotels. It was a good hotel, but not nearly as good a hotel as was the China World. Xian's population is 5 million. Although they are building numerous high-rises also, it obviously is not nearly so prosperous a city as is Beijing. Xian was a fairly dingy city. It was near Xian where we saw the terra cotta soldiers. The soldiers are indeed an awesome sight to see. On August 22 we flew to Chongqing and had lunch there and saw some of the city. The population of Chongqing is 8 million. It was called Chungking during World War II and was Chiang Kai-shek's as well as the Allies' headquarters during the War. There is a considerable amount of building there also. It is a big city, though it also is a fairly dingy city.

The temperature in these cities gets up to 110-112 in the summer, and people sleep out on rooftops and do everything they can to neutralize the heat.

We continued on our bus to Dazu, population 120,000. Dazu is famous for the stone carvings nearby, but that is its only claim to fame. It was a dreary city. Our three-star Dazu Hotel was the only decent hotel in town. The stone carvings were amazing, and the trip out through the countryside with all the water buffalo and manual labor farming was most interesting. Our beds at the hotel were very hard, and I tried to sleep, not too successfully, on pillows. Despite the stone carvings, which really were amazing, Dazu as Critchlow would say has been scratched off my list.

On August 23 we took the bus back to Chongqing where we had lunch at a different hotel and toured the city more extensively. The most interesting thing we saw was General Stillwell's Flying Tigers World War II Headquarters and Museum. An island in the river which runs through Chongqing was used as a Flying Tiger airbase during the War. Being an industrial city, Chongqing was heavily bombed by the Japanese in World War II.

That night we boarded our Victoria Cruises boat for an interesting trip down the Yangtze which included a side trip up the Daning River, a beautiful river gorge. The Daning River gorge, a tributary of the Yangtze, was as impressive as the gorges on the Yangtze. We were on the ship for the next three and a half days and four nights. It was fascinating to see all the cities which will be covered by water once the construction of the major dam project is completed. We spent several hours at the site of the dam construction. It is a truly remarkable project, actually larger than I expected.

Midday on August 27 we docked in Wuhan. We had a short tour of Wuhan, another very big city, before boarding a short flight to Shanghai where we checked into the five-star J C Mandarin Hotel. This was a very good five-star hotel but it is not quite as elaborate as the China World. We spent August 28 touring Shanghai. Shanghai is truly a world class city with enormous skyscapers being built everywhere. Among Shanghai's most impressive sights are the "New Bund" and the "Old Bund" which are divided by the Huong-pu River, a tributary of the Yangtze.

On August 29 we took our bus to Zhouzhaung where we spent a few hours and had lunch before boarding our Grand Canal boat for the trip to Suzhou where we checked into the four-star Bamboo Grove Hotel which was probably as good as any hotel in Suzhou. On August 30 we took a tour of Suzhou and its famous gardens. That afternoon we took the bus back to Shanghai and boarded our flight to Guilin where we stayed at the Sheraton Guilin Hotel which is a five-star hotel and the best hotel in town. Once again it was not as good as the China World. A former prime minister of South Korea was there at the same time we were there. The Clintons had stayed in this hotel on their trip to China. They had also stayed in our Xian Hotel. Guilin's claim to fame are the beautiful and unique mountains, some of which are inside Guilin itself, and the Li River Cruise through these mountains.

On September 1 we flew to Guangzhou (Canton) another enormous city, which we toured by bus. That afternoon we boarded a modern hydrofoil for a two hour trip to Hong Kong. We arrived in the evening and transferred to our Great Eagle Hotel, another five-star hotel which was comparable to the China World Hotel in Beijing, though not quite as grand. It was an ornate and very fine hotel and was well located in Kowloon, only two blocks from Nathan Road, two blocks from the Peninsula Hotel, one block from Ashley Road, a very good restaurant street, and three blocks from the Kowloon Ferry to Hong Kong Island. The shopping and restaurants were excellent. Hong Kong is an enormous city of 8 million plus and was by far the most fun place we went. I bought pearls for all the girls at the Trio Pearl Company in the Peninsula Hotel. I had bought pearls for Pat in this elegant shop when I was there on the 1974 cotton trip. The Peninsula is considered to be one of the world's extreme top hotels. I'd love to stay there some day.

In China we flew on China Airlines which allowed one carry-on and one checked bag of 44 pounds maximum (though mine exceeded 44 pounds). But we were allowed two check-in bags from Hong Kong back to the United States, each of which could weigh as much as 70 pounds. The idea here probably is to let people shop all they want to in Hong Kong which is indeed a shopper's paradise.

On September 4 we flew United Airlines direct to Chicago and then on to Memphis. I drove home, arriving mid-afternoon, and barely had enough strength to unpack.

It was an excellent trip. I have stayed in touch with and we have seen Philip and Ana Pappas and their children, Marcelo and Amanda, as well as Peter and Darlene Campanella, in Chicago. (Phil and Ana's older son, Tiago, an Agricultural Economics major at the University of Wisconsin, spent ten days with Will and me this summer (2003) learning about Tennessee agriculture. Tiago grew up on the north side of Chicago. Kenton must surely have been a cultural shock!) These folks are mighty good friends.

In April, 2000 Pat and I went with Robert and Jenny Kirkland to the Napa Valley. We stayed three nights in the wonderful Auberge de Soleil and we ate at several good restaurants. Unfortunately we could not get reservations at the famous restaurant, the French Laundry. Then we drove down to Yosemite Park and stayed two nights at the Ahwahnee Lodge, a beautiful old hotel. Then it was back to San Francisco and a night at the luxurious Ritz Carlton, followed by a flight to Los Angeles and one night in the famous Bel-Air Hotel with its unbelievably beautiful grounds.

The next day we met Johnny and Patsy Bruff, Bill and Shirley Kaler, Jim and Martha Rippy, and Bill and Ann Townes, all of Union City, for a cruise from the Los Angeles area port at San Pedro down the Mexican coast with stops at Cabo San Lucas, Mazatlan, and Puerto Vallarta. We sailed on Royal Caribbeans's *Rhapsody of the Seas*. We had a festive seven days at sea and in port with this fun group of friends.

Earlier in the year Pat and I had taken a cruise on a Princess ship. We had a great room with a balcony and the services of a butler. We were seated for dinner with some pleasant people including the brother of the famous crooner and husband (at different times) of Debbie Reynolds and Elizabeth Taylor (and other ladies), Eddie Fisher.

In June of 2000 we took a Tauck trip to the Canadian Rockies. First we spent two nights at Banff Springs Hotel, a magnificent and very large and famous old hotel which we thoroughly enjoyed. The next two nights were spent at Chateau Lake Louise which I remembered from a childhood trip through the northwest with Mother, Dad, Grandmother, and Sally. Lake Louise and its glacier had remained in my memory as the most beautiful spot that I had ever seen. My mind has not changed. Our room looked out at this captivating scene. Then it was on to Jasper Park Lodge, a lovely rather sizable lodge with a five-star restaurant. While there we took a 2-rated white water rafting trip on the Athabasca River. On the way back down to the Kananaskis Lodge we stopped at the Athabasca Glacier and drove up onto this enormous field of snow and ice on snowmobiles that ride on giant Goodyear tires. There are only 21 of these vehicles in the world, 20 at Athabasca and the other at a United States research station in Antarctica. (I sent pictures to Jimmy Cagle, Union City Goodyear's public relations man, and he put the pictures and my information about the tires and this glacier in their company newsletter.) The Athabasca Glacier is part of the Columbia Ice Field and is one of only two Triple Continental Divides in the world, the other being in Siberia.

Along our way north and back south to Calgary we saw spectacular lakes, Maraine Lake with its ten peaks, Peyto Lake, and Emerald Lake where we had lunch at the Emerald Lake Lodge.

One of the neat things about this trip was meeting a fellow Pike, Wade Jones of Colorado. At Banff I struck up a conversation with this very friendly man and asked him where he went to school. He said, "Pitt." I told Wade that I had known Johnny Majors (formerly Pitt's football coach) well at UT, though he was a Sigma Chi and I was a Pike. Wade said, "I was a Pike at Pitt." From that point on we really hit it off. We ate with Wade and his sweet wife, Eleanor, and his widowed sister several times and rode in the same raft with them on our white water trip.

In January 2001 my old McCallie and UT and PiKA roommate, Bill Monin, and I had a great time in Antarctica. (Pat and Bill's Christiane did not want to go.) We flew from Memphis to Miami to Buenos Aires which is one of the world's most beautiful cities. Pat and I had been there 12 or 15 years ago for a day or two and enjoyed it very much. Bill and I were there for two days on this trip and had a great time. It seems to me that a week or so in Buenos Aires would be great fun.

From there we flew to Ushuia for part of a day prior to boarding our Russian ship. We mailed postcards home from Ushuia's post office on February 6. They arrived in September! (Postcards sent from two Antarctica research stations took over a year to arrive.)

That afternoon we sailed for Antarctica, a truly fascinating continent (and my seventh continent). The icebergs are much more beautiful and numerous than I realized. At times we could stand on the deck of the ship and look in one direction and see probably as many as 100. The penguins are delightful. We saw tens of thousands of them. Sometimes they would walk up to within two or three feet of you. We also saw thousands of seals of different kinds and dozens, if not hundreds, of whales, mostly Minke, but a few Humpbacks. As one can imagine, the scenery was awe inspiring with enormous ice fields, glaciers, and mountains.

Our Russian ship was not too great but it was about what I expected. The food was better than I expected. We had one meal that I proclaimed to our table was the worst meal I ever had in my life. But for the most part, the food ranged from fair to real good. We had soup one or two times a day, and it was usually very good. We had two real nice steaks but the taste was different from what we are used to. They did not have eggs very often for breakfast, and they never had bacon or sausage but they did have some sort of ham which to me looked like what Ken Kirkland might have called "funny meat." So it was oatmeal with no ham for breakfast for me every morning. Fortunately the oatmeal was fine. The orange juice was also kind of funny, but it was better than nothing. The coffee was so strong that it was seldom part of breaking my fast.

As one might imagine on a trip of this sort, the passengers for the most part were very well traveled. Most of us had been in similar type situations somewhere in the world and there was very little complaining about anything. Our room was about what I expected, small and spartan. The bed was not real comfortable, but fair sleep was possible. My main objection to the whole deal was the bathroom which was tiny. The shower was not separated from the rest of the bathroom so the water just went everywhere. The bathroom was very much like the one we had on our Nile River trip.

The Drake Passage, possibly the wickedest seas in the world, was terribly rough for 36 to 48 hours going and coming. The 4000-ton ship had stabilizers but they were broken, so the ship pitched and rolled like mad for these three to four days. Taking a shower was a real challenge. At times you would be jerked literally from one bathroom wall to the other. Eating was also a challenge, and soup would slosh out both sides of the bowl onto the tablecloths. They dampened the tablecloths during these times so the dishes would not slide as badly as they would have if the tablecloths had been dry. Walking was also very hard. At times we would be thrown from wall to wall or table to table depending on where we were. It was pretty hard to sleep. But the Antarctic Sea was mostly calm during the ten days that we were actually down there.

The ship had a bar and a library. Wisely they never opened the bar until the last Zodiac (the little boats that carried us back and forth from the ship to land) was back to the ship. Cocktail hour was festive, as we met a lot of people that we liked. The people came from the United States and Canada and from several foreign countries including England, South Africa, Denmark, and Sweden.

On the front of the ship there was a lecture hall which had formerly been a lounge and dance floor. We had a fantastic staff, especially two older men who had spent many years in Antarctica as well as the Arctic. One of the men, Brian Shoemaker, is a former Navy commander who, for three years, was commander of the United States Research Station at McMurdo Bay, Antarctica. The other man, Laurie Dexter, a Canadian, was an Antarctic and Arctic historian who, during the next Antarctic summer, was planning to cross Antarctica on skis from one side to the other, crossing the South Pole. These men made Antarctica and its past come alive. We also were shown appropriate videos and movies.

It was a great trip and an unforgettable experience. Bill and I hit it off just like we had all those many years ago.

On May 24, 2001 Pat and I joined Newell and Bettye Graham and friends of theirs, John and Diane Scott and Dexter and Lee Ann Cleveland, of Indiana and South Carolina, respectively, for a trip to Italy. We flew to Rome where we spent three days and nights in a marvelous little hotel, the Lord Byron, and did the usual tourist things again. As always, the highlight for me was St. Peters. To me St. Peters

241

is far and away the most magnificent man-made thing in the world. Then we were driven to Umbria for a week's stay in a country house, Villa Salicotta, which sat high up on a hill overlooking a beautiful valley. The only crop was tobacco, and it was fascinating to see them plant, irrigate, and cultivate it. Robert and Jenny Kirkland met us at Villa Salicotta where they had spent the previous week with some of their family. While in Umbria we visited several fascinating towns. Gubbio was fun, and Orvieto's cathedral is one of the world's most beautiful. We bought ceramics of different kinds and pottery in Orvieto. We also bought and paid for a wire chicken in a shop there, but we never received it. We bought a terra cotta statue in Citta di Castello, and we bought ceramics for ourselves and the children in Deruta, a town world famous for ceramics. We bought our inlaid table in an antique store in Arrezzo. They did a terrible job of packing it, and it arrived in 20 or 25 pieces. We did have it put back together, and though the cracks show, we are still very happy to have it. Insurance paid a good deal of our loss. Then Robert and Jenny and Pat and I caught a train in Arezzo for Stresa on Lake Maggiore, a city that my 1956 college tour visited. The four of us had an enormous amount of luggage. We changed trains in the gigantic Milan train station. It took us a long time to figure out where our connecting train to Stresa was located. We walked literally miles back and forth looking for it, much of the time dragging all that luggage. We barely caught our train and headed north. The conductor told us that we had only one minute to get off in Stresa, and getting ourselves and all our luggage off in one minute was an almost impossible task. Again, we barely made it. Without the assistance of a helpful and friendly Aussie, we might still be on that train. Our Grand Hotel des iles Borromees was magnificent. We had mini-suites with sitting areas and balconies overlooking the lake, and our room was one of the finest we've ever had.

After three delightful days in Stresa we rented a car and headed for Lake Como. On the way we passed a large dealer of concrete and terra cotta statuary. We decided to turn around and see what they had. We spent about four hours there. The Kirklands bought a great deal of what turned out to be really good stuff, and Pat and I also bought quite a bit for our house and yard. Bob's CBK Ltd. made the arrangements to get it trucked to Genoa, shipped to the United States, and trucked on to Union City. We consolidated, at Deruta, our purchases from Deruta, Citta, and Arrezzo with the Kirklands' purchases at these same cities, and Bob and CBK arranged to have it all put into a container and shipped and trucked from Italy to Union City. Pat and I never could have made all these purchases had it not been for the Kirklands and their import expertise. Our table and a bust the Kirklands bought, which they also were able to repair, were the only things broken. We treasure everything we bought.

We then drove on to Lake Como and to our world-class hotel, Villa D'Este, where we spent three more days and nights. Villa D'Este, a beautiful and elegant hotel, has often been considered the world's number one hotel. The grounds of the hotel were the most magnificent hotel grounds we had ever seen — by far! They include a fortress that was built on the side of a hill by a long-ago owner of the property who was trying to appease her new husband's love of warfare. This former soldier enjoyed playing war, I guess with servants and/or friends. Cernobbio, the town where Villa D'Este is located, is a lovely little town just outside the city of Como, the namesake of Como, Tennessee, famous as the home of my Como Grain and Feed Company! One day we drove up to Bellagio, another picturesque town on Lake Como. Another day we drove to Campione, Italy, a neat little town on Lake Lugano and within sight of Lugano, Switzerland. Campione is completely surrounded by Switzerland, and the main attractions of Campione are its casino and the fact that it is a tax haven, much, we understood, like Monaco. The best meals we had on the trip were at a restaurant in Gubbio and at Da Candida Ristorante in Campione. From Cernobbio we headed for the Milano airport. After spending the last night at the spartan Jet Hotel in a town near our airport, we flew home from a great vacation.

Our most recent trip, in the spring of 2003, was with Robert and Jenny Kirkland to France. We first went to Paris where we stayed at the world class Hotel de Crillon. Paris is arguably the world's most beautiful city. Highlights were visits to the Louvre with its ever exciting Mona Lisa, Winged Victory, and Venus de Milo and to the Musee d'Orsay and its fabulous collection of Impressionists and Post Impressionists and other paintings and sculpture. We went there twice, the second time as guests of John and Betty Ann Tanner who were in Paris for a NATO meeting. The museum opened late for a privately conducted tour for the members of NATO. The Kirklands and we were greatly honored to have been included with this important group. Afterwards John and Betty Ann joined us for a very festive dinner in an excellent restaurant, Le Balzar, which had been recommended to them by a NATO friend of theirs.

Other excellent small restaurants with quick service were Minims, owned by the famous next-door restaurant, Maxims, and Brasserie Flottes, both near our hotel.

After four days in Paris we were picked up by Papillon and driven to Burgundy where we boarded our home for the next six days, the river barge, Le Papillon. (This Papillon barge operation is affiliated with the Papillon Company which hosted us in a country house on our 2001 trip to Umbria.) We began at Serre on the Soane River canal and switched to the Bourgogne (Burgundy) Canal at St. Jean de-Losne. We followed this canal up to Dijon, a fascinating city of 250,000, where we docked for a night in downtown Dijon. From there we followed the same canal which had turned south through the Ouche River Valley. We very much enjoyed our times in Dijon and Beaune (pronounced Bone). Beaune is in the heart of the Burgundy wine country and is an interesting city. A visit there to an old hospital-museum was fascinating. We disembarked at Pont-d'Ouche and were driven back to Paris from where the Kirklands flew to the Amalfi coast of Italy and Pat and I flew home. It was a very good trip and, as always, the Kirklands were perfect traveling companions.

Olympics Trips

In 1984 Robert and Christopher Kirkland and Will and I decided to go to the Los Angeles Olympics. We flew to L.A. and rented two cars and checked into the Del Capri Hotel on Wilshire Boulevard. Our hotel was near Westwood, a fun area of good restaurants and shops adjacent to the UCLA campus. The famous actor, Joey Bishop of Ratpack fame, was a guest of our hotel while we were there. We spoke with him a time or two at the pool and he was most cordial.

The infamous L.A. traffic was daunting to me, but as it turned out the traffic was no worse than normal. A fair number of locals "vacated the premises" during the Olympics, which helped, and other factors worked to hold down the traffic snarls that were predicted. We had no real problems in moving around the area to the different venues. Will and I saw volleyball twice at the Long Beach Arena, free-style wrestling (we saw two Americans win) at the Anaheim Arena, water polo at Pepperdine University, soccer at the Rose Bowl, diving at the University of Southern California diving arena, Track and Field two or three times at the Los Angeles Coliseum, the site of Los Angeles' previous Olympics, and baseball at Dodger Stadium. The boys had a great time buying and trading Olympic pins. While out there we did a fair amount of sightseeing, ate at many good restaurants, and we also took in Universal Studios and the *Queen Mary* and the *Spruce Goose* in Long Beach. It was a thrill to walk the decks of the *Queen Mary* after having sailed to Europe on her in 1956. I was able to pick out the table in the Observation Lounge in first class where our gang hung out for hours on end during that delightful voyage. After having seen the hull of the sunken *Queen Elizabeth* in Hong Kong Harbor on the 1974 cotton trip, I had now seen both *Queens* on which we had sailed in 1956. What wonderful memories those sights brought back.

Chris and Will and their Dads had a memorable time and came home tired but happy campers.

Will, Pat and I as well as Robert, Jenny and Christopher Kirkland went to the Olympics in Barcelona in 1992. We stayed at Salou, a very nice and sizeable beach town on the Costa Brava. Our hotel was not air conditioned and it was extremely hot. The hotel had a band every night, and the raucous music lasted until about 1:00 AM making it impossible to sleep, not only because of the heat but also because of the infernal noise. Nevertheless, it was a great trip except for the sad fact that Will was sick for a week with something which the doctor who was with our group was not able to diagnose. However, Will got well after a week and he was o.k. from then on. He did miss the majority of the events for which we had tickets and had to stay at the hotel. Pat stayed with him. We bought fans to put in the rooms which made it somewhat more bearable. Salou was a two hour bus ride from Barcelona. Fortunately the buses left at regular intervals and we had dependable bus service. Salou's 1992 year-round population was in the range of 15,000 to 20,000. However, during the summer when people come to their condos and tourists flock to the hotels the population swells to between 300,000 to 400,000.

Among the events we saw were Track and Field two or three times, volleyball, water polo, diving, and tennis. We sat directly behind U.S.A. tennis player Mary Joe Fernandez' mother and sister and had an ongoing conversation with them as Mary Joe won her match. Most of the venues were on the beautiful Mont Juic and the Plaza de Espana.

We went with *Track and Field News* (TAFNOT) which is the "bible" of the track and field world. They always have the largest groups of people at major track and field events around the world. TAFNOT gave us a day's sightseeing in Barcelona during the Olympics. The most interesting thing we saw in Barcelona was Gaudi's unfinished cathedral which is possibly the strangest and certainly one of the most impressive structures in the world. After our tour we stopped at a palatial estate about half way between Barcelona and Salou and were treated to a TAFNOT gala, one of the nicest and most fun parties that I have ever been to in my life. We had pre-arranged to meet a friend of Bill and Betty Gillett's (Union City friends) at the party, and "Goose" Campbell was a great guy. At the party we met famous decathlon winner, Bob Mathias and his wife, Gwen, and Milt Campbell and his wife (Milt was also a decathlon gold medal winner). On the way from the party back to Salou we sat in the back of the bus with the Mathiases and Campbells and we all sang songs including *I Don't Wanta go Home*. TAFNOT had a daily paper, *The TAFNOT Times*, and our group's singing made *The Times* the next day. The Mathiases and Campbells were extremely nice and cordial people. Their autographs and photos are in our trip album. Another former decathlon winner from the U.S.A. whom we saw but did not meet was Rafer Johnson. Despite Will's mysterious illness and the very hot and loud accommodations in Salou, it was a good trip.

We decided after Barcelona that we would go to the 1996 Atlanta Olympics. Coming home from the Barcelona Olympics on the plane with the Mayor of Atlanta and a good part of the Atlanta Olympic Committee just cinched the deal.

The word was out early that accommodations in Atlanta would be very hard to come by, so we started making calls long in advance. All the hotels I called said they were booked. We talked with two or three people with Agris (our agricultural software firm in Atlanta) and with some grain brokers we deal with in Atlanta about the possibility of renting somebody's home. The prices were ridiculously high and nothing came of that. So I called Zeta PiKA brother Dr. Richard Colditz of Carrollton, Georgia west of Atlanta. Richard's wife, Beverly, called the manager of the best hotel in Carrollton, a Ramada Inn, and he was entirely booked by a foreign country.

Beverly persisted though and finally several months later he let us have two rooms, saying that he had not heard from this phantom country. (After we got there, we found that we could have gotten rooms even in downtown hotels, right next to the Olympics main site, but that was water under the bridge as the Carrollton rooms were paid for entirely in advance.)

The first day the four of us, Kim and Will and Pat and I, took a shuttle service to the westernmost MARTA (the Atlanta subway system) train station and caught MARTA to the games. We noted that there was plenty of room to park in the many parking lots located in fields in the country where those who parked caught buses to the MARTA station, so from then on we drove to these parking lots. This saved money and gave us much more flexibility.

The games were very well organized and we had no trouble getting from one venue to another on Atlanta's rapid transit system's MARTA. Often our events were in the main area of the Olympic Park - the Georgia Dome, the Georgia World Congress Center, and the Omni, and we could simply walk from venue to venue. Just south by MARTA was Atlanta-Fulton County Stadium, where the Braves had always played, and Olympic Stadium, which later became Turner Field to which the Braves moved after Atlanta-Fulton County Stadium was torn down. We could simply walk from baseball to track and field. Just north by MARTA was Georgia Tech where we saw boxing and swimming. To the east by MARTA and bus was Stone Mountain and tennis. Will and I went to swimming finals while Pat, Kim, and Kim's parents, Eddie and Judy Oglesby, (who came down for a day of the games) saw the Dream Team (the men's basketball team) at the same time. I saw two women's basketball games (Will saw one of them) which we won handily. Two former Lady Vols, Carla McGhee and Nikki McCray, played for U.S.A. We saw the U.S.A. play baseball twice (won one, lost one to Japan), gymnastics, women's basketball (won twice), judo, track and field, (twice), weightlifting, swimming (U.S.A. won several events), field hockey (U.S.A. lost), tennis (U.S.A.'s Malavai Washington and Mary Joe Fernandez — we saw her win in Barcelona — both won their singles matches), and men's volleyball (U.S.A. lost).

By far our favorite and the most exciting event, other than women's basketball for me, was weightlifting. We saw at least three world records set as the "Pocket Hercules," Naim Suleymanoglu of Turkey, expatriate of Bulgaria, worked his way up to the gold in his third consecutive Olympics, and he was the first weightlifter ever to do so. His competitor from Greece, Valerios Leonidis, also set a world record on the way up in weight. His Greek fans were on the right (to us) of the platform, and the Turks were directly across from them on our left. The Turks and Greeks were very loud, as were all of the 5,000 (including us!) which filled the venue in the Georgia World Congress Center. The crowd (including us! LOUD!) sang YMCA time and time again. We had never been in such a festive crowd. Everybody was just plain happy and loudly and almost constantly were expressing that feeling. It was an experience we'll never forget.

We missed the famous bombing in Centennial Park (the Olympic Park) by an hour and a half or so. We had been at that exact spot just before leaving for the day. Each night on our drive back to Carrollton we listened to news of the Olympics on the car radio, and this is how we heard about it. That was a strange feeling.

Bowl Trips and Other Games

Mother and Dad and Sally and I went to several Tennessee bowl games. Dad and I often took in the old Delta Bowl at Crump Stadium in Memphis regardless of who was playing. We went to at least two Cotton Bowls staying with our Pharr relatives. The first one was the memorable January 1951 game in which we beat Texas 20-14. This was the game in which Hank Lauricella made his famous 75 yard run, running from one sideline to the other three times. Andy Kozar, whom I got to know well during my UT alumni days, scored a couple of touchdowns and played one of his best games. Texas beat us two years later in the Cotton Bowl. We saw that game, too.

We went to the Sugar Bowl on January 1, 1952, after our undefeated team had won the 1951 national championship. We played poorly and Maryland beat us 28-13. We again went to the Sugar Bowl on January 1, 1957. Our team was also undefeated and was ranked second in the nation. Baylor beat us, but I believe we would have won if Bruce Burnham had not been kicked in the face by a Baylor player. He had a convulsion on the field and was carried off unconscious. We didn't know until after the game if he was dead or alive. My close friend, the Jacobs Trophy-winning Blocking Back for Tennessee, Stockton Adkins of Union City, told me that the players were totally demoralized by Bruce's injury and their hearts were not in the game after this first half incident. I had a party in my room of the Jung Hotel after the game. 70 or 80 folks showed up. My old McCallie and UT friend who was in Pat's and my wedding, Mike Miller of Knoxville, spent most of the party standing in the bathtub; that's how crowded we were. Interestingly Bruce Burnham who married Katie Hess, a girl I knew at UT, later became head coach at Union City High School for four years or so. I don't know what ever became of him. In the 70s, Bill Glass, the star of the '57 Sugar Bowl and a giant Baylor All-American, was preaching in a community revival in Kenton. Mother and Dad had him and Stockton and Stockton's wife, Jenny, and Pat and me for dessert after one evening's services. Mother served her famous strawberry shortcake which everybody enjoyed immensely. Bill Glass who was not the game's culprit was an extraordinarily nice person.

When I was fairly young we played Rice in the Orange Bowl. We had a great team that year, but Rice beat us in a defensive struggle. This was probably my biggest disappointment in terms of bowl games that we saw. Certainly Tennessee plays on a much higher level now than does Rice.

Since college I have seen Tennessee play in several Liberty Bowls, Citrus Bowls, Sugar Bowls, and Fiesta Bowls. The most memorable Liberty Bowl was when we beat Arkansas on a last minute touchdown, 14-13. We just about froze to death at that game. The most memorable Citrus Bowl was when we beat favored Ohio State and Eddie George, 20-14. The most memorable Sugar Bowl was beating heavily favored Miami and Vinnie Testaverde, 35-7. Pat and I were in the official party for that game. We all stood for the entire scintillating game. Everybody, that is, but Pat. Pat usually sits through football games and more often than not reads a book or works a cross-word puzzle. I have never heard a louder crowd. The Tennessee noise started long before the kickoff and never abated. As we left the crowd was shouting, "It's great to be a Tennessee Volunteer, it sucks to be a Miami Hurricane." What a game!

By far the most memorable Fiesta Bowl game was on January 4, 1999, when we beat Florida State for the 1998 national championship, 23-16. Will and Kim and Pat and I went out with David Critchlow and the two Critchlow boys, David Jr. and Scott, and their wives, Heard and Heather. We had a great time in Phoenix and Scottsdale. Will, David, Scott, and Will's and my friend and fraternity brother, Jeff Abraham from Scottsdale, played golf three times on famous golf courses. The whole time out there was wonderful. After the game we drove to the UT and Vols headquarters hotel, the Scottsdale Plaza Resort, for the victory party after the game. What a blast! We saw Malcolm and Harriet Colditz, our fraternity brother and his wife from Houston, and John and Ann Michels, another fraternity brother and All-American Volunteer whose induction into the College Football Hall of Fame we attended in December 1996, and many other friends and acquaintances. The only part of the whole thing that wasn't just great was that it took me 45 minutes to get a drink!

The first Fiesta Bowl I attended was with Will and Kenton cousin, William Penn. I contracted some sort of flu out there and had to leave the game, which we lost to Penn State, at the end of the first half. We were sitting with cousin James and Mary Nell Hamilton from Trenton.

The last Fiesta Bowl I took in was with Pat and Patti and Rance. We stayed in the marvelous, world-class Arizona Biltmore which we thoroughly enjoyed. This time Nebraska beat us.

These were the highlights of many bowls to which we have traveled over the years.

Dad and I, sometimes with Mother, never missed a Vanderbilt game in Nashville or an Ole Miss game in Memphis. The Vanderbilt game I remember best was one which we lost badly to Vanderbilt which was coached by the famous Red Sanders who went on to coach at UCLA. I believe this would have been the '48 game. We drove back to Huntingdon where we had supper. There was a group of men in the restaurant who obviously knew each other but who were arguing vehemently. One of the Tennessee boosters challenged a Vandy booster to bet on next year's game. The Vandy booster told the UT fan that he was simply "betting on sentiment," to which the UT man said, "I'm not betting on sentiment; I'm betting on our damn freshman team!" They bet. Sure enough, Tennessee beat Vanderbilt handily the next fall. That freshman team went on to become national champs.

Tennessee played Ole Miss in Crump Stadium in Memphis every year for many years. For a long time we beat Ole Miss every year. Then they hired a new coach, Johnny Vaught. The last time we beat Ole Miss for a good while was my most memorable Tennessee-Ole Miss game. They had outplayed us throughout, but we were only down by 14-12 as time was running out. We had the ball at about mid-field but were going nowhere fast. Dad and I decided to leave the game a few seconds early. As we were leaving by the east end zone, a great roar erupted. We looked up just in time to see two hands high above the crowd, catching the football. It was the last of many Proctor to Powell passes in the game. We won, 18-14, as the clock ran out. Ole Miss still had never beaten UT. This was our 18th consecutive victory over them. We had almost miraculously seen the winning pass. J. B. Proctor and Jim Powell were a great combination for Tennessee that year. As an aside, as a youngster I was pretty good at drawing, and I drew a picture of one of these two players — can't remember which one — from a photograph in a sports magazine and mailed it to him with a short letter. He never acknowledged my drawing which was a great disappointment. My recollection is that it was a darn good likeness.

After that game Ole Miss became a football powerhouse. It seemed like forever before we beat them again. But I had to admit that most of the Ole Miss teams during that era were simply better than ours, especially the years when future New York Giant great, Charley Conerly, was their quarterback.

We saw many other great games through the years. One of the greatest was in Knoxville when we beat LSU which came into the game undefeated and ranked number one. We won that game by stopping their All-American running back, Billy Cannon, on fourth and goal on a play that they have always disputed. Another great one was in Memphis when we beat UCLA which was coached by Memphian Tommy Prothro, 37-34. In this game Dewey Warren, our great quarterback, scored on a run which UCLA claimed they stopped. This was probably the most exciting game I ever saw. Prothro said after the game that he was ashamed to be a Southerner. He lost a lot of friends that day. Our weigher at the gin, Delbert Orr, a longtime Vol fan, had never seen a college game. We took Delbert and his dear wife, Marie, to the game. Delbert must have thought that college football was mighty exciting in person. He saw what is still probably the most exciting of the hundreds of college games that I have ever seen. Delbert followed Tennessee football over the years and his all-time favorite Vol was great Neyland-era fullback, Andy Kozar. Andy and I became friendly during my time of heavy involvement in UT alumni work, and I told him of Delbert's great admiration for him. Andy wrote an exceptionally nice note to Delbert and autographed it. Delbert was overwhelmed when I gave it to him. Nothing could have pleased him more.

One of the neat things about going to games in Knoxville for the past 25 years or so has been staying at the Knoxville Hyatt Regency which recently has become a Marriott. The Hyatt always had the Pride of the Southland Pep Band, the cheerleaders, and the majorettes for two sets the mornings of the games. The Marriott did not bring them in last year (2002), but here's hoping they will have the good sense to continue this exciting tradition. We see lots of old friends in the hotel each football weekend which is another great thing about staying there. I have spent at least 200 nights, probably more, in that hotel and have met many interesting people there including Pierre Salinger of the JFK Administration.

I could go on for pages on end with great games I have seen, but the foregoing were some of the highlights of a phenomenon that has given me enormous pleasure ever since I was a little boy listening to the legendary Lindsey Nelson's calling of Tennessee games. Tennessee has had a series of unusually talented sportscasters over the decades, the most famous of whom was college friend John Ward who rushed me for Kappa Sig. My fraternity brother and friend, Bill Anderson, Vol and NFL great, was John's outstanding color man for those 31 years. Tim Priest, the current color man for the Vol Network, is a fascinating addition to Vol broadcast lore. Tim, an All-SEC cornerback from Huntingdon and the Vols all-time interception leader, is the father of Will's fraternity brother Adam Priest. Announcer Bob Kessling and Tim know the game, and they are able successors to John and Bill.

Tennessee Volunteer football games are just as exciting to me as they were 55 or 60 years ago. All Tennessee Vol sports, and the Lady Vols coached by legend-in-her-own-time, Pat Head Summit, have added a great deal to the quality and enjoyment of my life. My blood runs orange!

Cruises

We have been on many cruises in many places. The first cruise we took was with Mary and David Critchlow and Dale and Milton Hamilton on a small Norwegian-Caribbean ship of about 12,000 tons. We drove down from Nashville to Miami. On the way down I told them about a little friend of Lolly's whose family was relocating from Union City to Fort Wayne. They were Yankee folks and when the little friend told me where they were moving, she pronounced the "o" in Fort as "ah." Get my drift? We spent a night in Fort Pierce asking just about everybody we saw for directions to get there, and you can just imagine how we asked for those directions to Fort Pierce. I also told the gang about a Memphis man who had done some truck scale work for us who never said "yes;" he always said, "Right you are, yep."

But he pronounced it very, very fast, "Ritecharyep." It took me a long time to figure out what he was saying. Critchlow still says it to me all the time. When we pulled up to the Fountainbleau Hotel in Miami Beach, Milton got out of the car in his T-shirt and asked the liveried doorman in an exaggerated Tennessee twang, "Y'all got any overnite sleepin' rooms?" The doorman, who had no sense of humor, could not get rid of us quickly enough. We couldn't have afforded to stay there anyway. We stayed across the street at a very ordinary motel. We boarded the ship the next day. Pat ate mostly salads. We men drank a fair number of rum punches. One morning Critchlow had room service bring Pat and me a salad and a rum punch at 7 AM. We probably hadn't gone to bed before three or four o'clock.

We met an attractive couple whom we enjoyed a lot. The young man was a special agent for the F.B.I. We got a room steward to take a picture of all eight of us jammed into one of our tiny bathrooms in one of our tiny rooms. It wasn't an easy task. One night at the midnight buffet I ate some Limburger cheese. Pat made me face the wall all night long. Never again has Limburger cheese crossed my lips.

Several years later we took a four night cruise to the Bahamas on a very large old ship, *The Leonardo da Vinci*. Our family and the Critchlow family went, eleven of us in all. One of our favorite activities was Bingo. During the course of the cruise we must have won seven or eight, or maybe even more, games.

Three or four years later we took Patti and Will on a cruise out of Tampa during spring holidays. Will had recently broken his foot which was in a walking cast. There were a good many children on the ship, *The Veendam* of the Holland America line, which was great fun for Patti and Will. We entered every contest on the ship, some of which were for a parent and child. Will and I and then Patti and I finished second in their age groups in shuffleboard. They both were very disappointed not to win. They also had a talent show for children, and Will sang *Gary, Indiana*, dancing on his cast and one good foot. He had just sung this song in a play in Union City, and he did real well. The crowd loved him.

One winter Pat and I and the Critchlows went to Acapulco for a couple of days prior to boarding a ship for a cruise through the Panama

Canal and on through the Caribbean to Fort Lauderdale. Right after getting on the ship we saw a helicopter landing on a very small concrete pad on the side of Acapulco Bay. It slipped off the pad, but it appeared that nobody was hurt. As we were sailing through the Panama Canal, a fascinating day, our congressmen and senators were debating as to whether or not to give the canal to Panama. We were enamored with it and wrote our representatives when we got home asking them not to give it away. Senator Howard Baker was in the forefront of those in favor of disposing of it, which we later did, of course. This is one of the relatively few times that Howard really disappointed us.

On another Caribbean cruise we took with the Critchlows, David and I decided to take a tour that crossed the island of Jamaica. We went through the small home town of Harry Belafonte on their once-a-year big Festival Day. We went back to the ship and told Mary and Pat that we ran into Belafonte and, in fact, had a long conversation with him. I have never before told Pat that we were kidding them and trying to make them sorry that they didn't go along with us. (I ran into Belafonte in New York's JFK Airport a few years ago. Several people and I sat around and talked with him. True story — I swear!) On that same day tour we passed very near the Jamaica home of Ian Fleming, the famous writer of the James Bond novels (every one of which I read back in the 60s). David and I told Pat and Mary that we had a personally conducted tour of the house. Actually we didn't even see it. Surprisingly the girls didn't seem at all unhappy about the fact that they had spent a relaxing day on the ship.

On a Caribbean Cruise one winter I entered the ping-pong tournament. I got to the finals and played a Chinese man for the ship championship. He was by far the best ping-pong player I had ever seen. He beat me 21-3, and those three points were gifts. Afterwards I introduced myself and congratulated him, and he introduced himself, "My name is Ping Tom from Chicago." My gosh, no wonder he was such a great player.

On another cruise I entered the shuffleboard tournament. A Texan who obviously played a lot of shuffleboard wiped me out. On the last night aboard he and I happened to end up together in the line to buy Bingo cards for the final jackpot game. During our conversation we switched positions in line. Well, by George, he won the jackpot which was in excess of $2,500. This was a right long time ago, and that was a lot more money than it is today. That was indeed an expensive shuffleboard game. I entered many cruise contests over the years and enjoyed them and have several trophies for my efforts.

Pat and I were on a Caribbean cruise with UT, on the *Fairwind*. (We sailed on the *Fairwind* and *Fairsea*, Sitmar ships, several times, usually with the Critchlows.) Several colleges were aboard. We were seated one afternoon in the pizza lounge with a couple from Purdue, about our ages. In getting to know each other and after finding out that we were with UT, this gentleman said that he had a real good friend from Houston, where he used to work for Shell Oil, who went to all the UT football games. I said, "You must be talking about my good McCallie and UT — PiKA friend and fraternity brother, Malcolm Colditz." And he was! The next fall Malcolm flew up and got the Sowles, who then lived in Ohio, and brought them down to a UT game, and I went out to dinner with them. Pat was not with me that weekend.

One of the fun things to do on cruises was to buy a "race horse" at auction. The race was held on the last night out, and during the days leading up to the race the race horse owners took the little wooden horses with them wherever they went on the ship. The Critchlows and Pat and I bought a horse on this UT cruise and named her "Harass." We'd pull her around with us (she had wheels) as we walked the decks. We'd take her up to a group of people and Critchlow would announce, "Harass will not be scratched!" Harass was the crowd favorite but turned out to be an also-ran.

One winter the Critchlows and Al and Ruth Starr Strayhorn, also of Union City, and Pat and I flew to Los Angeles and checked into the world famous Beverly Hills Hotel for a couple of days prior to taking a cruise down the coast of Mexico. Pat and I stayed in one of their cottages. Right after going to bed the first night I felt like a coronary might be coming on. Remembering my wrestling with our very heavy bags at the airport and after hearing my symptoms, Pat had me lie on the floor with a rolled up towel under my neck. She got in touch with the hotel's house physician who verified Pat's diagnosis which was that

I was experiencing discomfort with my back. The doctor prescribed a muscle relaxant which we picked up at the famous Schwab's Pharmacy. The pills worked rapid wonders.

While at the hotel we saw Dustin Hoffman who walked through the lobby, Red Buttons in the barbershop, and Jacklyn Smith in the small coffee shop. We ate right across from her. She was a remarkably beautiful lady. The cruise was also great fun.

Pat and I have made many great purchases on trips. A cruise we booked one time took us to the San Blas Islands off the coast of Panama. The Cuna Indian women of these islands create beautiful molas, fabric panels which they wear on the front and back of their unique blouses. The sewing method they use is called reverse applique. We were fascinated with molas and wound up buying 70 or 80 of them. Pat came up with the idea of quilting them into large panels and using the resulting pieces as wall hangings. It is a beautiful way to display them, and some of our molas hang in the gallery of our home.

Another UT trip in 1981 was a Rhine and Mosel River cruise in Germany. T.O. and Carol Lashlee, Ted and Cathy Jones, and several others from Humboldt and Jackson were along. We flew to Lucerne and stayed in the world class Palace Hotel a couple of nights (I had stayed there in 1956) before embarking on our colorful cruise. We stopped at several picturesque German towns and visited several wineries. We bought some wine and packed it for our trip to Paris where we stayed at the Intercontinental Hotel. When my bag was unpacked, no bottles were to be found — just wine and tiny pieces of glass. We washed out the clothes in the bathtub and then hung them out on the window grate. Surprisingly nobody complained. We've never again packed wine bought on a trip.

In 1989 Pat and I flew to Rio de Janeiro for Carnival. We boarded our ship, Ocean Cruise Line's *Ocean Princess*, and then were taken to a grandstand where we saw a portion of far and away the world's greatest parade. Security was very tight. We even had to take a "body guard" with us when we went to the restroom. The beaches of Rio and the view from Sugar Loaf Mountain are fabulous. What a shame Rio is such a dangerous place. Our ship then called at Santos and Florianopolis, Brazil, and Mar del Plata and Buenos Aires, Argentina, another world class city, where we disembarked. Buenos Aires is one of my favorite cities. Strangely, both the toughest and the best steak ever, at least to that point, disappointed, then pleased my palate in Buenos Aires. A day trip to Iguassu Falls was offered. Pat didn't want to go, but I did. The falls were unbelievably big and beautiful — one of the most amazing sights in the world. An interesting thing happened on the way to Rio. We were flying Eastern Airlines out of Miami. Eastern was experiencing financial difficulties. We landed in Manaus, Brazil to refuel. We sat there for several hours. Finally they let us off to stretch and walk around in the terminal. When we finally took off we learned that the Manaus airport would not fuel the plane until the money for the fuel was in their hands.

Pat and I took a Danube River cruise on a Russian boat in 1989. We arrived at Kennedy Airport in New York, the starting point of our trip. When our flight was called we lined up for departure and to our great surprise, Judge Howard and Barbara Bozeman, our good friends from Knoxville, were on our trip. Howard was also a former UT National Alumni Association president. Their close friends, UT professor of History Dr. George Schweitzer and his wife, Verna, were with them. Dr. Schweitzer was the lecturer on the trip, and he was an absolutely great one. He knew the history of the countries we visited extraordinarily well, and he was also a marvelously interesting and entertaining lecturer. We began our trip in Vienna and went ashore in Budapest, Hungary; Bucharest, Romania; Bratislava, Czechoslovakia; Belgrade, Yugoslavia; and Plevin, Bulgaria. Belgrade was interesting, especially the Bohemian section. We bought a still life in a gallery and two naif, or primitive, paintings in the Bohemian section. All three paintings hang in our home. Budapest was a beautiful and interesting city, and we thoroughly enjoyed lunch and a wonderful folkloric show in a big cave outside Plevin. The most amazing thing we saw was the palace that Dictator Ceausescu built for himself in Bucharest. The gold displayed in the impressive Bucharest museum was a contradiction in this poverty-stricken country. At the mouth of the Danube we transferred from our boat to a Russian ship which took us across the Black Sea to Istanbul where we stayed in a very good Sheraton Hotel. We were fascinated with this world class city and purchased from an excellent rug shop, Ostarakci, a great looking camel back rug which also hangs in our house. Just a few weeks after we returned home the Iron Curtain fell and Eastern Europe was, almost overnight, changed forever. On television we saw Ceausescu executed. Our Romanian guide had indicated that the Romanian people were restless, and we had left Eastern Europe thinking that an uprising might be coming. Pat and I were observing more history in the making than we realized.

In 1990 Pat and her brother, Bob Thurmond, and I flew to Manaus again, this time to board the Greek ship, the *Stella Solaris*, and embarked on a trip down the Amazon River and out into the Atlantic and on to the Grenadine Islands before heading back home. The Amazon River is by far the world's greatest river. At times we could hardly see the banks of the river, and as we approached the mouth of the river we could not see either bank for several hours. We had been told that the Greek ships sometimes did not have very good food, but we thought the food on the *Stella Solaris* was excellent, as good, in fact, as we had ever had on a ship and better than most. Having Bob along added to a pleasant trip, and the couple with whom the three of us ate were very nice folks.

Prior to an Australia-New Zealand cruise Pat and I flew to Sydney where we spent two nights and a day at the plush Regent Hotel. Our room overlooked the harbor and bridge and the world famous Opera House. We saw a terrific one-woman show, Shirley Valentine, in the Opera House on our second evening. We greatly enjoyed Sydney. We left on a Royal Viking ship and sailed to Melbourne where we spent a day sightseeing. Melbourne was also a most impressive city. Then we sailed to Hobart, Tasmania where we took a day trip to the prison colony (a few years ago a deranged man gunned down a large number of tourists at this spot). Then we sailed to New Zealand and into Milford Sound and called at Christchurch and Wellington before disembarking at Auckland where we again stayed at a fine Regent Hotel. We enjoyed Australia and New Zealand very much, though we only saw the cities. Maybe some day we will be able to see more of Australia.

Another fine UT cruise was to Alaska. The Critchlows and Drerups were along, and Len Hoffman of UTM Development staffed the trip. We flew to Vancouver and then on to Fairbanks. Flying over hundreds of miles of glacier fields and mountains of Alaska was one of the most spectacular sights we had ever seen. We spent a night in Fairbanks and then boarded the train, *The Midnight Express*, which took us to Denali Park where we spent a couple of nights in the lodge. Critchlow and I took a helicopter flight up to Mount McKinley. What a view! We went outside late that night and saw the Northern Lights. Then it was back to *The Midnight Express* and on through spectacular mountains and scenery (Critchlow mooned a moose) to Anchorage where we stayed in the Captain Cook Hotel. Then we took the boat train to Whittier where we boarded our good Princess ship. Pat got sick with some sort of flu, so she couldn't enjoy our landings in Ketchikan, Juneau, Sitka, and Skagway. All these towns were fun stops. I organized the UT group for 5 PM gatherings in the lounge for cocktails and dancing to the ship's band. We met many nice UT and Penn State alumni (our counterparts on the trip). Pat was so sick that she forgot to pack all her hanging clothes. She later called the cruise company and they sent them to her.

In early January, 1994, before UT's winter/spring semester classes began, Pat and I took Will and Kim, his steady girlfriend, on a Caribbean Cruise on the giant ship, *Sovereign of the Seas*. This was Kim's first cruise, and she recently told us that she packed far more than was necessary in an attempt to be sure that she had anything that she might possibly need. For instance she packed 15 pairs of shoes! Rather than embarrass herself with the enormous amount of clothing she had brought, Kim attempted to pick times to open her luggage when Pat was away from their stateroom. Kim wasn't always successful in her approach, as one time Pat did come in just as Kim had taken out her 15 pairs of shoes and spread them on the bed thus revealing all 30 shoes to her roommate-soon-to-be-Mother-in-law. Shoes notwithstanding, the four of us had a marvelous time.

In 1994 Jack and Peggy Drerup, Bob and Jenny Kirkland, Barry and Lois White, and Pat and I took a Renaissance Cruise to the Greek Isles and the coast of Turkey. Our first day and night were spent at the Intercontinental Hotel in Athens. The Acropolis and Parthenon were breathtaking, and we enjoyed a trip along the coast to the Poseidon

Temple.   We boarded our ship and sailed for the Greek Islands, stopping at Santorini, Rhodes, Mykonos, and Patmos, and we called at Canakale and Kusadasi, where we bought five Turkish rugs, on the coast of Turkey.   Ephesus was unbelievably well preserved and enormously impressive, and the replica of the famed Trojan horse at the ruins of Troy was fascinating. The trip wound up with two days and nights in Istanbul where we stayed at the beautiful Conrad Hotel. The view of the Bosphorus from the lounge atop the hotel was spectacular. A fun group made this a great trip.

Our most recent cruise included Lolly and Don Bearden (our son-in-law who had never before cruised), Bob Thurmond (Pat's brother, of course), and Pat and me. This January 2003 Caribbean cruise was aboard the very nice *Sea Princess* and was a good one.

Chapter Twenty-One

Pi Kappa Alpha in Later Years

From the mid to late 60s until the mid 80s I was not very involved with Pi Kappa Alpha. Those years were spent pretty much exclusively working very hard in our business and helping Pat raise our family. (During busy seasons I often left home before the children got up and came home after they were sound asleep. Believe me, Pat deserves virtually all of the credit for raising three very fine children.). Nevertheless I had often daydreamed about getting our old Zeta gang together again. I had not laid eyes on most of them since college days and the thought of never again seeing many of these fellows was a most unpleasant prospect. After all, they were my best friends. To me the fraternity experience was an extraordinary one that, when practiced according to the Ritual, enabled fraternity brothers to become almost as close as blood brothers. To the uninitiated this phenomenon is impossible to explain.

In the summer of 1985 I decided to see if we could get together a reunion of us old Pikes from the 50s. I had addresses of 20 of them and daughter Patti had just graduated from Union City High School and had nothing in particular to do until she entered UT that fall. She could type and she went to work. We wrote those 20 men and heard from twelve of them very promptly saying they hoped a reunion could be organized for that fall. We went to work to accomplish that objective. We got addresses from Zeta Chapter, from PiKA National, and from the University. My old annuals and composite pictures enabled us to come up with other names of brothers who were lost. We wrote those with good addresses about these lost men and found, over a considerable period of time, almost all of them. Unfortunately several were deceased.

We planned our first reunion for Homecoming weekend of 1985 with headquarters at Knoxville's Holiday Inn World's Fair. 62 of the brothers and wives and dates attended. That Friday night many of us never left the banquet room for eight hours. It was a magical experience, almost as if those intervening 25 to 30 years, depending on graduation classes, had disappeared and we were once more at dear old 1305 West Clinch. During the course of the weekend we discovered that several of those present had never been initiated so we decided to reconvene the next fall and correct that situation. During Homecoming weekend of 1986, 46 of us gathered for another great reunion. We initiated, in what Pi Kappa Alpha calls Special Dispensation, five former pledges and a sixth posthumously. These fellows were very popular but either did not make their grades while pledges or transferred to other schools. But now they were brothers! The initiation took place in our old chapter room at 1305 West Clinch. For a number of years our old fraternity house had been operated as a rooming house of some sort. I slipped the manager a little cash to get the house cleared that Sunday morning, and the whole affair was a grand experience for old and new Pikes alike. Afterwards old pledge and new initiate Henry Davis and his wife, Nancy, gave me a lift to Nashville where Pat had gone on ahead with daughter, Patti, who was living there.

We then had smaller reunions in 1987 and 1988, and it became obvious that once every five years was often enough.

For several years George Campbell, who lived in Pennsylvania at the time, kept Super Group address records on his computer. When my company became computerized we took over this function. George's unselfish help was invaluable during those early years.

In 1990 we had a doozy of a reunion. 108 of the 50s era brothers came from 18 states. We had eight brothers in California, seven of whom came. Eight of the 50s Dream Girls came from all over the country, at our expense, with husbands in some cases. Five of these ladies, Fran Dominick Shackelford, Shirley Hendren Grant, Ginna Sanders Huddleston, Robbie Roberts Gray Willmarth, and Elaine Horton Sweeney were, and are, dear friends of mine. This was a happening the likes of which most of us had never experienced. To top off a marvelous weekend four more men were initiated in special dispensation, two former pledges, the son of a brother, and the son-in-law of a brother. One of the former pledges, Ron Lancaster, had been president of his Zeta pledge class. His older brothers, Bob and George Lancaster, both Zeta brothers, welcomed Ron into the brotherhood. In addition to being blood brothers, the three Lancasters were now also fraternity brothers. Wonderful! The initiation again took place at 1305 West Clinch in the old chapter room. I again greased the house manager's palm.

Son-in-law Rance Barnes, an Electrical Engineering graduate of The University of Tennessee, Knoxville, was not in a fraternity while at UT. We also initiated him in the 1990 initiation. He and I then drove from Knoxville together to Nashville where we met Pat, who had gone on ahead with Patti. Rance and I stopped in Lebanon to get gasoline and pulled in right behind a man who had a Pike sticker on his back window. He saw my fraternity pin and addressed me with the PiKA secret greeting and shook my hand with the fraternity grip. Rance must have thought the world was full of Pikes!

In 1995 107 of the brothers made their way to Knoxville. The featured attraction of this reunion was the recognition of Zeta brothers who had been varsity athletes. Zeta has had many Volunteer notables including football great All-American, Hall of Famer, NFL player, and long-time NFL coach John Michels; All-American, Hall of Famer, NFL player, and long-time college coach George Cafego (deceased); All-American and Hall of Famer Bob Suffridge (deceased); All-SEC and NFL great Jim Hill (deceased); All-SEC and college head coach Hal Littleford; and long-time NFL player and for 31 years the Color Man with John Ward on the Vol Network, Bill Anderson. John Michels has four Super Bowl rings, and Jim Hill wore an NFL championship ring. Wonder how many fraternity chapters have three brothers who are members of the College Football Hall of Fame? Zeta has had many varsity athletes among its ranks. In addition to football we have been represented in basketball, baseball, track, swimming, and tennis. Also two of the brothers, Gus Manning and Bob Davis, have worked for the UT Athletics Department for over 50 years each. Bob started at center on the 1951 National Championship team, and Gus started out as General Neyland's personal assistant. This grand reunion was climaxed by another moving initiation, this time of two fine old former pledges and the husband of one of Zeta's all time great Dream Girls.

70 of the brothers trekked to Knoxville for our 2000 reunion. Though it was a smaller group than the previous two reunions, many of the brothers thought this was the best one yet. The somewhat smaller numbers did afford us opportunities to spend more quality time with each other. David Fleming sat with me at the game which was a great opportunity for me to spend several hours with a great Brother. All the events were outstanding, and everyone left the Knoxville Hyatt Regency (where the last reunions have been held) with fraternal love in their hearts. Our special dispensation initiation brought two more former pledges and another son of a brother into the ranks of Pi Kappa Alpha. I am proud to say that we have now initiated 11 former pledges, all of whom were very popular undergraduates, another former pledge posthumously (I stood in for him, a great honor for me), two sons of brothers, and a son-in-law of a brother — 15 special dispensation initiates in all. That accomplishment is equally as important to me as the fact that I organized the Super Group in the first place.

Presently there are 152 brothers on my Super Group mailing list. 22 of the Super Groupers have died since our founding in 1985. 30 brothers whom I contacted, in most cases several times, simply had no interest. Some folks just don't care for reunions. The upshot of all this is that 204 of the brothers from our era were contacted. Of the 174 brothers who were interested in our doings, 136 of the brothers attended at least one reunion. The majority of those 136 attended several of our seven reunions. In addition, our getting together again has spawned dozens of mini-reunions that would not otherwise have happened. Examples are a trip Pat and I took to Naples, Florida two years ago during which we spent a good deal of time with Brothers Charles Lamb and Jack Puckett and their wives and Jack's daughter in their Naples homes. And on two occasions I have seen Dan Johnson, once with his wife, Linda, in California. Obviously many great old friendships have been rekindled.

The name SUPER GROUP seemed to me to be a "natural" as I became familiar with the unusual successes of our always diverse group. In addition to the varsity athletes earlier mentioned, we include several attorneys; two state senators, one of whom (Joe Haynes) is Chairman of the Democratic Caucus and one of whom is a Republican; several physicians, one of whom (David Stewart) helped treat Governor Connally at Dallas' Parkland Hospital on the day of the Kennedy assassination and who later worked on Lee Harvey Oswald after he was shot by Jack Ruby; several pharmacists (one of whom, Blair Harrison, followed his physician father into Zeta Chapter, and who was followed into PiKA by his son); several dentists; several Ph.D.s; several college professors (one of whom, recently retired John Davidson, is a loyal Super Grouper); an imminent psychiatrist at the world famous Menninger Clinic in Topeka (Jim Hasselle); a member of the Pi Kappa Alpha Supreme Council; a president of the Pi Kappa Alpha Educational Foundation; a former president of the UT National Alumni Association, as well as a former vice president of the same group (Malcolm Colditz); the CEO of a near-billion dollar company (Bob Hall) and vice presidents of several national and international firms (John R. Thomas, for example, was Senior Vice President of Associates Corporation of North America.); head of the Engine Division of Boeing Corporation (Granny Frazier); a novelist published by an international publishing house (Tim Sullivan); an oft-published poet (Bill Weller); president of a national engineering organization; several presidents of statewide organizations; mayors, aldermen, and county commissioners; the project engineer of what was to be the world's largest nuclear plant (Dick Swisher); Deputy Director of the California Department of Health; Assistant Secretary of Health and Welfare for the State of California; two brothers who held high positions of the Toastmasters Club, one being an international position; a man who had a great deal to do with bringing the first-ever school to a very remote area of southwest Texas (Tom Williams); a man who has lived in Memphis; Newport, RI; San Diego; Albuquerque; Concord, CA; Indian Harbor Beach, FL; Antigua, BWI; Trinidad, WI; Eleuthera, WI; Manitoba, Canada; San Salvador, WI; Meritt Island, FL; Las Vegas; Long Island; Northboro, MA; St. Mary, GA; Bay St. Louis, MS; and Estill Springs, TN for the third time (Mike McKinnon)!; presidents of country clubs, civic clubs, and great involvement and honors in church; university (UT and otherwise), civic, engineering, insurance, legal, health, and music circles; successful business ventures of all types imaginable (a good example of which would be John Drumheller's long time family business in Knoxville, Drumheller's, dealers in appliances, televisions, and video equipment, and audio equipment.); a self-employed truck freight broker (Bob Hambright); judges; several chambers of commerce presidents; chairman of a worldwide business forms organization; a highly decorated Ranger Company Commander in Vietnam who later served as a professor at the War College and who retired as a full Army colonel (Tom Johnson); a full Air Force colonel; several lieutenant colonels; an inventor, and I could go on and on ...No doubt the lessons learned at 1305 West Clinch have had a lot to do with all these success stories. There is no question in my mind but that any success I have enjoyed has been due in large part to the leadership training received at Zeta Chapter.

In the mid 80s it began to hit home with me that Will would soon be going to college, and I made contact with Zeta Chapter at UT and once again became involved with my chapter of Pi Kappa Alpha. Sure enough Will pledged Pike (which was discussed in an earlier chapter).

I served on the Zeta House Corporation Board for several years and took a leadership role in the very successful capital campaign for a total house renovation which took place in the mid 90s.

On August 7, 1989, I was invited to become a trustee of the Pi Kappa Alpha Educational Foundation. I served on this board from that point until the Atlanta convention of 2000, serving two-year terms each as secretary, treasurer, president-elect and president. For several years during my tenure on the board I served as chairman of PiKA's Annual Fund, now called our Pike Fund. I wrote handwritten letters to contributors of $200 - later $250 - or more. In the process I became good friends with several large contributors. Two in particular stand out: General Victor L. Cary of Houston, in whose home I have visited, and William C. (Wick) Watkins of Auburn, Alabama. I had the great good fortune to attend a fabulous Upsilon 50s reunion, organized by Wick. Chris Peters of the National Office accompanied me on both these memorable trips. These men are now among PiKA's greatest benefactors. My two presidential years were the most successful money-raising years in the history of the Foundation. In recent years I have attended conventions in Memphis, Chicago, Tampa, Kansas City, Toronto, Atlanta, and Palm Springs.

One time we Educational Foundation trustees had a meeting in Cincinnati at the home of long time trustee and past president of the Foundation and of the fraternity itself, Gary Menchhofer. Jeff Abraham, who ran the operations of the Foundation at the time, and I were able to get a commuter plane back to Memphis earlier than our scheduled flight, and we rode a bus out to the plane. We struck up a conversation with a man across the aisle from us who was a front man for the Harlem Globetrotters, and the conversation turned to Tennessee football. He asked me what Tennessee's chances were of recruiting the great high school quarterback, Peyton Manning, and I replied that it was probably a long shot. A young man about three spaces down from me said, "I'm Cooper Manning, Peyton's brother, and I have just been with him on his recruiting trip to Notre Dame. Peyton is extremely interested in Tennessee." Well, by George, we did get Peyton, and he was the best quarterback Tennessee ever had. Cooper, who had played football at Ole Miss until he was hurt, and I had parked side by side in the Memphis Airport parking lot, and we talked on the way to our cars. Having been convinced that there was a legitimate possibility that Peyton might become a Volunteer, my trip home was a pleasant one. This chance encounter was one of the neat little things that has occurred in my lifetime. After he was playing for the Colts I met Peyton on a Colts off weekend at the popular tailgate party adjacent to Neyland Stadium hosted by Will's in-laws, Eddie and Judy Oglesby. Pat and I had briefly talked with Archie, Peyton's father, several times at the Oglesbys' tailgates, well attended Saturday football events of many years standing, as well as at the UT parties given for Johnny Majors and John Michels, prior to their Hall of Fame inductions, at the Waldorf. One of the Oglesbys' friends is the sister of the famous actress and model, Andie MacDowell. She was at a tailgate party one time when we were all there. Andie was smitten with grandson Wilton, and she held him for a long time. Can't say as I blame her!

In 1994 at a luncheon at the Pike convention in Tampa, Florida Pi Kappa Alpha awarded Dad, posthumously, its highest honor, the

Order of West Range. I accepted this honor on his behalf; excerpts of my remarks on that occasion follow:

"Dad's family is truly a PiKA family, his older brother, his son, his grandson, his Dream Girl daughter, his son-in-law, a grandson-in-law, two nephews, one grand-nephew, and six cousins, 16 of us in all. His grandson, my son Will, was president of his very fine 1990 Zeta pledge class (of 32 pledges, all made their grades and were initiated after the first semester). Dad had pinned the PiKA badge on me in 1953. I felt Dad's presence when I pinned the Shield and Diamond on Will in 1991. Will has followed Dad's footsteps — all the way to the Supreme Council. Dad would have been overwhelmed with pride. I am.

Tom W. Wade was a loyal man. When he decided something was right for him, he never changed his mind: His God, his church, his family, his horned Hereford cattle, cotton, strawberries, The University of Tennessee, Pi Kappa Alpha. Most assuredly, his love for Pi Kappa Alpha came right behind family in the pecking order of his loyal ties. He was an unsung hero of Pi Kappa Alpha, always doing what he could do, usually behind the scenes, for the betterment of his beloved fraternity.

Certainly Dad's accomplishments do not approach the significance of those of many of the present and previous recipients of the Order of West Range. But in my heart I know that no other recipient of this wonderful honor ever loved Pi Kappa Alpha more deeply, nor more unselfishly than did my Dad. He was Phi Phi Kappa Alpha personified. To me, Tom Wilton Wade, my hero, will always be the quintessential Pike."

That evening at a convention banquet I received the 1994 Pi Kappa Alpha Loyalty Award which was a total surprise to me. Though three of my Zeta brothers, Bill Taylor, who was S.M.C. when I pledged, Roger Bradley, who was president of my pledge class, and Dave McSween, my pledge brother, were there for Dad's Order of West Range induction, they had actually come to the convention to see me accept the Loyalty Award. Dad's award was a bonus for them, as they knew and highly respected Dad. What great friends Roger, Dave, and Bill are!

Working on the PiKA Educational Foundation board with Pat Haynes and with his predecessor, Jeff Abraham, has been one of the highlights of my life. These two brothers were absolutely great to work with, as were these trustees: Jerry Askew, Knoxville; Richard Blatt, Chicago; Joe Brown, Kansas City; Marvin Dennis, Hillsborough, California; Phillip Goodman, Ponte Vedra Beach; Bram Govaars, Newport Beach; Garth Grissom, Denver; Craig Hoenshell, New York; Tom Husselman, Zionsville, Indiana; Bill LaForge, Washington, D.C.; Phillip Lighty, Burlingame, California; John Lisher, Indianapolis; Stanley Love, Denver; Rick McKinney, San Angelo, Texas; John McNair, Winston Salem; Gary Menchhofer, Cincinnati; Lynn Mulherin, Omaha; Bill Nester, Cincinnati; Richard Ogle, Birmingham; Ron Roark, Columbus, Ohio; Tom Tillar, Blacksburg, Virginia; Joe Turner, Clemson, South Carolina; Tommy Turner, Lubbock; and Bruce Wolfson, Scarsdale, New York. I consider these men to be among my very best friends. Good friends, John Bobango of Memphis; Pat Halloran also of Memphis; Richard Jackson (fellow Zeta brother) Columbia, South Carolina; and former U.S. Congressman, Ed Pease, Terre Haute, Indiana, came on the board right after my tenure.

Pat Haynes and I twice, and then my Pat and I spent time in Phil and June Lighty's lovely home in Burlingame. Phil and Miss June (an AOPi!) are great friends of ours and extraordinary benefactors of Pi Kappa Alpha. It is indeed an honor to have partnered with Phil to help make the Lighty-Wade Courtyard possible for our PiKA Headquarters in Memphis.

Two other Super Groupers have been heavily involved with Pi Kappa Alpha. Dan McGehee served two terms as National Counsel and two terms as a National Vice President on the Supreme Council. Dan has long been Zeta Chapter Alumnus Advisor and was selected as the fraternity's top advisor in 2002. Howard Hinds has served for several years as National Chaplain, a position that requires his attendance at many national meetings.

In 1994 I decided to organize a Northwest Tennessee PiKA Alumni Chapter. In talking with Pike alumnus and close friend Hamilton Parks of Trimble he reminded me that there was a dormant area chapter, The Reelfoot Alumni Chapter of the Pi Kappa Alpha

Fraternity, so we decided to revive that charter. Three of the signatories were original charter members, the others, including Dad, having passed on to their rewards. These three were Hardy Moore Graham, William Hamilton Parks II, and Winston Frederick Tipton. 61 additional alumni signed the charter, and these men elected me president. At the 1996 convention in Kansas City our chapter was named the outstanding chapter in North America. We had come a long way in a hurry. Fortunately Hamilton had kept all the old records, minutes, etc. which he passed along to me. Hamilton, Brother Graham, and his son, Hardy P. Graham, each bought benches in the new Lighty-Wade Courtyard at the Pi Kappa Alpha headquarters in Memphis. Hamilton dedicated his to the memory of my Dad. For this, we Wades will always be deeply indebted to Hamilton. Again, Phil Lighty and I donated the courtyard pavilion.

At an Officers Leadership Academy in Memphis a few years ago, famous PiKA coach of the Florida State Seminoles, Bobby Bowden, was presented with our Order of West Range. I shook his hand afterwards and talked with him briefly, telling him that if Tennessee did not win the National Championship that fall I would be pulling for Florida State to win it. He thanked me and told me, obviously referring to our very successful coach, Philip Fulmer, "You're in good hands." A couple of years later we played Florida State in the Fiesta Bowl for the National Championship and won!

At the 2001 Officers Leadership Academy in Memphis Dr. Gordon Gee was given the fraternity's number one honor, its Distinguished Service Award. Dr. Gee is presently Chancellor (President) of Vanderbilt University. Dr. Gee graduated from the University of Utah and has been president of West Virginia University, The University of Colorado, Brown University, and Ohio State University. I went up on the podium afterwards and introduced myself and told him that I was serving on The University of Tennessee Presidential Search Advisory Committee and wondered if he was happy at Vanderbilt. He started to tell me how much he liked Nashville, etc. when he abruptly stopped and said, "I walked right into that one didn't I?" We two had a good laugh. Dr. Gee is an enormously likeable and impressive man.

Pi Kappa Alpha has been an extraordinarily important part of the lives of many of us Wades. Uncle Eugene Wade was initiated at Tennessee in 1905 and was President of Zeta Chapter. Dad was initiated at UT in 1917 and was President of Zeta. I was initiated at Zeta in 1953 and was President of the Chapter. Son Will was initiated into Zeta in 1991 and was twice Vice President of the Chapter. My sister Sally was Dream Girl of Tau Chapter at North Carolina and was runner-up to the National Dream Girl. She married Pitt Tomlinson III who was president of our chapter at Emory University. My first cousin, Eugene Wade, Jr. was president of our chapter at North Carolina State. Another first cousin, Peter Pelham was initiated at Zeta and transferred to Mississippi Southern where he became president of the chapter there. As earlier told, my son-in-law, Rance Barnes is a Zeta special initiate. Seven other cousins have been Pikes at Tennessee, Tennessee Martin, the University of Memphis, and Florida Southern. Sixteen of us in all! And to this point I have five grandsons. No telling how many of us will eventually be initiated into the ranks of PiKA, all of which started with Uncle Eugene, Dad's brother, in 1905. Wouldn't he be amazed if he knew what he started?

On October 16, 2001 Pat Haynes, who most capably manages the affairs of the Pi Kappa Alpha Educational Foundation, called me with the exciting news that the Foundation had tapped me for membership in the Fraternity's Order of West Range, our Fraternity's highest honor for an alumnus. I was inducted into the Order on August 4, 2002 at the Palm Springs Convention. It was my distinct honor to have been inducted with the following great PiKAs: John W. Hein of Huntington Beach, California was a PiKA at the University of Southern California where he was a Phi Beta Kappa. His roommate in the Pike house was Fess Parker of Davy Crockett fame. John was one of PiKA's first traveling secretaries, now known as chapter consultants. He and I were good friends when I was in school and afterwards, and he and Dad were also good friends. Until retirement John was Director of the Metropolitan Water District of Southern California, obviously an awesome responsibility. What a pleasure to have been a part of John's Order of West Range class!

Kenneth W. Lowe is the President and C.E.O. of the E. W. Scripps Company, a *Fortune 500* media company founded in 1878. Scripps owns 21 newspapers including *The Memphis Commercial Appeal*, which I read every day, and *The Knoxville News-Sentinel*, which I read every day as an undergraduate at UT. Scripps also owns ten TV stations, Scripps Howard News Service, United Media, and 31 Websites. They have just bought controlling interest in the Shop at Home Network. Ken founded Home and Garden Television (HGTV), Fine Living, Food Network, and Do It Yourself Network, all four networks being now owned by Scripps. Ken and Pat had a great conversation at a party the night before our induction about these networks, two of which, HGTV and Do It Yourself, are probably Pat's favorite TV watching. Ken was at Tau Chapter at North Carolina. I told him about Sally's having been their Dream Girl and about cousin Bill Bevis' being a member of Tau.

Fellow inductee, Kenneth W. Simonds and his lovely wife, Sally, hosted a party for dignitaries (the writer excepted!) in their lovely home in Indian Wells which adjoins Palm Springs. Ken was a Pike at East Tennessee State and is good friends with Super Groupers Jay Searcy and Joe Taylor. Ken played football at State for Coach Hal Littleford, another Super Grouper! After a distinguished career at IBM Ken was named Executive Vice President of Amdahl Corporation in 1975. In 1985 he became President and C.O.O. for Teradata Corporation. Though officially retired Ken and his family are involved in several pursuits including ownership of a golf course in the Palm Springs area.

Rigdon O. "Rick" Dees is a nationally known entertainer and radio personality who lives in the San Fernando Valley. Our family happened to see his star on the internationally famous "Hollywood Walk of Fame" while in Los Angeles prior to going to Palm Springs. Rick wrote and recorded *"Disco Duck"* which became a runaway hit, selling 6 million copies, and which won for him a People's Choice Award. His radio shows have made Rick Dees a recognized name across America. I told him about how popular he was in my part of the world when he was with WHBQ in Memphis. Amazingly enough Rick and Ken Lowe were roommates at Tau Chapter and still count themselves as best friends. What a twosome!

Receiving the Order of West Range along with these four men was a humbling and most gratifying experience. There is no honor that I would rather have received.

Pi Kappa Alpha has been an important part of my life for 50 years. Joining Dad in the Order of West Range made it even more meaningful to me. We are the Order's first father-son combination.

Chapter Twenty-Two

UT in Later Years

Very soon after graduation from UT the Obion County UT Alumni Association elected me president of our local alumni chapter. One day Tom Elam, a longtime UT trustee and chairman of the UT Athletics Board, called to tell me that General Robert Neyland, storied Vol coach, was to be in town the next night. Saying that the General's health was deteriorating, Colonel Elam asked me to get together an alumni reception for him the next evening adding that this would probably be Neyland's last visit. I did, and it was. This was my first task on behalf of the University of Tennessee Alumni Association. Others would follow.

Some years later I was again elected president of our county alumni association. After my term ended our alumni chapter nominated me for our area's position on the UT Alumni Association Board of Governors. I was elected, on the second try, and spent many years on the board.

At a board meeting in Chattanooga in 1979 I was asked to assume the presidency of the UT National Alumni Association. I declined but the next day I called my good friend and PiKA brother from UTM, present Chancellor of the University of Tennessee at Martin, Nick Dunagan, and accepted. (Nick was one of the three-man committee which had asked me to serve.) I became president-elect in 1980, president in 1981, and National Chairman of Annual Giving in 1982.

My year as president of the alumni association involved spending all or part of 101 days away from home and traveling over 57,000 miles for and with the university. It was a hard but fun year. After my year as alumni president I automatically served a year as National Chairman for Annual Giving. My undergraduate days at the university and my alumni activities since have been most rewarding. In later years I was chairman of the national gifts phase of the 21st Century Campaign, a capital campaign headed by Bill Stokely in which we raised $433 million against an original goal of $250 million. $99 million was raised in my part of the campaign. About 20 years ago I served on a search committee for a vice president for the UT Institute of Agriculture. In 2001 I served on the search advisory committee for a new president for the University of Tennessee. Dr. John Shumaker was the popular choice. (Sadly, a year later Dr. Shumaker resigned because of some apparent improprieties.)

The University of Tennessee National Alumni Association is considered one of the best and most effective in the South, if not the best, and one of the extreme top associations in the nation. The reason is simple – the people. David Roberts, who along with his wife, Mary – Kate to many now – are among Pat's and my closest friends. David has run the association for many years. His long-time assistant, Lofton Stuart, an old West Tennessee boy, is as nice a person as one could ever know. Others in the alumni office who have been extraordinarily nice to Pat and me through the years are Bob Carroll, Steve Catlett, Betsy Child, Jacky Gullett and his wife, Nell, Carol Kirkland (a former Union Citian whose husband, Ron Kirkland, also a former Union Citian, was a recent UT National Alumni president), Becky Little (president of AOPi when Pat was in school; her husband is Super Grouper Joe Little whose father was a long ago UT National Alumni president; their PiKA son, Ford, has handled legal matters for us in Knoxville); Martha Massengill, Barbara McAdams, Susie Orr, Jeanna Swafford, and Kerry Witcher (with whom I worked closely in the last UT capital campaign).

Close friends who worked in UT Development are Charlie Brakebill, John Sheridan, and Jack Williams. We also know and admire their wives, Joyce, Carol, and Carolyn, respectively. Charlie headed this enormously successful operation, Jack heads it now, and John headed up the 21st Century Campaign which raised $433 million for UT.

In my opinion the main reason why UT has had such successful alumni and development operations has been the administration's dedication to these programs. Presidents Ed Boling, Lamar Alexander, Joe Johnson, and Eli Fly were proponents of alumni and development, and Pat and I consider these men and Carolyn Boling, Pat Johnson, and Catherine Fly our close friends. These four men fit admirably into the mold first created by Andy Holt.

Some of the living former UT Alumni National presidents and their spouses who have been important parts of our lives are Tom and Pattye Barnes, Howard and Barbara Bozeman, Dick and Nancy Cardin, Alan and Jean Cates, Floyd and Joann Crain, Gary and Betty Doble, Lew and Mary Jo Dougherty, Woody Forbes, Jim and Jo Hall, Jeannie and Jim Hastings, Barbara and Bob Higgs, Leonard and Nancye Hines, Lyle and Carolyn Key, Ron and Carol Kirkland, T. O. and Carol Lashlee, Hal Littleford, Ed Townsend, Betty and Kay Whaley, Bill and Patsy Williams, Tandy and Dai Wilson, and Hunter and Sylvia Wright. It is a delight to see these people most Aprils at the annual Past Presidents Council meeting.

I am a charter member of the board of directors of the UT Foundation which was organized in 2001 to further the interests of The University of Tennessee. Other directors of the Foundation are Neal Allen, Jim Ayers, Mark Dean, Jim Haslam (chairman), Ben Kimbrough, Fran Marcum, Ned McWherter, Clayton McWhorter, Sharon Miller, Bill Sansom, and Bill Stokely. Lamar Alexander resigned after being elected to the United States Senate, and Howard Baker resigned after being named Ambassador to Japan. How in the world did they ever pick me to be a member of this board? Beats me. The Foundation was set up to receive property, stocks, bonds, unrestricted cash gifts, and other types of gifts to the university for the purposes of creating scholarships, professorships, and endowments for the benefit of the students, professors, and other needs of the university. Eli Fly, originally from Milan, long-time executive vice president and then president of The University of Tennessee, is president of The Foundation. Eli and Catherine are old friends of ours, and he is an absolute delight to work with. He continually brings most attractive proposals to the board. There is no question but that The Foundation will be a great asset to a great university.

Following are some excerpts from an article entitled "Tom Wade: UT is a Family Commitment" which appeared in the fall, 1986, *Tennessee Alumnus*:

"Tom Wade's term as National Alumni Association president ... he received more than 700 letters from the alumni office during his year as president (1981-82) ... he spent 101 days away from his Union City, Tennessee home, ... he traveled 57,000 miles, including two international tours with alumni groups ... My primary interests (outside of family and business) have been UT alumni work and my fraternity, Pi Kappa Alpha ... a leadership role in the National Alumni Association is ... a three-year commitment — not just one year as president, and the following year as national chairman of annual giving. Wade agrees that there almost has to be an emotional attachment to an organization to motivate one to devote so much time and energy to it. 'There has to be some innate love of the institution,' he says. 'My whole family has gone to UT Knoxville, starting with my uncle in 1905. It's a tradition. There's no question about where we go to college.' Wade's ties to his college years are probably stronger than most. Last year he organized a reunion of Pi Kappa Alpha fraternity brothers from the classes of the mid-50s at UTK. The experience was profound. 'We met for a social hour and dinner in Knoxville, and many of us didn't leave the room for eight hours. I was really proud of getting that group together, and we're going to try to do it every five years for as long as we're able.' Lasting relationships mean a lot to Wade, and his relationship to the University of Tennessee is holding strong. He has confidence in the University academically, ... athletically, ... and alumni association-wise ('The single most important strength of the alumni association is the support of the University administration.') ... he was dedicated to doing a good job."

During my term as alumni president, UTK's and UTC's homecomings were on the same weekend. After I made a half time presentation on the 50-yard line of Neyland Stadium in Knoxville, the alumni staff carried me to the airport for a quick flight to Chattanooga to do the same at their later starting game. It so happened that Roy Acuff, possibly the most famous country music singer of all time, had been in Knoxville for the half time show and he and his nephew rode on the UT plane with me to Chattanooga. He was then flown home to Nashville, and the plane came back to Chattanooga to pick us up and take us back to Knoxville. On the way down from Knoxville to

Chattanooga I said something like, "Mr. Acuff, it is a great thrill for me to be riding on this plane with you. As a child I listened to the *Grand Ole Opry* on Saturday nights, and you've always been one of my heroes. When I get home and tell my children that I was on the plane with you and talked to you they simply won't believe it." Mr. Acuff said, "Your name is Tom, ain't it?" to which I replied, "Yes." He then said, "Give me that program," (the Tennessee football program in my hand) and he wrote on the center spread, "Tom was there and so was I. Sincerely, Roy Acuff." Upon arrival home and showing the program to my children they said, almost in one voice, "Who is Roy Acuff?" Obviously, unlike their Dad, Lolly, Patti, and Will were not country music fans.

During my presidency of the National Alumni Association I saw a Tennessee-Kentucky basketball game in UT's Stokely Center. I sat in President Ed Boling's box between Dr. Boling and Governor Lamar Alexander and enjoyed conversations with both. UT won! I remember hitting Dr. Boling (much too hard) on his back and yelling, "We beat Kentucky!" with the emphasis on "Ken."

In the early 80s Johnny Majors invited me to stand on the sidelines of a Tennessee-Vanderbilt game in Vanderbilt Stadium. Vanderbilt never has been known for their bands, but they pulled a stunt that day which is one that I often think about and tell people about. Just before the kickoff, half of the band came running out onto the field holding a long narrow banner that read, "Vanderbilt Culture." Right on their heels the rest of the band came running out with a banner that read, "Tennessee Agriculture." They thought they were insulting us Tennessee fans, but they tickled this one Volunteer half to death.

Pat and I enjoy going to Knoxville most years for the spring football Orange and White game and our annual Past Presidents (of the UT National Alumni Association) Council meeting. One year when Lamar Alexander was president of The University of Tennessee he challenged us former alumni presidents to come up with a concise phrase to describe UT and its myriad of functions. I came home and thought and thought and finally wrote Lamar and suggested "Lamar's One-Stop College." He wrote back, "The idea of 'Lamar's One-Stop College' would probably make a lot of sense to about half the people and a lot of nonsense to the other half! It's probably a lot clearer than anything I could come up with ... Hope the strawberries are coming in good."

I was a charter member of The Volunteer Alumni Network (VAN), a group of UTK alumni who recruit top scholastic students for The University of Tennessee at Knoxville. After a year or so I suggested we have a party for top high school students from Obion County and adjoining counties at our home. We had such a party, and it was a big success. Since then this approach has been the norm, and countless parties have been held in homes of UTK alumni across Tennessee and in other states.

One time Pat and I hosted the UT Development Council in our home. Then Governor Lamar Alexander (later to become president of UT, Secretary of Education in the first Bush Administration, viable presidential candidate, and United States Senator), UT president Boling, future UT president Joe Johnson, and many other dignitaries from the business world and other pursuits were there. We hosted the council another time when Governor Sundquist, UT president Joe Johnson, future UT president Eli Fly, and several giants of international business and industry were there. Among the many important American executives at our house was John W. Snow, chairman, president and CEO of CSX Corporation, the giant railroad company. Snow has been chairman of the influential Business Roundtable, an association of chief executives of major corporations, and is now Secretary of the Treasury in the George W. Bush Administration. We are honored to have hosted members of two U. S. cabinets. We have hosted UT presidents Boling, Johnson, and Fly and their wives, Carolyn, Pat, and Catherine on several occasions at 2022 Stonewall. UTM chancellors Larry McGehee, Charles Smith, Margaret Perry, and Nick Dunagan and their spouses, Betsy, Shawna Lee, Randy, and Cathy, and past UTK chancellors Bill Snyder and Jack Reese and their wives, Margaret and Nancy, have also been in our home.

One time at a UT Board of Governors meeting in Gatlinburg I was sitting behind Larry McGehee and UTK chancellor Jack Reese. Larry doodled constantly and doodled well. I leaned forward and asked him to sign the doodle he was working on which he had aptly entitled, "The

Great Seal of the Federal Bureaucracy." He and Jack chuckled, and he agreed. Someone else having overheard our exchange asked for his next one. I leaned forward again and said, "Don't let him have it. If you start giving them to every Tom, Dick, and Harry who asks, you'll diminish the value of mine." Larry and Jack got a kick out of this.

Larry over the years while he was chancellor at Martin gave me several more doodles, some in color. Unbeknownst to Larry, Pat and I had all of them framed, and we hung them in our family room. We had a going away party for Larry and his lovely wife, Betsy, prior to their leaving UTM and going to Wofford College in South Carolina. Well into the party Larry finally noticed all the framed doodles and he literally let out a piercing scream.

A few years ago Larry sent me some strawberry stationery. He designed it on his computer, and it is very clever. The logo is red, green, and black and features a man and woman picking strawberries with birds flying above, one of which is perched on the head of the man. At the bottom is the following quotation which we have long featured on one of our strawberry signs: "Doubtless God could have made a better berry, but doubtless God never did — English author William Butler (1535-1618)." This is a marvelous and accurate quote.

Larry's syndicated column, "Southern Seen," appears in our hometown newspaper, *The Messenger*, regularly and we enjoy reading those excellent writings of a truly scholarly man.

Between 25 and 30 years ago I started the tradition of an Obion County UT alumni bus trip to a football game each fall. This carried on for over 20 years before playing out. Dr. Jeff Triplett organized a bus trip to the Arkansas game in the fall of 2001, the first alumni chapter trip in several years. The first bus trip I organized was for a Knoxville football game weekend. Martha (Marty) Clendenin, Mary Jewel (Sapphire) Critchlow, Jody (Jo Jo) Hansen, and Pat (Trish) wore cute little waitress outfits and served food and libations on the trip to Knoxville. Mother always called Mary, Sapphire, from that point on. We stayed at the old Campus Inn on the edge of the UT campus. At one point on Saturday morning before the game several of us were in their bar. I started whistling to a song on the jukebox as I sometimes do, when this unattached girl came up to me and said, "You must have been eatin' birdseed." Ever since then some of the people who were there, Critchlow included, have on occasion called me Birdseed. That night we had dinner at Knoxville's City Club, and coming out of the club afterwards Pat's brother, Bob Thurmond, fell and broke his arm. It was an eventful weekend from start to finish. We charged $99 per couple $49 for singles for the weekend including the bus, food and drink on the bus and in the hospitality room of the hotel, the hotel rooms for two nights, and game tickets. The last full blown Obion County UT Alumni Association trip cost $500 or so per couple.

The single best party I have ever attended in my life was during a bus trip to Birmingham in our hotel's dining room after a loss to Alabama. We reserved a section of their dining room, and they set us up with a "U" shaped table. David Critchlow went straight to the center of the head table, poured the rolls out of the basket, placed the basket upside down on his head, and proclaimed that he was "king" of the group which he said was "no more than I deserve!" Turner Kirkland slid down off his chair and started crawling around underneath the heavily draped tables pinching the legs of the ladies. There were some shocked ladies sitting at those tables. Critchlow joined him. A very good looking blonde lady, an Alabama fan, also crawled under the tables, pinching legs of the men. At one point Turner turned around and to his great surprise ran smack into that lovely lady. And she was a beauty.

Rita Winter, who sings like an angel, sang *Summertime* as beautifully as it has ever been sung. Then our waiter, a big older black man with a deep bass voice, sang an extraordinary rendition of *Ole Man River*. Much champagne was ordered. Every single thing that happened at that dinner was as if it had been written for a movie script. It was the perfect party. Afterwards Critchlow went to his room, locked the door, and fell into a deep sleep, deep enough that his lovely wife, Mary, could not rouse him. She knocked on Pat's and my door, and we let her sleep on our second bed. This, incidentally, was the second time that Mary had spent the night in our room on a bus trip. David, after a good party, was a mighty sound sleeper.

We had many fun bus trips through the years. Attorney Bill Acree, now Judge Acree, when he was Obion County alumni president, started an award for bus trips entitled "Ass of the Year," the prize being a trophy fashioned as the back half of a donkey. Some of us normally fairly reserved people won it. Sometimes somebody would set out to win it and they were hard to beat.

Some of my other involvements with UT alumni work include having been awarded UTK Chancellor's Citation; having served a three year term on the UT Athletics Board; having served two different terms on the UT Development Council; having served three separate terms on the UTM Development Committee, once as its chairman; having served as Northwest Tennessee chairman for a UT Institute of Agriculture capital campaign.

As this book goes to print, Joe Johnson has once again assumed the presidency of UT, Eli Fly has temporarily moved back to the position of Executive Vice President and CFO of UT, Robert Harrill will temporarily manage the affairs of the UT Foundation, and Lofton Stuart has become Dr. Johnson's assistant.

The University of Tennessee has done a great deal for my family and me, and I think it's incumbent upon us to repay, to some degree, those institutions that have meant so much to us. My efforts on behalf of The University of Tennessee have been repaid many fold.

Chapter Twenty-Three

A Volunteer

I have always been a Volunteer, even after my UT days. Some of the positions and awards that have come my way follow.

Kenton's 1983 Man of the Year; member Kenton Lions Club; (several Rotarians have asked me through the years to consider joining Union City's Rotary Club. The time constraints of my business made it impractical, though I would have enjoyed that group very much); president of the Obion County Industrial Development Board; 1986 Obion County Conservation Farmer of the Year; member Union City Jaycees; president of Union City's Poplar Meadows Country Club; vice president of the Obion County Chamber of Commerce; University of Tennessee and Pi Kappa Alpha alumni involvements; member of Governor Sundquist's Council on Agriculture and Forestry; member of the Tennessee Board for Economic Growth; alternate delegate to the White House Conference on Small Business; twice president of the Tennessee Ginners Association; ginner, and later producer delegate to the National Cotton Council; Tennessee member of the National Cotton Council's Producers Steering Committee; chairman of the Tennessee delegation to the National Cotton Council; alternate director of Cotton, Inc.; director of the Southern Ginners Association; charter president of the Tennessee Grain and Feed Association; vice chairman of the Gibson County Railroad Authority; director and chairman of the board of First State Bank and vice chairman and later chairman of the Executive Committee of Community First Bancshares; member McCallie School (Chattanooga) Board of Trustees; 1997 McCallie Alumni Achievement Award; 2000 Cotton Carnival President's Award for Service to the Mid-South.

In this chapter I will elaborate on some of the above and recount some of the more interesting and amusing things that have happened to me.

In 1974 the National Cotton Council selected me to be the alternate Cotton Producers Steering Committee member from Tennessee. At the 1974 convention in St. Louis, due to the illness of Tennessee's Producers Steering Committee delegate, I was chosen to go on a cotton export trade mission to the Orient which was to be paid for by Elanco, a large agricultural chemical company. One delegate from each cotton producing state as well as the president of Cotton Council International and a National Cotton Council employee, the editors or publishers of each major farm and cotton publication, and three or four representatives from Elanco were invited.

With the exception of the writer it was a powerful group of men, several of whom later ascended to the presidency of the National Cotton Council. In fact we soon referred to ourselves as the Super Group, a moniker which eleven years later was also deemed appropriate for our 50s era Tennessee Pi Kappa Alpha reunion group. I have been a part of two genuine, in my judgment, Super Groups. My roommate on the trip to the Orient was a hard driving, hard drinking man from Georgia. After a first orientation night in Chicago we flew to Anchorage on Northwest Orient (now Northwest Airlines) where we stopped to refuel before heading on to Tokyo. My roomie told me, as we were flying high above the ice fields and glaciers of Alaska, that he had been up there the previous week in his jet. I was amazed when he told me that he had a great deal of stock in Texaco and that he was up there with some Texaco executives. It was also amazing to hear that he was farming 20,000 acres of cotton.

We checked into the Imperial Hotel in Tokyo and he and I, badly jet lagged, talked for some time prior to drifting off to sleep. It was at this time that he told me about having been grievously injured in Europe during World War II. He said he was in hospitals for a long time and was the only soldier ever to be awarded the Congressional Medal of Honor on foreign soil by a sitting U.S. President, Harry Truman. We had meetings in Tokyo in the U.S. Embassy, actually in their bombproof room where they kept sensitive records. One day we drove through the Japanese countryside visiting small farms of only an acre or two and a cattle feeding operation where the steers were fed beer and given manual rubdowns. We were told that the land sold for

$100,000 per acre! That day at lunch we ate at a traditional restaurant where we were served by geishas. Then we caught the bullet train to Osaka, stopping for a tour of Kyoto and speeding through Nagoya. The man who was the National Cotton Council's representative on the trip, a most attractive and pleasant individual, regaled us with stories of when he had been in the Army of Occupation after World War II and his experiences in the cleaning up of Nagoya Harbor. He was an officer and had a good deal of responsibility in this Herculean effort. We stayed in the Osaka Royale which was a fabulous hotel with a creek wandering through the lobby.

From Osaka we flew to Taipei, Taiwan where we stayed in the President Hotel, a nice enough hotel but nothing like the Grand Hotel where we had dinner one night. We were told that the unbelievably ornate Grand Hotel belonged to Madame Chiang Kai-Chek. While in Taipai we visited the National Museum. When Chiang Kai-Chek was forced off the mainland he took with him most of the movable treasures of China. This museum was enormous and impressive. They said that only 5% of its inventory was on display at any given time. On my trip to mainland China 24 years later in 1998, (Pat did not want to go) we saw no really impressive museums. Obviously Chiang Kai-Chek was very thorough in moving a great portion of history's important Chinese art and antiquities to Taiwan.

From Taipai we flew to Hong Kong where we stayed in the Hyatt Regency in Kowloon (I walked through its lobby while in Hong Kong in 1998). My shopping in this shopper's mecca would have done Pat proud! Dirty clothes were mailed home in order to make room for my Chinese purchases.

In each country we entertained and were entertained by cotton mill people and customers for U.S. cotton. We were in embassies and consulates and stayed in fine hotels and ate in great restaurants everywhere we went. We enjoyed a large number of ten course meals with numerous sake and rice wine toasts. We were treated like royalty and we thought that we represented American agriculture, specifically the American cotton industry, pretty doggone well.

At our final banquet in Hong Kong awards were given out. For rooming with my Georgia buddy I was awarded the Chinese

Congressional Medal of Honor which is draped over my photo of our Super Group which hangs in my office. This was one of the truly great parties I have ever in my life attended. (In later years another man from Georgia who was on the trip and who later served as deputy secretary of agriculture in the Carter Administration told me that he searched the Congressional Medal of Honor records in the Library of Congress and that our friend's name did not appear in them. I also later learned that he had no stock in Texaco and farmed about 2,000 acres of cotton.). Our room in the Hong Kong Hyatt Regency had a mini-bar. When we left our room the morning after the party the mini-bar was totally cleaned out. Roomie told me that he had paid for all the booze he drank from it. In checking out, the hotel presented me the bill for the entire contents of the bar, $75.00 or so which was a fair amount of money in 1974.

Roomie continued the party all the way from Hong Kong to Seattle. While we were in the customs line he simply slid down to the floor, out cold. The Elanco folks made arrangements to get him to a local hospital where he stayed for two or three days. He told me in a later conversation that he had to borrow $5.00 from a man in his hospital ward in order to pay for a cab to go to the airport and fly home to Georgia. This unforgettable character had spent lots of money, buying such major things as a full dining room suite, and he arrived in the good old U.S. of A. penniless.

I didn't arrive in such good shape myself after having contracted some sort of Asian flu or something on the plane and being as sick as a dog on the flight home. After arriving in Memphis I checked into a motel and had the worst night of my life with all sorts of demons and weird things in my crazy dreams. Sure enough I had to spend three weeks in Kenton with Mother and Dad. We were afraid for me to be around our children. One day Pat brought Will, who was two years old, down to see me. Will ran toward me but Pat held him back. Not hugging him was a very hard thing to do. That low-grade fever hung on for those three weeks and finally went away. How great it was to finally get back to my own home and family.

Once at a National Cotton Council convention in Phoenix in 1975 or 1976, in the early evening after all the day's business was completed,

I was having a drink with a friend in one of the hotel bars. Jimmy Carter was just beginning his campaign for the Presidency and my old Georgia roommate from the trip to the Orient had invited Jimmy and his wife Rosalynn out to the convention as his guests to stay in his hotel suite. He had reserved a meeting room for a little rally for Jimmy, and he was having trouble getting up a crowd. At that point nobody knew much about Carter though he was an announced candidate for the Presidency, so my old roomie came into the bar and asked my other buddy and me to come to the rally. To accommodate him, we did. Rosalynn was sitting at a card table printing name cards for the attendees while Jimmy was shaking hands and talking with the folks. There were probably 40 or 50 people there and Jimmy stood up on a straight chair and made a very short talk. Afterwards I shook his hand again and told him I was very much interested in seeing how this thing came along for him. He said he was, too. On the way back to the bar I put my arm around the shoulder of my buddy and said, "That son-of-a-gun has just about as much chance of being elected President as I do." Nobody has ever accused me of being a political pundit! Five years or so after his Presidency Jimmy came to The University of Tennessee at Martin, and his plane flew into and out of the Union City airport. The word got out that he would be leaving the airport at a certain time one night, and I took daughter Patti and son Will out there in hopes that we could shake his hand. Sure enough he shook the hands of everybody out there. I told him about having met him in Phoenix and he remembered the occasion. He's the only President with whom I have shaken hands.

Another time when at a Cotton, Inc. meeting in Dallas I had spent a good deal of time in the break room talking to another director. At one point this alternate director from Mississippi sidled over to us and said, "I declare, I do believe you two is steady breakin'." We had to admit that he was pretty much right.

I was charter president of the Tennessee Grain and Feed Association. There were twelve of us who organized the new association and they elected me to be their first president. Our office sent out the mailing and did the banking until we merged with a livestock feed organization, Tennessee Feed Dealers Association, and the new entity was called the Tennessee Feed and Grain Association. Many small grain dealers have dropped by the wayside as larger and larger dealers have come to dominate the grain business, and the association now is geared primarily to the feed industry.

Tennessee Governor Don Sundquist asked me to be a member of his Council on Agriculture and Forestry in 1995. This ad-hoc committee met often over the course of nine months, and, in my opinion we did some good things for Tennessee agriculture. Tennessee's most capable Commissioner of Agriculture at the time, Dan Wheeler, an old friend of mine from UT Alumni Board of Governors days, orchestrated our doings. His lieutenant, Joe Gaines, an extraordinarily capable Tennessee Department of Agriculture officer, was in charge of our day to day activities. Our nine months culminated with a highly successful Governor's Conference on Agriculture and Forestry in May, 1996. Several commissioners of agriculture attended our conference. I was privileged to sit next to a very sharp young man from Texas at one of the luncheons, Texas Commissioner of Agriculture Rick Perry. This young man is now Governor of Texas.

Governor Sundquist also asked me to serve on his Tennessee Board for Economic Growth. Dan Wheeler probably also made that appointment possible, and I served as the liason between the Council on Agriculture and Forestry and the Board for Economic Growth. This board met monthly for two days each time all across Tennessee. Though it was a hard working and effective group, I declined to be reappointed to a new term after my initial two-year term was completed. Joe Hollingsworth of Clinton was our first chairman, and Bill Morris from Memphis succeeded Joe. They are both extraordinarily capable men. It was my pleasure to represent Tennessee agriculture at the economic board's governor's economic summit.

I'm probably the reason why we have The WTNN, our shortline railroad, having made the initial contacts with folks that enabled the ball to start to roll. It seems that I have had a little talent at organizing, going back to my childhood days of organizing ball games, Halloween forays, etc. The following is the account of how The Gibson County Railroad Authority and the WTNN came into existence.

In the middle of the 19th Century the Mobile and Ohio (M&O) built the first railroad through Kenton, Rutherford, Dyer, and Trenton. The M&O continued through Humboldt and Jackson and on to Mobile. Later they added some trackage and renamed the railroad the Gulf, Mobile, and Ohio (GM&O). On August 2, 1972, the GM&O sold out to the Illinois Central (IC) which renamed itself the Illinois Central Gulf (ICG). In 1978 the ICG announced intentions to cut our railroad from Rives to Humboldt. The North Gibson-South Obion county areas pulled together and persuaded the ICG to leave service intact to Kenton, Rutherford, Dyer, and Trenton. But then in 1983 the ICG announced plans to cut service to these four towns.

The mood of the area seemed to be a mixture of "There's nothing we can do about it" and "Who cares?" I wasn't ready to give up. I knew that if the railroad left us we'd most likely never get it back. Without rail service our towns would forevermore be at a disadvantage in recruiting and keeping industry. More selfishly, my elevators at Dyer, Kenton, and Como (Como because most of its grain and soybeans are brought to Kenton and shipped by rail) would be at a competitive disadvantage to elevators on railroads. This would have hurt our business enormously, and it also would have hurt our hundreds of customers as lower prices for their grain and soybeans would have resulted.

During this period of time I owned an interest in a river grain terminal at Hickman, Kentucky (Bill Latimer was majority owner) and was invited to an affair in Hickman that celebrated the opening of a short line railroad, the TennKen Railroad between Dyersburg and Hickman. Governors, U.S. senators, congressmen, and Henry Hohorst were there. You ask, "Who's Henry Hohorst?"

Henry was the principal in the TennKen Railroad. I was very impressed with what Henry, a New Jersey maritime and railroad consultant and now a Tennessee businessman, had to say. After the party was over I introduced myself to Henry and asked if he'd have any interest in looking into our situation. He said that he would. I then contacted Ronnie Riley who was Gibson County executive at the time — and still is — and we organized a steering committee. The Gibson

County Railroad Authority (GCRA) consisting of the Gibson County executive, the mayors of Kenton, Rutherford, Dyer, Trenton, Humboldt, and now Jackson, and one mayor-appointed member from each of the towns, was organized. The Gibson County executive is chairman, and I was elected vice-chairman. We hired Henry as a consultant, and we all went to work. A study was done to see if a viable shortline railroad could operate between Kenton and Humboldt but not including Humboldt, and the answer was no. Then we figured on a shortline that included Humboldt and the answer was still no. It was obvious at this point that in order to make the shortline a viable operation, the possible new railroad would need switching revenue from Ameristeel, a large railroad customer at Carroll, a country point between Humboldt and Jackson.

Henry Hohorst and Ronnie Riley are masterful negotiators, and they ended up with an agreement with the ICG to sell the line all the way from milepost 394.5 at Carroll to milepost 431.31 at Kenton, a distance of 36.81 miles. They also negotiated trackage rights from the ICG on their line from Carroll on into Jackson.

Everything looked great. But where was the money coming from? Ronnie and some other political types and some of us plain folks had been working hard with the State of Tennessee and Gibson County to come up with the funding. Finally everything fell into place - $900,000 from the Tennessee Department of Economic and Community Development for part of the purchase, $1,000,000 from the Tennessee Department of Transportation for rehabilitation (the track was in deplorable condition), and $200,000 from Gibson County. This was enough money to purchase the railroad and rehabilitate it to a 25MPH line.

GCRA then contracted with Henry and his two partners, Bill Drunsic and Tony Linn, to organize a railroad operating company. I financed their first locomotives and a few work cars for them. They named their new shortline railroad The West Tennessee Railroad, the WTNN, and they began operating on August 31, 1984.

The WTNN has been very successful. The last full year the ICG operated our line, only 600 cars were shipped from Kenton, Rutherford, Dyer, and Trenton. In 2000, also counting Humboldt and

Ameristeel, WTNN handled 9,100 cars! How's that for a success story! Ameristeel is their largest customer. Our Dyer Grain Company is their second largest customer, and our Kenton Grain Company is their third largest customer. The WTNN is making our Gibson County (Kenton is one half Obion County, of course) towns much more prosperous than they would have been without a railroad. Henry is semi-retired, and his son, Bruce Hohorst, is now CEO of The WTNN and The TennKen. Bill Drunsic is no longer a partner (he owns and runs another Tennessee shortline), but Tony Linn remains a partner.

In 2001 the Hohorsts and Linn gained a long-term lease of the Norfolk Southern's line from Fulton, Kentucky through Jackson and all the way down to Corinth, Mississippi. They now control a considerable part of West Tennessee's intra-railroad shipments.

This shortline railroad is a textbook case of what can be done if people work together for the common good. The folks of Gibson County, and certainly I, owe a great deal to a few good people.

The most lucrative thing about living in Union City has been the business networking it has afforded me.

Dad had been chairman of the board of First State Bank of Kenton and his father had been chairman of the board of its predecessor bank. When Dad died in 1975 the board named me to replace him. In 1987 our most capable president, Andy Newmon, had suffered greatly with his heart, and I felt that we needed to do something with the bank. First American Bank of Nashville had pulled the charter from its bank in Union City and dismissed all the directors except for three who were named to a board in Jackson. Union City's capable and personable president, Dan Weber, was named branch manager, and most of the power to make decisions was sent to Jackson and Nashville. I knew that all this was very unpopular with the former board members and with Dan.

One Saturday night in 1986 at a wedding reception at Union City's Poplar Meadows Country Club I got Dan off to the side and explained my concern for Kenton's bank and asked if he might have any interest in helping organize a group of men to buy Kenton and branch into Union City. He jumped at the chance to make this change. Dan and I decided to talk to Jim White, my next door neighbor in Union City and one of the three men on the board of First American in Jackson. Jim came over to my house and almost immediately was ready to pitch in with Dan and me. Next Andy Newmon threw in with us. Later on Andy handled the Kenton situation brilliantly. Over a period of time we talked to one man at a time, men whom we thought would be interested and whom we would like to have aboard. I do not remember the order in which we approached the others but they were Lamar King of the Kenton bank, George Botts and Jackson board member Jack Drerup of First American, David Critchlow, Newell Graham, and Robert Kirkland of Union City's board of the Commerce Union Bank of Nashville, and Milton Hamilton and Barry White of the Union City board of Metropolitan Federal Savings and Loan of Nashville. These talks and our planning took place over a six-month period of time. Every single man invited to join with us did so. All the meetings were held in my house in our big room, and often in our driveway there would be a large number of automobiles. Yet nobody ever knew one thing about our plans — until one morning in 1987 at 10 AM when everybody went to their respective banks and resigned as directors and told them about our plans. Union City was not surprised — it was shocked. The fact that all this was kept secret attests to the great character of each of these twelve men. Our Kenton bank that we twelve men bought was a $25 million bank. Our First State Bank totals reached $285 million (just prior to the consolidation detailed ahead). In addition to Union City and Kenton, we had branches in Mason Hall, Rives, and South Fulton (and after consolidation also in Troy, Goodlettsville, White House, and operations in Brentwood and Nashville's West End).

The last 15 years have been great fun and very rewarding. Our net worths have benefited considerably as a result of those deliberations at 2022 Stonewall Drive in Union City, Tennessee. We were all good friends when it started, and the ten of us surviving remain so today. Lamar King and Barry White have passed on to their rewards. Milton Hamilton resigned after he moved from Union City to Nashville. Andy Newmon, who was chairman of our board from the beginning, has retired from the board. Additional current directors are Bob Cartwright, John Clark, Tony Gregory (who was brought in from

Goodlettsville four years ago to be president and CEO of First State Bank), John Miles, James Porter, Bill Simrell, and Bart White. Dan was moved up from the presidency of the bank to chairman of the board, replacing Andy.

In 1999 we entered into discussions with Sharon Bancshares, the parent company of Bank of Sharon, City State Bank of Martin, and Weakley County Bank of Dresden, and their branches and subsidiaries in Jackson, Dyersburg, Paris, Lexington, Greenfield, Union City, and Brownsville. Robert Kirkland, Jim White, and I were the non-staff members of the negotiating team. After several months of negotiations the boards voted to merge. Today our combined holding company, Community First Bancshares, has total footings of approximately $600 million and our subsidiary operations have expanded to Columbia, Franklin, and Dalton, Georgia. We are now in 22 towns in Tennessee and one in Georgia! Who would have thought it back in 1987? In my opinion a few years from now we will be a billion-dollar bank. Dad never would have believed it. His Dad would have thought that you were totally out of your mind to think that such a thing could ever happen.

The executive committee of Community First Bancshares was made up of six men from First State Bank: Newell Graham, Tony Gregory, Robert Kirkland, Dan Weber, Jim White, and me, as well as six men from the Weakley County banks: John Clark, Bill Liggett, James Porter, Joe Porter, R. D. Robinson, and Van Swaim. Mr. James Porter was chairman of the executive committee, and I was vice chairman. In 2002 Mr. Liggett resigned, and Mike McWherter was elected to replace him. Sadly, Mr. Liggett died in 2003.

All four banks and their branches and the subsidiaries were consolidated into one bank charter in late January of 2003. New 25 member bank and holding company boards were named and included the previously mentioned Obion County directors and the Weakley County members of the executive committee plus Chris Bell, UTM Chancellor Nick Dunagan, Keith Fowler, past Governor Ned McWherter, Terry Oliver, Jeff Perkins, and Mike Swaim, these last seven men all being from Weakley County. Total footings were $600 million. The new combined bank board chose the name of First State

Bank going forward and kept the charter of the Weakley County Bank since it was the oldest of the four bank charters. That charter went back well into the 19th Century. The board was kind to elect me as its chairman. Dad was chairman of the Kenton First State Bank Board, and my grandfather, C. R. Wade, was president of two different banks at different times in Kenton, one of them having been the predecessor bank of our original First State Bank. It is a great privilege to be the third generation Wade to be so honored.

A couple of months later new boards were named. George Botts, David Critchlow, Jack Drerup, Ned McWherter, and James Porter retired. James R. (Jimmy) White was elected as were all the other previously mentioned men. The bank and holding company boards consisted of the same 22 men. I was elected chairman of the executive committee.

In February, 2003, we organized a First State Bank – Kenton Community Bank Board for the Kenton/Mason Hall area. The charter directors are Richard Davis, Jack Finch, Jay Ray Hobbs, Bob Hollomon, Amos Huey, Mike Perryman, Bill Sanderson, Will Wade, and Coy Yergin. We are excited about the possibilities that this good group of men will bring to the bank and to the area. Andy Page from Greenfield is now heading the Kenton bank, and he will do a marvelous job. No doubt about it.

In 1987 I started looking at some farmland in the Dyer County Mississippi River bottom with Frank Burnett, a Dyersburg real estate broker whom I had known since his days with PCA (Production Credit Association). More and more land was added to a possible purchase, and it got too big for me to handle. I talked with friends and fellow First State Bank directors, Robert Kirkland and David Critchlow, about the possibility of going in with me and buying it. The upshot was that the three of us bought 3,561.64 acres. A couple of years later we bought an additional 725 acres, so our total holdings down there were, and are, 4,286.64 acres, most of it contiguous, the rest being within a mile or so of the big block. West Tennessee Farms, as we named our partnership, has been a very good investment.

Shortly after putting all this land together we three partners were in Dyersburg, and Frank Burnett joined us for a look around the territory.

When we got back to his office in Dyersburg we saw records and papers scattered all over the place and several new employees. We asked Frank what was going on, and he told us that he and his partner, Walter Hastings, had gone into the business of buying loans from the Resolution Trust Corporation (RTC) which had taken over loans from failed savings and loan associations. They were also buying loans from F.D.I.C. which it had taken from failed banks. Critchlow, Kirkland, and I talked about this business on our way back to Union City and decided to bring up the possibility of our bank's directors going into this business separate from the bank. We directors decided to give it a shot, and a new company which we gave the grandiose name of American Holdings, Inc. was formed. Eddie Carden, a talented banker and loan man, was hired to run the operation. It was profitable from the git-go, and the investments of us owners have been repaid many times over. If Kirkland, Critchlow, and I had not gone over to Dyersburg that day, the odds of our ever having gotten into the business of buying and flipping or collecting discounted loans would have been mighty slim.

The above three ventures — the bank, the Dyer County land deal, and American Holdings — probably never would have happened had it not been for my Union City networking.

A couple of years ago the president of the Tennessee Farm Bureau called to ask if I would consider serving as one of the three directors of TVA. This is a most prestigious position, but I had come too far down the road to take on such a momentous obligation. Most likely wouldn't have been asked, anyway.

Yes, in more ways than one I have been a Volunteer. The University of Tennessee reaches into every nook and cranny of our fair state. In my opinion my UT connection also has been a great advantage to me in terms of doing business in Tennessee and in terms of the quality of my life. If I had it all to do over, I'd do it exactly the same way.

Chapter Twenty-Four

Sally, After Childhood

After sister Sally's sophomore year in Kenton High School she entered Holton Arms, a private girls school in Washington, D. C. While at Holton Arms she became close friends with Nancy Gore and Beverly Baker, the daughter of Tennessee's Senator Albert Gore and the sister of Senator, Vice President, and presidential candidate Al Gore and the sister of Senator and White House Chief of Staff and Ambassador to Japan Howard Baker, respectively. In fact Sally visited in both girls' homes in Carthage and Huntsville, Tennessee. She also was friendly with the daughters of many other politicians from around the nation and the world. She was a member of the Holton Arms Student Council, sang in the Glee Club, and was dormitory chairman. She won a John Robert Powers modeling scholarship while representing Holton Arms in competition with girls from every school in the District of Columbia. During her senior year she was a D.A.R. page to Continental Congress in Washington.

At this point I'll digress and tell a couple of stories about Nancy Gore and one about Beverly Baker.

At UT I had a fraternity brother, Sonny Holloway from Monterey, Tennessee, a small town on the Cumberland Plateau, who was also a friend of Nancy's. One day Nancy was riding with Sonny in his big, very old Buick. Sonny was turning a corner in downtown Monterey when a log truck hit him on the passenger side literally peeling off that side of the car. Unbelievably nobody suffered even a scratch. Sonny seeing that Nancy was all right reached across and opened the glove compartment explaining, "Nancy, I've got a little booklet in here that explains what to do in case of an accident" with the emphasis on the last syllable. Though shaken Nancy collapsed into laughter.

Nancy and I also became good buddies. One time she came into Knoxville on a train and had a layover. Sonny and I picked her up before dawn at the train station and entertained her at the Pike house for a few hours until she caught her next train. Nancy was the campaign manager for her father for his last successful senatorial campaign when he had only token opposition. Nancy, in the process of visiting all 95 Tennessee counties, spent the night with Pat and me in our home in Union City. Tragically Nancy died of cancer at an all-too-young age. She was a highly intelligent and clever lady who was married to a Greenville, Mississippi attorney whom she met when they were both students at Vanderbilt.

Beverly Baker came to UT, joined Chi Omega, and she and I became good friends. I was defeated for UT's student body presidency by 53 votes. Chi Omega and PiKA were in the same political party, and Beverly was my champion. No telling how badly I would have been beaten had it not been for Beverly. She was a sharp and effective politician. She should have been. Her father was a congressman, and her brother, Howard, is a great statesman. Actually I could have won. My opponent worked hard for three weeks, and I campaigned only the last three days. Only 27 switched votes would have given me the win. Fortunately I seem to have done some things better than my representation of our Rebel (political) Party.

Sally became a member of the Children of the American Revolution, and on February 1, 1955 she was approved as a member of The National Society of the Daughters of the American Revolution. She was a member of the Elizabeth Marshall Martin Chapter of The D.A.R., her chapter's location being Trenton, Tennessee. In Sally's application papers her "Ancestor's Services" reads as follows:

"Kerenhappuck Norman Turner rode alone from Maryland to North Carolina to nurse a son wounded in the Battle of Guilford Courthouse and remained to nurse others. Her sons and grandsons served with General Greene at the Battle of Guilford Courthouse, North Carolina. A monument has been erected to her memory on the battlefield. She nursed back to health and service, her son, James Turner, in a log cabin on the site of the monument. From the rafters of the cabin she suspended tubs that she bored holes in and kept filled with cool water from the 'Bloody Run' near. The constant dripping upon the wounds allayed the fever, and she thus improvised a treatment as effective as the 'Ice Pack' of Modern Science. Captain

James Morehead was at the battles of Stoney Point and Elizabethtown. Kerrenhappuck Norman Turner lived to be approximately 115 years of age."

Sally's other "Ancestor's Services" reads:

"Tscharner de Graffenreid served in Revolutionary War as Sergeant. At battle of Guilford Courthouse, North Carolina he was shot through both hands and maimed for life being deprived by his wounds of the use of both hands."

After graduation from Holton Arms Sally entered Bennett Junior College of Millbrook, New York, a girls' finishing school. While at Bennett she was the school song leader, sang with the Novelettes, and modeled for the 1956 college issue of *Mademoiselle Magazine*.

After graduating from Bennett Sally entered the University of North Carolina, Chapel Hill in the fall of 1957 where she became a member of Chi Omega Sorority. She was selected Dream Girl of our PiKA Chapter, Tau Chapter, at UNC. During our college years PiKA's Dream Girls were a very important part of our chapters' operations.

Sally then was selected as one of three national Dream Girl Finalists and all our family went with her to the 1958 PiKA convention at the Shoreham Hotel in Washington, D. C. I had a big cocktail reception for her in my large room in the Shoreham. Hundreds of boys came by, and I thought Sally had it won. A friend told me later that she had finished second by one vote. I'll always think that Sally should have won!

At Carolina she sang with Circle Nine and was one of fifteen Beauties to appear in the school annual. Chi Omega also sponsored her as a Blue-White Beauty. She graduated with a Bachelor of Arts degree from the University of North Carolina in 1960.

During the summer of 1959 she and her old friend and roommate from Bennett, Flo Pittman from Memphis, attended the University of Hawaii in Honolulu.

A couple of years earlier Sally was selected as one of 23 finalists in the National Cotton Council's Maid of Cotton Contest. Back then all the activities, except for the final night which was held at the auditorium in Memphis before 5,000 people, were held at the Peabody. Sally was far and away the favorite of the auditorium crowd. This time she was selected as Second Maid to the Maid of Cotton. The winner was a girl whom I knew from Tennessee. Before the contest I told Sally that I didn't know who would win but it sure as heck wouldn't be that girl! She was a big girl and Sally was fairly thin. We were told later that the judges wondered if Sally would have had the stamina required for the job. The Maid traveled the world for seven months, meeting with kings and queens and heads of state around the world, and her schedule was murderous. Nevertheless, we Wades felt that Sally's not winning was a travesty. Our family was prejudiced, of course, but we all thought she should have been a shoo-in. According to applause received by the various girls the majority of the crowd felt the same way.

Sally is and always has been an extraordinarily beautiful, talented, and intelligent girl and lady. She was highly popular during every stage of her life and has hundreds of friends in the South as well as in the East.

Sally and Pitt, and Pitt

In 1956 PiKA had its national convention in Mexico City. Several of the brothers from Knoxville went. Malcolm Colditz and I left early and drove the RM3 to Laredo, Texas and caught a plane across the border to Mexico City. We went to convention headquarters, the very large del Prado Hotel, where we booked a trip to Acapulco through a hotel travel agent. The trip included flights to and from Acapulco, two nights in a nice hotel, and some meals, the total cost of which was less than $40.00! Man, we couldn't believe how cheap things were in Mexico. We came back to Mexico City the night before the convention and checked back into the del Prado. We then went into one of several bars and lounges in the hotel, a very large lounge, and picked out one table among many dozens, and sat down. It so happened that there were a couple of real sharp Pikes at the next table and they invited us to join them, which we did. They were from Emory University of Atlanta and were John Pitt Tomlinson III, chapter S.M.C. (President), and Charlie Gillespie, chapter I.M.C. (Vice President).

Mother and Dad and Sally and our great looking and extraordinarily sharp cousin, Jean Sanders from Memphis, were arriving the next day by automobile. I asked Pitt and Charlie if they would like to date my beautiful sister and cousin while they were at the convention, especially for the big Dream Girl Ball which would have hundreds of Mexican girls sitting around like wall flowers with their mothers as chaperones. As any good Pikes would have done, they jumped at the opportunity.

The conclusion of this story is that Pitt and Sally were married in May, 1964 and have a son, John Pitt Tomlinson IV. What an amazing thing fate can be. Malcolm and I picked out one of many bars in that big hotel. Then we picked one of many, many tables to sit at — a table next to Pitt and Charlie. If we'd chosen a different place to have our drinks or a different table in that gigantic bar at which to sit, Sally and Pitt would never have met. Ain't life grand!

Mother and Dad and Sally and Jean drove to Mexico City to the convention and enroute got lost in Monterrey, Mexico. Mother had studied high school Spanish but had forgotten almost all that she had learned. Mother asked directions of every Monterrey person that Dad would pull up alongside, thusly, phonetically, "May-he-co Hee Hee?" She got lots of puzzled looks and Dad said it took forever to get through Monterrey. Jean and Sally still laugh about this experience. We all do.

As was often the case back then, Pitt was drafted right out of Emory Med School. He was sent to Nellis Air Force Base near Las Vegas where he spent the next four years as a physician and member of the United States Air Force. Pitt and Sally married as Pitt was entering his last year of armed forces service, and they spent their first married year in Las Vegas. While they were there, Pat and I went out and spent a week with them in their apartment which was on Sahara Avenue, three or four blocks behind the Sahara Hotel which was one of the major hotels on The Strip. We had a ball. Pat's and my trip is discussed in some detail in Chapter 15.

After leaving the Air Force, Pitt, who grew up in Lake Wales, Florida where his father and grandfather lived and had been practicing physicians, and Sally moved to Jacksonville, Florida where Pitt reentered med school, this time at Duval Medical Center where he did his residency in pediatrics. Then they moved to Lake Wales where he practiced for two years in the family clinic after which time they moved to Dunedin for five years and later to Clearwater for five more years, and Pitt practiced those ten years in a large Dunedin clinic, the Mease Clinic.

After these years Pitt decided to consider going back into the service. He and Sally picked Williamsburg as a town in which they would enjoy living, and they went to Washington and talked with the medical branch of the Army which agreed to bring Pitt back into the armed forces and to send him to Fort Eustis which was only 16 miles from Williamsburg. So Pitt joined the Army, with credit for his four years in the Air Force, and they moved to Williamsburg. While they lived there Pitt went back to medical school to get a degree in preventive medicine, a much better discipline for the armed forces. He spent a year at The Johns Hopkins School of Public Health where he received a Masters in Public Health, and then a year at the Madigan Army Medical Center at Fort Lewis in Tacoma, Washington. After six years in Williamsburg, which they very much enjoyed, they were relocated to Columbus, Georgia where Pitt was Chief of Preventive Medicine at Fort Benning. Two years there and then they were sent to Washington, D. C. They moved into a house in Bethesda where they spent a pleasant ten years. Pitt was Chief of Preventive Medicine at Walter Reed Army Medical Center for nearly three years. Then he was assigned to the Pentagon where he was the Preventive Medicine Consultant to the Surgeon General of the Army for five years. Pitt was now the Army's chief expert in biological and gas warfare and was quoted in newspapers and appeared on television in those regards during the Gulf War. Pitt was then reassigned to Walter Reed where he was again Chief of Preventive Medicine for 27 months.

After a distinguished career in the service, Pitt retired as a full colonel in 1997, and he and Sally moved to Chapel Hill, North Carolina, Sally's old stomping ground and where their only child, Pitt IV, lives. Pitt III obtained a position in the Disability Office of the State of North Carolina. His commute to Raleigh is not a bad one, and he is enjoying his work.

John Pitt Tomlinson IV, born May 30, 1965, lives in Chapel Hill with his wife who is a dentist. Pitt IV attended private secondary schools and matriculated at the College of William & Mary in Williamsburg. After graduation he moved in with his parents in Bethesda and went to work for Riggs Bank in D.C. While Pitt IV was working for Riggs my first estate tax attorney and fellow McCallie graduate, Robert Benham of Memphis, was in Washington on business for his sister's estate and was at the bank. He met a young man who said he had relatives in Kenton and Union City. Bob said, "You wouldn't be talking about Tom Wade, would you?" Pitt IV replied, "He's my uncle." At Riggs Pitt worked with Anderson (Andy) Morse, a Pike alumnus from William and Mary who became national president of Pi Kappa Alpha. Andy is a good friend of mine who, in my humble opinion, will some day be president and chairman of Riggs Bank. After several successful years with Riggs, Pitt IV decided to go back to school to pursue an MBA. After looking at several schools he decided on Duke University and moved to the Research Triangle area and entered Duke's Fuqua School of Business. As was always the case with young Pitt, he graduated with high honors. My recollection is that he was second in his class. He then took a position with Duke's Development Office working in corporate relations. He traveled the eastern United States and occasionally as far west as California on behalf of Duke, calling on corporate clients, with very good results I'm told. As is the case with his parents, Pitt IV is an extraordinarily talented and capable person who is a dedicated Christian. In 1997 he married Sarah High who is now a practicing dentist.

While little Pitt was growing up, he and Sally spent several weeks every summer in Kenton with Mother and Dad. The Tomlinsons don't come back to Kenton very often now that Mother and Dad are gone. When Sally and Pitt do come they often eat lunch and dinner at R&J in Rutherford. R&J Restaurant has outstanding West Tennessee pork barbecue. Sally often refers to a book about good food, sometimes at out-of-the-way places, *Eat Your Way Across America*. She wrote the authors about R&J, and they paid a visit to this excellent restaurant, which is five miles south of Kenton. R&J has been recommended in their book ever since.   Their pulled barbecue and ribs are truly marvelous.

In 1995 Claudia Brush Kidwell, Curator, Division of Costume of the National Museum of American History — Science, Technology, and Culture, of the Smithsonian Institution, wrote to me as follows:

"Last week your sister, Sally Wade Tomlinson, brought a manicure set into the museum for possible donation. We would be pleased to accept this (c. 1920) set, which belonged to your mother, for the collections. Mrs. Tomlinson indicated that both you and she would be the donors. In order to complete our records, we need to have both of you sign a Deed of Gift which legally gives us the set ... We appreciate your family having made this manicuring set available to us."

Sally had found this old mint condition "art decoish" set in the attic after Mother died.

Sally and the Pitts live in a town widely considered to be one of the best places in America in which to live.

Chapter Twenty-Five

Mother

Patti Walker Wade, Mother, grew up in Dyersburg at 428 West Court, just west of the square and where St. Marys Episcopal Church now stands (other relatives lived on Dyersburg's Finley Street). Mother was the daughter of William Powell (Will) Walker and Kate Smith Walker, and she had one sister, Zedna, who was younger. Mother's name was Patti Louise Walker, but in later years she claimed that she did not have a middle name. For some reason she did not like the name, Louise. However, Louise must have been her legal middle name; the name on her 1920 Dyersburg High School diploma was Patti Louise Walker. We found it in some old papers where Mother had long ago carefully hidden it, and we had it restored and framed.

After graduation from high school Mother went to Hollins College in Roanoke, Virginia where she roomed with Nell Pflueger of Cincinnati. In an old album of Mother's, the title of which was *Stunt Book* (for some obscure reason), there is a letter from Nell to Mother thanking Mother for a baby gift for "Baby Patti." I suspect Nell named her first born for Mother. Mother and Nell stayed in close touch for many years but finally drifted apart.

Between Hollins and marriage Mother must have been a real gadabout. Her Stunt Book has memorabilia from trips to Cincinnati (she was in Nell's wedding and was there several times); Covington, Kentucky (where Nell later lived); Nashville, Memphis, Murfreesboro, Louisville (where Mother received a telegram from Aunt Zedna which read, "Send my junk. We miss you. Kiss my foot. Zedna."); Blytheville, Arkansas; Florence, Alabama; and Senatobia, Mississippi. The album also contains dozens of invitations to dances and parties. Another interesting item in the album is a bill to Dad from Methodist Hospital in Memphis for a two day stay, November 16 and 17, 1927. The charges were: 2 days @ \$6 — \$12; operating room fee - \$5; prescriptions - \$1.75; laboratory fees - \$3; total - \$21.75. The album also contains a bill for an Easter corsage that Dad sent to Mother on April 2, 1925. The Memphis Florist charged $10 for the corsage and 50 cents for delivery. It would seem that a florist shop was more valuable than an M.D. degree back in the 20s!

When she wasn't in school or visiting friends in the South and Midwest, Mother lived with her parents in Dyersburg until she married Dad on June 14, 1925. Mother and Dad were introduced at a Christmas dance in Union City, where Mother often visited relatives, by Dad's friend, Tom Owen of Brownsville. Oftentimes Dad would catch the little M&O Railroad passenger train to Union City for Saturday night dances especially in the winter when the dirt road became impassable. He would spend the night in the Palace Hotel, which was located beside the railroad in Union City and which was owned and operated by Fenner Heathcock's mother. (Fenner would soon become Dad's attorney. In later years Mr. Heathcock and Tom Elam, his younger partner, went their separate ways and Dad then dealt with Colonel Elam whose firm soon included Jim Glasgow and through the years also included Jim Glasgow, Jr., Bill Acree — now a judge, and John Tanner — now our Congressman and a distant cousin of ours. Speaking of Mr. Elam, he used to tell a story about when he was a little fellow and went to a funeral with his aunt. He had heard the grown folks talk about how terribly sick the deceased had been and that her death was a blessing. Little Tom and his aunt sat on the second row of the church and he suddenly blurted out, loud enough for everyone in the church to hear, "Ain'tcha glad she died, Aunt Chloe!") Dad would then catch the train back home to Kenton on Sunday. Tom Owen, a cotton broker, remained their dear friend for the rest of their lives. After I was out of college and working during cotton season mostly in the sample room at Wade Gin Company in Kenton, Tom bought lots of cotton from us. Often he would start "taking up" cotton late in the afternoon, and we'd invite him up to the house for dinner, an invitation he never declined. After a couple of highballs and one of Mother's wonderful meals, we'd head back down to the gin where his "takeup" was invariably "easier!"

My recollection is that Mother sometimes helped her father in his grocery store in downtown Dyersburg. Unfortunately, Mother never did talk much about her growing up years, though they were obviously very happy times. I didn't have enough sense to ask her more. We get too soon old and too late smart!

When Mother and Dad were a young married couple in Kenton her good friend from Dyersburg, Jere Cooper, came to them and asked them if they would help him in his first campaign for Congress. Mother and Dad organized a big rally for Jere on the strawberry platform in downtown Kenton where they set up hundreds of borrowed folding chairs and begged and cajoled people to attend the rally. This was Jere's first try for Congress, and his name was not a "household name" to say the least. They had a very big turnout, and Jere was received most favorably. He won this first race by the narrowest of margins, by less than he carried Kenton. From that point on until his death he credited Mother and Dad with his victory. Jere Cooper went on to become the powerful chairman of the House Ways and Means Committee and was a great friend of my parents to the end of his days. As a postscript to this story, my close personal friend and fraternity brother, John Hoff of Dyersburg, was close friends growing up with Jere's son who died young from a heart disorder.

Mother was always very active in our Kenton Cumberland Presbyterian Church and sang in the choir. In later years she and her close friends met just about every afternoon for coffee and pie, or something sweet, usually at Mother's or Miss Yetta Shatz's. Miss Yetta was arguably Mother's best friend, though Mother had many close friends. Mother loved to entertain with luncheons and dinners, and she was very involved with the Women's Club, both locally and with the Federation of Women's Clubs. She was also a member of the Daughters of the American Revolution (D.A.R.) and the Daughters of the Confederacy and often went to meetings of those organizations, especially the D.A.R. Mother loved to cook and was good at it. She did not like to clean house and almost always had maids to take care of the house and wash dishes and clothes. Regardless of who did it though, our house was always spotlessly clean. She made the world's best homemade ice cream from homemade boiled custard. As the ice cream neared perfection in consistency, Sally and I were wont to cry, "I scream, you scream, we all scream for ice cream." The two of us vied to see who was going to get the leavings on the dasher. Why is the ice cream on the dasher the best of all? Doesn't make sense. But it is.

Mother watered the gravel street in front of the house during dry spells, and during strawberry season she ran the picking and packing operation of Dad's strawberry patches. Dad was busy with the affairs of the Kenton Berry Growers Association and did not have time to look after both the association and his own berry deal, so Mother handled everything on the farm. Dad always admitted that Mother made far more money on the farm than he made in town.

Hobos, or tramps, in the old days would ride the rails in and out of town. Sometimes one would come to Mother's back door and ask her for food. She would always fix him a big plate of her wonderful cooking and he would sit on the back porch and enjoy a repast fit for a king. Oftentimes the hobos made camp in the little woodslot just north of the railroad platform. Some of them had small tents of the homemade variety, but most of them just slept in bedrolls. They cooked in cans on open fires. As a youngster their lifestyle seemed very exciting to me. Not any more! Hobos were the forerunners of today's homeless people who gravitate to our major cities. Hobos were kind of scary, but I don't recall their ever having caused any problems in Kenton. Maybe because our very stern policeman, Corb Barner (Carbarner to little sister Sally), kept a close watch on them.

The following article appeared in a late 19th Century issue of the *Kenton Enterprise Courier:*

"Tribulations of a Tramp

Tramp life is not what it used to be. What with quarantines and yellow fever, the irregularity of railroad accommodations and the continuous flow of charity in other directions, he dines but sparely, seldom sleeps on downy beds, and gathers few flowers along his rugged pathway.

Late Saturday evening, while Granville Powell, a grocer on Main Street, was putting up the outside blinds, he was approached by a real blue-blood aristocrat of the original tramp family. He carried his coat swung over his left arm, and in his right hand an empty oyster can. As he came up he hesitated a moment, then asked: 'Are you a feeling man?'

The grocer replied that he sometimes felt a little.

'Will you listen to the story of an unfortunate man?'

'That depends entirely upon how much you are able to condense it.'

He shifted his coat to the other arm and continued:

'Well, I'm disabled, discouraged, disjointed, dismounted, disturbed, disjuncted and disthroned. When I visited this town one year ago every back gate was thrown open to me, and I met a hearty welcome at every kitchen window. Now when I ask for bread they give me a stone or a brick-bat or any other missile that comes handy. I've only been in town two minutes and a half, and I've had thirty seven notices to leave. I don't feel right over it somehow; I feel distressed, disowned, disconnected, dismantled, disintegrated, disorganized, disinfected dis—disinclined to finish my narrative,' he said suddenly as officer McNeely was seen approaching. 'Here, give me five cents worth of good crackers and fill this oyster can with the commonest molasses you've got.' And he hobbled off in the direction of Union City, promising to call again after we have had three black frosts and a white snow.'"

Another thing that Mother was good at was "pickin' on me." This was my way of saying, "Scratch my back," or "Rub my head." I loved to be "picked on," and Mother would oblige if at all possible. Among my favorite memories were summer nights on the swing in our screened-in sunporch, with my head in Mother's lap, listening to the drone of the now nearly 100 years old (still working) ceiling fan, the squeaking of the swing, and the symphony of the crickets and frogs and other summer sounds while Mother "picked on me." What a sweet way to fall asleep.

Mother and Dad had several close friends in Kenton. These couples formed a loosely organized "club" which was basically a dinner club. Among Mother's and Dad's best friends were Wallace and Verna Mae Taylor who later moved to Trenton where Wallace was their long time postmaster. Also Shirley (a man's name in this instance) and Josephine Draper were close friends. They later moved to Shamrock, Texas where Shirley was a haberdasher. Mother and Dad visited them in Shamrock several times, always with others of the "crowd" as they termed themselves. Bill and Lorene Thweatt were in Kenton several years before moving to Union City. Bill was the Ford dealer in Kenton after having been a professional baseball player, a pitcher with the Memphis Chicks for several years. Bill died fairly young and Lorene was head of the Red Cross in Union City for many years. (Their great grandsons played baseball with my grandsons, Rance, Jr. and Walker in the Union City Minor and Little Leagues.)

Other members of the club were Harry and Margaret Dodson. Margaret had come to Kenton as a singer in a traveling show from Cincinnati and had fallen in love with Kentonian Harry Dodson whom she married. Harry served for a short while as Kenton postmaster. He was a Republican, one of very few in Kenton, and when a Democrat came in as President, Harry lost his job. Harry owned some land and worked for Dad at the gins in Kenton and Rutherford for years. He was the weigher and wrote checks. A particularly funny story about Margaret was that as a new bride she invited some of the local young couples, including Mother and Dad, to dinner. As she was making early preparations for dinner she called Mother for some advice. She told Mother that smothered chicken was to be her entrée and she was having a difficult time smothering the chicken despite the fact that she had a good tow sack over its head! Another time, when told that Laura Joyce and Jack Barton were going from Kenton to Chattanooga for a Lions convention, Margaret suggested that they stop by on the way for a visit with her daughter, Betty. Betty lived in New Orleans. Margaret thrilled us in church time and time again with her extraordinarily beautiful singing. What a voice she had! I can just hear her now, "Ah Sweet Mystery of Life..." Literally makes my skin crawl.

Sam and Yetta Shatz were members of the crowd. Sam was a merchant in Kenton and owned considerable property of different types. During World War II he sold the berries for Dad and Cousin Iman Freeman while they managed all the other affairs of the Kenton Berry Growers Association. During the war there was a ceiling price on most things. The ceiling price for a 24 quart crate of strawberries was $8.80. Sam found out that they could add 8 or 10 cents or some such amount to the ceiling price for a sales commission. This obviously did not cost Dad and Cousin Inman nor the growers a penny, so they were happy to oblige Mr. Shatz. After the war was over and ceiling prices were removed, Dad and Cousin Inman again took over the chore of selling the berries. Usually, however, they contracted with someone else to actually do the selling. For many years Mr. Shatz traveled the South and Midwest buying and selling produce.

Auntie Moselle and Uncle George Tucker and Cousins Inman and Reeves Freeman soon were part of the crowd. Cousin Inman is mentioned prominently in other chapters of this book. He and Dad partnered in several endeavors.

Mother and Dad were sad to see many of their best friends move away from Kenton, but they all stayed in touch as long as they lived.

Mother was very careful with money. She scrimped and saved in every way possible, but when she wanted diamond earrings or a fine fur coat she did not hesitate to buy them. Her parsimoniousness in some ways and extravagance in others rubbed off on me. I use soap until it is so tiny that it's ridiculous and squeeze the last little bit out of a tube of toothpaste, but I have bought Pat fine jewelry, and we have taken very nice trips through the years.

In their latter years Mother and Dad finally did some overseas traveling. After Dad died in 1975 Mother continued to travel as long as she was able to do so. Neither of them drank alcoholic beverages other than to have an occasional cocktail at a party. Mother got into the habit of ordering doubles on the overseas flights which did not charge for drinks, pocketing the full miniature bottles. Those stewardesses must have thought that she was a first class lush! Every time she came home from one of her trips she brought me a shoebox full of miniatures. Needless to say, they were put to good use! When she went to the Holy Land she brought home some water from the River Jordan — in a quart whiskey bottle! Pat ran across it recently — too late to christen any of our seven grandchildren. Maybe there'll be more.

Grace Gary from Union City, a distant cousin of Mother's, has information on Mother's genealogy showing that we are descended from Charlemagne, King of the Franks from 768 to 814 and Emperor of the Holy Roman Empire from 800 to 814. My goodness, we're only 1,200 years from royalty!

Mother was good to everybody, old and young, rich and poor, black and white. She was a wonderful Mother, wife, daughter, granddaughter, and friend.

Mother's Help

Mother had some really neat maids through the years. When I was real young a big black man named Gentry Powell worked for Dad. His mother, Cordelia or Cord, had been Sally's and my nursemaid when we were little, and Gentry's wife, Mary, a genteel person, was Mother's cook and maid. Gentry was the proverbial gentle giant. He worked at the gin, drove trucks, did work on the farm for Dad, and did odd jobs for Mother. Oftentimes when he would be at the house washing windows, cleaning out gutters, etc., I would give Gentry one of my cowboy pistols and ask him to play with me. I'd sneak around the corner of the house and "shoot" at him, and he'd shoot back. Sometimes Mother would tell me that my shenanigans were taking time away from Gentry's work. But that didn't stop our running gun battles, and Gentry kept on shootin' back.

Gentry and Mary left Kenton and moved to California. We were mighty sorry to see them go. Gentry got a job on one of the big railroads as a Pullman porter, and Dad always said that Gentry was bound to be a good one. He was always very polite and did his share of palavering and Dad figured that he would just rake in the tips.

Cord was with Mother for a long time. She babysat for little Patti, for me, and for Sally. One night when I was two years old Mother and Dad left me in Cord's care while they went to a party. They came home to find me wheezing and breathing hard. They were distressed, of course. Cord told them that she thought my problem was asthma, something they had never suspected. It turned out, of course, that Cord was exactly right. From then until about the age of ten, asthma was an ongoing problem for me. At that point I began to "grow out of it," though I have always been a highly allergic person who is subject to an asthma attack if the conditions are just right. Or wrong! In the late 30s Cord died suddenly in church while testifying. Mother and Dad said that this was the way that Cord would have wanted to go. Her death was almost as if a member of the family had died.

Maggie O. Lancaster worked for Mother and later for Pat for many years. She was a sweet and gentle person and a marvelous cook. Her fried chicken and pies were simply the best. Actually everything she cooked was wonderful. Her husband, Sammie Lee Lancaster, worked for Dad for most of his life. Sammie Lee died fairly young. Maggie, who continued to live on the lot in Kenton where she and Sammie always lived, later in a neat new house the government built for her, passed away on January 24, 2003.

One maid who was particularly fun was Charlie Ruth Lee. She pretty much taught Sally and me how to dance. And could she dance! She talked pretty fast, and sometimes it was a little hard to understand her. One day at lunch Dad asked her what she had for dessert. She said something like, "Bernaller ice cream." Dad told her to bring him some. Dad ate bernaller ice cream for quite a while until one day Charlie Ruth was not at our house at noon and Dad asked Mother for some banana ice cream. Mother said we didn't have any. Dad told Mother that Charlie Ruth had been giving him banana ice cream for several weeks. Mother said, "Tom, we have never had any banana ice cream in this house." They quickly figured out that Charlie Ruth had been giving Dad vanilla ice cream all that time.

When Mother would ask Charlie Ruth to do something her answer was always, "Wellum, O.K, sure will." She was an extraordinarily sweet and cooperative soul who made our lives more pleasant.

Another great maid was Ida Jackson who was a peppy little lady always "full of herself." One Saturday night Sally and I had several people for dinner at our home prior to a black tie party. One of the girls was Nancy Boone from Trenton who was wearing a lovely strapless evening dress. At one point Ida was passing something and Nancy, engrossed in conversation, had not noticed the proferred dish from Ida, so Ida, to get Nancy's attention, touched her back with her cold hand and Nancy just about jumped into the chandelier. After this experience the next time Ida had something to offer she opened the door from the kitchen to the dining room and almost yelled in her little, high pitched voice, "Anybody want any butterbeans?" Our fancy dinner party was no longer very fancy. Ida was mighty good to Mother, and Mother was crazy about her.

Another funny one was Inetta from Dyersburg. Mother, whose health was not good, was desperate for help, and Inetta, who worked for Mother's sister, our Aunt Zedna in Dyersburg, was available. Dad had Sammie Lee go get her and take her back home to Dyersburg at night. One night, right after entering the Dyersburg city limits, Inetta said to Sammie, "Sammie Lee, I do believes I hears a ambulanch." It turned out to be a Dyersburg policeman who stopped Sammie for speeding. Inetta told Mother the story. Sammie never mentioned it.

Bobbie Sue Bardwell was another one of Mother's maids. She was a quiet spoken, very capable person who was also a favorite of our family. Bobbie Sue worked for Mother for several years, and we all hated to see her go.

Chapter Twenty-Six

Grandmother and Jennie

Cousin Mai Alexander wrote the following priceless information and remembrances for my cousin, Martha Frances Craig Tickle: (Mother and Martha Frances were first cousins.)

"Baron Christopher de Graffenreid, born in Bern Switzerland 1659. He had a son, Baron Christopher de Graffenreid VI. He had a son, Tscharner (the first de Graffenreid born in America). He was born in Lunenburg County, Virginia, was married five times and had twenty-two children. His son, William had six children. One of his children, Nancy Ann, married James Smith of Lunenburg, Virginia. Nancy Ann de Graffenreid Smith and James Smith's oldest child, Martha Ann Smith, was born in Lunenburg, Virginia. They came to Dyer County in 1825. Martha Ann, born in Lunenburg, Virginia, 1818, married Asa Fowlkes, born in Lunenburg, Virginia 1809. They had eleven (11) children. *[Our Fowlkes ancestors also came to West Tennessee in 1825.]*

Their first child, Mary Ann Fowlkes born 1855 in Dyer County married Dr. Jim White just after graduation from Philadelphia School of Medicine. *[His diploma was from the University of Pennsylvania Medical School which is and was located in Philadelphia. Many southern boys were trained in medicine there.]*

Jim White was born 1818 – died of food poisoning in Civil War. They had one child, Jennie White, born 1858. She married Jim Smith 1876. *(These were Sally's and my great grandparents, Mother's grandparents.)*

Jim Smith born 1853, son of Joe Smith, born 1823.

Jennie White Smith had three daughters

1. Madie died when a child.

2. Kate Smith born 1879 married William P. Walker 1899.

(They had two daughters, Patti and Zedna. Patti born 1901 married Tom Wade [(they had two children)] {*They actually had three children, their first little Patti having died at age 22 months, a victim of sudden* dehydration, *young Tom, and Sally},* Zedna born 1905 married Gordon Pelham. They had one son, Peter.

3. Martha Ann Smith born 1884 married William Hall Craig.

They had four children: Jennie White Craig born 1908, married Everett Eugene (Dock) Watters.

Estelle Craig born 1910 married Louis Norvell. They had two children.

Martha Frances Craig born 1912 married Pinkney Tickle, had three children.

William Hall Craig Jr. (Bill) born 1918 married Nancy Peeke Cook."

(Martha Frances survives.)

Excerpts from life of Jennie Smith by Mai Alexander:

"Dear Martha Frances,

You seem so interested in the postal cards Sister Jennie (*"sister" and "aunt" were often used as terms of endearment in those days*) wrote me from time to time I shall try to write the story of her life for you.

Of course, you, Estelle and Bill knew her much better than I in her late years but I well remember her when your Aunt Kate and your mother were young girls and have been told many incidents of her life which I so clearly recall. There never was anyone like Jennie Smith; she will be long remembered. She was the only child of Mary Ann, oldest child of Martha Ann Smith Fowlkes and Asa Fowlkes both born in Lunenburg County, Virginia, later came to Dyer County. Her father, Dr. Jim White married her mother, Mary Ann just after his graduation from Philadelphia School of Medicine. He died of food poisoning while serving in the Confederate Army. Mary Ann and their only child, Jennie, age 4, continued to live with her parents, Martha Ann and Asa Fowlkes. They had eleven children. All the aunts and uncles were devoted to Jennie. When old enough to leave home she went to her Aunt Noon White's, then living in Union City. Aunt Noon, whose real name was Sarah Jane, had first married Josiah Benjamin Hibbith. He was killed while serving as Captain in the Civil War, and she later married Patrick White, brother of Jennie's father, Dr. Jim White. She had two sons, Ben and John Hibbith. They lived in Union City after her marriage to Patrick White.

Jennie was a pretty child with brown eyes, dainty features and had reddish brown hair and she had a wonderful personality, and all the family loved her as did anyone who ever knew her, even when she was an old lady. Aunt Noon wanted the jolly, pretty little niece to be a real "lady" and Jennie was given every advantage. She was very musical and one story that has come down through the years is that Aunt Noon had a pretty dress made for her first piano recital. It was a big event in Jennie's life (probably her mother and aunts living in Dyersburg were there for the recital). When the teacher called her name, expecting her to play the classical number she was expected to play, Jennie walked out on the stage, made a deep bow and played 'Listen To the Mocking Bird', a very familiar but beautiful song of that day. The teacher was surprised and Aunt Noon was disappointed and disgusted, but Jennie enjoyed the applause so much she sat down again and played and sang: 'Ole Dan Tucker'. I do not remember many of the words but it ran something like this: 'Ole Dan Tucker was a bad old man, washed his face in the frying pan.'

When she was a young lady, she joined a large group of Dyersburg young people to go on an excursion on one of the big boats that went from Memphis to St. Louis. On the boat Jim Smith (aged 23) fell in love with her (she was 18) and their marriage later was a happy event (in 1876), for both their families. Jim took his bride to his father and mother's beautiful country home that was built by a St. Louis architect with slave labor in 1854. They had lots of visitors and pretty Jennie added much to the pleasure of every party. She and Jim had a happy life and continued to live on in the old home after his mother died and his father married again. Jennie's mother had died at her grandfather's home before her grandparents, Martha Ann and Asa Fowlkes died — after Jennie's children were born. There in the old house their daughters, Kate, Martha and Madie (who died when a child) were born and reared and all of Martha's children were born there. In the Parlor was a beautiful built-in bookcase. The lower part was a cabinet where valuable old family papers were kept. Jennie always cautioned all children, "Don't ever open the bookcase", but it was locked anyway. In it were papers Jim's grandfather had brought in a big box on an Ox cart when they came to Dyer County from Virginia in 1825 where he became a prominent landowner. In 19–, the old house burned. It is tragic that the old bookcase was lost, for in it were letters dating back to the time of the French and Indian Wars. There were letters Jim's father had written his father when he was a young boy when he was sent to Nashville, to learn the Saddler's trade. In one letter was his description of the big celebration of James K. Polk's election as president. He did not learn the Saddler's trade for he had to return shortly after that to look after his father's estate. The house was built on a high hill on a 59 A. lot with many old forest trees. From the front porch there was a clear view of the countryside in three directions for many miles.

Jennie and Jim had more company than any couple I ever heard of for they were both very gracious and enjoyed people. In those days people had plenty of colored help and Jennie didn't take cooking and housekeeping as seriously as most people. They both loved young people of their generation and later their girls' friends. Jennie would sit on the porch and when she saw a buggy or wagon turn the corner (almost a quarter of a mile below), she would call to the cook: "Put some more beans in the pot" for it was nearly always friends or relatives and she would be on the front doorstep to welcome them. When they were not entertaining their many guests, Jim loved to read. Jennie told someone later: 'I don't know why Jim loves to spend so much time reading; I read but one book after the children and grandchildren were born. It was the story of an old Ape bringing up a child (she referred to 'Tarzan and the Apes'). It was so exciting, I could not put it down. If any of the children came to me crying, if they had cut their finger or were hurt, in any way, well I would just read on and let them cry, so I thought if books affected me that way, I'd not read any more books.' She told me once that after a hard rain Jim said: 'Well, I saw something today I never saw before, a bunch of frying size chickens could not pull their feet out of the mud.' Jennie didn't say anything but she remembered she had forgotten to feed the chickens for several days, but when a big cloud came up she thought of them and let them out; they were too weak to walk in the mud.

When Kate and Martha were past the Primary department of Smith's School nearby, a teacher was hired to live in the home and teach History, Music and Art and several of the cousins their age would stay with them for months to take advantage of the lessons. At the close of the sessions, they always had a big picnic in the yard, when all the parents, Kinfolk, and neighbors brought dinners which were spread under the trees. 'Dinner on the Ground' was a real joy to everyone and after dinner, the pupils would play the piano, and recite poems and say dialogues the teacher had had them rehearsing for many weeks.

Jim loved to play Dominoes and often a group of men came out from town. Uncle Al who lived near, always joined them. Several young people, friends of the girls, would often spend nearly all of Christmas week with them. There was nothing Jennie liked better than having a crowd of young people in their home. If there were not enough beds, she made pallets on the floor and they kept the big open fire going all night. During the day, they would go rabbit hunting and many a night all sat around the fire where Jennie basted the rabbits hanging over the open fire with a seasoning of sweet pepper, vinegar and mustard and they would have a feast late at night.

They had a cottage at Curtainer Springs, a place near Reelfoot Lake where the big Revival was held every summer under a big Brush arbor. Many of the relatives and friends joined them and many brought tents, but all ate together. When their oldest daughter (*my grandmother Kate*) and Will Walker married they had a Wedding supper for 200 guests. A week before the wedding, Aunt Noon and some of the other good cooks in the family came out to oversee and helped prepare the food. Jennie let them have complete control of the preparations. Negroes on the place boiled hams in a big iron kettle and barbecued a whole hog over a fire in a barbecue pit. The kinfolk made all kinds of cakes and pies and had boiled custard for all.

After Jim died, and the old house burned, Jennie, Martha, Hal and the children moved to town. They continued to have lots of company and when Bill, the youngest and only boy started to school, Jennie would have the colored man walk with him to and from school. When he first entered school, she wrote the teacher a note saying: 'I don't care if Bill doesn't learn to read and write just so he can learn to go to school and back, will be enough learning for a while.'

I've almost forgotten one of the funniest things she ever did was after Bill (the adored only boy in the family) entered training in World War II and wrote home that he had kitchen duty — she wrote to his Commanding Officer: 'Dear Sir: Please take Bill Craig out of the kitchen, he never washed a dish in his life. He is over there to help fight the War and not to cook.'

She, Jennie, often visited Ben Hibbitts in Nashville. He and his wife knew lots of stylish folks and Jennie said: 'When I go to Ben's and stylish company were there for meals, I always put my knife way off in front of my plate so I would not forget and eat with it.

When Algenon Rucker got the first motorcycle in town and passed their house, she said: 'If I could just put a side saddle on that I could ride as fast as I've always liked to ride.'

Martha had the reputation of being the worst spoiled child in the family. She had Colic at night and they had to walk her. Jim carried her all over the house and Jennie came right behind with a lighted coaloil lamp and Martha would howl loud when her father turned a corner and she could not see the lamp light. Once she rode her pony at the Dyer County Fair. She had a long riding habit just like the grownups and a hat with a plume in it. When she won the prize for being the best child rider in her age group, Jim gave her a ten-dollar gold piece and she stamped her foot and threw the coin on the ground and said: 'I don't want that penny, I want a nickel so I can ride the Flying Jennie.'

Kate was a gentle child, interested in school and was unspoiled and was one of the most charitable women in Dyersburg. There were no hospitals then and she would go to the homes of the poor and help nurse their sick. When her girls were growing up they had lots of company and had good times just as she had when young and Martha, the 'spoiled brat' grew up to be one of the most unselfish women I have ever known.

A family Christmas dinner at Martha's where Jennie lived and was the 'Queen of All' the annual Christmas family dinner was looked forward to from year to year. Jennie was the center of attraction all her life. When she died her funeral was one of the largest ever held in the

Cumberland Presbyterian Church for she had loved people of all walks of life all the long years."

Jennie wrote the following letter to Master Thomas Fred Johnson, Jr., my Pat's first cousin, on the occasion of his birth. It goes:

"Dyersburg, Tenn.

Sept. 30, 1945

My dear Fred, Jr.: I am so glad you have arrived safe in our city. Best of all you're a Boy. someday you can be our Congresman or our President. You have a great future being a Boy. No hair to curle, no Jettie coats to wear. Best of all no baby to squall when you go to play ball. A little girl's future to be some laizy man's wife a cook in his kitchen. The cradle to rock while your darning his socks. A man's work from Sun to Sun. A woman's work is never done. See what you have missed by being a Boy.

Love,

Aunt Jennie Smith."

The following was written on a card by Jennie for Grandmother. I don't know when Grandmother received it but wonder if it was after Jennie's death.

"June 18 – 1948. Kate and I Rooming here at Mrs. Wil Tuckers. I have saved this <u>one hundred dollars</u> for <u>Kate Walker</u> when I die. Now Kate you may need this. Come in handy for Shows. Put this <u>one hundred dollars</u> right in your own <u>Pocket Book</u> for I have saved it all for you. You shure bin good to cook clean house not let one do a thing You saw to me in evry way Mama always came first with you. I am 90 years old and childish but you nevver tierd waiting on me. I love you lots Mama.

Mrs. Jennie Smith

Dyersburg, Tenn. – Troy St"

As is obvious from the foregoing, my Great Grandmother, Jennie White Smith, just plain Jennie to her great grandchildren, Grandmother to her grandchildren, was an unforgettable character. She grew up in the Dyer County, Tennessee rural community of Hurricane Hill, a few miles north of Dyersburg. Her father was a country doctor, and her husband was a country doctor, both practicing at Hurricane Hill. Her ancestors, Charles H. and Mary (aka Polly)

White are buried seven or eight miles west of Union City. It is only a hop, skip, and a jump from their cemetery to Hurricane Hill. I have been told that this couple was my Great Great Great Great Grandfather and Grandmother, but recent things I have read indicate that they may only be three greats away from my generation. If three greats are correct they would have been Jennie's Grandparents. If this is true, Jennie's father would have been Dr. James A. White. Sally has Jacobeum H. White's 1859 medical graduation certificate from The University of Pennsylvania. My guess is that he might have been a brother to James A. White.

Jennie, whose full name was Sallie Jennie Nooney White, was born on May 8, 1858. She married Dr. James Joseph Smith. They had two daughters, Kate Fowlkes Smith Walker, my Grandmother, who was born on February 14, 1879, and Great Aunt Martha Smith Craig, who was born in 1884. James Joseph Smith died on July 18, 1909. Jennie lived on to November 28, 1948, so she was a widow for over 39 years. Jennie always said that she did not want people to grieve for her when she died; she wanted them to rejoice that she had entered into Heaven. She wanted Dyersburg's bells to toll when she died. They did. She wanted people to be happy at her wake. They were.

Being the daughter and later, wife, of doctors meant that Jennie had the opportunity to live pretty much as she desired. She did. She never learned to cook. She told me that if she had learned how to cook people would expect her to cook, so she opted out of cooking. She never learned how to keep house. She told me that if she had known how to keep house people would expect her to sweep, vacuum, dust, wash windows and clothes. She didn't want to do those things, so she didn't. She lived with Grandmother or Aunt Martha in Dyersburg all her widowed life. During her childhood her mother always had help, and during her married life she always had help. Aunt Martha, with whom Jennie lived after her husband's death, always had help. After Aunt Martha died, Grandmother waited on Jennie, hand and foot. Jennie didn't turn a tap. Didn't want to, and didn't have to.

Grandmother's husband and Sally's and my Grandfather, William Powell (W. P.) Walker, was a grocer in Dyersburg for 31 years, and from all accounts was a very fine gentleman. He was an alderman for the City of Dyersburg and was an elder of the Dyersburg Cumberland Presbyterian Church. His sisters were Ethel and Mary Gee Walker. Neither of them ever married, though Mary Gee, as a young woman, fell in love with a man on an ocean voyage. He broke her heart, and apparently she never got over it. My Grandfather's brothers were Mann and Brown, both of Dyersburg, Grover of Memphis, and Harry of Washington, D. C. Grandfather Walker developed tuberculosis and fought it for several years before succumbing on January 14, 1935, three days short of his 60th birthday. Dyersburg's bank, offices, and stores closed for his funeral. Grandmother and Grandfather Walker had spent several winters in Tucson for his health. I remember when we spent those winters in Tucson for my asthma our highway often paralleled the old one-lane highway that they took west. Grandmother would comment time and time again about the highway that she and her Will drove on. In my mind's eye I can still see sections of that old highway mostly covered in drifting sand. When Grandfather Walker died, Grandmother moved in with Jennie and Aunt Martha and Uncle (in-law) Hal Craig. When Aunt Martha died, Jennie and Grandmother moved into their own apartment. Grandmother did not have help, but she took care of Jennie. Jennie lived over 90 years, hardly ever hitting a lick at a snake!

Jennie and Grandmother both would leave on a trip, long or short, at the drop of a hat. Consequently they took many trips to Memphis or to St. Louis or to Arizona or to other places in the United States and Canada with Mother or with Mother and Dad. They loved to travel.

After a trip to Memphis the following letter was written by Jennie to Cousin Katherine Ann Dietzel Cox who now lives in Union City with her daughter, Pam:

"Kenton, Tenn. May 9, 1935. Dear Katherine Ann,

Child, I looked Memphis over jest for ruffled drawers every thing clerks showed me were good quality and not much fixing to them so they would say this is the style but when I was a girl I wore ruffled drawers. I then looked for stockings not a red silk pair could I find so all I know to do Just send a dollar for each leg.

I am so proud of you hope you some day get a good husband one easily henpeck always figure to that end of the line in matrimony.

I love you

Aunt Jennie Smith"

One time Sally went with Mother and Grandmother and some other relatives for a few days to Dawson Springs, Kentucky. Jennie and Great Grandfather Smith often vacationed at Dawson Springs. I have a postcard entitled "Camp on Mountain Side — Dawson Springs, KY" with a photograph of Jennie and Great Grandfather Smith and some other people. As was often the case with Jennie in old photographs, she was holding a fan high in her left hand. The card was dated July 23, 1911, and postmarked Dawson Springs, KY. It is addressed to Mrs. J. J. Smith (Jennie) Dyersburg, Tenn., care of W. P. Walker, and signed by "Mai" who obviously would have been Cousin Mai Alexander from Dyersburg. It reads, "Can you imagine my surprise when I found this postcard down in one of the stores? Am having a fine time here. My love to Martha, Kate, the children and you."

I have another postcard having to do with Jennie. This one showed a crowd of people, Americans and Mexicans, in The White Horse Café, Nuevo Laredo, Tamps. Mex. The people were standing in front of a large bar. On the back of the card is a 4 Centavos stamp and the following written by Jennie in her distinctive handwriting: "Larado Old Mexico, I drank the real whiskey at this Bar Feb 5/1928. Had beer for supper. Kate Walker made trip with me. Mrs. Jennie Smith."

One time early in Mother's and Dad's marriage, before Dad knew Jennie very well, the three of them were driving to Memphis. Jennie rode in the back seat. Several times on the trip Dad mentioned to Mother that they must be driving by a still as he could sure smell alcohol. When they got to Memphis and Mother and Dad were alone, Mother said, "Tom, we weren't passing stills. That was Jennie taking sips from her flask." Jennie never went anywhere without her little leather-covered flask which she always carried in her purse and from which she nipped often throughout the day, every day. After she died Mother found a pint bottle of bourbon hidden back in a closet. On the label in Jennie's unmistakable handwriting was, "for medical purposes only." Sally has this unopened bottle in her home in Chapel Hill, North Carolina. Obviously Jennie didn't want anybody to get the wrong idea when she died. Wonder how many times she wrote that inscription on bourbon bottles? My guess is that it would have been a bunch.

Jennie loved her snuff. When I was young but big enough to reach up into a tree she would get me to walk with her back in the alley behind their house in Dyersburg and break off little twigs for her. She would fray the ends of one-and-a-half inch twigs and with them brush the snuff into her gums. This is the way she enjoyed dipping her snuff. She carried a little spittoon with her when she was in a place where it was not handy to expectorate — spit to us rednecks! One time we great grandchildren got into her snuffbox, and we all decided to see what it was like to dip snuff. Talk about a sick bunch of younguns! It's doubtful that any of us ever again put snuff into our mouths. I certainly didn't.

Jennie and Grandmother spent lots of time in Kenton. We used to slip into Jennie's bedroom while she was still asleep (she liked to sleep late) and tickle her feet. Our across-the-street neighbor, Laura Joyce Howell Barton, was one of Jennie's favorites and Jennie always called her Laura George. We put up with it for years and finally I said, "Jennie, her name is Laura Joyce, not Laura George." She replied, "I know it but I'm gonna call her Laura George." And so she did. The same exchange occurred after Jennie had called Hitler, Hilter, for years. She never called him anything other than Hilter or Ole Hilter.

Jennie and then Jennie and Grandmother lived in two big old houses in Dyersburg with the Craigs. The first house was just across the Illinois Central Railroad tracks, due east of the square. This big house sat back off the highway on a big lot with very large oak trees. It was either at this house or at the Hurricane Hill house they lived in before moving in to Dyersburg when one day Jennie had some of her friends over to play cards, and the ladies kept hearing a strange noise. Jennie told the ladies not to worry about it, it was just one of Hal's dogs scratching around. Well pretty soon the "scratching" broke into a roar and the ladies fled the house which had almost burned down around them. (Both the Hurricane Hill house and the house east of Dyersburg's square burned to the ground.)

After the Dyersburg house burned they all moved to another big house on Sampson Avenue in Dyersburg. As was the case with many of the houses back then, every room had a coal fireplace. Jennie had a habit of backing up to the fireplace in her room and hiking the skirt of her nightgown when she got up on winter mornings. One morning somebody turned on a radio within hearing distance of Jennie just as she hiked her skirt, and a man on the radio blurted out, "Good morning, ladies!" This was the talk of the town for weeks.

One time I was spending the night in this house while Mother and Dad were away for the night. A cousin, an older man named Fowlkes, came into the house drunk. He probably was trying to be nice to me, but never before having seen a drunk person, he scared me to death. I ran upstairs and hid and later slipped back into the upstairs hall and peeped at him through the stair rails. When Grandmother found out how much he had scared me, she was furious and ran him out of the house. Never again did I see this very nice cousin drunk.

Mother, Dad, Sally, and I spent part of every Christmas Day in this old Sampson Avenue house. We had Santa Claus and opened gifts at 405 Maple Heights in Kenton. Then by mid-morning we'd pack up and head to Dyersburg. Actually we spent one Christmas Eve on Sampson Avenue, but it wasn't the same as spending this magical night at home.

We always had Christmas dinner at the Watkins Street Dyersburg home of Sally's and my Great Uncle Brown Walker, a bachelor who lived with his old maid sisters, our Great Aunts Ethel and Mary G, both of whom lived to be about 90. When they were no longer able to host the big meal, we began to have Christmas dinner with Peter Pelham and his family in their big Oak Street home. This continued until Pete died in 1976, and from then on Pat has hosted Christmas dinner in our home for our family and for her family and my Mother for as long as her parents and Mother lived. (Dad died in 1975, a few months before Pete's death.) This tradition continues with Pat's brother, Bob, Patti and her family, and Will and his family. Lolly and her family now spend Christmas Day in their Shreveport home, coming to Union City for a few days after Christmas.

During World War II the Craigs rented a room to two girls who had moved in to Dyersburg from the country to work. Of course, girls and women were counted on to help the war effort by doing work of kinds that had never before been done by women. There was an air base out at Halls where soldier boys were taught to fly, and pretty soon some flyboys were coming to see the girls. There was a little grassy area behind the house which had hedges around it and which was fairly private, and this is where a good bit of their courting took place. We little ones loved to "spy on" these nice young couples.

Years ago this Sampson Avenue house was bought by the wealthy road builder, Kent Ford, and he and his wife completely renovated it. A few years ago it was converted to a Bed and Breakfast called Aunt Ginny's. (I wonder if they really meant "Aunt Jennie's." Many Dyersburg people, whether related to her or not, called Jennie "Aunt Jennie.") Pat and I went to see it four or five years ago, and it is very nice. For the most part the rooms are as they were long ago, and seeing it brought back a rush of wonderful memories. It's mighty good when these fine old substantial structures can be saved rather than being torn down.

After Jennie died, Grandmother lived by herself in her Troy Avenue apartment until she died at age 83. She was a dignified and strait-laced lady, entirely different in some ways from Jennie. However, their values were the same. They were both devout Christians. They just practiced their religion a little differently.

After Aunt Martha died Jennie and Grandmother first moved into an upstairs apartment on McGaughey Street in Dyersburg. When the stairs became too much for Jennie to negotiate they moved to a duplex apartment on Troy Avenue. In 1948 Jennie fell down the front steps of this apartment and broke her hip. They took her to the Baptist Hospital in Memphis where she died on November 28, 1948. The last conversation we had was in the hospital, just after she had eaten her last meal which was chicken. I asked her how she liked it. She said, "No good at all. Tasted like a ole rooster, half cooked." She carried her good humor to the very end. I had just turned 15 and was trying to convince myself that she would be all right as Mother, Dad, and I left the hospital. They told me that Jennie had had an injury that was just too great for her old body to overcome. She died that night. Never before had I experienced that kind of helpless feeling.

In some ways Jennie might not have been totally admirable to good but narrow-minded people. But she had a positive impact on hundreds of lives. Jennie was loved by many. It takes all kinds to make the world go 'round. Jennie's mold was broken.

One winter when there was lots of snow on the ground Grandmother Kate drove Sally and me from Kenton to Dyersburg. As she was driving between Dyer and Yorkville, the windshield kept icing over. She stopped in Yorkville, and a service station attendant poured Coca-Cola on our windshield to break up the ice. It seemed to work pretty well. She slid around the roads and "scared me half to death," which was one of our family's sayings, but we made it intact.

Grandmother discouraged us from writing the word, "Xmas." She said that Christ should never be left out of Christmas. Never have I written Christmas any way other than Christmas.

Grandmother started giving us three grandchildren subscriptions to *National Geographic* about the time we went to college. I have continued the subscription ever since she died, and we have enjoyed it immensely all these years.

Grandmother died on January 13, 1963, ten months after Pat and I married. She left Mother one-half interest in two Kenton area farms (Sally and I owned the other half interest by virtue of gifts from Dad). She left a farm in Dyersburg to Aunt Zedna Pelham. This farm is where the shopping mall in Dyersburg is now located. It was then left to Peter Pelham, and his widow sold or leased it to the developers of the mall. It is prime real estate. Jennie and I walked on it many times during the 30s and 40s.

Grandmother thought we three grandchildren could do no wrong. She was always our champion and told us often about how bright and good looking we were. With the exception of Sally, love was certainly blind in terms of the latter trait! And maybe the former trait. Grandmother referred to Peter and me and to other men and boys whom she held in high regard as "Chesterfields." This word was a complimentary term for males in days gone by.

Grandmother was one of the most unselfish people who ever lived. She spent her life doing for others. Dad did a great deal for Grandmother who always said that Dad was the perfect son-in-law.

Certainly Grandmother was an exemplary daughter, wife, mother, mother-in-law, and grandmother.

Chapter Twenty-Seven

Dad

Tom Wilton Wade was the son of Charles Richard Wade and Lyda Belle Elder Wade. He was born August 28, 1897 in Kenton. He had one sister, Moselle Wade Tucker, and one older brother, William Eugene Wade.

When Dad was a little boy growing up in Kenton he loved animals of every sort. He had a pony named Maud and a regular menagerie in the lot behind their house. He had just about every kind of domesticated animal that one could think of except for a goat. He wanted a goat to pull him in a little wagon. His mother, my Granny Nanny, drew the line with goats. At one time he raised squabs (young pigeons) supposedly for his mother's dinner table, but Dad could not bear to let Granny Nanny kill them so all his squabs flew off as grown pigeons. When he was real young he called water "dottu." When he was a little older he called it "walra." One time soon after he had graduated to the pronunciation of walra he announced at the dinner table, "When I was little I called it dottu, now I call it walra. When I get big I will call it water." Another of Dad's young sayings when he was conveying the fact that he was giving up was, "I give a cup." Our family always used this expression. I still do. Dad and his sister and brother called their mother, Mama, and their father, Papa.

Dad said that when he was a young fellow he hated to get up in the mornings. He asked his Mother to wake him on Saturdays so he could enjoy the luxury of going back to sleep and sleeping until he wanted to get up. That certainly changed as he aged. All my life he was a very early riser.

One time Dad and his folks went to Jackson, Tennessee for the Ringling Brothers Barnum and Bailey Circus. They went the night before and got up before sunrise and watched the circus train come in, unload, and proceed to the circus site. The circus always had an organized parade from the railroad to where the tents were pitched.

Long ago most people took vacations at places that had mineral water springs. It was thought that these waters had curative powers, and people would go to these places to "take the waters." Dad told me that his Mother and Dad and siblings and he spent time during several summers at Gibson Wells in Gibson County. Hotels grew up around these springs and they became important vacation destinations. One would have to presume that they had plenty of good country cooking in those big old hotels. And surely there must have been lots of rockin' on their front porches after dinner.

The Wades had a big family reunion on August 10th and 11th, 1911 at the Gibson County Fairgrounds in Trenton. The invitation read,

"As one in whose veins such blood flows or one who was so fortunate as to have bound himself, or herself, to the family by bonds of matrimony, you are invited to be present that you may know your kinspeople. R. W. Wade, Chairman."

Wallace Wade, the enormously successful football coach of Alabama and Duke, was there. Cousin Wallace was an outstanding guard on the 1916 Brown University team that played in the Rose Bowl. Then he was a very successful high school coach for several years. His first two college coaching years were as an assistant to the storied Dan McGugin at Vanderbilt. Then he went to Alabama in 1923 as head coach and athletics director. He took their lackluster program to the heights of college football including three Rose Bowls when the Rose Bowl was the only bowl and the victor often was considered to be National Champion. (There were no college football polls back in those days.) Then in 1931 he moved on to Duke as head coach and athletics director. He took Duke to two Rose Bowls, again having brought a downtrodden football program to the pinnacle of the college ranks (and in the process making a total of six Wallace Wade appearances in the Rose Bowl!). In 20 years as a head coach, Cousin Wallace won three national championships at Alabama, one at Duke, eleven conference championships, and in 1937 he graced the cover of *Time* magazine. After retiring as a coach, he was Commissioner of the Southern Conference for ten years. Cousin Wallace was the first man to officially enter the College Football Hall of Fame. In his latter years Duke's football stadium was named Wallace Wade Stadium, and the

University of Alabama football stadium in Tuscaloosa is at the corner of 8th Avenue and Wallace Wade Drive. Just another ordinary run-of-the-mill Wade!

I carried on a short correspondence with Cousin Wallace in his latter years. He retired in Durham and died in October, 1986, at age 94. I wrote Cousin Wallace in 1984 and received this reply on Wadehill Farm, Registered Herefords, Durham, North Carolina, stationery:

"Oct. 18 1984

Dear Tom:

I appreciate your letter very much. It was kind of you to write. I have thought for some time that we Wades should get together more often. I remember that many years ago a Wade reunion was held in Trenton Tenn. And it was a tremendous occasion. I hope that you will come to Durham and visit us. I am past 92 years and have not been well for some time. I appreciate your writing me and with best wishes, I am sincerely, Wallace Wade."

On October 23, 1984 I replied:

"Dear Cousin Wallace:

Thank you so much for your letter of October 18.

My Dad, who died in 1975, often talked about the Wade reunion in Trenton which you mentioned. He did remember that occasion well with wonderful memories. We are all proud of our Wade heritage.

I have heard my Mother and Dad tell the following story dozens of times, with much relish. Tennessee played Southern Cal in the Rose Bowl (their first trip) just prior to World War II. It must have been in 1939 or 1940. They and my Mother's sister (from Dyersburg) and brother-in-law decided at the last minute to go, and they drove non-stop for 48 hours or so without reservations. Upon arriving in Los Angeles, they went straight to the Biltmore Hotel and inquired about rooms. The room clerk told them that they had no rooms left, so Dad asked him if he would mind calling around and trying to locate some rooms for them somewhere else. He agreed and asked Dad's name, to which Dad replied, Tom Wade. Knowing my folks were from Tennessee, of course, the room clerk asked if by any chance they were related to Wallace Wade — to which Dad replied that he was actually a fairly distant cousin of ours. This was the magic word. Suddenly they found that they had two extra rooms for the Wades and the Pelhams, and the West Tennessee foursome were minor celebrities. The hotel personnel were even able to get four tickets for the Jack Benny and Edgar Bergen/Charley McCarthy radio shows, much sought after plums. Obviously, the esteem with which you were held in California because of your teams' trips to the Rose Bowl was largely the reason why this trip was probably the most memorable in my parents' lives. A person in your position of national prominence touches lives in ways that he cannot imagine.

Johnny Majors was in my home for a reception a year or so ago, and a group of neighborhood boys found out about it and intercepted him in our front yard and spent several minutes getting autographs. I thought I could tell that Johnny probably would have been just as happy not to have gotten involved with them. I probably shouldn't have done it, but I told him later that I felt that people in his position might eventually lose touch with reality to the extent that it might be hard for them to know in what esteem people such as himself (and you, as for that matter) are held by ordinary fans — children or otherwise. He took it in the spirit it was intended and cited an example of a time when he and a couple of his brothers, when they were real young, took a bus from their little hometown of Huntland, Tennessee to Atlanta to see Charley Trippi (I believe it was) play baseball with the Atlanta Crackers in the old Southern League. Before the game, the three little boys asked him for his autograph, and he refused and was rude to the boys. He said this made a lasting impression on him, obviously, and he was very aware of my thrust.

I am sorry you do not feel well, and I hope you soon feel much better. My sister graduated from Chapel Hill. My own main connection with North Carolina is that I sell lots of cotton to some fine folks in Wake Forest and truck it direct over there from my gin at Kenton. My other three gins are now dormant, and my main business now is grain and farming. I guess I'm the second largest independent country grain elevator operator in Tennessee. If I ever have an occasion to be in Durham, I would very much enjoy an opportunity of visiting with you. Who wouldn't!

Your 'fairly distant' cousin, Tom Wade, Jr."

Our Wade family has been prominent in southern football. Bill Wade of Nashville was a great quarterback for Vanderbilt and was acknowledged to be one of the best quarterbacks in the NFL with the Chicago Bears. One time he played in a charity tennis tournament in Union City and I met him at a party after the tourney ended. He also owned the book by Aunt Zade, *The Wades–The History of a Family*, and we quickly established the fact that we were related. My Yellowstone football story further reinforces the fact that the Wade name and southern football are synonymous!

Dad's best friend growing up was Hal Bogle. One time Dad and Hal rode their horses down to Trenton for First Monday which was the biggest flea market type of activity anywhere around. First Mondays remain Trenton's traditional trading day. Dad said he followed Hal around as Hal bargained, cajoled, and out negotiated person after person, coming home with goods worth far more than those he had taken down to Trenton. Dad said Hal was a natural born trader who never failed to get the better of the person with whom he was trading. Dad said that Hal contracted tuberculosis and at age 19 left Kenton on the train with $200 and a fairly poor prognosis. He settled in New Mexico where he married a lady who was worth a good little bit of money — not too much — but some. Hal's health improved and his TB was licked. He parlayed that small nest egg into a giant fortune. His money was in oil, land, cotton gins, alfalfa mills, and countless other enterprises in New Mexico, Arizona, Colorado, Missouri, and other states. When he retired from the board of the Dallas branch of the Federal Reserve Bank, his 18 years of service made his tenure the longest in the Dallas bank's history. His grand nephew, Johnny Bogle, once told me that Hal had bought a 250,000 acre ranch in Colorado which was the largest land transaction in the history of the state. Johnny also said that this acquisition brought his total land holdings to over one million acres! In the 1950s Hal sold Dad our 621 acre Bruce farm for $50,000. He told Dad that it was worth more than $50,000 but that if he were going to give anybody a bargain he'd rather it be

Dad than anybody he knew. They really had been close childhood friends. Hal told Dad that he would like to hold one-half of the mineral rights. Dad told Hal that would be fine with him and that with Hal's luck they probably would strike oil! Hasn't happened yet. Hal also owned thousands of acres of fine land in the Bootheel of Missouri. One time he bought an alfalfa mill or two in Lake County, and Dad said that Hal sold them after owning them for only a year or so for an enormous profit. No telling what he was worth when he died.

Dad graduated from Kenton High School in 1915 as Valedictorian. He was also last in his class. You see, he was the only member of the class of 1915. They asked him to make the valedictory address, but he declined and would not allow the school to have any sort of graduation ceremony just for him. He then entered Castle Heights Military Academy in Lebanon for a postgraduate year. He had an English teacher at Castle Heights who, when he would get angry at a student, would growl, "You pusillanimous rat!" Talk about from the sublime to the ridiculous! Dad's Castle Heights dormitory burned to the ground, and he lost all the clothes and possessions he had at school. During his one year at Heights (in Lebanon, Tennessee) he won both the Spanish and French medals. He again was Valedictorian (class of 1916), this time with plenty of competition.

Dad entered the University of Tennessee in the fall of 1916, his declared major being Engineering. He said they surveyed The Hill in just about every way possible. In fact one of his surveys of The Hill is framed and hangs in my office. A very well known professor of Engineering at the time, Red Matthews, was considered to be an extremely tough taskmaster. After his freshman year, Dad switched to agriculture and studied Animal Husbandry, now known as Animal Science. Dad always said, "Red Matthews made a farmer out of me." At the University of Tennessee, Dad was president of Pi Kappa Alpha Fraternity, president of the Glee Club, and sang in the University Quartet. A member of the Reserve Officers Training Corps, he was drafted to attend Officers Training School at Camp Pike, Arkansas, near Little Rock, in the fall of 1918, which was during his junior year at UT. Before Dad was commissioned as an Army officer, Armistice was signed and World War I ended. He elected to leave the service immediately but always said he wished he'd stayed long enough to get his commission. Dad's time at Camp Pike threw him one semester behind, and he decided to enter summer school at the University of Wisconsin at Madison where they had an excellent Animal Husbandry program. Then he went back to UT, graduating with honors in 1920 with a B.S. in Agriculture, having majored in Animal Husbandry.

While at the University of Tennessee Dad was one of a handful of students to hold a student membership in the Cherokee Country Club which was, and remains to this day, Knoxville's most prestigious private club. Student memberships were long ago discontinued. At UT he belonged to a secret organization, so secret that its existence was known to nobody outside its membership. He told me its name, but I will not divulge it. Who knows? Maybe it still exists! Several of Dad's friends have told me that he was one of the most popular and respected students on campus.

When Dad was a freshman at UT one night he was crossing the football field (which were tennis courts on the corner of Cumberland Avenue and 15th Street during my years at UT, and which is now the Walters Life-Sciences Building) when he was accosted by an armed robber who demanded his valuables. Dad had a new watch which had just been given to him by his parents and he quickly threw it into the bushes (he went back the next morning and found it). The robber did get his money, but there was not very much of it. The next day in the Knoxville paper the headlines were to the effect that "UT Freshman Foils Robber." The story told how Dad threw his valuable watch away and lost only a small amount of money. An upperclassman who was a IIKA fraternity brother of Dad's, upon reading the story, laughed and told Dad in the presence of several fraternity brothers that he would never let a robber get anything at all from him. That very night, that cocky upperclassman was crossing the same football field and was accosted, apparently by the same robber, who took everything of value that he had including his watch. Sometimes he who laughs last, laughs longest. Or is it loudest?

Dad had a fraternity brother from Mississippi named Joe Dean. Dad said that when anybody asked Joe where he was from he'd reply,

"I'm from Hushpuckna, Mississippi, right around the corner from Vinegar Bend!" Joe came to Knoxville one time in his latter years and I met him. Sure enough, he was a card. He told me about driving to a party at a Knoxville country club one time. Occasionally he would take a swig from his fruit jar of white lightnin'. One swig was swugged just as he crossed a railroad track and the fruit jar, which had a crack in the top, was bumped up into his brow and cut it badly enough that he had to have stitches. He swore that a week later he was crossing the same track and swigging from what must have been the same fruit jar and reopened the cut. Dad said later that it probably was a true story.

Dad told the story of going to a ΠΚΑ convention in New York City and staying at the Pennsylvania Hotel. On the train going to New York he met a fraternity brother from Wichita Falls, Texas who was also going to the convention. His name was Waggoner, and Dad learned in later years that he was an extremely wealthy man. When they got to the Pennsylvania Hotel, a fine hostelry, Waggoner strode up to the desk and said to the room clerk, "Round me up a room, by golly."

Another story in connection with the same convention was that some of the fraternity brothers decided to play a prank on one of the other brothers who was a quiet and reserved boy. They called room service and asked for a valet, telling him that their friend was drunk and needed help in getting dressed for a party. When the valet knocked on the door, Waggoner intercepted him and told him that their friend would protest and claim that he was sober, but not to believe him and to undress him and then dress him in his tuxedo, whether he liked it or not. In other words, if it had to be done forcibly, that's what would have to be done. Of course, the quiet boy protested vigorously and finally convinced the valet that he was cold sober. During the same trip, Waggoner, whom the boys called Tex, called room service for some ice water. They told him that ice water came out of a special tap in the bathroom, to which Tex replied, "I want real ice water. I want to hear the ice tinkle in the glass, podner."

My good friend and fraternity brother, Jim deRopp of Knoxville, found an almost mint-condition Zeta Chapter of Pi Kappa Alpha Minute Book from 1914-1916. Some of what I read in these minutes, nothing secret, of course, was amusing and since they also included mention of Dad, I thought it would be appropriate and interesting to include excerpts from the book. They follow:

"October 1, 1914 – It was decided definitely that we give a house dance November 27... Brother Leach made a talk concerning the courtesy due wall flowers at the dance ... Brother R. Slagle asked that the freshmen be subdued and made to be more gentlemanly around the house.

March 22, 1915 – Motion made and passed that some system be gotten up by which all could do their part toward calling on the girls. Brothers McLean, Jacobs, and Kilpatrick were appointed to make out a list of girls whom we should call on.

October 24, 1915 – Brother Landess reported he went to a wiener roast last Monday night and had a 'doggone' good time'.

November 21, 1915 – Brother Rawlings reported that he had an exceptionally good time at the dance. Brother Jacobs said that he also had a good time. Brothers Bayer and Phipps made similar reports. Brothers Wexler and Leach were equally pleased. Brother Landess reported that he was unable to attend. Brother Brown also was pleased. Brother Shadow attended but didn't dance, doing his share of entertainment in conversational lines. Brother Henson was in the same category as Brother Shadow and was in the same automobile as Brother Ochs (of the *New York Times* and *Chattanooga Times* Family). Brother Hopkins enjoyed dancing. Brother Wilson regretted that he was unable to enjoy the dancing feature of the occasion, but he enjoyed the ladies. Brother Kilpatrick had a good time as did Brother Sorrells. Brother Ochs reported his enjoyment of the liquor as refreshment.

September 19, 1916 – The object of the meeting was the consideration of new material. Mr. Wade's name was brought up by Wexler. He was discussed by different members of the fraternity and a motion was made to vote upon him. Brother Leach reported that Mr. Wade had passed and that Brother Wexler pledge him ... Brother Landess proposed the name of Mr. Bond ... Both men were favorably discussed, and a motion was made to vote upon them ... Both passed.

October 23, 1916 – A motion was made that all swearing and petty actions be abolished and that we take off our hats when we enter the house and that if a member is corrected be it resolved that he take it good naturedly and profit by his mistakes."

I remember the names of all these men as Dad often talked about his experiences at Zeta Chapter. Dan Wexler became a very wealthy tire dealer in East Tennessee. At one point I heard that he had 16 stores including one in Johnson City, his hometown and headquarters, and more than one in Knoxville. The name of his company was Free Service Tire Company. His son and daughter went with us on our 1956 college tour of Europe. His son roomed with Peter Pelham on the trip. The Wade mentioned was, of course, Dad. Dad said that Dan pinned the PiKA pledge pin on him on the Clinch Street bridge. Dad and Dan remained close friends throughout their lives. The Bond mentioned was Cy from Little Rock who joined Dad in forming a cotton brokerage partnership, Bond & Wade, in Dyersburg the first year after they graduated. After one year, Cy went home to Arkansas and Dad moved back to Kenton and continued operating the business by himself out of his parents' home until he married Mother. Dad and Cy saw each other occasionally through the years. I think I met him only once, though I saw Mr. Wexler on several occasions.

After graduation from The University of Tennessee in 1920, Dad went to Dallas and squigged (an apprenticeship to learn cotton classing) for his older cousin, Gus Pharr, who was the second spot cotton broker in Dallas and the first president of the Dallas Cotton Brokers Association. Dad spent the summer in the lovely Highland Park home of "Cousin Gus and Ida." After learning the cotton business in this manner, Dad came back to Kenton and went into the cotton brokerage business after turning down an offer to be County Agent at Wickliffe, Kentucky.

When Dad first started buying cotton for mill accounts in the Carolinas and Georgia he called on an old bachelor ginner whose gin was up in Kentucky. One of Dad's mills told him not to let any of that man's cotton get away from them. The grizzled old ginner had an old-timey slow gin which ginned between one and two bales of beautiful character cotton per hour. The first time Dad called on this old fellow and introduced himself, the old man quickly said to Dad, who was fairly baby-faced at that young age, "What'll you give, Tom?" Dad was kind of hesitant and started off by saying, "Well, I don't know ...," to which the old man immediately asked, "Does yo Mammy know?" Dad bought the old man's cotton that day, and from that day forward, until he gave up the brokerage business for the gin business, Dad bought every bale the old bachelor ginned. But he never again hesitated to quickly quote a price.

When Dad was a young man there was a drummer (a traveling salesman) who came through Kenton fairly regularly selling a cheap kind of life insurance. When asked about the coverage he always replied, "It pays the full benefit if you drown in a pitcher of buttermilk."

Dad's young friend, Dave Shatz, got a new car. Dave asked Dad if he would like to take a spin with him. Dad agreed and they took off for Trimble, ten miles to the west of Kenton. Dad said that Dave floorboarded the car and raced across country on that little gravel road. All the creek bridges between Kenton and Trimble were raised considerably higher than the roadbed itself, and Dave didn't slow down a bit for them. Dad said that he hit the ceiling of the car on every bridge. Dad never again rode with Dave. Dave was always a dangerous driver. In his latter years in Union City, where he lived all his adult life and accumulated a fortune, folks would slow down and pull over when they saw Dave coming.

Dad and Dave entered UT at about the same time. They both took ROTC, and Dad's unit was adjacent to Dave's. Apparently Dave's marching ability closely paralleled his driving ability, as he was relegated to what the Army folks termed their "odd squad." Dave was never particularly well coordinated, except with money.

After college Dad wasn't all work and no play. He was a good baseball player when he was a young man and played third base on the very good Kenton independent team.

Tom Wilton Wade married Patti Walker of Dyersburg on June 14, 1925.

Mother and Dad waited for several years for their first child, Patti Walker Wade, born March 16, 1931 in the Methodist Hospital, Memphis, Tennessee. Little Patti, as she was called, was a beautiful fair-haired child and the apple of the eyes of Mother and Dad. In early

January of 1933 Little Pattie developed some sort of mild illness. On January 10 Grandmother Walker was in Kenton and stayed with Little Patti while Mother and Dad went to the house of friends for dinner. Soon thereafter Grandmother called to tell them that Little Patti had suddenly gotten worse. Mother and Dad called old Dr. Gray who met them at their home, and he quickly told them Little Patti was becoming dehydrated and to get her to Memphis to the Baptist Hospital as fast as they could (back in those days there were no hospitals up here in the country). Little Patti's breathing became more and more shallow as Dad sped toward Memphis. Dad screeched to a halt at the hospital and Mother rushed in with Little Patti who breathed her last breath just as she and Mother entered the hospital. She died in Mother's arms. That was a terrible time for my parents. Dad told me that for months afterwards he didn't care whether he lived or died. Mother always seemed reticent about Little Patti. Though Mother and Dad didn't talk much about Little Patti with Sally and me, it was obvious to me that her deth created great sadness in their hearts that followed them to their graves. Little Patti lies beside Mother and Dad in Sunnyside Cemetery.

I've often wondered what it would have been like to have had a big sister. Little Patti's tiny baby footprint is in a concrete step of the Eddie Jones house across the street from Sally's and my homeplace which is now Will's and my office. I go over to look at it every now and then.

Another reason Mother and Dad took Little Patti to the Baptist Hospital was that our cousin, Polly Elder, was chief pediatric nurse there. When any of us Wades needed to go to a hospital, we always went to Baptist where we were treated like royalty. We three children were born at Memphis Methodist Hospital because that's where Mother's noted obstetrician, Dr. W. T. Pride, practiced.

Dad's sister and brother-in-law, Moselle and George Tucker, lived on Cowden Street in Memphis when all three of us children were born. Mother would move in with the Tuckers and Granny Nanny, Dad's mother who was living with them at the time, a while before her due date. When Mother went to the Methodist Hospital to give birth to me, Dad was in some Kentucky town buying cotton. The family got in touch with him and told him that my birth was imminent. Dad said that he ran every stop sign between there and Memphis, not even slowing down for the towns. He got there on November 23, 1933, probably in time for my birth.

I don't know a story in connection with Sally's birth, but she also was born at the Methodist Hospital, and her date of birth was October 4, 1936.

Granny Nanny lived on until February 28, 1939. I can remember her but not well.

Except during the hottest part of the summer Dad always wore a suit and tie and hat to work. Many were the times I've seen him take off his coat, roll up his sleeves, tuck his tie into his shirt, and start ginning. He could run the gin as well as anybody, and he knew what to do when it broke down. Long ago I often worked with the Wade Gin night crew. If we broke down in the middle of the night, and that happened fairly often, Dad would invariably show up within five minutes. He slept well as long as the gin was running, but when that faint drone stopped, he immediately woke up and came to the gin. He was mechanically inclined. I'm not. During my junior year at McCallie we were given aptitude tests. My lowest score on the test came in mechanics, which was no surprise to me. Things mechanical have never been very interesting to me. Fortunately for my business we have been blessed with many mechanically gifted employees down through the years. The aptitude test indicated that the legal profession would be right down my alley. I have always thought that a law degree would be excellent training for a businessman. As our society has gotten more litigious, such a degree certainly would have become more valuable.

Dad always shopped for his clothes at Beasley Bros., Jones, and Ragland, a men's shop on Main Street in Memphis. I remember going there with him often. In the old days he always gave his employees shirts for Christmas which he bought at BJR. Their pneumatic system of zipping money and invoices around the store always fascinated me. In later years Dad bought Christmas shirts at Bennett's Men Store in Union City. He always bought Pendleton shirts for the managers and

Andy Newmon, our Kenton bank president who kept Dad's books for many years.

Long ago Mother and Dad were contacted by the "Edwards Heirs," a family from whom we were supposedly somehow descended. The 3,260 members of the "Association of Edwards Heirs" claimed ownership by birthright of 77 acres of prime real estate in New York's lower Manhattan. The association's claim was derived from a common ancestor named Robert Edwards who was an 18th Century pirate who supposedly held legal title to the tract. The Edwards claim has been disallowed by three courts as well as by the New York State Legislature. Mother and Dad debated as to whether or not they should invest money in a class action lawsuit in hopes of winning and becoming part owners of some mighty valuable property, but they decided not to part with any of their hard earned money. Nothing has ever been realized from this claim.

I also heard that somehow we were related to the two Taylor brothers who were early governors of Tennessee, Robert Love Taylor who was elected in 1897 and again in 1899, and Alf A. Taylor who was elected in 1921. I don't know if the relationship was on Mother's or Dad's side or even if it is true, but it was discussed in our family quite a bit during my early years. Then during the time shortly after my graduation from college Tip Taylor unsuccessfully ran for governor. I met him a time or two and was told that we were related.

In 1991 a former Kentonian, Flora Spencer Handley, wrote a sweet letter to me. She wrote that Dad did much truck farming, with her help. She said he was "young and nice" and that he grew strawberries, okra, cabbage, sweet potatoes, tomatoes, corn, onions, and butterbeans. She said that my Grandmother Wade had beautiful white hair and a flawless complexion and that Grandfather Wade had a big roll-top desk with a swivel chair in the back of his store. Flora went on to say that she got a nickel for lunch and that often she had a big dill pickle or a Moon Pie. She was not allowed to walk on the street in front of the poolroom. Her Dad worked for my Dad for many years, and one time he hauled a load of berries to St. Louis for Dad. The truck was real hot, and he took off his shoes, one of which promptly fell out of a hole in the floorboard and was lost forever. Flora said Dad got a big kick out of this story. She said she used to play with my first cousin, Lydabeth Tucker Nordman. Flora said she was always amazed at Lydie's perfect grammar. Flora's Mother told her that the reason why was that good grammar was all that Lydie ever heard at home.

Additional recollections of Flora Spencer Handley are as follows:

"Your Dad taught me many farm chores such as putting a teaspoon of fertilizer around a cabbage plant, how to cut them when they matured, how to hoe strawberries and place a lump of soil on the runners to keep them on the row. Your Mother <u>always</u> placed the strawberries I picked on top (back then the berries were packed in 24 quart crates, three tiers of eight quarts. It just made sense to put your best foot [*best strawberries*] forward" [*on top!*]).

Flora grew up, married, and moved to Chicago. Her remembrances continue.

"After World War II you could not buy a new car here unless you made a big payoff under the table. I told your father we would sure like to buy a new car without a bribe and he said the next one he received we could have and sure enough - a new 1948 Plymouth for about $1,600. Your Mother brought your older sister [*Little Patti*] out to the farm [*where Flora lived with her parents and siblings*] in a bassinet for me to hold and cuddle. How I cried when she died. I was so glad you were born and the Wade name could go on — I hope you have a son [*I do, of course*]. When my Mother died, your Mother visited me for several hours. I loved her for it. I saw you at my Dad's funeral and he had worked for your Dad more than 45 years and enjoyed every hour he spent in those gins. Once your Dad brought in about 50 hands to chop cotton. They were bad about spending a lot of time leaning on their hoes. Your Dad asked me if I could lead them, and I did stay in the lead of all of them all day long even though I was only about twelve years old."

Dad always had several laborers on the farm, some of whom were paid by the day and some of whom sharecropped as well as worked by the day. Tenant farmers usually had a cow for milk as well as big gardens, chickens for meat and eggs, hogs for meat, and they really did not need to buy many groceries. Mostly they bought in bulk such things as flour, cornmeal, sugar, and salt. Mr. Ellis Hobbs once told me that he and Mrs. Hobbs moved onto Dad's farm when they first married, and Dad paid him 50 cents a day, from "can to can't." These wages were customary during those times. According to Dad he paid farm labor 50 cents a day, gin labor $1.00 a day, and the ginner $1.50 a day. (Mr. Hobbs' sons, Jay Ray, Teddy, and Joe, are big and loyal customers of my Kenton Grain Company, and Teddy Hobbs worked for me as manager of the grain place for 17 years soon after he came home from Vietnam after having lost his right arm in battle. I hated to lose Teddy to full time farming.)

One time a new man and his family moved onto Dad's railroad farm. Dad didn't know anything about them other than the fact that the man had a ten or twelve year old son named Arlie. Arlie had a dog but Dad didn't know its name. One of Dad's all-time favorite greetings was, "How's Tricks?" Well, one day Dad went out to the farm and saw Arlie and said, "Arlie, how's Tricks?" Arlie replied, "I don't know, Mr. Tom. Last time I seen 'er, she wuz running down the railroad track." Needless to say the dog's name was Tricks, and she must have had a "fit." It took a while for Dad to figure that one out.

For a few years Dad had a most cooperative farm employee named Chock Simpson. Every time Dad asked Chock to do something, Chock's reply was, "Anything suits me suits you, Mr. Tom." Dad said that after awhile Chock's acknowledgement made perfect sense. Chock passed away in 2002.

One of Dad's farm hands never didn't have a cigar in his mouth. Dad always called him "Seegar." The first name of one of our good cotton customers was Orange Mays. Dad often called him "Grapefruit." A cotton gin employee's name was T.C. Pitts. Dad called him Tennessee Central. Dad had a great sense of humor and constantly good-naturedly kidded with folks.

Dad served on the Kenton School Board, was a city alderman, and a charter member of the Kenton Lions Club and later president of the Lions Club. In 1958 he was elected delegate to the National Cotton Council. He owned cotton gins in Kenton, Rutherford, Dyer, and Como and had interests in six other gins at various times. He was a planter, owned and operated automobile and implement interests in Union City, and owned land near Kenton and Union City. He was a stockholder and director of the Mason Hall Bank, later to be renamed First State Bank of Kenton, later becoming chairman of the board.

Dad was a member and served as an elder of the Kenton Cumberland Presbyterian Church. He was president of the Kenton Strawberry Growers Association and president of the West Tennessee Hereford Breeders Association. In later years, he served on The University of Tennessee Development Council.

At age 72 Dad contracted leukemia. It was diagnosed at Mayo Clinic, and they gave him five years or so to live. He had periodic blood transfusions which kept him alive until he was 78. Early on Dad was suspicious of blood from people "off the streets," so I worked out an arrangement with our Pike chapter at UTM whereby brothers with the same blood type as Dad's would give blood which would then be transfused into Dad. Though it wasn't necessary, we made a monetary gift to the chapter for each pint of blood received. This went on for a couple of years or so and then finally played out. At that time our fraternity National Office in Memphis put out a notice to Mid-South brothers about this need which received some response. When a brother responded, we told him of our intention of making a gift to his chapter, a kind of a love offering, for each pint donated. A story about one of the latter donors follows:

December, 1974, a letter from Dad to Bill LaForge, a Pike from Delta State of Cleveland, Mississippi who was in law school at Ole Miss, an excerpt from which follows:

"I want to extend to you my sincerest thanks for your gift of blood. Also I want to assure you that we accept it in the spirit of brotherhood, which is, I am positive, the way in which you meant to give it. I will get to Memphis within the next few days for the transfusion ... As you can imagine, our family will be eternally grateful to you."

Fourteen years ago I became a trustee of the Pi Kappa Alpha Educational Foundation. Bill LaForge was a trustee also and went on to become president of the Foundation. He had formerly been president of the Pi Kappa Alpha Fraternity. I had not known Bill before, and he became a close friend.

Excerpts from my letter to Bill, dated September 7, 2001 follow:

"Dear Bill: I am writing a book about growing up in Kenton, my times since, and about my family. In going through some old files I ran across a copy of the enclosed letter *[the one just above]* that Dad wrote to you in 1974 thanking you for a pint of blood that you gave for him when he had leukemia. His great fear was getting hepatitis from a transfusion, and we were able to get many pints of blood from PiKAs, primarily from Epsilon Sigma Chapter at the University of Tennessee at Martin. These sources finally played out, and, sure enough, he contracted hepatitis from a transfusion about mid-year 1975, and he died that October.

I am ashamed to say that I had forgotten that you gave blood to Dad. I presume from the address that this occurred when you were a law student at Ole Miss. The letter (from Dad to you) properly expresses the feelings we had at the time and that I still have. What a wonderful tribute to you.

You are one of my favorite people and always will be."

Bill's answer to me:

"Dear Tom: You were so kind and thoughtful to write and remember about my giving blood for your Dad. You certainly have no reason to be ashamed of 'forgetting' that I gave blood, Tom. You and I had not even met then. But, this is a good story.

What I want you to know, however, is that I profoundly appreciate your thoughts about this event and about me. I well remember the occasion, as an Ole Miss law student, when I was simply responding to a call to any and all brothers in the Mid-South to help out. I had forgotten, frankly, that it was for your Dad, although I well remember his generosity to my chapter which I thought was well beyond and above any expectations. It seemed to me truly to be the gift of life for your Dad.

Thanks for sharing this fond and touching memory with me. Now we know that, in addition to being PiKA brothers, we're also 'blood brothers.'"

Every time I read this last sentence, and I have read it many times, it brings tears to my eyes. A finer person than Bill LaForge has never lived, and I consider him not only a fraternity and a "blood brother," but also a very dear friend.

Dad

Dad was more expressive with his love for us than was Mother, though nobody in the family readily expressed our love for each other. It was hard for us Wades to say, "I love you," though it was unequivocally understood that great love did exist among us. Many people in those more puritanical times were very private with their feelings, and our family fit that mold, for better or worse. It was especially hard for many men and sons and brothers to openly express love for each other. I do not ever remember Dad telling me that he loved me, or vice versa, until he was on his deathbed, just a day or two before he died. He was in the Union City hospital, and the two of us were the only ones in his room. I said, "I love you, Dad" to which there was no immediate reply. Then I asked, "Do you love me, Dad?" He said, "I sure do" with the emphasis on "sure." This exchange has been a very important part of my memories of Dad. Dad died on October 19, 1975.

Pat's and my family have told each other often that we love each other. But I don't tell the children nearly often enough.

Chapter Twenty-Eight

Aunt Zade; Her Book,
The Wades — The History of a Family; and
William Brawner Wade

According to *The Wades—The History of a Family*, written by Zada Wade Beadles and published in 1963, "The origin of the Wades is lost in the mists of history." The name is believed to be derived from the ancient Anglo-Saxon word, "wath," which was the word for "ford," and probably was first taken by one who lived near a ford of a river or creek. Spellings have included Wadde, Wad, Waude, Wath, Waythe, Waad, Waade, and Wade. Armagil Waad of an ancient Yorkshire (England) family was thought to have been the first of our family to be granted a coat-of-arms. He was born in 1511 at Kilnsey, near Coniston. He died at Belsize in 1568 and was buried in Hampstead Church. The second Waad of record was Armagil's son, Sir William Waad who was born in 1546. He was one of 20 children born to Armagil's two wives. William's life was spent serving the Crown. He served as clerk of the council and as lieutenant of the tower, and he traveled widely on the continent in diplomatic service. He also served several terms in Parliament. He was granted knighthood from James I. Sir William died in 1623 at his Manor of Battailes, Essex. Aunt Zade said, "It is said that the Wades of Virginia claim descent from Armagil Waad, but the question remains as to whether this descent was through Sir William or through another of the six surviving children." Aunt Zade goes on to list several supporting reasons for the above assumption and then continues, "Tradition has it that at an early age two brothers came from England, from Buckinghamshire, and settled in the Colony of Maryland ..., and from these have come the Wades who moved ever westward and contributed their share of the making of many of these United States."

355

At this point Aunt Zade begins with what she calls "The First Generation," Zachary Wade, who was born in 1627 and came to Maryland as an immigrant and accumulated 3,000 acres of land including a large tract in what is now Washington, D. C. Zachary became a member of the first Maryland General Assembly. His name appears on a monument in the park south of the White House commemorating the original patentees to the land now comprising the District of Columbia. Zachary's son, Robert, was also a landowner with 1,650 acres of land. His son, Richard, inherited the family plantation, "Friendship," and continued an agrarian lifestyle. Richard's son, John, was born in 1735 and served as a soldier in a "marching militia" under General Washington in New Jersey in 1777-78. John's son, William Wade, was born in Maryland in 1762 (or 1763) and moved to Rutherford County, Tennessee, near Murfreesboro, in the early 19th Century, became a large landowner, and sired 15 children. Beginning in 1828, eight of them with their families moved to Gibson County, Tennessee where their father had acquired a considerable acreage of land. One of the eight, Hilleary Wade, was born on Christmas Day of 1797. Hilleary had six children, one of whom was my Great Grandfather, William Brawner Wade, who was born near Winchester, Tennessee in 1826. William Brawner moved from the Trenton, Tennessee area to the Macedonia Community in Obion County just east of Kenton where he accumulated 5,000 acres of land and was the largest landowner in the Kenton area. He had five race horses and a race track on his estate. William Brawner Wade married Sallie T. Morton on June 20, 1849. One of his great achievements was that he supervised and largely financed the digging of the Obion River Rutherford Fork canal, the creation of which greatly reduced flooding in that river bottom. This canal was cleaned out and redug about 40 years ago. Dad said that William Brawner often went to First Monday in Trenton. The story was that one First Monday he made the rounds of the saloons, offering to pay for his drinks with a thousand dollar bill. Of course, nobody had enough change so he drank free all day long. Another handed down story is that one day he was riding in his buggy when he was stopped by a little but feisty man who bore some kind of grudge and invited Mr. Wade to get down off his buggy and square off with him. Mr. Wade, being a big man, said, "Dick, it wouldn't be any honor if I whipped you, but it'd be a helluva come off if you whipped me!" Needless to say, my Great Grandfather rode off leaving Dick fuming in his dust.

William was a big, braggadocio kind of man and when he married he told his friends that he was going to sire 26 children and give them names starting with all the letters of the alphabet. William and Sallie T. had eleven children including my Grandfather, Charles R. Wade, and then Sallie T. died. William remarried to Emily McNeely and she soon became pregnant. When she gave birth to my Aunt Zade, actually Zada Wade, William said that he had enough children and he gave her this name starting with a "Z" and proclaimed that Zada was his last child. A few years later Emily again became pregnant with William's 13th child. When this little girl was born he named her "So Forth." This was her legal name until she came of age and had her name changed legally to Mabel Clara. Aunt Mabel had a happy life, and in her later years she was the housemother of the Delta Upsilon Fraternity at the University of Oklahoma. When she visited in Kenton during my teens and early twenties I would take her around to see her old friends, white and black, and they all called her Soph or Sophie or Miss Soph (pronounced like sofa without the "a") or Miss Sophie. She obviously had been a popular girl growing up in Kenton.

Aunt Zade was the postmistress in Kenton for a while and then she married Jesse Beadles and moved to Cairo, Illinois with him where he became president of a bank and owned a large lumber business. He was very successful, and they lived in a big house that was raised high off the ground, as were all the houses in flood-prone Cairo which lays on the banks of the Mississippi River. These "tall" houses were built before the big levees and floodgates were built around Cairo. We used to go to Cairo every year or two for Sunday dinner, and I always enjoyed listening to Aunt Zade tell stories of her young years in Kenton. (Aunt Zade had a delightful big black maid who always told me I looked like a congressman. Must have been my prematurely gray hair. I sure liked her!) Aunt Zade did a wonderful job on the Wade book which she researched for a good many years, traveling extensively in the United States in the process of writing it. She had a very nice summer home on Kentucky Lake on Jonathan Creek which she called "Wadewood." The Gus Pharrs from Dallas, the George Tuckers, the I. W. Freemans, our family, and other relatives gathered at Wadewood for overnight stays many summers. Aunt Zade died at age 97 and is buried in Sunnyside Cemetery in Kenton alongside her husband, Jesse, and their daughter, Louise. Her surviving child, Tom Beadles, lives in Cairo. His wife, Virginia, died in 2003. Tom, an accountant, was once mayor of Cairo. His brother, Robert, and Robert's wife, Adelaide, died years ago. Robert, like his father, was in the lumber and timber business.

I often wish I had had the sense to ask Aunt Zade why she did not spend more time in attempting to trace our family back into England or Wales as my family once thought might be the case, but I didn't. So one time when Pat and I were in London with our close friends, David and Mary Critchlow, we went by the College of Arms. We talked with a genealogist there and I later wrote him from home sending him copies of some of the pages from Aunt Zade's book. I received the following letter from this gentleman. The letterhead address was

"P.Ll. Gwynn-Jones, M.A.   The College of Arms
Lancaster Herald   Queen Victoria Street
Telephone 01-248-0911   London EC4V4BT.
24 March 1982
Tom W. Wade Esq.,
Kenton,
Tennessee 38233
U.S.A.
Dear Mr. Wade,
Thank you for your letter of 12 March.
In the first instance, it would seem desirable for a complete search to be made among the official records of the College of Arms in order to see what Wade pedigrees have been registered here over the centuries, and whether your own known forbear appears therein. In

this respect, it would help considerably if you could let me have details of your emigrant forbear, such as his full name and approximate dates. The fees payable in respect of the above search and report will be $125.00; and if you would like to let me have your cheaque in that amount, made payable to the College of Arms, I will be pleased to have the work put in hand for you.

I would be grateful if all future correspondence could be addressed to me personally, as this will avoid unnecessary delay.

Yours sincerely,

P. Ll. Gwynn-Jones,

Lancaster Herald."

Later a Mr. Paston Bedingfeld wrote and told me that without any information at all tracing our ancestry back into England, it would be virtually impossible for the College of Arms to give me anything definite. He did tell me that if he had to guess where we Wades came from it would be north of London where he found records of two Armagil Wades. We have an Armagil Wade in our ancestry, and these two Armagils were the only ones that Mr. Paston Bedingfeld had ever run across. I gave up the quest for my "roots," at least for then and for now. Maybe again in the future I'll pursue them. (I do not know why Mr. Gwynn-Jones passed me off to Mr. Paston Bedingfeld. A copy of their research is in my lockbox.)

Our Wade Coat of Arms is different from several Wade Coats of Arms that the College of Arms sent to me. However, the one we have goes back several generations, and I suspect there was a legitimate basis for it. It's certainly one of the prettiest ones I've ever seen. From an old somewhat damaged Wade Coat of Arms, Mother had a Wade Coat of Arms as well as a Walker Coat of Arms (I have no idea where it came from) painted in 1957 by Algin H. Reeves of Stanford, Kentucky. This one, along with the Coat of Arms of the Walker family (which Mr. Reeves also painted) hangs in our Union City home. The description of the Wade Coat of Arms follows:

FAMILY OF: WADE

Arms: Azure, a saltire argent, between four escallops or.

Crest: A dove with an olive branch in beak, all proper.
Motto: <u>Vincit qui pattitur</u> (He who endures conquers).
Authority: Burke's "General Armory," 1844&1878 Editions.
TINCTURES AS SHOWN BY DESCRIPTION:
The shield is blue. Bars of gold and blue.
The saltire is silver.
The helmet is steel color.
The dove holding a branch of olive in beak are of natural color.
The scroll with the motto is gold.
The mantle (leaves around the shield) are all blue.

NOTES:
The arms, described above, is recorded by BURKE, the best considered and most authentic of all British Published Heraldic Authorities on English, Scotch and Irish family arms for the family of Wade of York, Warwich, Middlesex, Essex, Durham and London, (all of England also one branch of Montreal, Quebec, and of Ireland, granted in the year of 1768). The Wade Arms was also granted to the Rev. Thomas Wade, of Tottingham Bury County, Lancaster, England.

Chapter Twenty-Nine

Grandfather C. R. and Granny Nanny Wade

Charles R. Wade was born on March 12, 1858, the fifth child of William Brawner Wade and Sallie T. Morton Wade. Miss Lyda Belle Elder and Charles R. Wade were married by the Reverend J. T. Rothrock on October 6, 1886 in the Trenton home of Miss Elder's mother, Mrs. Mosie Watkins.

The only story I remember from the childhood of Grandfather Wade was that when he was a little boy he had a poem to recite in a program of some sort. One of the lines was, "Snowflakes on their backs." He thought it should rhyme so he recited it, "Snowflaks on their backs." Nice rhyme.

Unfortunately I know very little about the family of Lyda Belle Elder Wade, Granny Nanny to us grandchildren. Tom Watkins was her stepfather, and Eugene Elder was her brother. We had several Elder cousins in Kenton when I was growing up, but nobody ever told me or, to my knowledge, wrote anything about her family. What a shame. How fortunate we Wades are that Aunt Zade made it her business to record the American history of our branch of the Wade family

Dad's older brother, William Eugene Wade, was born on July 21, 1887.

Dad's next brother tragically died as a little boy in 1891. In those days death notices were sent to family and friends. Little Charlie's death notice follows:

FUNERAL NOTICE

The friends of the family are requested

To attend the funeral of

CHARLIE MORTON

Infant son of C. R. and Lyda Belle Wade

on Thursday, Feb. 26, '91.

Services at the Presbyterian Church at

9:30 o'clock, a.m., conducted by

Rev. J. T. Rothrock.

I have a wonderful photograph of this beautiful little boy in my Kenton office/homeplace.

Dad's sister, Moselle Wade, was born on September 24, 1894, and Dad was born on August 28, 1897.

Grandfather Charles R. Wade was a highly respected man and was wealthy in his day. He had a large general mercantile business, was a farm implement dealer, a grain buyer, a cotton buyer, a landowner, a cotton ginner, and was once mayor of Kenton. He sold everything from ladies hats to giant steam engines. At one time or another, he had interests in three cotton gins in Kenton and at different times was president of two Kenton banks and was later chairman of one of the predecessor banks of our present First State Bank. For fifty years he was an elder of the Kenton Cumberland Presbyterian Church. He and a cousin of his named Johnson owned a gin, Wade Johnson Cotton Company which was located on the site of our present gin. In addition, he owned a gin where Shatz Gin stood as well as another gin, the press being powered by mules, where the Verne Tomlinson house stands, just east of where the Kenton Schools stood. (Danny Jowers bought and refurbished the Tomlinson house in 2002.)

C. R. Wade's stores burned once or twice, but he rebuilt them. I have a photograph in my office of the rubble of a complete burn down with immediate family members, including a very young Tom Wade, and employees standing in the fallen bricks and concrete. What a poignant picture.

My Aunt (in-law) Carrie came to Kenton as a young lady from St. Louis, if my memory serves me correctly, as a milliner for the store. Back in those days, all the nice stores had their own millinery department where they had women who did nothing but design and make hats for ladies. While working for C. R. Wade, Aunt Carrie married into the family.

Billy Reid, a cousin of the Wades from Oklahoma, lived with the C. R. Wade family in Kenton for a period of time while he was clerking in C. R. Wade's store in Kenton. He was a witty young man. One time when Tom Wade and his sister, Moselle, were young, unexpected guests arrived for dinner. Granny Nanny took Tom, Moselle, and Billy into the kitchen prior to dinner and told them that she would be short of bread and that they would be given crackers to eat. She then instructed the children and Billy to decline bread when it would be offered by the maid, and crackers would then be passed. The first time the maid offered bread to Billy, his reply was, "No thank you; I prefer a cracker." Needless to say, this "cracked up" Dad and Auntie Moselle. Cousin Billy repeated his performance every time the bread was passed, and his young cousins spent the whole evening trying to hold back laughter.

One of my Grandfather's greatest accomplishments involved Sunnyside Cemetery which lies on a gentle hill in the western edge of Kenton and which was incorporated on January 21, 1899 by my Great Uncle, Wilton Hilleary Wade; my Great Aunt, Mattie Bell Wade Pharr; my Grandfather, Charles R. Wade; J. A. Reeves; and J. W. Clayton. I am justifiably proud that three of my ancestors were among the five people who organized Sunnyside, a lovely little cemetery that is certainly one of the prettiest and best kept cemeteries in this area. Standing adjacent to the Pharr and Wade lots in Sunnyside is a giant and stately old magnolia tree. If it could speak I wonder about the things it could tell from the many years it has stood within the borders of this serene final resting place of so many. Many of our ancestors are buried at Sunnyside as well as at Walnut Grove Cemetery east of Kenton and in Oakland Cemetery at Trenton.

In my early days of working at the gin in Kenton, old customers who had known my Grandfather, "Mr. Charlie," and had done business with him often told me about what a wonderful person he was. More than one told me that they simply could not have made it without his help. Dad told me that he really was too "easy" in extending credit which cost him a great deal of money in bad debts. Dad said he overheard his Mother, Granny Nanny to us grandchildren, tell Grandfather Wade, upon his extending credit to a known slow payer, "Charlie, you know he won't pay you," to which Grandfather Wade replied, "He said he would."

His easy ways finally cost him most of what he had accumulated, and he died at home in 1930. Granny Nanny moved to Memphis to live out her life with her daughter, Auntie Moselle, and Uncle George Tucker. I was five years old when Granny Nanny died in 1939, and I barely remember her. My recollection of her is that she was a soft spoken and gentle lady. Dad did tell me that she was a good businesswoman who was a great help to Grandfather Wade in his various business pursuits. Dad's parents had enough money to put him through college, but when he got back home from Knoxville and went into the cotton business he received no help financially from his family. He had to do everything that he accomplished on his own, from scratch. He inherited nothing when they died. Auntie Moselle inherited their furniture and whatever else they may have had, and she certainly deserved it.

The following was a feature story in the *Kenton Enterprise Courier,* circa 1890:

C. R. Wade

"Among the businessmen of Kenton there has never been a more prominent figure than C. R. Wade. He was born in Gibson County in 1858 and reared on a farm. In 1880, at 22 years of age he commenced business in Kenton in the line of groceries and hardware. Since that time he has steadily grown in popularity and his business has increased year by year. His success has been almost phenomenal. This success has been due mainly to the innate spirit which characterized Abon Ben Davis, "Write me as one who loves his fellow man." Few men have been blessed with such an even temper, such liberality of views and thought and such philosophical ideas of social and business life as C. R. Wade, and few men in any community have unconsciously established such a reputation for honor and integrity. The name of Charley Wade, as he is familiarly called is a synonym for all that is honorable, honest, and conscientious. No matter whom he has business with, no matter whom he settles with, everything is always satisfactory, and that special class of people who are constitutionally predisposed to dispute their bills find themselves amazed at the easy, smooth, and pleasant manner in which they have settled their annual accounts. Every reliable and responsible man who wants a favor goes to him instinctively and gets the favor.

Mr. Wade was married in October, 1886, to Miss Lyda Belle Elder of Trenton, Tenn. And has one son living, Eugene, who is already a familiar character in the town; a second son having died in his first year. *(Auntie Moselle was born in 1894 and Dad in 1897).*

He is an elder and active worker in the Cumberland Presbyterian Church, in which work he has had the valuable aid and cooperation of his estimable and devoted wife. Notwithstanding the financial depression of the past year, Mr. Wade's business has steadily increased. As agent for the celebrated McCormick Reaping and Mowing Machinery and J. L. Case & Co., threshers and other prominent farm implements and machinery he has established a very permanent and profitable trade which is increasing every year. He buys and ships annually about a hundred carloads of wheat and the same amount of corn. He at present occupies a large two story brick building on College Street with two warehouses and will at early date add another brick building to accommodate his increasing business. He is a stockholder and director in the Kenton Bank and holds the important position of member of the Finance Committee *(later he was president of this and then another bank in Kenton).* He owns and occupies a handsome residence on College Street ..."

The following obituaries which appeared in *The Kenton Press News* and *The Union City Daily Messenger* eloquently tell the story of a kind and generous man.

From the *Kenton Press*:

IN MEMORIAM
CHARLES R. WADE

"On Tuesday, May 27, the people of Kenton and surrounding country met under the shadow of a death which has caused more real sorrow and grief than any in Kenton for the last forty years. This statement is no exaggeration, but in my humble judgment is veritably true. I have known Charlie Wade for an unbroken term of forty years. Many have known him longer, but few have known him better. In early life he cried out in the language and wisdom of Jeremiah, the oldest and wisest of the Hebrew prophets, "My Father thou are the guide of my youth." How well he has stuck to this resolve, everybody knows full well. It has led him to long life, to honor, to success and finally to heaven and God. Aside from his active and well known Christian life, coupled with a spotless domestic life, I believe the two most outstanding characteristics are innate goodness of heart and downright honest all through life. His character is as white as a white light of a cloudless day, not a shadow falling to dim the deeds of a day. His democratic spirit and unassuming manner greatly endeared him to all classes of people. He had no new religion to experiment with, but held to the same old gospel in which he had been baptized. He believed in that religion that the Master sent the Son to preach upon and down the banks of the hisotric (sic) Jordan. He believed in the Fatherhood of God and Bro- a good Samartan (sic), where the priest and Levite passed a stranger he would have graciously cared for him. He was loyal and faithful in all the relations of life. He was a pattern of domestic life and an example of right living. He bowed in simple faith to the divine decree. He met death with unfaltering front, and unshaken faith and without the fear of the judgment of God. By the memory of our dear friend let us resolve to cultivate and preserve the qualities that made him useful and believed by all. That he was a near approach to a model man and citizen is the verdict of all who knew him best. He had the enjoyment of the love admiration and affection of all our people, white and colored, to a degree rarely ever permitted to anyone. 'But he has gone where the redeemed are keeping a festival above.' The Saviour's heart is glad — 'a younger brother has reached the Father's home.' He was honest and upright as a citizen tender and devoted as a husband, truthful, generous, unselfish, moral and clean in all relations. The collection of flowers was in generous profusion and perhaps was the most beautiful ever seen in Kenton. Evidently the elite of the gentler sex had been vying with each other, both as to the variety of selection and beauty of arrangement. The colored people were there to contribute their mite and to show that they, too, respected merit, worth and friendship. The remarks of the clergy, Revs. Spence, Oakley, Reynolds, and Cunningham were strong, well chosen and particularly appropriate. Now in conclusion let us indulge the hope and cherish the wish that all may join in the prayer that our Heavenly Father will be very gracious to his beloved companions and precious children and that he will comfort them as he alone can. This is not the first time that she has been known to nurse him tenderly and lovingly, often bending over him with tearful eyes and throbbing heart. I loved him living and honor him dead. JNO. C. PARIS"

From the *Union City Daily Messenger*
May 27, 1930

CHARLES R. WADE
DIED YESTERDAY

"Kenton's Most Highly Esteemed Citizen
Reached Ripe Old Age.

Charles R. Wade, highly esteemed citizen of Kenton, died at the family resident in Kenton yesterday afternoon following a brief illness. Funeral services were conducted this afternoon at three o'clock from the Cumberland Presbyterian Church of Kenton by the pastor Rev. O. D. Spence assisted by the pastors of the other churches of Kenton. During the funeral hour every business house in Kenton was closed as a mark of respect to Mr. Wade.

Surviving him are his widow, and two sons, W. Eugene Wade, a manager of a Memphis department store and Tom W. Wade, cotton buyer of Kenton and one daughter, Mrs. Geo. E. Tucker of Kenton.

Mr. Wade who was seventy two years of age, was a pioneer merchant of Kenton, having been engaged in business there for fifty years. During this half century of activity he made a wide circle of friends throughout this county and surrounding counties where he did business as a merchant, cotton buyer and grain buyer. Among these friends and acquaintances he made a reputation that few men establish for themselves for integrity, morality and high ideals of life.

Speaking of Mr. Wade this morning to a Daily Messenger representative C. O. Ramer, prominent Kenton banker, said "Mr. Wade was one of the most public spirited citizen I have ever known, one of the best business men this town has ever had, and one of our best citizens. And the greatest citizen our town has known during my lifetime. He fed the hungry, clothed the naked and gave homes to the homeless. Mr. Wade was known throughout this section of West Tennessee and wherever he was known he was beloved for the fine type of man and Christian he was. He had been a ruling elder in the Cumberland Presbyterian church in Kenton for nearly fifty years.

During his active business career he had helped organize the old Kenton Bank and was its president and was later president of the Peoples Bank of Kenton until ill health forced his retirement."

Dad followed in the footsteps of his father and had an impeccable reputation. I have done my best to live up to Dad's and my Grandfather's legacies. There is absolutely no question whatsoever but that Will Wade is cut from their molds.

Chapter Thirty

Uncle Eugene and Aunt Floye Wade

Dad's older brother, William Eugene Wade, was born on July 21, 1887. He graduated from Kenton High School with five other boys (no girls) in 1904. He did a post graduate year at Castle Heights Military Academy in Lebanon, Tennessee, graduating in 1905. He entered the University of Tennessee, pledged and was initiated into Pi Kappa Alpha in 1905 and then graduated with an L.L.B. degree in 1910. He was the first Pi Kappa Alpha in a long line of Pikes in our family. He married Floye Johnson on September 21, 1911.

Aunt Floye was the daughter of E. R. and Virginia Askew Johnson. She graduated from Peabody College for Teachers of Nashville. She taught school in Kenton for two years.

One of Uncle Eugene's closest PiKA friends was Hub Walters of Morristown. Dad also knew Hub very well. Mr. Walters went on to become a United States Senator from Tennessee. One of the large buildings at the University of Tennessee in Knoxville is named for him.

After graduation from UT Uncle Eugene came back to Kenton and worked with his father in their firm, C. R. Wade & Son, for 18 years. In 1928 the Eugene Wade family moved to Memphis.

Uncle Eugene and his family later moved to Humboldt for a few years, and they moved to Raleigh, North Carolina in 1938 where he worked for the Farmers Home Administration. He later became the top man in FHA in the state of North Carolina.

In late 1944 or early 1945 Uncle Eugene and Aunt Floye moved to Union City, and Uncle Eugene went into the automobile and implement business with Dad and Cousin Inman Freeman.

Uncle Eugene and Aunt Floye had three children: Virginia Lyda Wade, born July 31, 1912; Charles Rightman Wade, born January 22, 1920; and William Eugene Wade, Jr., born August 1, 1923.

Uncle Eugene and Aunt Floye's older son, Charles Rightman (Charley) Wade, received most of his elementary schooling and did part of his high school work in Memphis and Humboldt. The family moved to Raleigh in 1938 where Charley finished high school. He then entered North Carolina State in Raleigh and studied Aeronautical Engineering for two years after which time he volunteered for the United States Air Force in 1942. Charley was fairly short, and Dad told me he lacked just a little bit of being tall enough to be a pilot. Dad went on to say that Charley did some sort of stretching exercises in hopes of making himself tall enough to be able to fly Air Force planes. But it didn't work, and Charley graduated as a second lieutenant with the first class of navigators at Mather Field in California. He was sent to Hickam Field in Hawaii.

While stationed at Hickam, Charley took part in the first bombing of Wake Island, for which he was awarded the Air Medal. On February 13, 1943, his flight of Liberator Bombers was sent to bomb Japanese ships in Shortland Harbor off Bougainville. His plane was shot down and his parents were notified that Charley was "Missing in Action." On September 23, 1943 Uncle Eugene and Aunt Floye were notified that Charley was listed as "Killed in Action." The Purple Heart was awarded for Charles R. Wade, Lt., 307th Bombardment Group, 424 Squadron, APC 953, by Colonel J. A. Matheny. (My memory of Charley's death appears in Chapter 8 about World War II.).

From everything I have always heard, Charley was an unusually good, kind, and generous person. What a terrible loss.

Uncle Eugene and Aunt Floye gave a beautiful framed print of a Raphael Madonna to her Union City First United Methodist Church (our family church) Sunday School Class, the Queen Esther Class, in memory of Charley. Our church has built a new building, and our Sunday School classes have been moved around. This picture now hangs in Pat's and my Upper Room Sunday School Classroom. It is a poignant reminder of Charley's sacrifice.

Eugene and Floye's younger son, William Eugene (Gene) Wade, Jr., attended elementary school in Memphis and later in Humboldt when his Dad and my Dad bought a cotton gin (Will and I presently own one-third interest in this same gin) which Uncle Eugene ran for a few years before moving to Raleigh. Gene finished high school in Raleigh and followed his older brother to North Carolina State from which he graduated Cum Laude with a B.S. Degree in Aeronautical Engineering, a degree which his brother did not live to receive.

I remember hearing a story about Gene who, when he was a little boy, loved to wear cowboy clothes, and Cousin Lydabeth Tucker. Gene was almost two years older than Lydie. One time Dad went out into the yard and found Gene dressed up in his cowboy outfit, holding a lasso. He was lassoing Lydie and jerking her to the ground time after time. Lydie was crying uncontrollably. Gene said in his very matter-of-fact slow southern drawl, and this is a true quote according to Dad, "Don't cry Lydie. Genie's just apracticin' lassoin'," pronouncing the last two words with broad A's.

While at North Carolina State Gene played trombone in a band and was president of Pi Kappa Alpha Fraternity, the same national fraternity that his Dad had served as president after his 1905 initiation at The University of Tennessee.

After graduation Gene immediately went to work for Grumman Aircraft Corporation in Bethpage (on Long Island), New York. After a distinguished career with Grumman Gene came back south and lived in Union City and later in Dresden. He married Iantha Domer, and they had one daughter, Sabrina GeneAnn Wade Moore. Sabrina's two children are Alex and Rachel.

Tom Watson, Jr., the son of the founder of IBM, owned a yacht which he raced each year in the Bermuda Yacht Race. Gene was a personal friend of young Tom's. Gene lived on Long Island, and I presume Mr. Watson may also have lived there. At any rate Gene was a Bermuda Yacht Race crewman on the Watson yacht, which Tom Watson captained, on more than one occasion.

Naturally I knew Gene much better than Charley, whom I barely remember. In fact Gene worked for Dad in the automobile and implement business for awhile during which time I was also working there. I remember Gene coming to Union City on vacations from Grumman. He was ten years older than I, and I absolutely idolized him. Gene was very bright and had an incisive kind of wit. I simply thought he was the sharpest fellow I had ever known. My opinion in that regard never changed.

Gene died on April 1, 1994. I placed a Pike pin in Gene's lapel as he lay in his casket.

Virginia Lyda (Jennie Lyde) Wade grew up in Kenton and Memphis. She played basketball for the Kenton High School team, and Dad remembered with much affection and pride that Jennie Lyde had been selected as the county's prettiest player. I can certainly imagine that to have been the case! After graduation from high school she attended Memphis State for two years, during which time she accompanied, on their concert Steinway, the Memphis First Methodist choir. On October 10, 1935, she married a 1930 Southwestern graduate, Memphian Herman W. Bevis. Herman had received an M.B.A. in Accounting with High Honors in 1932 from Harvard Business School, and he had gone to work for Price Waterhouse, an international accounting firm, in New York City in 1933. Herman and Jennie Lyde moved to New York City to an apartment building that at the time was the largest in the world. Herman insisted that they have an apartment with a piano for Jennie Lyde, an accomplished pianist who loved her music. They managed to rent an apartment with a beautiful Steinway piano!

Eighteen months later Richard Wade (Dick) Bevis was born on June 4, 1937. Jennie Lyde and Dick traveled south to Humboldt and spent the rest of the summer with her parents. Soon the Bevis family moved to an apartment in Kew Gardens, Long Island. They lived in two other apartments in Kew Gardens before moving to a rented house in Westchester County. After nine months in this house Herman and Jennie Lyde bought a very large house in Greenwich, Connecticut in which they lived for 34 years.

Herman had a remarkable career with Price Waterhouse, culminating in his being named Senior Partner, or CEO, in 1961, a position he held until his retirement in 1969. While running the international affairs of Price Waterhouse, Herman found time to serve the American Institute of Certified Public Accountants (AICPA) as a member of their Board of Examiners, their Commission on Standards of Education and Experience, and many other committees, his service culminating with the vice presidency of AICPA and finally with his receipt of their 1969 AICPA Gold Medal for Distinguished Service.

Herman was very much involved with Greenwich activities, serving on the board of his city's Community Chest and as a member of Greenwich's Charter Commission. He served on national boards such as the American Arbitration Association, the United States Chamber of Commerce's Task Force on Economic Growth and Opportunity, the President's Task Force on improving the prospects of small business, and the National Budget Committee of Community Chests. Herman also did his share for national government. He served as consultant for financial management for the Assistant Secretary of the Air Force as well as for the Assistant Secretary of Defense. He also served as consultant to the Comptroller General of the United States. Herman wrote a book which I have and which I read, *Corporate Financial Reporting in a Competitive Economy*, 1965. This book was widely used as a college textbook and was published in English, Spanish, and Japanese editions. Herman also wrote numerous articles that were published in magazines.

As Price Waterhouse required retirement at age 60, Herman found himself at loose ends at a fairly early age. But not for long. From 1969 to 1971 he served on the President's Advisory Council on Minority Business Enterprise, and he later served on a task force that studied and advised New York City's Chamber of Commerce. He also served as a member of the city's Industry and Economic Development Council in 1978-79.

Herman's primary post retirement pursuit was serving in the most prestigious position of Executive Director of the Banking and Securities Industry Committee (BASIC). BASIC involved Interindustry Teamwork and was sponsored by The American Stock Exchange, The National Association of Securities Dealers, The New York Clearing House Association, and The New York Stock Exchange. BASIC was organized on April 1, 1974, and the Bevis's friend, John Meyer, also of Greenwich, was its first chairman. Mr. Meyer was chairman of Morgan Guaranty Trust. The following quote explains the reasons for BASIC's having been founded. "Conceptually, the problem with which the Committee is concerned is the inability of the present system accurately to execute, record and settle securities, transfers, and dividend claims within acceptable limits of time and expense." Jennie Lyde said that BASIC was a big success. She also said that this extremely challenging position was exactly what Herman needed. Jennie Lyde wrote, "I knew my husband wanted something rather important to do all the time. BASIC came — a stranger it was, but a savior it became, because Herman found it to be as interesting as Price Waterhouse had always been."

Jennie Lyde and Herman sold their big Victorian house in Greenwich, where they had raised their children, in 1978 and moved to a smaller one. In 1988 they moved to Colorado to be closer to their children. In April of 1989 Herman died. Jennie Lyde died in Colorado Springs on May 31, 2003.

Dick Bevis was graduated with Highest Honors from Country Day School of Greenwich and then from Phillips Academy of Exeter, New Hampshire. He graduated from Duke University, where he was a member of The Pi Kappa Phi Fraternity, and spent that summer abroad. One of the cities which he visited on his motor scooter was Beirut, Lebanon, a city he very much enjoyed. Prior to entering The University of California at Berkeley that fall, Dick and Vivian Leamer, also a graduate of Duke, were married in her New Jersey hometown. From Cal Berkeley Dick received a Masters Degree and a Ph.D. in 18th Century English Literature. Dick and Vivian's daughter, Linda, was born during this period of time. After graduation from Berkeley, Dick was offered a position at American University of Beirut, and he moved his family overseas. Vivian also found an English teaching position in Beirut. They were in Beirut from 1965 to 1970 when the unrest there became too dangerous for Dick and his young family, so they moved back to North America, this time to The University of British Columbia in Vancouver where Dick taught English Literature until his retirement at age 60. Vivian, an accomplished artist, has also taught English, for the most part, all these years. Dick decided he would rather write and travel than teach and grade papers, so he is now indulging himself in these two pursuits. Both Dick and Vivian are intrepid souls who are enjoying life to the fullest.

Dick has written three scholarly books which have been published. His first book, which I have read, was *The Laughing Tradition* published in 1980 by The University of Georgia Press. The second one (a

Longman Literature in English Series, The University of Lancaster) was published in the U.S.A. by Longman, Inc. New York, in 1988, and in England by Longman Group U.K. of London, also in 1988, and is titled *English Drama Restoration and Eighteenth Century, 1660-1789*. His third and last book was *The Road to Egedan Heath* published by McGill-Queen in 1999.

I confess that Dick's *The Laughing Tradition*, having to do with 18th Century English stage comedy, was not exactly the type literature that I normally read, but reading it had to have been good for me. I'll bet I'm the only person from Kenton ever to have read it. Jennie Lyde told me that she had told Dick some time ago that she was reading it, and Dick exclaimed, "Mother, I wrote this for teachers, not for people!" Well, guess I didn't have to read it after all.

Herman and Jennie Lyde's second son, William Wade (Bill) Bevis was born in New York City on June 25, 1941.

Bill also graduated with Honors from Country Day, and then he attended and graduated from Phillips Academy at Andover, Massachusetts. While Bill was at Andover he and some of his buddies wrote and recorded a song, the main words of which were, "You drive me crazy, Baby. You drive me crazy, Baby. I'm comin' home." I still remember the tune. Isn't it amazing how some fairly insignificant things stick with you? Actually their song was good. The right producer could have made a hit out of it. Bill, son Will has a fraternity brother who is a music producer in Nashville, and we'll be glad to send your song(s) to him!

Bill then headed for North Carolina, as had big brother Dick, but to The University of North Carolina, Chapel Hill, where he was a member of Tau Chapter of Pi Kappa Alpha, the chapter for which my sister Sally served as Dream Girl of PiKA. While at Andover Bill was goalie of their ice hockey team, the same position he had played at Country Day. During Bill's senior year Jennie Lyde and Herman attended Andover's big game with Exeter when Bill's play was so outstanding that the Andover student body chanted, "Bevis for President, Bevis for President." Jennie Lyde and Herman were mighty proud parents. This adoration may have been the impetus for Bill's having been the driving force in organizing a University of North

Carolina hockey team. He succeeded and became goalie for the Tarheels. Bill also followed big brother to Cal Berkeley where he obtained a Masters and Ph.D. in American Literature. Bill caught on with a hockey team in Berkeley which Jennie Lyde said "saved him."

Bill married Lee Kohn, also a North Carolina graduate, the summer after graduation, and they have two daughters, Sarah and Karen. After graduation from Berkeley, Bill taught for two years at Williams, but the West had gotten under his skin. He found an opening for an American Literature teaching position at the University of Montana at Missoula, and he took it and moved to Big Sky County. Bill and Lee had gotten a divorce, and he met Juliette Crump who had come to the University at the same time to teach dance. She had two daughters. Bill's two daughters were back in Berkeley with their Mother. Bill and Juliette were married in 1974. Alas, Missoula did not have an ice rink. Bill, with the help of some interested friends, built a rink in his own back yard where many a child has learned to play hockey on the Bevis Rink.

Bill and Juliette have a second home, and second rink, at their cabin down in Big Hole. They have a third home, an automoble anchored to the ground, with a stove, that sleeps two. This abode sits atop a Gold Mine that never produced any gold. Wonder if they bought this property from Shorty, the subject of Bill's great novel *Shorty Harris, or The Price of Gold* (published by The University of Oklahoma Press in 1999). As this is being written, Bill and Juliette will be retiring within a few months.

Bill has also written several other books. His first one was *Mind of Winter – Wallace Stevens – Meditation and Literature* published in 1988 by The University of Pittsburgh Press. Next came *Ten Tough Trips – Montana Writers and The West*, a McLellan Book published in 1990 by The University of Washington Press. Then came *Borneo Log – The Struggle for Sarawak's Forests*, published in 1995 in Seattle and London by The University of Washington Press.

As was the case with Dick, Bill has done all this writing while teaching as a professor of English.

The third Bevis child, Virginia Ann (Ginger) Bevis was born in Greenwich on January 2, 1951.

Ginger also attended Country Day. Dick and Bill left Country Day after the ninth grade to move on to Exeter and Andover, respectively, and Ginger also left Greenwich after the ninth grade and went to Ethel Walker School in Simsbury, Connecticut. After graduating from Ethel Walker (I had a great aunt on Mother's side named Ethel Walker, but she lived in Dyersburg!), Ginger, after an intensive search of schools around the country, decided on Lawrence University in Appleton, Wisconsin. She majored in Music Education, which she thoroughly enjoyed, and graduated with Honors. Then she headed — where else? — to Berkeley. Ginger called Lee, who by this time was separated from Bill, and Lee invited Ginger to move in with her and the girls. Ginger took a job teaching music at Head Royce School in Berkeley, and then she enrolled in Holy Names College, also in Berkeley, where she remained until she had a Masters in Kodaly (pronounced KO DI E), a highly acclaimed music teaching method. She stayed in Berkeley, teaching and studying, for five years, and then took a teaching position in Colorado Springs in 1980.

Ginger had always loved to skate, and she was a very good skater. She heard about a situation there in Colorado Springs where she could take free lessons taught by excellent skaters. Jennie Lyde says, "She particularly liked one tall, dark, and handsome young man who was one of the teachers. She noticed that when one of his pupils fell, he carefully helped her to stand up again. After a bit of thinking Ginger managed to fall right in sight of Mr. Littleton. And he did, very kindly, pick her up — several times." They talked. Ginger told him that her father was an accountant. He told her that his grandfather was an accountant, but "mostly he wrote books about accounting." Ginger called her Dad and told him about meeting this boy whose grandfather, A. C. Littleton, wrote books about accounting. Herman exclaimed, "Of course! Finest books on accounting ever written!" From skating to accounting, Ginger and Bob had a great deal in common, so much so that they became husband and wife. Their daughters, Peggy and Gayle, owe their very existence to some carefully orchestrated falls on ice! Ginger still teaches elementary and high school music and has done so since an eight year hiatus when the girls were young.

Ginger not only teaches music but she also writes it. Three of her songs for children have been published.

Jennie Lyde said, "Ginger is a born teacher, just as her brothers are and just as her Grandmother (my Aunt Floye) was. Herman and I were both pleased that our children turned to teaching."

Certainly Herman and Jennie Lyde's children are remarkable folks, as were their Father and Mother. They have made considerable contributions to mankind and continue to make the world a better place. I pray every day that my children and grandchildren will do the same. Happily they also seem to have the right stuff.

Uncle Eugene and Aunt Floye were mighty proud of their family. They had every right to be.

Chapter Thirty-One

Auntie Moselle and Uncle George Tucker

RECOLLECTIONS OF MOSELLE WADE (AUNTIE MOSELLE) TUCKER:

Her recollections (for me):

"Papa and Mama [*my paternal grandparents*] had a big playhouse built for Tom [*Dad*] and me in the back of the store. I was five, and Tom was two, and we played together constantly. We each had a nurse. Tom's was named Ray, and mine was Mertie. They were about 13 and 14 and were the daughters of our family cook whom we called Aunt Liza. At that time and until I was 13 years old, our Grandmother, Mrs. Rachel Mosella Carthel Elder Watkins, had lived with us. She died when I was 13. One of her sons was named Tom. He died in Louisville, Kentucky of typhoid fever. Your father, and you [*me*] were named for him. Your middle name is for Papa's brother, Wilton. Yours is a name to be very proud of." [*I am.*]

Continuing Auntie Moselle's memories:

"I still remember my graduation year when I was awarded the medal for best grade in bookkeeping. I didn't even know there was to be a medal given so when my name was called and I was sitting back in the audience with Mama and Papa and Tom, I was so excited I could scarcely make my way up to the stage to receive it. It was given by the bank, but Papa didn't know anything about it even though he was president of the bank at that time. I didn't think I was dressed up sufficient to go up on the stage to receive it, but your father [*Dad*] said, 'Go on, Sister. No one will pay any attention to what you have on.' So I did." [*Uncle Eugene and Dad always called Auntie "Sister." Auntie and Dad always called Uncle Eugene "Brother." Auntie and Uncle Eugene called Dad "Tom." Sally and I called Uncle Eugene "Bubba" until we were teenagers. We grandchildren called our Grandmother Wade, Granny Nanny.*]

For several summers as a young lady Auntie Moselle went to Chautauqua in upper New York State to take voice and piano lessons. She was always accompanied by Granny Nanny or some other older female relative; no genteel young lady ever went anywhere unaccompanied. (For years I have wanted to take our entire family to Chautauqua which has been operating for 150 years or so. Maybe we'll do that one of these years.)

Cousin Margaret Biggs' husband died at a very young age, and she was distraught. Granny Nanny sent Auntie Moselle to Memphis to be with Cousin Margaret during her time of grief. Cousin Margaret was a friend of George D. Tucker's father, and she thought it would be nice if Moselle could meet the young George, so she had father and son over for dinner. Moselle and George hit it off famously, and it wasn't too long until Moselle Wade and George deSausure Tucker were husband and wife. They were married on Easter Sunday, April 8, 1917 at Granny Nanny and Grandfather Wade's home in Kenton. Uncle George's father had recently died, and they didn't think a big wedding would be in good taste. Uncle George came from a very prominent family in Charleston, South Carolina. As Uncle George termed it, he grew up "on the Battry," no "e" in the pronunciation. His mother died when he was only 18 months old, and his father moved them to Memphis when Uncle George was a teenager. His father was president of the Virginia Carolina Chemical Company which made the nationally famous VC fertilizer, a brand we saw until not too many years ago. Uncle George was sent to prep school at Sewanee Military Academy and then attended Georgia Tech where he was a Sigma Alpha Epsilon. At one point his father also owned one-sixth of the Delta and Pine Land plantation in Scott, Mississippi. This company is now traded on the New York Stock Exchange and is the world's largest breeder of planting cottonseed as well as being a large breeder of soybean seed. Too bad Mr. Tucker divested himself of this stock many decades ago.

When Uncle George was courting Auntie Moselle he was in very good shape financially and was the Stanley Steamer dealer in Memphis. Stanley Steamers were cars that ran on steam and in order to run fast, the steam had to be built up real well. He told me that when he drove up to Kenton the first time to call on Auntie he stopped just south of the hill on the south side of Kenton and built up his steam and then roared into Kenton, making a big impression on everybody, especially Auntie. During his business career after they married, Uncle George owned a Ford franchise in Forrest City, Arkansas. In addition, at one point he was in the contracting business, owning large dirt moving equipment.

Lydabeth (Lydie to all the family) Tucker was born to Moselle and George Tucker on April 26, 1925, in Memphis at Baptist Hospital. (Cousin Polly Elder, who never married, was the daughter of Cousin Jessie Wade Elder, the very good painter, and John Carthel Elder. Cousin Polly for many years was Pediatric Supervisor for the Baptist Hospital of Memphis. She always took extra good care of us Wades and Tuckers.) Lydie started to school in Kenton with Laura Joyce Howell (Barton), our across-the-street close friend, and Billie Thweatt (Dickerson), the daughter of Mother's and Dad's very close friends, Bill and Lorene Thweatt. The Tuckers then moved to Memphis where Lydie started the second grade. They lived in Memphis through Lydie's sophomore year in high school, and then they moved back to Kenton for a year. Lydie remembers "being with a bunch of friends at Mark Shatz's house on the Sunday afternoon of the Pearl Harbor attack, December 7, 1941." The Tuckers then moved to Cairo, Illinois in 1942 where Uncle George worked at the Edison Plant which made munitions for the Navy during the war. Auntie Moselle and Uncle George moved to Union City a few months after Lydie and Ernest Nordman, Jr. were married on November 7, 1946, and Uncle George went to work for Dad, Cousin Inman Freeman, and Uncle Eugene as parts man in the automobile and implement businesses which were called Freeman and Wade. A short time later, Auntie Moselle went to work for them as the head bookkeeper. Auntie and Uncle George lived in their Union City, East Main Street home until Uncle George's death on February 8, 1975. Auntie stayed in their home for two or three years and then she moved to Cairo to live with Lydie. Auntie, who first saw the light of day on September 24, 1894, died on August 17, 1986. Auntie's Mother, Father, and older brother had all died at age 72, and she was convinced that she would also die in her 72nd year. She lacked one month of beating that by 20 years!

Ernest (Ernie) Nordman, Jr. was a civil engineer who had graduated from the University of Illinois. During his engineering career he worked for Edgar Stephens Construction Company and for Illinois Minerals Company, both of Cairo.

Lydie and Ernie had two children, Ernest Nordman III and Elizabeth Ann (Libby) Nordman, born April 26, 1948 and November 26, 1950, respectively. Little Ernie married Judith Ann Wissinger on May 22, 1970, and they have three children, Rachael Ann, Gretchen Rene, and Ernest Todd, born March 22, 1972; November 20, 1973; and July 29, 1976, respectively. Rachael married Joseph David Narsh on May 20, 1995, and they have two "adorable" (according to Lydie) daughters, Riley Rose and Dylan Renee. Gretchen married Andrew John McMillen on September 16, 2000. Todd is unmarried as of this writing. Ernie's and Judy's two daughters graduated from Southwest Missouri State University in Springfield, and both live in St. Louis. Todd graduated from Southeast Missouri State in Cape Girardeau where he has bought a home.

Little Ernie was not little. He was a big boy and an excellent athlete. He was a particularly good baseball pitcher. I remember catching him in the alley behind the automobile place in Union City, when he was probably 12 or 13 years old, as he fired one fast ball after another. My hand stung for days. Ernie has long been a pharmaceutical salesman for what is now GlaxoSmithKline. He and Judy have lived in Cape Girardeau for many years.

Libby married James Kenneth Sharpe on July 22, 1972 (permit me a little bragging here — Jim is a Pike from Murray State!). Libby works for LEXMARK, a successor company to IBM in Lexington, Kentucky, where she and Jim live. Jim is a consultant, owning his own firm, JKS Consulting. Both Libby and Jim have Masters Degrees, hers in Business Administration from the University of Kentucky and his in Economics from Murray State University. Libby and Jim — and also Ernie — did their undergraduate work at Murray State. Libby and Jim have two children, Erica Lee Sharpe, born December 22, 1978, and Lindsey Erin Sharpe, born February 20, 1982. Erica married Gregory

G. Gates on February 5, 2000. They have one daughter, Evelyn Leigh. Erica graduated from Vanderbilt University, and she and her husband now live in Charlotte. Lindsey is presently in school at Vanderbilt.

Big Ernie tragically had a massive heart attack and died at 60 years of age at home on August 2, 1977.

My earliest recollection of Auntie Moselle was in her home in Memphis when I was very young. I believe they lived on Cowden Street. I barely remember Granny Nanny who lived with the Tuckers. This was after my Grandfather C. R. Wade had died.

Auntie Moselle came up from Memphis to Kenton and stayed with us in our home for four weeks or so for several years during strawberry season. She kept the books for Dad and Cousin Inman Freeman and the Kenton Berry Growers Association. For a couple of years or so Cousin Dayle Wade of Amory, Mississippi also came up and stayed with us and helped keep the books.

Auntie told me a great deal about the family, and I have been working through a voluminous file of this information in the course of writing this book. She gave me a painting of a little girl with rabbits and strawberries (of course!) which was painted by my Great Grandmother, Mosella Rachel Carthel Elder Watkins in 1861, the first year of the Civil War. Mrs. Watkins was the mother of Granny Nanny. I believe the story goes that her husband, who was my Great Grandfather, was in the War as a Confederate soldier at the time Mosella painted this picture. She had gone to a young ladies college in Columbia, Tennessee and while there she studied art. This painting always hung on the wall in her bedroom which she shared with Auntie Moselle beginning when Auntie was almost three years old. Auntie said, "I was 13 years old when she died at age 64. I loved her devotedly and would not sleep in 'our' room for about six months after she left us." The painting now hangs in our home, and it is one of my most prized possessions. Auntie said Granny Nanny took art lessons from an art teacher who came to her home. The artist's name was Miss Mamie Archibald and she was considered very good. Auntie said that Aunt Minnie, Cousin Jessie, and a Mrs. Odom, all from Kenton, also took lessons from Miss Archibald. We also have four oil paintings that were done by Granny Nanny and three paintings by Cousin Jessie

Elder in our home. Two of Granny Nanny's paintings, still lifes of strawberries and peaches, were in Mother's home on either side of the sideboard in her dining room. We have these paintings on either side of that same sideboard in our dining room! The other two, one of sparrows in snow and the other of a castle in a pastoral setting, hang in our library. The two still lifes painted by Granny Nanny are dated 1894 when she was pregnant with Auntie Moselle. Auntie told me that ladies often painted when they were heavy with child, as it was thought more proper back then for these ladies not to get out in public any more than was absolutely necessary during those delicate months. I also have a pastel, which I think is a retouched photograph, of my Grandfather Wade which Auntie said was painted by Cousin Emma, in my office. I was able to buy three of Cousin Jessie Elder's paintings in Kenton estate sales, and they hang in our home. Two of her paintings are small and are of flowers. The third painting is larger and appears to be a European village on a river with a bridge. I remember going up to Cousin Jessie's home on West College Street (which we used to call Quality Hill) in Kenton and watching her paint at her easel in the entrance hall of their home.

Uncle George was a dapper southern gentleman if ever there was one. He was charming in every way, easy going, and everybody liked him. He used to say that Auntie Moselle worried enough for both of them, so there was no point in his doing any worrying. After the world became so litigious, his parting shot was often, "I'll be suin' ya." Ask him how he was doing and he often would say, "All right, if there's any difference." I never did figure this one out. He referred to our really very good Union City newspaper, *The Daily Messenger*, as "The Daily Mess" or the "Daily Disappointment."

Uncle George never lost his love for Charleston and finally was able to go back one time in his latter years. Sally sent Auntie a picture of the St. George Tucker House in Williamsburg, where Sally and Pitt lived for six years. Auntie said that St. George Tucker was a member of Uncle George's family. Uncle George's father had a framed picture of that house. He also had a picture of Thomas Tudor Tucker's house. This relative of Uncle George's was Treasurer of the United States during George Washington's presidency. Pat, the children, and I saw the famous Tucker House in Bermuda, which also belonged to an ancestor of Uncle George. He and Auntie are buried in Kenton's Sunnyside Cemetery in the Wade lot.

Chapter Thirty-Two

The Pharrs

William C. Pharr, first mayor of Kenton, married Mattie Bell Wade, sister of C. R. Wade. One of the children born to William C. and Mattie Bell was Gus William Pharr, our Cousin Gus. W. C. Pharr came to Kenton as a grain buyer and later was a banker and the M&O Railroad agent, thereafter becoming editor of *The Kenton Reporter*. The following excerpts from *The Kenton Reporter* appeared after Pharr became editor in the late 19th Century.

"The Kenton Reporter, owned by Col. Ozier and edited by one J. T. Long, has changed owners and editors. Long the great temperance advocate got on a ten day drunk and skipped out for parts unknown. W. C. Pharr, is the present editor and under his management, we predict for the *Reporter* a long and prosperous life.

Alfonso: Your 'poem' on the 'Rise and Fall of Lick Creek,' is first rate — never better — but we cannot use it because you wrote on both sides of the paper. Write it again and put it on two sheets of paper so our foreman can use one sheet to light his pipe while Tom utilizes the other in kindling the fire — our wood is green.

He was eating dinner the other day around at the Commercial Hotel, and his companion, across the table, having finished his meal and growing impatient to leave the table remarked: 'You needn't lay in a two days' supply, they are going to have supper here at the regular hour this evening.' 'Well, they may, and they may not,' he replied, 'something may turn up to prevent it, and I never take such chances. Will you please pass me them perturnips?'

A pound's a pound the world over, but when your wife pounds you over the head with a one-legged frying pan you are apt to see the difference between that and a pound of fine-cut tobacco.

Vanderbilt is worth $100,000,000, and yet he don't have a bit more fun than poor folks.

387

On the 4th, inst., Deputy Ramsey arrested George Smithers at Dyer Station for carrying a pistol, Smithers proposed to give bond if the Deputy would accompany him to his home in the country. They went to the livery stable and procurred horses. Ramsey went up town for something and Smithers while he was gone proposed to trade for the horse Ramsey was going to ride. Ostensibly to try the horse's gaits, he mounted and rode back and forth in front of the stable a few times. Finally he rode a little further than usual and putting whip to the horse was soon out of sight. Ramsey pursued but did not overtake him. Next day the horse and Ramsey's saddlebags were found three miles from Dyer, but Smithers has not been heard from.

A scientific journal says the standard length of the human form is six times the length of the foot. This won't do. We publish this paper next door to a shoe shop and we propose to know a thing or two about the size of people's feet ourselves. If some human forms we have seen leaving that shop were to be stretched out to six times the length of their feet the 'milky way' and 'seven stars' would have to be moved up a story or two higher to prevent a derangement of the planetary system.

Near Walnut Grove, five miles from this place, stands an old house built by Davy Crockett and near that house stands a beech tree on which his name is carved by his own hand. It seems to us a block of that tree, containing the name, wouldn't be a bad thing to send to the Nashville Centennial.

Mr. Blake Flowers was intimately associated with Davy Crockett in his young days, and gave us many interesting reminiscenses of the early settling of this country. The last time he saw Davy was when he passed his house on his way to Texas, dressed in a hunting suit, wearing a coon skin cap with the tail on it, and carrying a very fine rifle.

Walking hats are advertised in the *Madison County Herald*, but their speed is not given. For summer wear the distance around the brim ought to be at least two 'running feet.'

Twenty cats for sale by Tom Bogle at so much 'purr' cat.

Obion County has a population of 22,466 with 5,042 voters. (*This late 19th Century fact strongly indicates that our 2002 population of approximately 32,000 is nothing to brag about*).

On the 6th, inst., near Mason Hall, Mr. Lewis Jonakin, a veteran of 62 years, and Miss Mattie Motley, a maiden of 17, were married by Rev. Martin Busick. It has only been a short time since the bride's father was married to a daughter of the bridegroom. The bride was the niece of the bridegroom and he is now the son-in-law of his own son-in-law. (*This story reminds me of an old song that recounted a similar strange set of marital circumstances and wound up, "I'm my own grandpa. I'm my own grandpa. It sounds funny I know, but it really is so ... Ohhh, I'm my own grandpa."*)

A few months ago stock in the Edison electric light ran up to enormous figures, and it is now charged that he intentionally manipulated it in the interest of stock speculators. Future developments may throw more light on the subject, and prove that his boasted discovery of the electric light was all gas."

Gus Pharr was Dad's older cousin, and he and his wife, Cousin Ida, lived in Dallas. Cousin Gus suffered reverses during the depression of the early 30s and moved into an apartment in the Dallas Country Club in order to live more frugally. Tough living! After times turned good again, the Pharrs built their second house in Highland Park, still one of the most prestigious addresses in Dallas, and lived there until Cousin Gus died. Their home was a big substantial two-story brick house in one of the fine old sections of Highland Park. Soon after Cousin Gus' death, Cousin Ida moved into a nursing home in Dallas. Their son, Bill Pharr, and his wife, Betty, lived in University Park, another nice part of Dallas, in a lovely home. Betty still lives there; Bill is deceased. Bill and Betty's children are Elizabeth (Betsy) Pharr Hedges, William (Bill) T. Pharr, Jr. (who sadly died as a young child), and Margaret (Peggy) Pharr Wilson. (See Chapter 27 for more Wade/Pharr involvement.)

"Cousin Gus and Ida," as we always referred to them, visited and stayed with us almost every summer. Cousin Gus who drove Chrysler New Yorkers which he bought from our dealership, always loved Kenton and enjoyed coming back here. Kenton seems to have that effect on anyone who's ever lived here.

William C. and Mattie Bell Wade Pharr are buried in Sunnyside on the southwest corner of the circle in the center of the cemetery. Bill and Betty Pharr were kind enough to sell to me the other six burial plots of the eight plot Pharr lot which lies next to the C. R. Wade family lot. I will be buried there between the Pharrs and the Wades. Others of my family may also be buried there.

Chapter Thirty-Three

Cousins

I have been blessed with many cousins who were and are wonderful people and who were and continue to be important to me. Though I have known at one time or another literally hundreds of cousins, many of whom have been mentioned in this manuscript, the cousins with whom Sally and I were closest were those with whom we grew up. Charlie Freeman and James and Tommy Hamilton of Kenton, somewhat older, are mentioned in several chapters. James was kind to ask me to serve as a groomsman in his and Mary Nell's wedding in Trezevant. Their two sons, both of whom live and work in Dyersburg, are James A. (Jim) Hamilton III, a practicing attorney, and John Edward Hamilton who owns and manages two Subway restaurants. Each of James and Mary Nell's sons has two daughters. Tommy and Ruth have a daughter, Nancy Hamilton Wilburn, and a son, Jerry Hamilton. Nancy has one son, and Jerry has two daughters. Charlie and Joyce have two daughters, Janice Freeman Jenks and Linda Freeman Stavropoulos. Janice has one daughter and two sons, one of whom, Jeff, was a friend of Will's at UT. Linda has one daughter. William Penn has also been mentioned briefly. William died a few years ago and left a son, Alan, and a real void in Kenton. William was loved by all who knew him. The two of us traveled quite a bit together. His older brother, Joe Ferris Penn, also mentioned in this book, preceded William in death leaving his widow, Nell, and two children, Joe, Jr. and Carol. William and Joe's younger sister, Lelia, died not long ago from ALS, Lou Gehrig's Disease. She left three sons, David, Terry, and Barry White. These Kenton cousins are from Dad's side of the family.

A great deal has already been written about Peter Pelham.

The three daughters of Mother's first cousin, Martha Frances Craig Tickle, also of Dyersburg, were very important to Sally and me. The oldest, Jennie Craig, now of Ripley and the wife of Dr. Sonny Tucker, was probably Sally's best friend growing up. Sally and Jennie Craig were about the same age. One of Jennie Craig's sons, John, is a loan officer with First Citizens National Bank in Dyersburg, and Will and I have had pleasant dealings with him in that capacity. Take it from me, John's a comer. John has two brothers, Craig and Jeremy. Martha Frances' middle daughter, Corinne, was one of my all-time favorite cousins. Corinne and I had a certain rapport, almost like brother and sister. Corinne is married to Bob Leggett who has long been an English professor at The University of Tennessee in Knoxville. They have two children, Leslie and Will. Martha Frances' youngest daughter is Martha Lynn Templeton who has lived in Memphis all her married life. Martha Lynn is considerably younger than Sally and me, and we didn't "pal around" together too much. Martha Lynn and my Pat were childhood playmates, though, and she has also been important to our family. Martha Lynn and Joe have three children, Tracy, Todd, and Scott. These cousins are from Mother's side, of course.

Other cousins who have not heretofore been mentioned in this book and who come to mind are and were from Mother's side: Johnny and Mike Walker from Memphis, both PiKAs from UTM, their sister Lynn, and their parents, J. P. and Betty; their uncle Grover, and their aunt Jane Walker McGoldrick; Grover and Mary's sons are Lee and Scott, and Jane's children are Art and Paula; Katherine Ann Dietzel Cox and her daughter, Pam, from Union City; Cousin Mai Alexander and her son, Bill (my long time accountant), and his son, Bill, Jr.; Grace Dietzel Sibley Gary and her daughter, Grace Sibley, and her son, Dan Gary, Jr.

And from Dad's side: Wilton Elder (a Pike from Memphis State) and his sister Suzanne; Tom and Virginia Beadles and their children, Patricia Wade (Patti) Beadles Bangert and her younger brother, John Asa, and younger sister, Louise Gail; and Robert A. and Adelaide Beadles and their one child, Robert W. Older cousins whom I knew or know: Beulah Hamilton, Laura Lou Hamilton Russell, Leila Hamilton, Jim Hamilton, Reeves Hamilton Freeman, Charles Montgomery, Evelyn Montgomery Alexander, Frances Montgomery Pennell, Beulah Montgomery Moffit, David Montgomery, Fanny Montgomery Bogle, Sarah (Bitsy) Bogle Karnes, Margaret Pharr Nelson, Sallie T. Kerr

Skinner, Virginia Holmes Freeman, George William Freeman, Mabel Wade Senter Jarrell; Carthel Wilton Elder, Mary Dean Glisson Williams, Mary Ellen Williams. Cousins of my approximate age and younger whom I knew or know, also from Dad's side: Martha Ellen Davidson Maxwell, Jo Alice Houston, Glenda Houston Caudle, Ann Alexander Hamilton, Thomas Clarence (T.C.) Karnes, Mary Frances (Sissy) Karnes Coleman, Ella Patricia (Pat) Nelson Coleman, William Peterson (Pete) Nelson, Albert Biggs, Elizabeth Josephine Pharr, George William (Bill) Freeman III, James C. (Jim) Bethshares, Jr., Charles Moffit.

Two cousins-in-law who surely seemed like cousins to Sally and me were Cousin Anna Mae Hamilton (Cousin Jim's wife) and Cousin Inman Freeman (Cousin Reeves' husband).

There are several reasons why so many more cousins have been mentioned from Dad's side than from Mother's side. First, Aunt Zade's book, *The Wades–The History of a Family*, is a wonderful resource simply to remind me of cousins whom I have known or met at one time or another. Secondly, I grew up in Kenton, a hotbed of my Wade cousins. Third, the Wades have been a more prolific group. My Great Great Great Grandfather Wade had 15 children, my Great Great Grandfather Wade had six children, and my Great Grandfather Wade had 13 children. 'Nuff said!

Since some of these cousins' names came from Aunt Zade's 1963 Wade book, and since I haven't seen or heard from some of them in many years, some of the females' names may not reflect later marriages. My apologies for any such inaccuracies.

Taking author's privilege I have decided to feature three of my cousins in this chapter — Estelle, Jr. (Fire) Norvell Cruxent from Mother's side of the family, and Frances Wade Caldwell and Ruth Wade Kane from Dad's side. After reading about them I believe you readers — if there are any readers! — will understand why this decision was made.

Estelle Norvell, Jr. (and her younger brother, Louis G. Norvell, Jr.) grew up near Newbern, Tennessee. Estelle, Jr., now known as Fire, attended Camp Nagawicka at Delafield, Wisconsin and Holton Arms in Washington, D. C. (Sister Sally attended Nagawicka also and graduated from Holton Arms. Lou G., as we called Louis, Jr. as a youngster, attended The McCallie School in Chattanooga and The University of Tennessee in Knoxville, also my alma maters. Obviously the Norvells and we Wades took similar scholastic paths.) Fire then matriculated at Wellesley, near Boston, and later at the Boston Museum School of Fine Art.

After her formal education ended, Estelle began to travel the world. She first lived near Veracruz, Mexico and then in San Francisco, Memphis, and then back to Boston for awhile. Then she headed for Europe and Tangier, Morocco and then back to San Francisco and then Manhattan Beach, California. Europe called again and she moved to Paris, then Rome, then Istanbul which is part Europe and part Asia. From Istanbul she moved to London and then to Malaga, Spain on the Mediterranean where she met Jorge Cruxent who was destined to be Estelle's husband. From Malaga, Estelle and Jorge moved to Tangier, Estelle's former home. From there they moved to Barcelona, Jorge's home and the home of his family. They moved into La Pedrera, a building designed by the world famous Antoni Gaudi. Their first child, Jorge Bel, was born in Barcelona. Wanderlust again hit the Cruxents and exotic homes were in their future. Their first stop was Sardina in Las Palmas de Gran Canarias. Then it was on to Rebola and then Bata, both in Spanish Guinea. The equatorial climate drove them away, this time on a freighter to Malaga again from where they later went to Casablanca. Madeiras, Portugal was their next home. Then Rio de Janeiro became their home for a time. Their next homes were Santa Cruz and La Paz, both in Bolivia. From Bolivia the Cruxents moved to Lima and then later to Iquitos, Peru. After Peru they moved to Boston and then Long Island and then back to Spain, this time Figols near Barcelona where their second child, Isis, was born. Jorge's mother, Mrs. Cruxent, had fixed up the house in Figols where she was born, as a summer retreat. Fire and Jorge lived there for two years. They then came home to the Norvell's lake house at Kentucky Lake near Paris, this time the one in Tennessee. Three years stateside is all they could take, and they moved to Crete, Greece. From the beautiful island of Crete they moved back to Figols where they stayed for four years. From there they moved to the metropolis of Roellen,

Tennessee. After a couple of years they moved to Seattle in 1987 where they lived until 1998 when they moved to Dyersburg in order to take care of Estelle, Sr. who had become virtually blind. Big Estelle died in 2000 at 90 years of age, and Fire and Jorge now plan to be in Dyersburg during the winters and to spend their summers elsewhere. The summers of 2002 and 2003 were spent in the mountains of Mexico. Fire and Jorge are undeniably world-class movers!

Jorge Bel lives in Stuckdorf, Germany, and Isis is married and lives in Seattle. Both children were educated abroad and in the United States and are multi-lingual.

Both Fire and Jorge Cruxent are artists. They have many other traits in common, and these intrepid souls plan to see much more of the world before they are finished. Fire and Jorge collaborate on what Pat and I think are beautiful paintings. Jorge normally does the drawing, and Fire fills in the colors. Seventeen of their paintings and drawings hang in our house and are among our favorite possessions. Until July 2003 Fire and Jorge lived in the large second story loft of a building in Dyersburg's square. This big room with very high ceilings and an enormous skylight was the sample room of Fire's Dad's cotton business. It made for a wonderful artists' studio. They then relocated to Newbern.

Estelle, Sr. (Big Estelle) was my Mother's first cousin. She was one of the children of Martha and Hal Craig of Dyersburg. Fire's and Louis' father, Louis G. Norvell, Sr., was a prominent and wealthy cotton man, landowner, and investor.

One of my favorite stories involving Estelle, Jr. (I use her old and new names interchangably) is about one time when she brought a fancy school friend of hers home during a vacation. We have a good friend named Larry Joe Ray from Finley, Tennessee, a very small town just west of Dyersburg. Larry Joe was a great guy with a terrific sense of humor and no pretensions whatsoever. Estelle arranged a blind date for her friend with Larry Joe. Obviously her friend knew nothing about this area. When Larry Joe and this girl met, in breaking the ice he asked her where she was from. Well, she commenced to tell him that she lived in one place during the winter, another place during the spring, still another place in the summer, and she wound up by telling

Larry Joe where her family spent their autumns. After going into all this detail about their seasonal homes, she said, "And where do you live, Larry Joe?" He quickly replied, "I live in Finley, all year 'round."

We Wades consider ourselves fortunate that the Cruxents found their way back to West Tennessee. We wish they would stay forever. Fire is unquestionably my most amazing cousin.

In the spring of 2001 former Kenton mayor, Damon Cross, brought me an article from the *Amory Advertiser* about Mrs. Frances Caldwell, 100 years old as of March 1, 2003! Knowing that some of my Wade ancestors moved to Amory, Mississippi a long time ago and started growing strawberries, I made inquiry of Mrs. Caldwell about the possibility of our being related. We are. That newspaper article and letter have spawned a steady correspondence between Cousin Frances Wade Caldwell and me and her sister, Cousin Ruth Wade Kane of Crescent City, Florida, and me. Cousins Frances and Ruth have shared with me many of their recollections about the Wade family, their families, and Kenton.

Martha Frances Wade Caldwell was born in Kenton on March 1, 1903. Cousin Frances' parents were William Powell Wade and Beulah Dayle Rodgers Wade. (Cousin Dayle helped keep the strawberry books for Dad for several years when I was young, see Chapter 3.) Cousin Frances graduated from Kenton High School and attended Stetson University in Deland, Florida, The University of Chicago, and graduated from Peabody College in Nashville. In 1928 the family, including Cousin Frances, moved to Amory, Mississippi where the Wades picked up their strawberry business and continued to be very large growers as they had been in Kenton. Cousin Frances taught English and History in Jacksonville, Alabama and in Amory.

In 1930 Cousin Frances married William Stanley (Stanley) Caldwell, and they had three children, Marianne Caldwell, William Stanley Caldwell, Jr., and Charles Anderson Caldwell.

Their first child, Marianne, was born in 1932. (If the following are not known by their first names, the name by which they are known will be in parentheses.) This Ole Miss graduate married Joseph Michael (Joe) Raper, a University of Tennessee Dental School graduate who practiced dentistry in Amory. Marianne and Joe's children were Joseph

Michael (Joe II he was called as a youngster) Raper, Jr., a Mississippi State graduate, and Cynthia Caldwell (Penny) Raper. Joe II married Janet Sue (Jan) Renfroe, and they had a child, Joseph Michael (Michael) Raper III. Penny married Jack Jenkins Sherman, a Mississippi State graduate. They have two children, Richard Erik (Erik) Sherman and Hillary Jane (Jane) Sherman.

William Stanley (Billy) Caldwell, Jr. graduated from Mississippi State. He married Margaret Jean (Marjean) Toney, a Mississippi Southern gal. Marjean has been my contact with Cousin Frances, as Cousin Frances is now blind. I have talked with Cousin Frances by telephone a few times, and she carries on a beautiful conversation. Billy and Marjean are retired and living in Germantown, Tennessee. They have done and continue to do extensive traveling. They recently visited mainland China for the third time. Billy and Marjean have three children. Their first child, William Stanley (Bill) Caldwell III, another Mississippi State graduate, married a Mississippi State graduate, Pamela Alice (Pam) Ford. Bill and Pam have two children, William Stanley (Stan) Caldwell IV, who is presently attending Mississippi State, and Abby Kathryn (who is called Abby Kathryn) Caldwell. Billy and Marjean's second child, Bridgette Cameron (Cameron) Caldwell Spell, a Mississippi State graduate, married Hugh David Spell, likewise a Mississippi State graduate. They have two children, Brenna Corinne Spell and Graham Powell Spell. Cassandra Jean Caldwell is the third child of Billy and Marjean.

Charles Anderson (Charley) Caldwell graduated from Ole Miss and married Sandra Delores (Delores) Leech. Delores is deceased. Charley lives in Amory. Charley and Delores had three children. Diane Leigh Caldwell Noe, an Ole Miss graduate, married Phillip Scott (Scott) Noe, a Mississippi State graduate, and they have two children, Leigh Ellen (called Leigh Ellen) Noe and Liza Kathleen Noe. Charley's and Delores' second child, Kimberly Frances (Kim) Caldwell Farrar, married Micheal Stanley Farrar, and they have one child, Amy Frances Farrar. Amy Frances is known as Amy Frances — I love those Southern double names! Charles Anderson (Chuck) Caldwell, Jr., an Ole Miss graduate, is the third child of Charley and Delores, and he married Tiffany Joan Lacey, a Mississippi State graduate. I had no idea I had so many

Mississippi State and Ole Miss cousins. Y'all got us Rocky Toppers outnumbered big time!

Cousin Frances is a member of Amory's First Presbyterian Church and taught Sunday School for many years. She served as president of the Presbyterian Women's Group and in 1968 became the first woman to be elected an elder of her church. Bammy, as Cousin Frances is known by her family and in Amory, was also the first Presbyterian female elder in the State of Mississippi. In 1975 she served as Commissioner of St. Andrews Presbytery to the 115th General Assembly. She also served on the board of Chamberlain Hunt Academy, a renowned Christian military academy in Port Gibson, Mississippi. She is a member of The Daughters of the American Revolution.

Cousin Frances' husband, Stanley Caldwell, died fairly young, so it became her sole responsibility to raise their children. From everything I have read, she did a remarkable job in that regard. All the time she was seeing to the upbringing of her children she ran the family furniture business in three towns and looked after their farming interests. Stanley's parents lived with Cousin Frances and Stanley until Stanley died. Then Cousin Frances' mother, my Cousin Dayle, moved in with her. I have heard, and it is quite obvious from the way she lived, that Cousin Frances is a genuine lady, a devout Christian, and was a smart and hard working businesswoman. To put it plainly, like many other true Southern ladies, she was sweet but she was tough. My understanding is that she has passed down through the generations these admirable qualities. Cousin Frances is just another typical Wade!

Cousin Ruth Rodgers Wade Kane, Cousin Frances' younger sister, was born on March 11, 1906, in Kenton. She is now 97 years old. She graduated from Kenton High School and attended Stetson University, Peabody College, and the University of Chicago.

The following is an excerpt from a July 10, 2001, letter from Cousin Ruth Wade Kane.

"Dear Tom: I can't tell you how much I have enjoyed your 'Growing up in Kenton' (Chapter 1 of this book). It brought back so many happy memories of my own as I read about yours ... I suppose we all should keep a journal or write our life histories for our children to know what it was like in our time ... Just last week I discovered that my granddaughter, Robyn, who had named her son Samuel Wilton because Wilton is his grandfather, did not know it was also her great grandfather's name! She is very pleased to know it has been in the family so long, and especially happy that it is being carried on down by Wades in Tennessee... I'm glad you wrote about Cord who looked after you when you were little. I assume she was the same Cord I knew, who used to houseclean for my Mother at regular intervals. Once I asked Mother why anyone would give a baby girl such an ugly name, and she answered, 'Oh her name is not Cord, her name is Cordelia, and she was named for my Aunt Cordelia!' Cord in Kenton was named for my great aunt who lived in Henderson (Tennessee)... Cord was an excellent cook. I know that because of the excellent meals I enjoyed at Aunt Lyde's table. Her delicious little yeast rolls would delight any gourmet."

I responded to her letter:

"I'm delighted that Robyn named her son Samuel Wilton. Please tell her that. I remember very well that Cord's real name was Cordelia. One of those childhood moments for me, when people somehow think they remember something from a very young age, is a vague memory of Cord bathing me in a little baby tub that Mother had and which Cord used on a porcelain table in our kitchen. I still have that table in the same kitchen of our old home in Kenton which has long been my private offices. Another thing about Cord is that I remember Mother telling me about Cord's death which occurred in her church while she was standing up and excitedly testifying. Mother always talked about what a devout Christian Cord was and that the sudden heart attack death in her church was a most appropriate way for her to have died. I am fascinated to hear about Cord's being named for your great aunt from Henderson. I agree that Kenton's Presbyterian Church was a beautiful building and that it is also a great shame that it was torn down."

Excerpts from a letter of February 15, 2002 from Cousin Ruth:

"I'm very thankful that I grew up in Kenton. Life there seemed so safe and secure and everyone seemed to operate from a firm foundation of values ... I hope we can hold onto enough of those early ethical and spiritual values to guide us through the many current problems."

Amen, Cousin Ruth.

Cousin Ruth met Bernard E. Kane at Stetson University in 1922 when she was a 16 year old freshman. Both their families had spent some winters in Cocoa and Daytona Beach which was the reason that Ruth and Bernard (and Frances) chose Stetson of Deland, Florida. (At the time they were in Cocoa, it was simply that — Cocoa. The beach could be reached by boat [motor launch] only, down the Indian River, around the south tip of Merritt Island, up the Banana River to the beach port opposite the town of Cocoa. It was a fun trip, but required all day from very early to very late. It was easier to drive up to New Smyrna Beach or Daytona Beach. Cousin Ruth remembers that school children from Merritt Island came to the Cocoa school by motor launch. She says now there are bridges across both rivers, and the whole Space Center Complex occupies that area.) Cousins Frances (Boe to Ruth) and Ruth were both at Stetson, but financial constraints required their leaving there early and going back to Tennessee. Bernard left Stetson after his junior year and transferred to Stanford University.

Though Bernard was from Pennsylvania, he "dropped in" on Ruth on his way back and forth between Pennsylvania and California, and they soon decided to get married, which they did. He then entered Vanderbilt, and Ruth entered Peabody also in Nashville. Then the Kanes went to Chicago where they both studied at the University of Chicago where he received his Bachelor of Science degree. They returned to Vanderbilt where Bernard received his Masters in Bacteriology. Then it was back to Chicago where Bernard received his M.D. degree from the University of Chicago. He practiced for a while in Haskell, Oklahoma, and then they moved to Amory, Mississippi where Ruth's family lived, and he practiced there. Their son, Wilton, had serious sinus and other allergy problems, so Ruth took the children to Daytona one winter, and Wilton had no trouble at all. The same thing happened the next year, so the Kanes decided to move to Florida. After looking the state over they decided to move to Crescent City, a decision they never regretted. Cousin Ruth still lives in

Crescent City where she has always been very active in her Presbyterian Church.

Bernard practiced in their Crescent City home. Cousin Ruth was his only office help. Cousin Ruth wrote,

"We liked to have patients in our home, and I could be office help and oversee the family at the same time. Our children were very sociable, so we had a lot of activity here all of the time. In the summers we had from five to eight grandchildren at a time, and we called our place Kamp Kane. It was a wonderful and happy life, with the cousins getting to know each other like siblings. We have a wonderful lake for swimming adjoining our back yard and a park with tennis courts across the street — an ideal place for kids."

Obviously the Kanes have had rewarding lives. And obviously Cousin Ruth has had a remarkable life, juggling the running of a medical office with the raising of her children and, to a degree, her grandchildren and great grandchildren. I'd say those 97 years have been jampacked with good things for her family as well as for mankind. We Wades have what it takes!

The Kanes had four sons: Wilton who was born in Nashville, Jean who was born in Oklahoma City (where Bernard did his internship), Barney who was born in Amory, and Wade who was born in Florida. Four sons, four states. All four boys graduated from Crescent City High School. Wilton, Jean, and Barney all graduated from the University of Florida, and Wade graduated from Embry Riddle in Daytona Beach. Wilton went to Jefferson Medical School in Philadelphia and did his residency in Jacksonville. (My brother-in-law, J. Pitt Tomlinson, III, was drafted right out of Emory Med School and spent four years in the Air Force after which time he and Sally moved to Jacksonville where he did his residency in Pediatrics. Pitt knew Wilton there, and in fact, Wilton was once in the Tomlinson's home. Sally and Wilton had no idea that they were related. It is indeed a small world.) Wilton married Nancy Finkelstein of Philadelphia and practiced medicine in Live Oak, Florida for ten years, and then they moved to Tallahassee where he still practices seven days a week at 75 years of age. A man after my own heart! Jean is a museum director, having worked in museums in Gainesville, Florida; Springfield, Illinois;

Daytona Beach; Raleigh, North Carolina; Richmond, Virginia; Nashville, where he was director of the Tennessee State Museum; and finally back to Richmond as director of the Valentine Museum. While in Gainesville he met and married Judith Ann (called Judith Ann, J. A., or Judy mostly) Flatter of Toledo. Barney married Emilie Schmidt of Brockport, New York. Both Barney and Emilie are Ph.D.s. Barney has taught Environmental Biology at East Carolina University for many years where he is now approaching retirement. Wade first married Susan Campos. They were divorced several years later, and then Wade married Sarah Swanson from Crescent City. They now live in Alaska where Wade is a member of the Alaska Air Guard. Wade volunteered for the Army in 1966 and was sent to Vietnam in 1967-68 during some of the heaviest fighting including the Tet Offensive. He was Crew Chief on a Chinook helicopter and received 21 medals. In Alaska he helped rescue four downed scientists who were doing research on polar bears and who went down in minus 20 weather and winds of 70 knots. The pilot, co-pilot, and Wade each received a Commendation Medal of Valor. Wade, you are a great credit to our name.

Wilton Rodgers Kane and Nancy had four children. Their daughter, Lisa Ruth Kane, an attorney from Florida State, married Ralph DeVitto, also a Florida State grad. Their second daughter, Robyn Dale Kane, a Florida State graduate, married Judge Lawrence Stevenson, a graduate of the University of Florida. They have two children, Katherine Alyne Stevenson and Samuel Wilton Stevenson. Wilton and Nancy's third child is Clinton Sean Kane, and their fourth child is Jeanette Ceceil Kane, a Florida graduate.

Jean DuVal Kane and Judith Ann have two children. Their son, Elisha Kent Kane IV, married Dahna Raur. Jean and Judith's second child, Aletris Anne Kane, married Shawn Cobb. Aletris and Shawn have five children: Matthew, Amber, Heather, Benjamin, and Rebecca.

Bernard and Ruth's third child, Bernard Evan (Barney) Kane, married Emilie Schmidt. They have two children, Elizabeth Ann, a graduate of the University of Florida, and Evan O'Hara who married Deborah Trusdell.

Wade O'Hara Kane and Susan Campos had one child, Mary Margchet (pronounced Marshay). After a few years they were divorced, and Wade then married Sarah Swanson. Wade and Sarah had two children, Michael Wade Kane and John Evan Allen Kane.

Cousin Ruth has four children, eleven grandchildren, and seven great grandchildren. It is quite obvious from our correspondence with Cousin Ruth that she and Bernard were devoted to each other, to their children, and to their grandchildren. Bernard died in 1984, before any of his great grandchildren were born, but Cousin Ruth obviously loves them enough for both Bernard and herself.

Even though I am a loyal Volunteer whose blood runs Tennessee Orange, I would love to get to know my Florida cousins despite the fact that many of them are Gators and Seminoles! Maybe I'll be privileged to meet some of them one of these days. I surely hope so.

Surely you readers will have to agree that Cousin Fire, Cousin Frances, and Cousin Ruth are all three truly remarkable ladies.

Chapter Thirty-Four

The Automobile and John Deere Places and Other Businesses

This chapter will be devoted to the history of the business endeavors of us Kenton Wades. On March 1, 1941, Dad and his friend and cousin-in-law, I. W. (Inman) Freeman, bought the property on the west side of the highway in Kenton where the Kenton Dairy Bar is now located. A brick building which formerly housed the Obion County Oil Company stood on the property (the concrete pad and foundation of the original building could still be seen at the Dairy Bar until it burned in April, 2003. The owner, Scott Whitworth, is going to rebuild from the ground up and has torn out the old foundation which I, selfishly hated to see go.) Freeman and Wade Implement Company opened up as a John Deere dealership. Ferris Penn was the manager. That fall the company bought property across the highway where the First State Bank drive-in and Exxon station are presently located. On that property a mule barn and business was established. Mules were traded by farmers for their first tractors. Mr. Will Lane was employed as the mule trader. I remember driving up to Anna, Illinois, a noted mule market, with Dad and Mr. Lane. They also bought and sold mules at Memphis, Shelbyville, and Columbia as well as at other big mule markets. Columbia was considered to be the nation's largest mule market. Our mule business flourished for several years, but mules were, of course, eventually totally supplanted by mechanized farming.

We young boys hung out at the John Deere place a good deal of the time. Carl Swink was the head mechanic. This "gentle giant" was a big and very strong man. I watched him work on the big old steel wheeled two-cylinder John Deere tractors for hours at a time. Occasionally I would "knock off" to go next door to play basketball with Billy Thetford. The Thetford house now belongs to Beulah Hill and is just north of where the "implement place," as we called it, was located.

I can remember "pitchin' pennies" in the showroom with Ferris Penn, Charlie Freeman, James and Tommy Hamilton, Charles Emrich, Bruce Lane (Mr. Will's son), Cousin Inman, Dad and others in the showroom, the winner being the one closest to the concrete seam at which we were pitching. We boys enjoyed stooping down on the portable platform scales, grabbing the bottom and pulling up as hard as we could to see who could generate the most pounds on the scales.

John Deere Day was something we children looked forward to from year to year. Long ago John Deere put on big "Days" at their dealerships. John Deere Day consisted of food and Cokes at the place of business and a movie, a combination of advertising and a feature picture show at the local movie theater. For a few years the Kenton school "let out" part of that day so all the children could go to the free movie at the Horse Opera. We had "Days" at Kenton and at Union City, where the movie was shown at the Capitol Theatre. Literally hundreds of farmers, wives, and hired hands would attend both events. John Deere Day was a marvelous sales tool for John Deere and for their dealers.

In 1944, anticipating the end of WWII and the revival of automobile manufacturing, Uncle Eugene and Aunt Floye met our family and Cousin Inman, Cousin Reeves, and Charlie Freeman in Knoxville for the purpose of exploring the possibility of opening a John Deere and automobile franchise in Union City. They decided to "go for it" and the Eugene Wades moved to Union City and a new Freeman and Wade was organized with the three men as equal partners in the Kenton John Deere store as well as in Union City. The new company rented the three-story triangular Deering Building on the north end of Union City's First Street business district next to the railroad, and their new John Deere agency was established. (This building still stands today, and although the upper stories are in need of revitalization, the lower story has been renovated somewhat and houses a couple of businesses.) Later that same year they signed a contract to become a Chrysler-Plymouth dealer.

On June 1, 1945 the partnership bought a lot two blocks north on First Street. A couple of years later a new modified art deco building was built, and the company moved into the new quarters. A few years later, in order to accommodate John Deere's wishes, they built another smaller building just north of the big building and next to the First Presbyterian Church (now the First Street Church of Christ) and moved the John Deere business next door. The Chrysler-Plymouth business remained in the big building.

As a youngster I wrote an advertising jingle for Plymouths when we were in that business. It went like this:

Look at that auto agoin' by.
Looks right good but looks can lie
Now listen to me while I tell you why
Plymouth is the best car that money can buy.
It's got everything and a little bit to boot
If you step on the gas it really will scoot
And I'm sure you'll like it if you give it a try
Plymouth is the best car that money can buy.
It's got shock absorbers that can't be beat
Its got an air conditioner if you're bothered by the heat
It rides like a cloud floatin' through the sky.
Plymouth is the best car that money can buy.
Go to Freeman and Wade and let 'em tell you why
Plymouth is the best car that money can buy.

I composed the tune with the help of my ukulele, a little musical instrument that gave me many hours of pleasure.

In the late 40s Dad and Cuddin' Inman, being caught up in the publicity of the supposedly soon-to-be revolutionary Tucker automobile, decided to pursue a franchise. They took me with them to Chicago to the fabulous first showing of the Tucker. I remember how great it looked on the stage of the opulent theater, slowly revolving on a turn table, a beautiful model standing beside it and almost caressing this sleek and spectacular automobile. I remember how disappointed and hurt I was to learn later that the car (which nobody was allowed near) was only a shell and had no motor or mechanical parts. This charade became one of the most famous events in the annals of the automobile business and the Tucker never got off the ground.

In 1948, Charles Emrich became parts and front manager at the Kenton John Deere place and later became manager of the shop. Then in 1950 Charles Inman (Charlie) Freeman, Inman Freeman's son, graduated from Florida Southern University (where he was a Pike!) and moved back to Kenton with his lovely bride, Joyce. After working with manager Ferris Penn for a few years, Charlie and his father bought the interests of the Wades in the Kenton store and operated it until it burned to the ground in December, 1956. The Freemans opted not to rebuild, and Dad opened a branch John Deere place in the building on the lot presently occupied by the Kenton American Station. After about a year this store was closed and Kenton no longer had a John Deere agency.

Earlier in 1956, anticipating my graduation from the University of Tennessee, Dad bought out the interests of Eugene Wade and Inman Freeman (who incidentally served for many years as president of Kenton's Mason Hall Bank, later to be First State Bank) and renamed the company Tom W. Wade Motor and Implement Company. This move took place in order to give me a business into which I could go. We all thought that my allergies would preclude my being able to work in the gin and farming businesses. At that time we were not in the grain business. As it turned out I was able to work in these other businesses and actually enjoyed cotton ginning, grain elevator operations, and farming, especially strawberries, much more than I did the trading and credit aspects of the implement and automobile businesses.

A few months earlier, again succumbing to great publicity for a new auto, Dad, close friend and PiKA Brother Hamilton Parks of Trimble, Carl Hayes of Union City (our automobile manager), and I journeyed to New Orleans for the introduction of Ford Motor Company's much heralded Edsel. We somehow got crossed up down there and ended up in the Lincoln-Mercury show and never even got to see the Edsel. However, Ford's famous TV personality of the time and other Ford folks convinced us that Edsel would make us rich! So we signed up. Carl reminded me that at one point on the way home when he was driving while we three others were asleep, that he was pulled over for speeding. Carl did some fancy talking and got off without a ticket. As he drove away, Dad opened his eyes and told Carl that he had handled the officer so well that we three thought it best "not to wake up!" Carl said that shortly after the New Orleans trip, he and Dad went to see an Edsel in Dyersburg, and Carl told Dad that he had serious doubts about the radical design. We made the switch anyway. Not our most astute business move! (As an aside, Carl lived to be 94 years old. He left $310,000 to our Union City First United Methodist Church.)

It became obvious in 1953 that I could take the minimum of 12 hours per quarter and Dad would keep on sendin' money, so my college career stretched through another football and basketball season, and my graduation was pushed back to March of 1957. After a temporary job raising money for a new fraternity house for my Pi Kappa Alpha Chapter at UT, I came to work for Dad in the late summer of 1957.

Bill Rudd worked for us on the farm and at the gin. After we gave up our Chrysler-Plymouth franchise and took on Edsel-Lincoln we sent Bill to Detroit with parts to be returned to Chrysler Corporation. As Bill pulled out from Union City he said, "Let's see now, we go through Memphis (110 miles due south of Union City), don't we?" We wondered if he'd ever find Detroit. Surprisingly, he did.

Six months and many thousands of dollars later we wisely decided to call it quits. That sixth month we sold our last ten new Edsels at whatever it took to "get rid of 'em." The Edsel folks were very excited about our sudden spurt of sales and wanted to send us a bunch more. Dad said, "No way! Why do you think we've been selling them at big losses?" It took another year or so to wind up the used cars and the business and we left the automobile world for good, a decision I have never regretted.

In 1958 we sold a big old used car to a distinguished looking man who claimed to be a preacher. We took a little money down and financed most of it, selling the note with recourse to Union City's Old & Third National Bank. This man drove to Philadelphia and wrote the bank and told them where they could pick the car up in Philly. He addressed the letter to "The Old Fashioned Bank." As I recall, we had it picked up and sold there. It wasn't worth sending after.

Another time I sold an old car to a man from Hickman, Kentucky. He became delinquent and I wrote him a strong collection letter. He immediately sent a $5.00 payment by <u>air</u> <u>mail</u> — from Hickman to

Union City, a distance of 15 miles. He meant for us to get this payment quickly. He didn't want to lose that car.

After cleaning up the used cars I went back home to work at the gin in Kenton and never again worked in Union City. We continued to run the John Deere business for awhile and then around 1960 or so, sold one-half interest to Bill Stephenson who earlier had come to work for Dad in the John Deere business. The new company was named Stephenson and Wade. We operated this business for just a few months, and Bill was dissatisfied with the situation and wanted all of it or none of it, so Dad bought him out. A short time later Dad sold one half interest to Bill Dilday, a young John Deere blockman, and Dilday and Wade took over.

In 1962 Dad bought six acres on Highway 51 South on the southwestern edge of Union City, from Edwin Stone, selling the back two acres on Old Rives Road to Bill Stephenson who soon opened a parts store there. In the mid 60s, Dilday and Wade built a new John Deere faclity on the four acres fronting Highway 51S and operated the franchise very successfully until Bill's tragic death of a massive stroke on June 14, 1973. Bill's young widow, Peggy, and Dad sold the company to Red Hunt and Johnie Dodds on September 13, 1973 ending Dad's 32 year career with John Deere. The building is now home to Aloha Pools and Spas. So ends the saga of the Wade's involvement in the farm implement and automobile businesses.

Other Businesses

From 1957, my college graduation year, through 1969 Dad made no financial progress. For those 13 years Mother and Dad and Pat and I and our family had lived out of the business, but Dad's net worth in 1969 was almost exactly the same as it had been in 1957. Obviously Dad was worth less in '69 than he had been in '57 because inflation had eaten away at the value of those dollars. Most of my UT friends had taken jobs with big companies and were making great progress in their careers. I felt like a total failure. When things weren't going well I worried almost constantly about such things as "How are we going to cover these losses, Dad?" Dad would always brush off my concerns with quiet reassurances, and sure enough things always did work out.

Fortunately Dad's ability to cope with setbacks has, to a degree, rubbed off on me as the years have rolled by. Now it seems that Will does a lot more worrying than I do. Maybe he will also mellow as time goes by. I believe he will.

In 1970 things for us turned on a dime, and we had a better year than we ever would have thought possible. With the exception of 1991, a very low volume handle year, and 2001 when my biggest corn customer went bankrupt and did not pay me for 100 carloads of corn and about 15% of another 25 cars, every year since 1969 has been a good one. How fortunate we Wades are that we just kept plugging away right here in our little corner of the world. It is very unlikely that almost any other pursuit would have done as much for us as have our efforts here at home in Kenton, Dyer, and Como. We owe a great deal to these communities.

History of the Wades in the Cotton Business

My Great Grandfather, William Brawner Wade, moved from the Trenton area to the Macedonia area east of Kenton in the middle of the 19th Century. He was a cotton grower and owned 5,000 acres in and around Macedonia. He had 13 children, one of whom was C. R. Wade, my Grandfather. C. R. (Charlie) Wade was a Kenton merchant and owned land on which cotton was grown, and he had other business interests including, at various times, three Kenton cotton gins. In the late 19th or early 20th Century, C. R. Wade was financially interested in two Kenton gins. The older one was located on property later owned by Miss Verne Tomlinson, between the Gray Clinic and the school. The press was powered by mules. His other gin was on property later owned by Shatz Gin Company. C. R. Wade and a cousin, E. R. Johnson, purchased the present Wade Gin Company in 1923 and they operated as Wade-Johnson Cotton Company.

In 1930 Wade-Johnson sold out to Dad and J. Wilbur Dickson of Rutherford. Dickson then sold his interest to Dad in 1932. Our family has operated a gin on our present lot for 81 years, and Will Wade is now the fourth generation Wade to gin cotton in Kenton.

In 1933 Dad, Rankin Mathis of Milan, and C. V. Alexander, also from Milan, bought Farmers Gin Company in Rutherford from the

National Cottonseed Products Corporation. In 1934 Dad and Mathis traded for Sharon Gin Company. Apparently Wade, Mathis, and Alexander decided in that same year to do some swapping, the results being that Dad and Mathis ended up with the Rutherford Gin and Alexander with the Sharon Gin.

In 1934 Dad purchased a gin in Humboldt, also from the National Cottonseed Products Corporation. Dad's older brother, W. Eugene Wade, was financially involved in this gin and managed it for several years. They sold it to the Trenton Cotton Oil Company in 1941 for a tidy profit. Will and I presently own one-third interest in this same gin (entirely different machinery and buildings, of course) and in the Humboldt Cotton and Commercial Warehouse. We, along with the John Shoaf family (John, Maureen, Ruth, Hedrick, Holt, and Vance) of Milan and Allen Espey of Huntingdon, bought into Humboldt in 1997.

In 1935 Dad and Rankin Mathis built Como Gin Company at Como, Tennessee from the ground up. In 1947 Dad bought out Mathis.

Dad, Rankin Mathis, and R. H. Owen in 1942 bought what is now Trenton Gin Company from V. B. Banks, the J. A. Hammond Estate, and Katherine Crafton. On December 10, 1945, they sold out to E. C. (Slim) Charlton and Paul Kinsey.

On June 31, 1954, Dad, Robert Patterson of Trenton, and Robert Wilson of Jackson bought Dyer Gin Company from L. A. Thornton of Dyer. In 1956 Robert Wilson sold his 1/3 interest to Robert Phebus of Dyersburg. In 1960 Robert Phebus (1/4), Buck Patton (1/4), Arthur Patton (1/4), all of Dyersburg, and Dad (1/4) bought Yorkville and Mason Hall Gin Companies. Shortly thereafter Dad and Phebus purchased Tip Top Gin Company in Dyersburg. Then in 1966 Dad swapped his 1/4 interest in the Yorkville and Mason Hall Gins to Phebus for his 1/3 interest in Dyer Gin Company. About this time Dad sold his interest in Tip Top to Phebus. In 1973 Robert Patterson sold his 1/3 interest in Dyer Gin and Tom Wade sold 1/6 of the total shares to me so that Dad and I owned Dyer Gin 50-50.

In 1997 Will and I bought one-half interest in Yorkville Gin Company, so we Wades are again in the gin business in Yorkville. The Shoaf family are our partners.

Dad continued to operate Wade Gin Company, Como Gin Company, Farmers Gin Company of Rutherford, and Dyer Gin Company until his death in October, 1975. I bought Wade, Como, Farmers, and Dad's one-half interest in Dyer from the Tom Wade Estate in 1976.

My saddest times, from a business standpoint, occurred after the 1976 season when we had to close down Como Gin for lack of cotton to gin and again after the '78 season when Rutherford and Dyer Gins were closed for the same reason. Fortunately for us, Como and Dyer's grain business took up the slack. Wade Gin Company was barely able to survive during those years when so little cotton was grown around here. For two years it was operated at zero cash flow and for several years with very little profit. Happily for us Wades, cotton came back around here in the 80s and at one point Wade Gin Company was ginning 50% more cotton than all four gins combined used to gin. Dyer was a double battery gin — two gins under one roof — so in effect they actually amounted to five gins.

Through the years Dad was involved in a total of ten West Tennessee gins.

Ginning

There's no telling how many gin fires we've experienced. Dad lost entire gins and parts of gins. Soon after my graduation from college we had a major fire at our Rutherford gin that burned the press end of the gin and the bale platform and all the cotton on it. This, as was usually the case with a gin fire, was in the middle of the season. We determined the parts and equipment that would have to be replaced and Dad sent long time employee, Sammie Lee Lancaster, to Prattville, Alabama to the Continental Gin Company to pick up a new DFB lint cleaner and other machinery and equipment. Sammie was told to "turn your hat around," or get there and back as fast as he could. A policeman somewhere in Alabama stopped him for speeding in his trailer truck and Sammie Lee said, "Mr. policeman, our gin done burned down!" The policeman let him go, and Sammie made the trip in record time. While on this trip he called us collect, and the operator said, "Collect call from Mr. Lee." Dad said, "I don't know any Mr. Lee," to which Sammie Lee excitedly said, "Tell 'em it's Sammie Lee!" Sammie Lee got the machinery to Rutherford and soon we got the gin running again, dropping the bales off the end of the gin into the mud while a crew was rebuilding the bale platform.

At Wade Gin Company in Kenton we had an incinerator for many years which was not very far from the bale platform. We had bale fire after bale fire, sometimes burning every bale on the platform. Finally we put in a trash house and the bale fires ended. When we have a suspected fire bale we religiously stick it out by itself for at least 96 hours before sending it to the warehouse. We do the same with the following bale and with the mote bale that happened to be in the mote press. Occasionally fire does break out in one of those bales at which time we break it down and salvage most of the cotton or motes.

One time, back in the 40s, the cotton house caught on fire when it was full of cotton. Dad's men worked those stalls out one by one by feeding cotton into the gin until they hit fire. They would put out that fire and then start on another stall and work in it until they hit fire there. They would put out that fire and then start on another stall and work in it until they ran into fire again. Mother stayed at the gin for hours at a time making hamburgers and coffee for the gallant crew. They ate and worked in heavy smoke and finally the cotton was emptied from the house and all the fires were put out. The next summer the house was repaired.

Not too many years ago the cotton house caught fire one night and burned to the ground. Modern methods of harvesting had made the building obsolete, and it was being used only for storage of such things as bagging and ties. With all its history we hated to see it go, but it was replaced by a modern fire proof warehouse and roof system. It was determined that the fire was arson. We've had our share of those.

We used to send cotton into the compresses in Jackson by rail. In Kenton we used the old strawberry platform for storage and then shipping by rail. In Rutherford we loaded into railroad cars directly from the gin platform, and at Dyer we loaded cars from trucks onto which cotton had been loaded at the gin We stacked cotton on the floor of the cars. Then we rolled cotton over a bale laid flat and one laid on its "ball" to the top of the cotton already loaded. Then we rolled it by hand to the back of the car and set it up straight on top of the bottom layer. In the door of the car we lifted the bales from the floor to the top of bales already in the car. All this was done by hand. The freight to Jackson was $1.00 per bale, but we got credit for this money when the cotton was shipped out of the press. So, in effect, with the use of these freight bills it cost us nothing to get the cotton from our gins to the compresses. Carthel McNeely loaded the Kenton cotton, filling up the floor only, and he was a wizard with a dolly (hand trucks) and a hook. But when we began having to fill the whole car, top and bottom, in order to get the same freight deal, we started using high school boys after school and on weekends to do this hard work. When the railroad backed up on this "sweet" deal, we started delivering the cotton on trailer trucks. In earlier days the cotton not delivered to the compresses by rail was delivered on bob trucks, for instance from Como Gin which was not on a railroad. Dad told me that in the real old days some farmers would haul four bales of cotton on a wagon pulled by a team of mules to Hickman, Kentucky which was an important Mississippi River port at that time. They would sell the cotton to a buyer in Hickman and the cotton would then be loaded onto river boats for delivery to mills up and down the river or to New Orleans for ocean delivery to New England mills or for export to Europe. Dad said the farmers would camp out on the way to Hickman and on the way back home on what amounted to a three or four day trip. Hard to imagine, isn't it?

When Dad first bought the Kenton gin, the seed house was on the ground. Seed was scooped out onto wagons pulled by mules. The wagons were taken to the railroad where the seed was scooped out and into the railroad cars, scooped to the back of the cars, filled up, and shipped by rail. I asked Dad why in the world they did not build the seedhouses up on stilts and load out by gravity. He said that labor was so plentiful and cheap that it didn't matter. And, besides, people needed the work.

When I was young and until several years after college we had overhead wooden seed houses. The trucks would drive underneath the houses, and doors would be opened to let the seed out into the trucks. One night at Kenton the bottom literally fell out of our seed house. Sammie Lee had just pulled his truck out from underneath the seed house. I saw it happen. Another time I happened to be at Rutherford and watched as the seed house slowly started leaning to the west, toward the gin building, and then fell in a big cloud of dust. Again, nobody was hurt. Neither instance caused us to stop ginning. While new steel seed houses were being erected, Dad rigged up portable augers, turned the seed onto the gin floors, and men scooped the seed into the augers which augered it into trucks just outside the gin. There's always more than one way to skin a cat!

Long ago some people sold their cotton "in the seed." In other words they sold it to us before it was ginned. One Kenton customer who always came to the gin after dark put a heavy piece of iron in his load of cotton. After his load was weighed he threw the iron into a ditch on the dark back side of the cotton house as he was on his way to the cotton house suck where it was unloaded. His wagon was then weighed back empty, minus the cotton and the piece of iron. He then came back during the night and retrieved the iron for use in his next load. There's no telling how much Dad paid for this piece of iron. Dad never revealed the fact that he discovered what the man was doing other than to him, and never asked for any money back. He just told the man to "cease and desist," and I'm sure he did. This man remained a loyal customer until the day he died.

We had a tall, skinny man named Coy Exum who worked at the gin as a suck man for many years. Sometimes when Coy would get real tired he became a little irritable and uncooperative. We had a cotton house with twelve stalls into which we blew cotton when we had long lines of loads to be ginned. We would gin the cotton out of the house when we caught up with the loads of cotton on the yard. One time the house was pretty much filled up when we needed to get just one more load unloaded into a particular stall. Coy told those in charge that this customer's stall was jampacked full and there was no way that he could get another load into that stall. We were later told that one of the other employees, in order to get Coy to try his best to get all that man's cotton into his stall, gave him a little "nip." Coy got the full load into that stall. Our weigher, Delbert Orr, asked Coy what in the world he did with all that cotton that was already in that stall. Coy replied, "Oh, Mr. Delbert, I just kicked it into the corner."

We used our cotton checks as weigh tickets as well as customer checks. The weigher would enter the gross, and tare, and net weights of the seed cotton on the checks and then post the bale numbers and lint cotton weights after the cotton was ginned. Then when we knew the price for the cotton the check would be filled out with the price and total dollars for each bale. Once upon a time Tommie Rudd, one of our long time gin employees, inadvertently threw away several of the checkbooks which had slid off the weigher's desk and into a cardboard box that we used for trash and which was sitting directly beside the desk. As was always the case back when we burned all gin trash in our incinerator, we simply threw the paper and other trash into the incinerator. When we discovered the checkbooks were missing I immediately ran out to the incinerator and, sure enough, they were in there around the outside edge to the right of the door. I tiptoed into the incinerator and grabbed all the books and pieces of books and then spent several days poring through them and piecing together the gin receipts represented in them. So far as we could determine, we were able to pay every farmer for every bale despite the fact that some of the books were about half burned. Not a single farmer indicated that he was dissatisfied with the reconstruction of our receipts. If we had discovered what had happened just two or three minutes later it would have been too late. What a nightmare that would have been!

At the gin in the fall we enjoyed playing a Coca Cola game whereby those playing would put a nickel into our Coke machine and then check the name of the city on the bottom of the 6-1/2 ounce bottles. On the bottom of each bottle the glass manufacturers put the city and state of the bottler to whom that batch of bottles was shipped. The man with the bottle with the nearest city had to reimburse the other players. The nearest plant was Union City, and we all dreaded getting one of their bottles. Some of those bottles had come from very long distances away. It was amazing how Coke bottles were carried back and forth across the United States. Interestingly, Union City still has one of the very few independently owned Coke plants left in America. The Union City plant and the Coke plant in Meridian, Mississippi are owned by our close friends and PiKA brothers, Hardy M. Graham, Hardy P. Graham, and Newell Graham and Mrs. Hardy M. Graham's family, the Poindexters.

Wade Land Company

Dad bought land, as he was financially able to do so, beginning in the 20s and going on through the 50s. He always farmed it himself. Dad said that insurance companies and other lending agencies long ago would sell farms to anybody on credit if they thought there was any chance at all that they would ever be repaid. The reason for this was that so many people during the hard years had lost their farms, and these financial institutions had repossessed many of them.

Mr. Ellis Hobbs, the deceased father of Kenton Grain Company customers and good friends, Jay Ray, Joe, and Teddy Hobbs (who was manager of Kenton Grain Company for 17 years), told me that when he and Mrs. Hobbs married they moved onto one of Dad's farms, and Dad paid him 50 cents a day. Can you imagine? Most of us can't. When I got out of college in 1957 we were paying our farm laborers $5.00 per day (and those days were from sunup to sundown) and furnishing them with a house in which to live. None of those houses had indoor plumbing. Obviously back in those days people could survive on such wages. In the early days every town had an ice plant, and ice was trucked to farm folks who had iceboxes. At that time there were no refrigerators in the country, as electricity did not reach beyond towns' city limits.

Many years ago a straight ditch was blown out by dynamite in the Bruce farm bottom. When we cleared the Bruce bottom, we used one section of this ditch as part of our drainage system. This ditch was always referred to by the local people as the "blowed ditch." Delbert Orr said that he and lots of other people used to "put in" to fish and hunt ducks in this area. He told me about a snake that they killed in the blowed ditch that "purt near" filled up a good sized wash tub. The Bruce bottom at one time was a haven for duck hunters. We cleared it about 35 or 40 years ago, and there's no hunting or fishing there now. We presently have fine crops growing in this bottom on well drained, level land. It could also be used again for duck and goose hunting with a minimal amount of work, and we're giving some thought to getting into the commercial hunting business. This land lies adjacent to the Gooch Wildlife Preserve.

When Dad bought the Brick House farm it had a double row of big boxwoods all the way from the house clear down to the road. An old man, Mr. Holland Reed, told me about the history of the Brick House which is on our "Brick House Farm" about a mile north of Kenton. This is the oldest house in the Kenton area. It has solid brick walls, is two-story, and has a breezeway, or dogtrot, separating it into two sections. Not too many years ago it still had several very large boxwoods around the front of the house. A professor of history at UTM, Daryl Hadden, once told me that he could definitely get the house on the state registry of historical buildings and probably on the federal registry. I told him that if that could be accomplished we would fix it up, according to their specifications, for posterity. Unbeknownst to me, some young people who were apparently into witchcraft and drugs had decided it was a haunted house and had been using it for some time for their parties. During these "parties" they tore it all to pieces, tearing bricks from around the windows until they were big round gaping holes and they covered the inside walls with graffiti and vulgarisms. We were sad to have to abandon the Brick House. It is still standing, but the area around it is grown up and the tin roof is about to fall in. I was told that George Pieper, who married Mary Jane Gordon on May 15, 1856, built it. Their son John later lived in it. Vade and Lon McNeely lived there for awhile. (This is the Miss Vade who lived next to us when I was growing up.) A Mr. Bruce probably bought it from the Piepers. "Uncle Pete" Carroll, who was Frank Johnson's wife's father, lived there in the 20s. Lon Tanner owned it in '35 before Dad bought it. Supposedly this is the history of The Brick House. One time a tornado came through and did considerable damage to it. Two by fours were driven through the brick walls of the house and were imbedded in a big oak tree that was just west of the house. One summer Clyde Vickery and I painted the big old barn that was in the lot west of the house.

Dad gave Sally and me half interest in the Union Grove and Railroad Farms. I ended up with the Bruce farm, the Railroad farm, the Union Grove farm, a farm we called the Carson farm, and half interest in the Brick House farm, and Sally owns the White Barn farm (where Dewey and Modine Bradley live) and the other half of the Brick House farm. I sold the Carson farm to Jack Allen and have bought from others the rest of my present land holdings.

Since Dad had once owned citrus grove land in the Rio Grande Valley, the idea of my owning some Valley land appealed to me. Frank Burnett, a Dyersburg real estate broker, had a listing on a 520 acre farm down there that once had belonged to my good friends, the Davis family of Roellen, near Dyersburg. Frank asked me if I'd like to go down there and look at it, so we flew to Harlingen which was the closest city to the farm. It was dryland, but it was flat and on a good highway only one farm away from a picturesque little town, Bayview, which had been developed on a resaca (a former section of a river that had been cut off from the main river long ago). The popular resort, South Padre Island, was only ten miles away. I bought it and still own it.

Including half interest with Will in a 210 acre farm south of Kenton, my one-third interest in the Dyer County land (see Chapter 23), the 520 acres in the Rio Grande, and land in Obion, Gibson, Weakley, and Henry Counties in West Tennessee, I now own 6,005 acres of farmland. The land in Obion, Gibson, Weakley, Henry, and Dyer Counties is all within a 40 mile radius of Kenton. One of the farms, the Railroad Farm as we call it, has been in the family for nearly 100 years. Other area farms that I own are known as the Allen-Kenton farm, Baker farm, Bingham farm, Brotherton farm, Bruce farm, Como farm, Concord farm, Dodson farm, Duren farm, Freeman bottom farm, Freeman highway farm, Grant tracts, Lumpkin-Carroll farm, McCullar farm, Orr farm, Paschall tract, Penn farm, Pierce farm, Sunnyside farm, Trimble farm, Weakley County farm, and the Westvaco farm. The only thing I actually farm is strawberries. The rest of the land is rented for cash or for part of the crop, to my son-in-law,

Rance Barnes, and to Jack Finch, Tommy, Tracy, and Brent Griggs, Don Hastings, Teddy and Jay Ray Hobbs, Bob Hollomon, Amos and Daniel Huey, Danny Jowers, Jimmy Joe Welch, and Larry and John Wylie. Rance farms most of the land around Kenton, the Wylies farm my Weakley-Henry County land, and Hastings and Welch farm our Dyer County land. The other renters farm land around Kenton and Rutherford. The Texas farm and about 100 acres of my Weakley County land are in the Conservation Reserve Program (CRP). A few years ago my total acreage got up to about 6,400 acres before selling several hundred acres and then buying a little land in the last few years. My own renters grow, in order of importance, cotton, corn, soybeans, wheat, and milo.

Up until a couple of years ago a good bit of my Obion County land was leased for a pittance for oil rights. There has been some thought for a long time that there might be oil below land that runs from around Trimble back across to my land north of Kenton. Supposedly there is some kind of ridge through there that has oil possibilities, and long ago some unsuccessful wells were drilled near Trimble. However, since those folks are no longer sending annual payments to hold the oil rights, they must have, at least for now, given up hope of finding oil around here.

During the energy crisis of the 70s a western man came to Kenton and talked with several of us landowners around here about buying the rights to lignite which lays under several thousand acres north of Kenton. He offered $15 per acre per year, and then if the lignite were ever mined it would be very lucrative for us. The lignite is pretty far below the surface of the ground and would require very extensive stripping of dirt to get down to it. My impression is that this mining would leave deep depressions in the land and that it would end up either being lakes or virtually worthless. Regardless of that, our interests in the lignite would have made us wealthy folks. Meetings were organized with area landowners, and this fellow sold several of us on his proposition. We were to meet him one morning in the office of my Union City attorney and friend, Tom Elam, to finalize the deal and receive our first year's payments. The man from out West was late. Thirty minutes or so after the appointed time Colonel Elam received a call from an attorney for the energy company telling us that they had backed out of the deal and were no longer interested in the rights to our lignite. We were a disappointed bunch of men. Our pie in the sky had suddenly crashed to earth.

In 2001 Will and I formed Wade & Wade, LLC and bought a 210 acre farm from Randy Harris south of Kenton. We then partnered with The Erora Group of Louisville, power generation consultants, in an effort to sell an opportunity for a gas-fired electricity generating plant to one of the world's major power generating companies. TVA power lines cross this farm which is in a fairly remote part of Gibson County. The idea would be to pipe natural gas from the Williams Companies gas transmission lines which run 3.5 miles north of this farm. Their natural gas would be used to power the generators.

We were successful in getting the farm's zoning changed from agricultural to industrial. In fact, not only did the Gibson County Court vote unanimously to allow the zoning change, they gave the Erora man and Will and me a standing ovation! The county magistrates were most interested in the tremendous tax revenue that this potential $200 to $300 million plant would generate for the county, to say nothing of the 150 to 200 part time jobs required to build the plant and the 15 to 35 high paying permanent jobs, depending on the type of plant that might be built, that would be created for area people. We had some big energy folks interested in our site and were very encouraged about our possibilities when we received the bad news that Tennessee had put a temporary moratorium on the building of such plants. However, the moratorium was lifted in April, 2002 for four applications only. We worked feverishly, and our application was the first one received! Though the energy industry is presently in the doldrums, ours is a viable situation and might possibly come to fruition some day. Maybe so, and maybe not ...

History of Kenton Grain Company

Buying into Kenton Grain Company made me the fourth generation of Wade agribusinessmen in Kenton. Will is the fifth generation Wade doing the same things in northwest Tennessee. Tom Wade Sr., along with W. G. Dement, a prominent Kenton farmer and close friend of the Wade family, originally built the first grain elevator in Kenton in 1959, the plant consisting of two 5,000 bushel bins and one 2,000 bushel per hour (BPH) elevator. These two men operated the business as a 50-50 partnership for two years at which time they sold out to a partnership of three men — Dad, Hamilton Parks of Trimble, and Kyle Bugg, now of Dyer, each partner owning 1/3 of the business. That partnership operated for four years and then sold out in 1968 to Dad and me as equal partners. The company operated this way until October, 1975, when Dad died. At that time I bought the estate's interest in the business, becoming the sole owner.

About 30 years ago a major expansion was undertaken. Two 60,000 bushel grain bins, a new 3,000 BPH elevator, and a 500 BPH autonomous drying system were installed.

In 1975 new 60' automatic scales were installed by Richard Davis, a very successful local farmer who used to do a little contracting, and 1976 additions included a 126,000 bushel bin, a 7,000 BPH leg (replacing the 3,000 BPH leg), and a second 500 BPH dryer.

In 1981 a 226,000 bushel bin along with another 7,000 BPH elevator and a large gravity flow dump pit were added. This system was located across the street from the existing facility giving the company much more flexibility.

In 1982 a modern office and an all-metal shop were constructed. Also in 1982, on January 8, Kenton Grain Company obtained a USDA license and the company has operated since as a federally licensed warehouse, storing grain for Commodity Credit Corporation as well as for area farmers and issuing bonded warehouse receipts for same.

In 1983 one of the 5,000 bushel bins was removed and replaced by two new bins totaling 44,000 bushels capacity. The two new bins and the remaining 5,000 bushel bin have drying floors and are used for storage as well as for wet holding space for the drying system.

In 1984 a 750 BPH dryer was added to the drying system.

In 1985 the company's most ambitious expansion to date took place. A new 226,000 bushel bin, a 5,000 bushel overhead hopper tank for truck loading, and a 4,000 bushel overhead hopper tank for loading railroad cars were added. A 32,000 bushel hopper tank for wet grain supported the new 2,500 BPH Berico grain dryer, giving us two separate drying systems. Two new legs — a 110' 5000 BPH wet leg and a 155' 7,000 BPH dry leg made the system autonomous. A reversible 10,000 BPH conveyor was constructed high over Main Street in order to totally connect every single bin and operation to each other. Rail loadout was increased dramatically with a new 14,000 BPH conveyor.

It was decided in 1986 that the area between the two 226,000 bushel bins and the shop should be utilized for storage. The decision was made to erect a 360,000 bushel bin which was the largest bin we had at our three elevators. In doing the dirt work for the foundation we ran into a rather large soft spot close to the shop. The contractor began digging in order to get to firm ground and soon dug into an enormous old septic tank built with large timbers, many of which were still sound. It turned out to be the septic tank for the old Kenton Hotel which had served the traveling (railroad, of course) public in the old, old days. Extensive further digging was required to get to good dirt, and the price of the bin escalated considerably.

In 2000 two 400,000 and one 250,000 bushel bins and a 15,000 BPH elevator were constructed over an eight foot tunnel east of the railroad tracks. Separate conveyors to and from the east side joined the old and new operations. A new enclosed rail loadout with a weighing system was built. Dust suppression systems were added to both unloading pits. The new, cleaner operation now totals approximately 2,250,000 bushels.

Kenton Grain's handling of corn, soybeans, wheat, and milo has increased from the old days some forty to fifty fold, as this area's former modest grain acreage has evolved into big-time commercial grain and soybean farming.

Ed Sims is Kenton Grain's most capable manager. He graduated from UTM one day and came to work the next day, in 1976.

Dyer Gin and Grain Company

In the same year, 1959, that Dad and W. G. Dement built the first grain elevator in Kenton, they likewise built Dyer Grain Company. It originally consisted of two 5,000 bushel bins and a 1,000 (BPH) elevator. In 1961 Mr. Dement decided to go back to farming full-time, so he and Dad sold out to the adjacent Dyer Gin Company which was owned in equal shares by Wade, Robert Patterson of Trenton, and Robert Phebus of Dyersburg. In 1966, Dad bought out Mr. Phebus. Then in 1973 I bought out Mr. Patterson. At this time Dad sold 1/6 of the corporation to me so that Dad and I were equal stockholders. Dad died in October, 1975, and I bought out the estate in 1976 and became the sole owner of Dyer Gin and Grain Company.

The two original 5,000 bushel bins and 1,000 BPH elevator were followed by two more 5,000 bushel bins in 1962 and then two more in 1964 at which time Dyer Grain Company's total capacity was 30,000 bushels. The company operated that way until 1979 when a new office and 70 foot set of scales were constructed along with two 75,000 bushel bins, a 12,000 bushel wet holding tank, a 3,000 bushel truck loadout tank, and a 10,000 BPH elevator. In 1980, another 75,000 bushel bin and a 1,000 BPH drier complete with all supporting equipment were added. In 1982 a 175,000 bushel bin was built, and in 1984 a 313,000 bushel bin replaced the old gin building which was leveled. (Dyer was without a cotton gin for the first time in over 100 years!) Then in 1985 a major project to speed up and increase flexibility and sophistication was undertaken. A 7,000 BPH elevator replaced the old original 1,000 BPH leg, giving the company a total unloading capacity of 17,000 BPH. In addition a 32,000 bushel wet holding bin was constructed alongside a new 2,500 BPH Berico drier. The rail loadout was upgraded to an 8,000 BPH operation, and a 4,000 bushel rail loadout tank was added. At this point, counting the three original bins still standing, now rated at 4,000; 4,500; and 4,500 bushel capacities, the total holding capacity at Dyer Grain Company stands at 777,000 bushels. How 'bout that for a lucky number!

In 1981 Dyer Grain Company became, and still is, a fully bonded and licensed Federal Warehouse.

During this period of time until retirement on December 31, 1989, William McFarland was manager of Dyer Grain Company, as well as of Dyer Gin Company, and Mrs. Edna Earl McFarland was bookkeeper. When Mr. McFarland retired he had been at Dyer Gin and Grain Company for 53 years! Mrs. McFarland had also been there for most of that time.

After Mr. McFarland's retirement, Johnny Martin assumed managerial responsibilities after having worked at Dyer Gin and Grain since 1977. Johnny's able assistant manager is Chuck Whitaker.

Como Gin and Grain Company

Dad went to a ginner meeting somewhere in West Tennessee in 1934. He and a fellow ginner, Dutch Barger, were talking. This gentleman told Dad that he planned to build a gin at Como. Dad said, "Where's Como?" Mr. Barger told Dad that it was halfway between Dresden and Paris. Dad then proceeded to tell Barger that he was thinking about building a gin at Crystal. "Where's Crystal," Dutch asked. Dad explained to him that it was a country point in Obion County, etc., etc. The meeting ended, and soon thereafter Dad heard by way of the grapevine that Dutch Barger was building a gin at Crystal! So, by George, Dad decided to build a gin at Como! Crystal operated only a year or two and insufficient cotton in that area forced Mr. Barger to tear down the gin. On the contrary, Como Gin operated profitably for 42 years, beginning in 1935, and Como Grain and Feed Company has operated profitably every year since. In that case fate was mighty good to Dad.

There was no telephone at Como that first year, and the only way Dad could find out about what was going on at Como was to drive up there. The roads were mostly dirt and some gravel in those days, and when it rained they turned to mud. It was a nightmare. So the next year Dad approached the local phone company about putting a telephone line from Ore Springs, the easternmost point on that line for phone service, to Como. They agreed to run the line if Dad would furnish the poles. Dad agreed. Until 20 years or so ago, one could still see some of those old poles occasionally alongside Highway 54. They were, for the most part, small tree trunks from which the limbs had barely been trimmed. Why in the world didn't I retrieve one of those poles and preserve it in some sort of monument-type way? Why do we so often put off the important things until it's too late?

When Como Gin was being built, Dad took his old Kenton ginner up there one day. The Como territory is entirely different from the Kenton territory. Down here just about all the land is tilled or grazed.

Not true around Como. Lots of the land up there is in trees, and sometimes cultivated fields are few and far between, especially along the main road that day in 1935. When they got to Como, Dad said, "Well, Dick, what do you think?" Dick replied, "Well, Mr. Tom, I seen 'bout a half a day's run." Reckon Dad, at that point, wondered if he had made the right decision?

Well, he did, Como actually has been profitable every year since 1935. Some years it didn't make much, but it was always in the black. As mentioned above, Como Gin operated for over 42 years. In the middle 60s, Dad decided to build a little grain elevator on the gin lot. The grain business grew steadily as cotton, unfortunately, began to decline in the Como area. The gin was finally closed after the 1976 season, but Dad had gradually added to Como Grain as the grain business grew, and at that point the grain business was sufficient to support the operation. The last and largest expansion took place in 1979 when two 127,000 bushel bins, a second 8,000 bushel per hour elevator, and a second dump pit were added. Presently our USDA warehouse license lists Como's total capacity at an even 500,000 bushels.

For some time we looked for ways to better utilize our personnel and facilities at Como Grain Company. After investigating several possibilities we decided that there was a need in and around the Como area for a modern livestock feed facility. Como's Darryl Sims and his brother, Ed, inspected commodity blending operations in Middle and East Tennessee, southwest Missouri, and Virginia and settled on a plan for Como which includes a new building and blending, loading, and delivery equipment. The McCord family kindly agreed to sell us 14 acres of land directly behind us, so we then had plenty of room on which to build and, hopefully, to expand in the future.

We opened up our feed operation in late 1996, and we work primarily with the dairy and beef cattle industries. We also sell horse, sheep, and goat feed and pet food from a retail store. We buy truckload lots of all types of commodities — corn gluten, alfalfa hay cubes, soybean meal, cottonseed meal, cottonseed hulls, whole cottonseed, wheat mids, brewers grain, distillers grain, hominy, etc. We blend these commodities or sell raw commodities. Feed is delivered to farmers or picked up by them at Como. We also stock concentrates, medications, and feed additives that can be precisely blended into a balanced ration for specific livestock needs. Our sales have far exceeded my expectations, and Como is now well established in the livestock feed business.

The secret to Como's success can be summed up in one word — PEOPLE! Mr. Charlie Davis opened up Como Gin for Dad and managed it ably until his retirement in 1960. Harrell Peery went to work at Como in 1950 and his wife, Margaret, started working there in 1964. This "salt of the earth" couple, along with the talented Van Howard, long time ginner, took over the reins. They capably managed Como until their retirement in 1982. Darryl Sims, Ed's younger brother, went to work at Como in 1982 and has done an excellent job of managing the business ever since. He is ably assisted by assistant manager, Janice Vogel.

There have been plenty of bumps along the business road.

The most heartrending bumps have been accidents on the job. The worst accident we ever had cost J. C. Betts, our employee for 56 years, both his hands. He got them caught in a lint cleaner at Wade Gin Company. He died at age 83 in January, 2002. It was remarkable what J. C. was able to do during the years between the accident and his passing. He was a man with an enormous amount of willpower. Another horrible accident occurred at Dyer where a young man lost his foot to a railroad car. He was just not paying attention. There have been several other accidents, but none nearly so bad as the two mentioned.

There have been lots of other bumps. Through the decades we have had literally dozens of significant gin fires, all the way from total gin burndowns to several dozens of bales of cotton burning up. Insurance covered the losses, but great heartache, much hard work, and loss of business were caused by those fires.

On several occasions I lost fair amounts of money on cotton and grain positions. Then on December 1, 1980, after a long bull market in soybeans and grains, the bean market dropped the limit. We had a fairly small long position. The market also dropped the limit for the next two days, three days in row. I reasoned that this was too much of a correction and closed out some hedges on beans. The market dropped again the next day. More hedges were dropped. It dropped the next day, Friday. I spent a sleepless weekend. It opened the limit down the next Monday. We continued to increase my long position hoping to "double up and catch up." It dropped, either the limit or near the limit, every day that week, the first time in history, at least to my knowledge, that the market had dropped ten straight days. I had hardly slept for two weeks and was a nervous wreck. On the next Monday the decision was made to cover our large (for me) long position. 1980 had been a very good year up until December 1, but in those ten market days half of what we had made all year was lost. I learned my lesson. We decision makers signed up for marketing seminars, learned exactly what we should be doing, and have never since taken a position in the markets. When we buy 5,000 bushels we hedge 5,000 bushels. Our strategy is simply to be totally hedged at all times. We sell futures as we buy the cash grain, and we estimate what we think we will buy from the market close each afternoon to the opening of the next market, and we sell that amount on the close that afternoon, evening up the next market morning. Sometimes now we also hedge on the new overnight market. A fully hedged life has been much more pleasant, and we have never again taken a market loss on our grain, soybean, and cotton handles.

In 1985 William McFarland, my Dyer manager, called me in the middle of the night. He said, "We're in Trouble." "Why?" I asked. He said, "Our big bin is on fire and part of the top has been blown off." I rushed to Dyer and found the fire departments of Dyer and several nearby towns pouring water on the bin and the burning milo inside it. The bin was red hot and steam was rising in a great plume. In all the excitement we did not turn off the fans on the adjoining bin, and they were sucking steam and hot moist air into and through the corn in that bin. Insurance did cover the milo and the damaged bin. A few weeks later I was summoned to Dyer again. This time the problem was black corn being drawn out of that adjacent bin. We figured we knew the reason why — all that steam and damp air coursing through the corn. We attempted to tie the damage to the fire, but the insurance company disallowed the additional claim. They did settle, but for only a fraction of the loss we had in the ruined corn. My loss was the largest I had ever taken to that point.

Things went fairly smoothly with no great losses from that point on until late November, 2001. Pat and I had been in Memphis and were on the way home when Will called. He said, "Dad, pull over. Nobody's hurt, but I have something to tell you." (I've always told my people to start off bad news with information on people first and then get into monetary losses.). I told him to spit it out. Will told me that one of our biggest customers had declared bankruptcy. They owed us for many carloads of corn. As I write this, the final results of the bankruptcy proceeding are not known. It is certain that we will collect relatively little of the money owing me. This has been far and away my biggest loss ever. We are presently collecting much more credit information than we've had in the past on all the people to whom we sell grain, cotton, and cottonseed. We simply must be much more careful in extending credit. Credit can be a cold, cruel world.

There has been a lot more good than bad, though, through the years. I was most fortunate to have had such a wonderful Dad, a good and highly respected businessman who left me with a nucleus on which to build. Dad willed half the businesses and land to Mother and a quarter each to Sally and me. I bought Mother's and Sally's shares of the businesses and land on credit except for a farm and half interest (with me) in another farm which Sally retained. I made notes with interest to them and paid them off over a period of time. Sally wanted to keep some of her Dad's land which certainly was her right. We all look after her farming interests and are delighted to do so.

Kenton, Dyer, and Como have been mighty good to my family and me.

Chapter Thirty-Five

Managers and Employee Friends

Obviously we could not have succeeded in business without the dedicated service of excellent employees whom we consider to be good friends. We are deeply indebted to the following key employees who have been with us for a good number of years. Some of them have been with us for a very long time.

Dewey and Modine Bradley

On December 7, 1944, Dewey Bradley came to Kenton with his mother and father and four brothers and sisters from Clifton, Tennessee. They moved onto Dad's farm where Dewey's first job was pulling corn that winter. So Dewey has been with the Wade family for over 58 years!

He and his wife, Modine, tell the story of staying with our children one time when Will was very young. Will said, "Dewey, you worked for Granddaddy, didn't you?" "Yes," said Dewey. "And now you work for Daddy?" "Yes," said Dewey. "Don't let anything happen to you; I want to be your boss someday." Sure enough, Dewey is now working with the third Wade generation.

On March 28, 1948, Dewey and Modine Ray married. They have three fine daughters, Taricia, Voinda, and Katrina, five grandchildren, and four great grandchildren.

Dewey and Modine made a four or five acre cotton crop, the first of several, in 1949. Modine picked the crop and it cleared $400, lots of money in those days. Dewey's wages for a seven-day work week were $17! In 1949 Dewey began working full time with Dad's registered Horned Herefords. For many years he was our herdsman. Modine was always heavily involved with our strawberries. Except for two years, she worked in our packsheds from 1949 to 1999 or a total of 49 years! She was in charge of the packing operation for over 40 years, having taken over from my Mother.

431

In 1977 we sold our cattle and bought a dozer to convert pastureland to cropland. Dewey still operates the third dozer we have owned, pulls cotton trailers in the fall, works in strawberries, and generally does a little of everything. His retirement a few years ago only lasted for a few weeks. He continues to work most of the time. In addition to his former farm duties Dewey started ginning in the 60s and ginned continuously for us until 1993 a good bit of that time as head ginner.

We Wades have always depended on the Bradleys. To illustrate just how much, in the early 70s Dad broke his hip and was in Baptist Hospital in Memphis in traction and could not get comfortable. One day he said to Mother, "Get Dewey! He can fix it."

The Bradleys are religious, loyal, conscientious, hard working folks who live exemplary lives. This fine family has positively touched the lives of countless Kenton area people.

Lilia Clanton

Lilia Gabel Clanton was born in Gibson County, Tennessee to Joel Aaron Gabel of Yorkville and Martha Page Gabel of Mason Hall. She was their fifth child; Lilia has two older brothers and two older sisters. Lilia grew up in the Mason Hall — North Union Church area where her father was a farmer and fruit grower. She attended Mason Hall School until it closed after her 4th grade year, Kenton School for one year, and then finally Yorkville School where she graduated in 1975. Lilia attended Dyersburg State Community College where she obtained a degree as a paralegal. She then worked for an attorney in Dyersburg for several years and later for Legal Services of West Tennessee.

Lilia is married to Danny Clanton of Trimble who has been told that his ancestors are quite possibly the infamous Clanton Gang of OK Corral fame. Not to be outdone, Lilia tells her own tale of an interesting ancestor. Mr. Joel Gabel, Lilia's dad, told her about J. B. Simon, his great-grandfather. Mr. Simon was a brick mason and was known for being quite a character. Upon finishing bricking a chimney he would set his mortar board on top of the chimney and then do a hand stand. Mr. Simon reportedly built the first hoosegow (jail) in Newbern. After he had finished the structure, he was reimbursed by the city and, being the good citizen that he was, decided to spend some of his money in town. He visited a local drinking establishment where he enthusiastically proceeded to partake. J. B. soon was arrested and became the first resident of Newbern's brand new jail. It does sound like Danny and Lilia have a lot in common.

The Clantons have two children, Candace and Abby. Candace is attending the University of Tennessee Health Science Center in Memphis where she is pursuing a Doctor of Pharmacy degree. She and Robin McCaig of Dyer were married in the summer of 2003. Abby is attending Gibson County High School where she will graduate in 2005.

Lilia came to work for Wade Gin Company in 1990 initially to do cotton settlements in the fall. After their children were older Lilia began to work full time at Wade Gin/Kenton Grain Company. Danny works for Ford Construction in Dyersburg. Their family attends the First Baptist Church in Kenton. The four Clantons are extraordinarily nice folks.

Johnny Martin

Dewey Bradley, herdsman for Tom Wade Herefords, crushed his ankle in an accident in the summer of 1972. Dad remembered a conversation with longtime cattleman and former Obion County resident, Jack Martin, at the Obion County Fair the previous summer in which Jack told him that he would like to come home from North Carolina. Dad called Jack, told him what had happened to Dewey, and asked if he could come to Kenton right away. Jack said, "Get your truck here; I'm ready to come home." We did. He did. That's how Jack's son, Johnny Martin, got to Kenton.

Johnny was born in Obion County on March 8, 1953. The Martins moved to North Carolina in 1969 and Johnny graduated from Cherryville High School in 1971 where he was delegate to the 4-H Congress in Chicago. He attended North Carolina State for one year and then transferred to the University of Tennessee at Martin where he graduated in 1975 with a major in Animal Science. While at UTM Johnny was a member of their first livestock judging team and was a charter member of the Block and Bridle Club. He worked while in school for UTM Farms under the direction of the venerated Doc Robinson.

Johnny worked for us in the construction of our new high capacity Wade Gin Company in the summer of 1973. I never saw a man work harder or better than Johnny worked that summer. I knew I wanted him to work with me permanently. But I had to wait a while.

Johnny and Kay Sisco were married on August 2, 1975. (Kay's sister, Julie Sisco Parker, now works as an assistant to Will and me.) Johnny and Kay moved to Shelby County where Johnny managed Wortham Polled Hereford Farms while Kay studied medical technology in Memphis. Kay graduated and on Labor Day, 1977 Johnny came to work for us at Dyer. My wish had been fulfilled. Johnny became manager on January 1, 1990. Johnny and Kay live on Reed Road just south of Dyer with their three beautiful and talented daughters, Emily, Lauren and Ali. This remarkable family attends the Dyer Church of Christ. Johnny, Kay, Emily, Lauren, and Ali, Dewey's bad luck turned out to be your Red Letter Day! Talk about fate!

Federico Mendez

On April 27, 1962, Federico Mendez was born in Coahuila, Mexico. At age five Federico and his family moved to Michigan where he did fieldwork. It was there that Fred (as we call him) met Nora Villegas who was to become his wife.

In 1981 Fred worked for one year at the Shallowater (Texas) Co-op Gin where Fred's cousin, Alberto Leyva, was superintendent. Then it was back to Michigan until 1985, when he came back to Lubbock, Texas. Then the next year he went to work again at the Shallowater Gin which is seven miles outside Lubbock. He started as a sweeper but was fascinated with the gin and soon realized that he wanted to be a ginner. Alberto told Fred that he needed to learn every aspect of the ginning procedure if he really wanted to run all the complicated machinery. Under the expert tutelage of Alberto, the excited Fred worked hard and studied carefully every detail of what is a sophisticated manufacturing process. To make a long story short, Fred became an accomplished ginner.

In 1993 Fred and Nora and their family came to Kenton for the summer repair season at our Wade Gin Company. After our gin was ready for the '93 season they went back to Shallowater where Fred ginned. Then in 1994 they moved back to Kenton for good, and Fred went to work for us full time. In addition to gin work and some fabrication work he repairs and maintains machinery, equipment, vehicles, etc. at Kenton Grain Company, Como Grain and Feed Company, on the farm, or wherever he's needed. Fred is the quintessential jack-of-all-trades!

Fred and Nora have three fine sons, Christopher, Federico, Jr., and Ramon.

We Wades are indeed fortunate that Fred's path, which started in Mexico and wound its way through Michigan and Texas, finally led to Tennessee.

John Lee Mitchell

John Lee Mitchell, the son of Haywood and Gladys Mitchell, was born in 1937 on Herbert Taylor's farm north of Kenton. John attended school in Kenton through the eighth grade and graduated in 1957 from Trenton's Rosenwald High School. Just like all schools around here, John's schools "let out" in the spring for strawberry picking and cotton chopping and then reconvened during the hottest part of the summers, "letting out" again for cotton picking. Since his Daddy's main crops were cotton and strawberries, these times weren't by any means vacations for John and his seven siblings. At one time John's Dad, Haywood (better known as Skinny), had 18 acres of strawberries — nine acres at Mr. Herbert's and nine acres at Cleatus Caton's.

Later the Mitchell family moved to Will Fowler's place south of Kenton. John remembers the family's hitching up the team to their wagon and coming to town on Saturdays just like everybody who "lived in the country" did. They tied up the horses in the vacant lot that was directly behind what are now C. W. Sanderson's, Hollomon Insurance Agency, and Country Expressions. After moving back to Mr. Taylor's for awhile, the family moved to town.

John's sister, Virginia Ann, died young leaving four little children. John and his wife, the former Rosie Skinner whom he married in 1960, took them to raise. No four children ever had more loving parents than John and Rose. John says that Rose deserves most of the credit, as he was "on the road" so much of the time (John has driven a truck for us for 30 years). But all of us friends of John's know that he also deserves plenty of credit. Just ask our customers. Often they tell us, "Send John!"

John served in the Army for two years. He is a deacon of Kenton's St. Paul Baptist Church, having served his church as Sunday School superintendent, Sunday School teacher, and chairman of the board of deacons. Rose looked after Miss Verne Tomlinson and later Mrs. Vera Stephens in their last years. You've heard the expression, "stars in their crowns?" John and Rosie have a galaxy of them!

J. C. Reed

J. C. Reed was born and reared in the Morella community southwest of Kenton where he is a lifelong member of Morella Cumberland Presbyterian Church and is an elder. He attended Morella School through the 8th grade after which he attended Mason Hall High School where he played basketball and softball and boxed.

He graduated in 1942 and joined the Army that September. After basic training at Fort Benning, Georgia, it was on to Germany by way of ship to Scotland and a boxcar from there across England and France. His H Company of the 8th Infantry Regiment of the 4th Infantry Division fought in the infamous Battle of the Bulge, the ferocious Battle of the Hurtgen Forest, and in the Rhineland and other campaigns. J. C.'s ultimate commanding officer was General George S. Patton. One time on the front line during the Battle of the Bulge, General Patton drove right up to where his company was dug in and visited with them. Another unforgettable experience occurred one night when Company H was at the Rhine River. J. C. and another boy volunteered to swim the Rhine with ropes which they attached to trees on the other side. Then, under the cover of darkness, their company crossed the river in rubber rafts pulling their way across with the ropes. J. C. served as a machine gunner, a mortar gunner, and a rifleman.

He was awarded the Bronze Star for bravery beyond the call of duty. He lost some mighty good buddies and had some close calls himself.

In 1946 he was discharged and came home to the farm. In 1948 he and Lafayne Pruitt were married. In 1956 he went to work for Kellwood in Rutherford. In 1966 he was employed by U.S.M. in Kenton where he stayed until they closed in 1984. All this time he also farmed. J. C. then came to work with us in '84 and continues to look after our strawberries and pull cotton trailers in the fall.

J. C. and Lafayne have four children, Ricky, Terry, Robin, and Pam Reed Moore. J. C. and Lafayne's four children have provided them with 12 grandchildren!

I'd like to think that when I'm J. C.'s age (if I make it that far) that I'll be able to work one-tenth as hard as J. C. works right now.

Darryl Sims

Darryl Sims, the manager of Como Grain and Feed Company, was born July 11, 1959, in Selmer, Tennessee and was raised on a small family dairy and row crop farm. After graduation from McNairy County Central High School in 1977, Darryl entered the University of Tennessee at Martin where he majored in Animal Science, graduating in 1982. While at UTM he was a member of the Block and Bridle Club, the Rodeo Club, and the Ag Club.

In order to help pay for his education, Darryl worked on and off for Tom Wade Companies in Kenton. Immediately upon graduation, Darryl went to work at Como Grain Company. Under the fine tutelage of Harrell and Margaret Peery and Van Howard, Darryl became the Manager of Como Grain Company where he has always done a marvelous job and has been greatly admired and liked by our literally hundreds of customers.

A former member of the Paris Jaycees, Darryl co-chaired their World's Biggest Fish Fry Rodeo Committee for two years and chaired it for four more years. Darryl's outside interests include team roping with his big brother, Ed, and rodeo in general, and he enjoys camping and trail riding with his three children, Kate, Lawrence, and Thomas. He also enjoys watching Lawrence and Thomas, who are teammates, play baseball.

Ed Sims

In the late spring of 1976, I was far behind in my work. Dad had died the previous October, the business had grown, and I was running basically a one-man operation in Kenton and for Como. One of our good friends was "Doc" Robinson, popular Animal Science professor at UTM. I called Doc and told him I just had to have some help. He replied, "I'm looking at a good man across my desk right now. He will work." Ed Sims came over and we talked. I offered him a job. He had also been offered a job by Tennessee Governor Ray Blanton in their cattle operation. I told Ed he'd better come to Kenton. He did, and history has proved that my advice was mighty good. Ed graduated from UTM and was on the job the next day. I soon realized that Doc (now deceased) was right. Ed will work!

Ed grew up in Selmer. Ed is 6'4" and weighs well over 200 pounds, so early on I naturally asked him if he played football and basketball at McNairy Central High School. He said, "No, I worked." When Ed was 10 years old, his Dad entered the hospital for eight weeks. Mr. Sims had five sows which Ed looked after, and on the day Mr. Sims left the hospital, Ed presented him with $500 he had accumulated from selling pigs. Not bad for a ten year old! From ages 12 to 16 Ed worked after school and on weekends for his grandfather and uncle in their farming and dairy business. From ages 16 to 19, he worked for Ashwood Farms of Selmer in their cattle and worm operations. No, those worms had nothing to do with those cattle. Ashwood raised two acres of redworms! I'd say it's understandable why Ed is a workaholic in the grain and cotton business; anything is easy after handling two full acres of worms! He then entered UTM and worked all four years for the UTM Experiment Station. His last three years he also worked every available minute for a Martin farmer. Ed put himself through school.

Ed is a former Obion County Commissioner (for 19 years) and served on the Obion County Budget Committee. He was five times president of the Kenton Lions Club, he is captain of the Kenton Fire Department and serves as a director of the UTM Equine Center. His favorite pastimes are watching his daughter, Vera, in her rodeo

438

activities, team roping with brother Darryl, and trail riding. Ed, his wife, Beverly, and Vera live four miles north of Kenton. Vera, like Ed, loves horses and has become a very successful junior rodeo performer. In fact, Vera was selected as 2002 Tennessee Junior Rodeo Queen. As Ed recently said to me, "Vera is my pride and joy." No wonder, Ed.

Susie Sturdivant

Susie started working with us in Kenton in September, 1974. She supplanted me as head bookkeeper, and was I glad! Susie was born on April 5, 1947 at the old Dyer Clinic, the daughter of Wray and Imogene Newmon. She graduated from Kenton High School in 1965 and has lived in Kenton almost all of her life. Her son, Tim Workman, also graduated from Kenton High School and now lives in Kenton with his wife, Tabatha, who is known to her friends and family as Tabby. Tim has worked at Goodyear in Union City since 1988. Susie and Terry Sturdivant of Mason Hall, the son of Donnie and Vernelle Sturdivant, were married on October 7, 1977. They settled in Kenton and Terry works for the Tennessee Department of Transportation in their engineering office in Jackson.

Susie's younger brother, Johnny, died on February 22, 1973. Her father, Wray, longtime Kenton grocer, died on April 8, 1989. Her mother, Imogene, lives in Kenton very near Susie and Terry.

Susie and Terry belong to the New Salem Baptist Church in Mason Hall where both have been and continue to be very active. Susie is church clerk and organized and teaches their Young Adults Sunday School Class. She has served as church treasurer, has worked in the church youth program and as director of the Senior Adult program, and has taught other Sunday School classes.

Susie has always worked in the office in a wing of the house where I grew up and where Mother and Dad lived until they died. Dad lived little more than a year after Susie came to work for us. She says that oftentimes Dad would come down to her office and just sit there. She remembers one time when Dad talked her into driving him out to the strawberry patch (his last strawberry season) and persuaded her to drive on around our Bruce farm, over the cattle guards, to see the cattle.

Susie said it was the dustiest, bumpiest ride she'd ever had. But Dad loved it.

Susie and Terry are "salt of the earth" folks. We Wades are fortunate to count them as our friends.

Janice Vogel

On October 5, 1989, a great thing happened to Como Grain Company. Janice Vogel went to work for us! Janice is a wonderful person, and all our Como customers like her very much. She is a Christian lady and an exemplary mother – her daughter, Amanda, was born in 1988. Janice is honest and has excellent people skills. She brightens our days, and we are lucky to have her.

Janice was born on January 4, 1961 in Henry County to Ralph and Deola Farrar. She grew up in Cottage Grove and went to school there where she graduated from eighth grade, second in her class. She went to Paris Grove High School for the 9th grade and then graduated from Henry County High School.

She bought a little store at Ore Springs and ran it for four years. In October, 1989, Janice was visiting with Margaret and Harrell Peery, Como's manager and office manager, while Margaret was in the hospital and they asked her if she could help out until Margaret came back. On October 5, 1989, Janice became an employee of Como Grain Company.

Janice is now the assistant manager of Como Grain & Feed Company. She is as popular with our customers as anyone could ever be. Janice is very intelligent and accurate and is a most important part of our Como operation. How lucky we are that she made that trip to the hospital!

Chuck Whitaker, Jr

Chuck Whitaker, Jr. was born on September 28, 1965 in Gallatin, Tennessee. He was raised on a small family farm which emphasized diversified livestock production. He and his father ran a registered quarter horse operation which included breeding, training, and showing. Chuck graduated from Gallatin High School in 1983 and attended Volunteer State Community College part-time while working to finance college expenses. Later he enrolled at the University of Tennessee at Martin where he graduated in 1988 with a B.S. in Animal Science. While attending UTM he was an active member of the Block & Bridle Club, Rodeo Club, and the Interfaith Center. Upon graduation he had the good sense to go to work for us at Dyer Grain Company! In addition to being Dyer's assistant manager, Chuck is our yard supervisor, overall safety director, manager of Dyer's Livestock Feed store, and has numerous customer service and clerical responsibilities.

In June, 1988 he married Gaela Potts, also of Gallatin. Gaela and Chuck moved to Dyer and joined the Dyer Cumberland Presbyterian Church where they are actively involved in the youth ministry. Chuck was elected to serve on the board of deacons in January, 1993. They make their home in the Beech Grove Community near Dyer with their two children, Lee and Leah. Chuck's interests include production agriculture, sports, horses, hunting, fishing, and working with children.

It is obvious that our Dyer customers are very fond of Chuck. He really is a personable young man, and he continues to do a great job for us.

Other Employees

We have several excellent employees who have been with us at least two years whom I will mention. Andrea Reese is office and clerical employee at Dyer Grain Company and a very nice and sweet lady. She has been with us since 1996. Pat Halliburton works in the office at Kenton Grain Company and has been with us nearly three years. She is a very pleasant lady who is popular with other employees and customers alike. Pat Patterson has been with us at Kenton Grain Company for three years. Pat is in charge of the yard and loading and unloading grain. He also does some repair work. Julie Parker has been working for Will and me for about three years. She was Tom Elam's legal secretary for 20 years and until his death. Julie was a Sisco who grew up in Kenton. She works about half a day when her children, Logan and Katherine, are in school. This arrangement is perfect for us at our private offices. Julie and her husband, Nick Parker, guidance counselor at Obion County Central High School, own and live on a cattle farm outside Union City. Juan Manuel Mendez is Federico's brother and has worked part of the year for us for several years. In the fall he is assistant ginner at Wade Gin Company, and he helps get the gin ready in the summer and sometimes works at the grain company after ginning season is over.

As this book is going to print, Ronnie Workman has joined our staff at Kenton Grain Company. Ronnie comes to us extraordinarily highly recommended. He has been in the grain business for a good many years and is fully qualified to move into our computer program and to do just about anything that needs to be done. He will make Ed's and Will's lives easier.

Former Employees

There are also several former employees who were most important to our past successes.

Trent Allman worked for Kenton Grain Company for a few months. He left for a better job at Cargill in Hickman. He was great help and we hated to lose him.

Keith Cardwell worked in our Kenton Grain office for 20 years, the last half of which time he was assistant manager and chief computer person. I hired him right out of Gibson County High School. He left us to accept a job with Caterpillar.

Herbert (Shorty) Hill was a longtime strawberry and gin employee. He retired a couple of years ago. Shorty lives next door to our Kenton office and kept up the grounds for us as long as he was able to do so.

Teddy Hobbs managed Kenton Grain Company for 17 years. He is mentioned in the story of Kenton Grain Company. Teddy lost his right arm in Vietnam. One day I went by the grain place and he was on top of one of our big, tall bins. When he came down I told him to, please, never again climb those bins. He said, "Mr. Tommy, if I hadn't gone up there to see how all the valves worked I couldn't have told the boys what to do when there was a problem." Of course, he was right, but it did worry me. Teddy had been right handed so he had to learn to write with his left hand. This bothered him a lot more than anything else about the job. But in no time he was writing checks as well as anybody. Never in my life have I admired a person more than

Teddy Hobbs. He and his lovely wife, Norma, have three fine children, Billie Jo (who wrote me sweet notes when she was a little girl), Bobby Joe, and Bradley Joe. Teddy left us to farm full time with his older brothers, Jay Ray and Joe.

Julie Jordan, daugher of Freddy and Marilyn Jordan, worked in the office of our Kenton Grain Company for two or three years. Though she was almost blind from a childhood brain tumor, she was able to compensate for this disadvantage and was an outstanding and very popular employee. Her marriage and move to Humboldt left a big void.

Edna Earl McFarland worked alongside her husband, William, for many years and was, and is, a highly respected Dyer lady. She is the quintessential Southern Lady. Miz Mac, as I often call her, was also a tremendous asset for Dyer Gin and Grain Company. She retired when William retired.

Steve Moore worked for Dyer Gin and Grain for many years and for a short while at Kenton Grain. He was Dyer's computer person, and he could do just about anything else that needed doing. He left us a few years ago to pursue other opportunites.

Harrell Peery was longtime manager of our Como Gin and Grain Company. As mentioned in the following story of his wife, Margaret, Harrell came to work at Como in 1950 and retired in 1991. He is a veteran of World War II. Harrell lives on a farm close enough to Como that he says he could hear the gin's old giant two-cylinder engine from his home back in the old days. Harrell and Margaret's son, Steve, who has three children, lives in Lexington. Harrell is as fine a person as ever walked the face of the earth.

James Turner was a jack-of-all-trades who worked for us for nearly twenty years. He was our ginner at Dyer and later at Kenton and was our trouble-shooter. James is a mechanically talented person who until recently ran a service station and auto shop in Kenton. We were mighty sorry when he left our company, but it seems to have worked out well for him.

Deceased Former Employees

For a company that has been operating as long as ours, there have obviously been numerous wonderful employees who have passed on to their rewards. It is only fitting that I remember some of those people who were very important to us in the operation of our business pursuits.

J. C. Betts worked for Dad at our gins, almost all of the time as head ginner, for 56 years. He was a mechanical genius. Give him a little baling wire and a little time and he could make almost anything work. I have never known a more dependable person. One morning J. C. was not at the gin at 7 AM. I told Delbert Orr that something bad had happened to J. C. or that he had died. Sure enough, a little while later J. C. drove in with the front end of his car badly damaged. He had run into a deer on the way to work. This was the only time he was ever late, and he never failed to show up for work. Apparently he never got sick during the summer repair season or the fall ginning season. J. C. died in January, 2002, at age 83. He left a widow, Martha, now of Milan, a daughter, Lee Sharp of Jackson, and a son, Jackie, also of Milan.

Van Howard, long time Como Gin and Como Grain Company employee, died October 15, 1994 at Como, Tennessee and was buried on his 69th birthday at Olive Branch Cemetery north of Como. Van started working at Como Gin at night and on weekends while he was still in high school in 1942 or 1943 and worked on until 1985. So his tenure at Como covered 43 or 44 years. Van was an outstanding ginner and later was equally important to our grain operation. For many years he shared in Como's managerial responsibilities. Van also farmed and enjoyed raising cattle and hogs. He liked to hunt, fish, and read. Van's widow, June Davis Howard, was the boss's niece. June's uncle, Mr. Charlie Davis, was Como's first manager and her father, Dennis Davis, also worked at the gin. In addition to June, Van also left two UTM graduate sons, Greg and Jeff.

Sammie Lee Lancaster, who is mentioned in the Wade Gin Company story, was a truck driver and general employee for Dad for a long time. He was a good natured and pleasant person with whom to work. His widow, Maggie, helped Mother, and then Pat, for decades. Maggie, a delightful person, was a great cook. Maggie lived in Kenton until her death on January 24, 2003. Sammie Lee died in 1979. I was pleased to put a headstone at their graves.

J. William McFarland was a very close friend, confidant, and company manager for the Wade family for a long, long time. William met his Maker on March 9, 1998.

William, who worked at Dyer Gin and Grain Company for 53 years, most of that time as manager, was a master of psychology. He had a way of calming people down. One time Dad came down to Dyer Gin Company a little peeved for some reason. While Dad and William were talking they saw a cat coming down the railroad, walking the rails headed south. Dad asked, "Where's that cat going?" William replied, "To Trenton." Dad, "How do you know?" William, "Because the cat's headed that way." The cat got off the railroad at the intersection south of the gin and walked east. Dad, "I guess he decided not to go to Trenton." Dad was happy.

Another instance of this talent of William's concerned a customer who came in a little upset about something. William saw him coming and tried to dodge him, but this ruse didn't work. William knew the man had a beloved female dog which was pregnant. He said to the customer, "Did Fido have her puppies yet?" Customer, "Yes." William, "How many did she have?" The customer told him, and they continued to talk about the dog and her pups, and the customer left completely happy.

On another occasion, a customer came in, a grizzled old man who wore a John Brown type overcoat in the winter. At that time Delta & Pine Plantation (DPL) had a series of seed with an "A" in the name (something like DPL 54A variety). The customer said to William, "Say boy, you got any of them A Model seed left?" William didn't and said, "Naw sir, but we've got a good pile of them V-8 seed left." This was of course, a made-up name, but William thinks it was probably Stoneville seed. The customer bought $300 or so worth of "them V-8 seed." Wonder if he raised little Fords?

One time a disgruntled customer was complaining to William about his turnouts (the percentage of the seed cotton that ends up as the lint in the bale). Dyer Gin was a double battery gin and had lots of outside exhausts and pipes leading to the incinerator. The man told William you couldn't expect much turnout, "After all," he said, "you've got one pipe going in and 16 coming out."

One night about 9 o'clock at the gin Farmer Jones said to William, "William, I'd like to talk to you a little bit. John Armstrong told me he was saving all his cottonseed to plant. John's got a load coming under and I wonder if I oughta save some for myself. He says his seed makes good cotton, says he ordered them special from up in Newbraskey. But ain't that 'way up north where it gets awful cold?" William said, "Yes, it is." To which Farmer Jones said, "He lied to me, didn't he?"

William got a kick out of telling the story of an employee — we'll call him Georgie, a fictitious name — who had very little education. In the old days we sold fertilizer in 50 pound bags, and William thought his inventory count was not always working out right. He called Georgie into the office and asked him, "Georgie, how many bags do you give a customer when he wants 100 pounds of fertilizer?" Georgie replied, "Two." William said, "That's good, Georgie. Now how many do you give him if he wants 200 pounds?" "I'd give 'em fo." "Very good, Georgie. Now how many would you give him if he wanted 500 pounds?" Georgie scratched his head, thought a minute, and said, "Uhh, I'd give 'em 'bout seben uh eight!" True story.

Delbert Orr worked in our Wade Gin Company office for 40 years. Delbert was a farmer who owned land north and northwest of Kenton. He was a loyal customer of Wade Gin Company. Forty years prior to Delbert's retirement from the gin he asked Dad if he would consider loaning him some money to buy a farm and Delbert would then work in the gin office, weighing and paying for cotton, reimbursing Dad that way. They struck a bargain, one which turned out to be one of the best deals Dad ever made. Delbert was an accurate and popular office manager for all those years. He was the kind of person who would do anything for a friend, and he became one of my best friends. Delbert was known to cuss a little, but he had a heart of gold.

In Kenton High School Delbert was a very good basketball player on a very good team. One of his best friends and a teammate was Earl Ramer (mentioned in Chapter 2) who went on to become a Ph.D. He also became Professor of Education and Chair of the Department of Continuing and Higher Education within the College of Education at UT and was twice president of the NCAA (National Collegiate Athletic Association)!

Delbert married Marie Vaughn and they had three children. Pat Orr Pierce and Lourita Orr live just north of Kenton in a house on a lot that Delbert bought from Dad and which was a part of our Brick House farm. Pat's daughter, Donna Pierce Ashe, lives in Kenton and has a son, Jeffrey Shayne Pickard. Delbert and Marie's third child, Carlton Shayne (Buster) Orr, and his wife, live in Tucson, Arizona. Buster's three children and one grandchild also live in Tucson.

Delbert died on July 28, 1990 and is buried in Kenton's Sunnyside Cemetery beside his Marie.

Margaret Peery, beloved wife of Harrell Peery, died on January 2, 1996. Margaret and Harrell were married for 58 years. They were a "team" in more than one way. Harrell went to work at Como Gin Company in 1950. Margaret joined him at Como in 1964. When they retired in 1991, Harrell had been there for 41 years and Margaret for 27 years! Once he was old enough to do so, their son, Steve, rode his bicycle to the gin in the afternoons after school and was a big help at the bale press. For the Peerys, Como Gin (and later Grain) Company was indeed a family affair. Margaret was a sweet person and a dedicated employee.

Aubrey (Pud) Phelan, known to his myriad of friends as "Pud", died on July 21, 1993. Pud was manager of our Farmers Gin Company at Rutherford for many years. His lovely wife, Armelia, also worked at the gin for most of that time. In all my years I have never known finer people than Pud and Armelia. They have meant a great deal to the Wade family, not only in a business way — and they were terrific in that regard — but more importantly for their sincere and dedicated friendship. Pud's passing left the world a poorer place.

Arthur Sisco was another of Dad's farm employees. Arthur and his wife, Pauline, who still resides in Kenton, raised six extraordinary children, one of whom is Will's and my assistant, Julie, who is typing this manuscript. Arthur, like most folks around here, was a big St. Louis Cardinals fan. I remember how much he enjoyed going to St.

447

Louis with other employees and Dad and me for games at Sportsman's Park. One of his sons, Marty, was the successful basketball coach mentioned in Chapter 2, and another of his daughters, Kay, is married to our Dyer manager, Johnny Martin. Arthur died in 1998.

James Turner's brother, Donald Turner, drove a truck for Dyer for many years and was an excellent driver and a loyal employee of longstanding. Donald was a big, raw boned man, but he was as gentle as a kitten.

Tom Wheatley drove trucks for us for many years. He owned his own truck for a long time and hauled grain for us for hire. Then he sold his last truck and drove for us until his health forced him to retire. Soon thereafter he died.

There are many other deceased former employees who worked for Dad and who were very important to him. Columbus (Lum) Bradley was a farm employee and the father of Dewey Bradley. James B. Bradley was another of Mr. Bradley's sons who worked for Dad on the farm and at the gin. Ulysses Dennison was Dad's longtime herdsman. His daughter, Melba, and I were classmates in school. Melba's son, Dwight Phillips, owns an engineering firm in Union City as well as land adjacent to our Bruce bottom. Harry Dodson weighed cotton and wrote checks at the Kenton and Rutherford gins for many years. Dad and I often noticed that Harry would drift off into a world of his own and smile when pleasant things would cross his mind. He was a real gentleman.

Jack Hanks worked for Dad in many capacities and lived on his farms for a good many years. His daughter, Joyce, was my classmate. Harry Landrum managed Dad's Rutherford gin for a long time and was, in fact, a partner for a few years. His son, Don, has helped us out on several occasions when we badly needed his assistance. Charlie (Skunny) Mitchell drove a truck for us. Tommie Rudd was a long time suck feeder at Wade Gin Company and worked on the farm. Enloe Spencer was Dad's long time Kenton ginner. His son, Sonny Spencer, drove a truck for Dad. Sonny's daughter, Barbara, was also my classmate. She married Ralph Perryman, and they have two children. One of them, Mike Perryman, is administrator of Baptist Hospital

Union City. I serve on his Indigent Care Fund Board. Mike is also chairman of our First State Bank of Kenton Community Bank Board.

Chapter Thirty-Six

Local Folks

Leaving Kenton and moving to Union City was a hard decision to make. I love Kenton, always have and always will. I come to Kenton six days a week, often seven, and will as long as my health allows me to do so. My toes will be turned up in Sunnyside Cemetery where my Mother, Dad, little Patti, paternal grandparents, and many uncles, aunts, and cousins are buried. My friendships with Kenton people, from long ago as well as those made in more recent times, are all important to me. It would be unconscionable for me to write a book about us Wades that did not include the names of those fine folks from the Kenton/Mason Hall area who have been and continue to be important in my life, and in many cases, the lives of my family. Another reason for including their names is that most of these people have never been mentioned in a book. They deserve such mention, and by George, they are now part of an honest-to-goodness book — one that will reside in the archives of the Library of Congress! The following list is a lengthy one; nevertheless there will be some people who should be listed but who have inadvertently been left out. You people know who you are; please forgive my oversight.

One category purposely left out are customers of ours who are not in the Kenton/Mason Hall area per se. These customers are among our good friends. After a great deal of soul searching and considering that we have literally hundreds of customers/friends at our Como, Dyer, and Kenton operations, I have reluctantly made the decision to stick with friends from the Kenton/Mason Hall and Union City areas only since these are the areas about which this book is written. If any of you customers from outside the Kenton/Mason Hall area ever read this modest epistle, please know that we are totally aware of the fact that the only reason we are able to survive in business is you. We are enormously grateful to you for what you do for us.

First State Bank of Kenton has been very important to the success of my company, and the man primarily responsible for the long-term viability of the bank is Andy Newmon. He and Ann are enjoying a much deserved retirement. Those at the bank now, all of whom are very helpful to us, are Andy Page, David Quinn, Brenda Allen, Brooke Cardwell, Debbie Denning, Deborah Eddlemon, Tracye Fender, Cassie Langston, Layne Randolph, Jennifer Russom, and Sis Tate. Thanks to each of these folks for their kindnesses through the years.

Will and I occasionally eat lunch at the Kenton House Restaurant, but most of the time we eat either at the Kenton Dairy Bar which is owned and capably operated by Scott Whitworth, or at Reed's Market. One of the pleasant aspects about life in Kenton for me is the bantering I get involved in with Reed's regular coffee customers. Some of these good men are Jack Allen, Charlie Ashe, Melvin Brooks, Harold Buchanan, Ronnie Hunt, Freddy Jordan, Tom Kasun, R. L. Landrum, Charles Needham, Ronnie Reeves, Bob Summers, and B. T. Yates.

Names of some others of Kenton's good people who have not otherwise been mentioned in this book follow: (In many cases I do not know spouses.)

Billy and Treva Adams, Kyle Agee, Delores Agee, Frank and Sarah Allen, Jane Allen, Michael Allen, Thomas (Butch) Allen, Donald and Mary Asbridge, Lee and Patty Asbridge, Jeff and Margie Asbridge, Pat Ashe, Peggy Baker, Harold Banks, Robert Banks, James and Elaine Barber, L. M. Bardwell, Harold Lloyd Baucom, L. A. and Rebecca Baucom, Jack and Sue Bell, Tom and Betty Bock, Marie Boucher, Gary Boyett, Quinton and Norene Boyett, Tom Bradford, Howard Brown, Geraldine Brown, Sue Buchanan, Jimmy Burress, Willie Burress, Gary Carson, Jeff and Rhonda Chandler, Natalie Chandler, Todd and Jennifer Chandler, Pat Chandler, W. A. and Shirley Clark, Roger and Beth Cochran, Eva Coday, Jay Cooley, Danny Cooper, Mark Cooper, Joey Cooper, Junior Cooper, Tommy Corley, James and Carolyn Covington, Ken and Nancy Covington, Damon and Marjorie Cross, Joe and Carrie Davis, Doug Davis, Randy Davis, Ricky Davis, Bruce and Virginia Davidson, Helen Dillon, Lualice Dodd, Wilbur Doran, Ben and Sherri Drake, Jerry and Ella Jean Dunn, Frances Dunn,

Wayne and Barbara Dunn, Jeff Duren, Jerry Duren, William Duren, Bob Eddlemon, Joe Eddlemon, Betty Eddings, William Edmonds, Michael Elder, Tim Ellison, Annie Mae Emrich, Louie and Gail Emrich, Mike Farrar, George Farris, Kerry Freeman, Ethel Galloway, Helen Garrett, Norma Jean Garrett, Frankie Glisson, Jere Gordon, Wayne and Ann Grant, Winfred Graves, Don Green, Jerry and Peggy Green, Mike Green, Haywood Green, Jo Griggs, Brenda Griggs, Tim and Julie Griggs, Ann Griggs, Christine Griggs, Curtis Halford, Steve Halford, Tom Halliburton, Mickey Hanks, Max Hardin, Darlene Hayes, Terry and Betty Hicks, Dennis and Regina Hixson, Sarah Hobbs, Michelle Hobbs, Lee Jay and Heather Hobbs, Ronnie Hobbs, Evelyn Hollomon, Lisa Hollomon, Mark and Cindy Hollomon, Jesse Horton, Reece and Helen Houston, McKinley Huey and Phyllis Huey, Debbie Huey, Vickie Huey, Barbara Hunt, Chad Hunt, Jimmy Hurt, Norman (Tooter) Jackson, Jimmy and Nadine Jackson, David Jacobs, Dickie Jacobs, John Wayne and Jackie James, Iona Johns, Tim Johns, Charles Johnson, Harrell Johnson, Jimmy Johnson, Dennis Jones, Harry Jones, Johnny Jones, Sheila Jones, Walter Jones, Danny Jowers, Jack and Nancy Kastorff, Barry and Amy Keathley, Betty Jo King, Dallas King, Harry King, John Kuykendall, Quentin and Amy Lee, Donny and Linda Little, Marilee Little, Mickey and Gail Little, Jason Little, Jody Little, Tommy and Kim Litton, Lurliene Long, Margaret Long, Mark Lumpkin, Jerry Lynch, Dale and Cara Marvin, Ed and Mary Ellen Marvin, John Maughan, Frank and Estelle May, Evelyn Mayhall, Susie McCleish, Kenneth McGregor, Steve McGregor, Billy McKenzie, Mac and Tina McMackin, Rodney and Joyce McMackin, Tammy McMackin, Roger Meeks, Steve Meeks, Connie Miller, Dorothy Moon, Lloyd and Bonnie Sue Moon, Eugene and Vivian Moore, J. T. and Bobbie Ruth Mullins, Leroy Neil, Imogene Newmon, Ralph and Peggy Nichols, David Northam, Robert Norton, Bobby and Peggy Owens, Gary Owens, J. B. Owens, Ray Parker, Mark Paschall, Johnny and Benny Patterson, Geoffrey and Lynn Payne, Gail Perryman, Donald Pierce, Ed Pierce, Franklin Pierce, S. T. Pierce, Billy and Penny Petty, Matthew and Laura Pitts, Randy and Mary Pitts, Michael Pitts, Stacy Pitts, Tracy Pitts, Katie Lou Polsgrove, Charles and Linda Pratt, Douglas Prince, Thomas Proctor, Cecil and Joann Ray,

Chris Ray, Grady and Peggy Ray, Jo Ann Reed, Johnny Reed, Patricia Reed, Randy Reeves, J. R. Roden, Mike and Laney Rogers, Damon and Myrtle Ross, Jerry Rudd, Terry Rudd, Curtis Russom, Joel Russom, Leo Russom, Valerie Sanderson, Helen Sanderson, Louis Sawyer, Bernice Sawyer, Gerald Schaeffer, Daniel and Faye Sharp, Joe and Peggy Sharp, Neil Sharp, Sam Shoulders, Jack and Joy Siler, Arnold and Sandy Simpson, Charlie Roscoe Simpson, J. W. Simpson, Norma Simpson, Mike Simpson, Wade and Cindy Simpson, Dianne Sisco, Marilyn Skiles, James and Sarah Skinner, Jonathan Skinner, Carl and June Smith, Mike Smith, Kenneth and Wanda Smithson, Kent and Jill Smithson, Rob Somerville, Max Spence, Allen Stephens, Joe Stephens, Bob Summers, Gayle Tankersley, Travis and Nancy Tankersley, Wendy Tate, W. C. Tate, Nellie Taylor, Howard (Pitt) and Broecksie Taylor, William and Beverly Taylor, Pam Tilghman, Janie Tilghman, Skip Tilghman, Robert Todd, Bruce and Betty Trout, Jim Turner, Sandy Upchurch, Clyde Vickery, Buddy Vinson, George Wade, Jeremy Warren, Jerry and Sherry Warren, Paula West, Tommy and Janice Wheatley, Stacy Wheatley, Clyde (Bill D.) Whitworth, Grady Whitworth, Harold Whitworth, Ray Whitworth, John and Lavenia Wiese, Lavan and Lisa Williams, Paul and Janice Williams, V. L. Williamson, Darryl Wilson, Zula Witherington, Emily Woods, Russ and Deb Woods, Tim Workman, Tim and Tabitha Workman, Woodrow and Kathryn Workman, Woodrow Workman, Jr., Helen Wylie, Billy and Faye Wyrick, Floyd and Lavonne Yarbro, Carlton Yarbrough, Reed and Neva Yarbrough, Mary Lou Yates, Barry and Carla Yergin, Billy and Ruby Yergin, Betty Yergin, Joe Mack and Reba Yergin, Jackie Zaricor.

Certainly one of the best things about moving to Union City has been the many good friends we have made. Almost as soon as we moved to Union City we began having Christmas Eve parties inviting some of our closest Union City friends and their families. This party has become a Wade tradition, and those who have joined us through the years are the David Critchlows and their children and now grandchildren, the Robert Kirklands and their children and now grandchildren, the Jack Drerups and their children and grandchild, the Milton Hamiltons and their children and grandchildren (until they all moved away), Harold and Mary Nell Butler, Kathleen Elam, Rick and Betty Smith, and the John Miles and their children. In recent years my cousin, Estelle Norvell (until she died) and her daughter Estelle, Jr. (Fire) and her husband, Jorge Cruxent, and big Estelle's son, Louis Norvell, Jr. and Ginger Guthrie, and Pat's lifelong friend, Tippy Moody Roach, all from Dyersburg, have become a part of our Christmas Eve tradition. Our Patti when she was a little girl, confused the greeting, "Merry Christmas!" with the name Mary Critchlow. When the Critchlows made their entrance into our home some long ago Christmas Eve, Patti spontaneously greeted them with a hearty "Mary Critchlow!" "Mary Critchlow" has been our standard Christmas greeting ever since. All of these old friends have added immeasurably to the quality of our lives through the years.

In addition to Jenny and Robert Kirkland, Lois and the late Barry White have been among our best friends. Robert and Barry, back door neighbors and best friends, were always great practical jokers. One time when Lois and Barry were out of town, Robert had a sign painted something like this:

Soon Coming to This Site
Cluck Cluck Farms
(phone number 885-xxxx)
6 Environmentally Friendly Chicken Houses

Robert had this rather large sign erected on part of a fair sized farm that is next to Barry's house in Sherwood Hills. Robert included his children's phone number and instructed Jenny to answer simply, "Cluck, Cluck." Barry came home and was incensed with what he saw. He called 885-xxxx. Jenny answered, "Cluck, Cluck." Barry asked another question. Jenny replied, "Cluck, Cluck." Barry, growing more upset by the second, slammed down the phone and called Robert at work to tell him about this unbelievable development. Robert agreed with Barry that the last thing they needed was a chicken operation next door to their homes and suggested that Barry might organize the Sherwood homeowners in an effort to put a stop to this outrageous turn of events. Barry called Bob Cartwright who lived down the street.

Bob sympathized with Barry, promised his support, and suggested that he carry on with his organizational efforts. Barry again called 885-xxxx, and his impassioned argument against building a chicken farm next to his property was simply answered, "Cluck, Cluck." Another stronger statement from Barry. "Cluck, Cluck," so he once again hung up and then called Robert who by this time was at home. Robert, upon hearing Barry's voice and being concerned that Barry might have a heart attack, answered his and Jenny's telephone, "Cluck, Cluck." Barry was taken aback and when it rapidly dawned on him that Robert was the source of his great consternation, he said, "Kirkland, you son-of-a-__, you oughta be shot!" So ends the saga of Cluck Cluck Farms. Or did it?

A short time later Jenny and Robert left on a trip. They returned home to find hundreds of baby chicks in their back yard. Guess who sent them? They had been put in a makeshift pen but had escaped. Robert and Barry, with the help of neighbor Jim Rippy, started scurrying around catching the chicks and throwing them back into the pen. For a while they did not realize that the chicks were coming back out as fast as they put them in. The reason? The openings in the wire sides were bigger than the chicks. Robert and Jenny have lived in their new fabulous home west of Union City for a couple of years now. I'll wager there are still some "free range" chickens pecking around Sherwood.

Speaking of the Kirkland's new home, which is the finest home in a big chunk of Tennessee, when the black under-roof was completed and before the tile roof was put on, Robert painted a big "See Rock City" on it. Some people thought this was the permanent roof. Guess they figured Kirkland was helping to pay for his house with advertising income.

In the early days of Kirkland's stores, headquartered in Jackson, and a little later CBK, Ltd. of Union City, Robert and Carl Kirkland's retail gift stores and wholesale gifts importer, Robert opened an office for himself on the second floor of one of the old buildings on Union City's First Street. One of the ways that he exaggerated the fact that theirs was still somewhat of a fledgling business was by making his desk out of some planks atop two sawhorses. When Pat and I received word of Robert's meager office furnishings we called Hattie Lou Brown and had her make up and deliver a floral arrangement of dead flowers in honor of his grand opening.

As all Union Citians and many Jacksonians now know, Kirkland's became a large chain of gift shops in major malls throughout the South and Midwest. Robert and Carl sold Kirkland's a few years ago, and Carl has stayed on to help the new owners for a while. My understanding is that these two first cousins still own a small part of Kirkland's. Several years ago Robert bought Carl's interest in CBK, Ltd., and Robert recently sold out.

Jenny and Robert and Pat and I have traveled together rather extensively. Two more pleasant travel companions never existed. They are highly intelligent, witty, and great fun to be with, and they simply "wear well."

Other great friends in Union City have been the Critchlows, about whom much has been written in various parts of this book, and Jack and Peggy Drerup, with whom we have often traveled. Both David Critchlow and Jack, partners with each other in several enterprises, were directors of our bank, as is Bob Kirkland and as was Barry White. Peggy Drerup and Diane Critchlow are delightful ladies and close friends of Pat's and mine.

Other close friends are Milton and Dale Hamilton. Milton, long time Tennessee state senator and later Tennessee Commissioner of Environment and Conservation in the Sundquist Administration, and Dale have recently moved from their lifelong home of Obion County and Union City to Nashville. We and all of Union City and Obion County were sorry to see them go. They are now nearer to two of their children, Mickey and David (who for several years was head of the Obion County Industrial Development Corporation), so they had a good reason to relocate to Middle Tennessee. We do miss them. Milton was also one of the original organizers and directors of our bank.

George and Edith Botts are without a doubt two of the nicest people Pat and I have ever known. George was a strong director for the bank, and we have enjoyed many occasions with them, business and social, on trips together and at their Rives lake house, Windy Hill. They are outstanding hosts and true friends.

Barry, another director of our bank who is now deceased, and Lois White were also delightful trip companions. This devoted couple has added to the quality of the lives of every single one of the literally thousands of people with whom they came in contact through the years.

Jim and Carol White are also great friends. Jim and I went to Camp Hy-Lake in Middle Tennessee together when we were small boys. Jim and Carol and their children, Jimmy and Linda, lived next door to us for many years. Jim and Carol moved several years ago so as to be across the street from Linda. Jim was also one of the originators and directors of our bank.

Newell and Bettye Graham are fine friends with whom we have traveled some. Newell was also one of our bank's charter directors. They have recently built a fabulous home southeast of Union City.

Bob and Brenda Cartwright and Bill and Linda Simrell are also mighty good friends. Bob, a great raconteur and owner of three Navistar truck dealerships, and Bill, who along with his family owns internationally known Jiffy Steamer, are newer directors of our bank. Pat and I value our friendship with these four attractive people.

John Miles and Bart White are also directors of the bank. They are excellent directors and good friends whom I admire and respect. Kristin Miles and Jean Ann White, their wives, are great assets to the community.

Dan Weber, a former president of the Tennessee Bankers Association and a charter director of the bank, did a marvelous job of organizing and leading First State Bank to bigger and better things. This good friend has been helpful to me in many ways. A great example of this fact can be found in Chapter 20 having to do with Pat's and my trip to Wimbledon. Dan and his wife, Jean, are civic-minded, popular Union Citians.

Tony Gregory, another director, came to us from Goodlettsville, Tennessee and has done a yeoman job as C.E.O. of our bank. Tony, an outstanding banker, has also been helpful to me personally in many ways. He and his wife, Amanda, and their two children live three houses from Will and Kim.

James R. (Jimmy) White is our newest director. It is obvious to all of us on the board that this well-educated, highly intelligent young man will be a great asset to our board.

Other good Union City friends from our Union City bank and holding company staffs as well as from our Rives and Troy offices are Chet Alexander, Kim Bacon, Larry Baker, Pam Baker, Kathy Barber, Alice Barron, Eric Beardsley, Amy Brown, John Bruno, Bonnie Brown, Bonnie Brunswick, Rana Buchanan, Joy Carson, John Clark, Amy Dickson, Jim Douglas, Jerry Forrester, Ken Garrigan, Bill Harrison, John Horner, Lisa Isbell, Tressa Jacobs, Janice James, Loretta Jercinovich, Christy Johnson, Sandra Joyner, Lynda King, Jody Kizer, John Liggett, J. C. (Pip) Little, Barbara Long, Maudie McCullar, David Moore, Chuck Oliver, Marlene Ring, Michele Siler, Don Stephens, Bill Townes, and Christa Walton. Good bankers can come in mighty handy!

Of course, we have many good Union City friends who are not directly associated with our bank.

Harold and Mary Nell Butler have long been close friends. Harold was for many years our outstanding and talented family doctor. We are delighted that he is again practicing in Union City. Mary Nell is one of the best friends Pat has ever had. She is true blue. A marvelous cook, Mary Nell, along with good friend, Gail Latimer, have accompanied Pat and me to New York a couple of times. Both Mary Nell and Gail have done a great deal, in their own ways, to make this a better world.

Jim and Martha Rippy are two great folks. Jim, the current president of the Insurors of Tennessee, is our insurance agent and a darn good one. Martha and Pat have also been close friends over the years. We have traveled with the Rippys, and they are both a lot of fun to be with. Jim has been an extraordinary leader in Union City and Obion County, as evidenced by his selection one year as "The Pride of Obion County," a richly deserved wonderful honor.

Paul (Pete) Tate is a close friend. In addition to being the world's best painter (houses and interiors, not canvases!), Pete has been our "house sitter" who lives in and looks after our house when we are away.

He has also been a true friend to our children and grandchildren. Pete is simply one of the world's good people.

Other Union Citians with whom we go out to dinner fairly often and whom we enjoy being with very much are David and Sheila Parks. David was our family dentist from the time we moved to Union City until he retired. We miss David's dental attention, but our new dentist, Jerry Sullivan, is terrific. We also value Jerry and Charlotte's friendships.

It is impossible to write a chapter about our Union City friends without leaving out some folks who should have been mentioned. Since some oversights are inevitable, please forgive me, and bear in mind that I do not know all spouses. A book about our lives would not be complete without mentioning the foregoing and following who have made our lives more pleasant and who have not been mentioned elsewhere in this book: Ginny Acree, Ralph and Bobbie Adams, Roger and Janie Alexander, Ron Arant, Trent and Leslee Arnold, Richard and Patty Arnold, Craig and Christy Atwill, Mackey Austin, Johnny and Kathy Bacon, Nancy Jo Bacon, Robert Bagwell, Jere and Nancy Baldridge, Wayne Barber, Harold Barham, Hattie Barham, Bim Barker, Bryan and Kathey Barker, Wayne and Judy Barker, Randy and Sharon Barnes, James Batey, Bentley and Celene Beard, John Bell, Pete and Vicky Blanton, Ron and Carolyn Bloebaum, Joy Bloodworth, Jim and Mary Nita Bondurant, Franklin Botts, Kevin Bowden, Lynn and Debbie Bowlin, Dan Boykin, John Brannon, Eric Brooks, Gordon and Amanda Bruff, Stacy Bruff, Tracy and Jennifer Bruff, Larry and Rita Buckles, Mary Burchard, Bill and Billie Burkett, Peggy Burnett, Perry and Linda Burnett, Wynn Burnett, Russell and Donna Caldwell, Lanny Callicott, Damon Campbell, Ray and Pat Capps, Eddie and Betty Lee Carden, Millard and Marian Carman, Bob Carpenter, Sam Carpenter, John and Sammie Castellano, Victor and Laura Castro, Terry and Glenda Caudle, Eddie and Rachel Chancellor, Randy and Paula Chapman, Bob and Pat Cherry, Richard Chesteen, Art Chivers, Tommy and Glenda Chrisp, Martha Clendenin, Chuck and Christy Cloud, Charles and Sandra Cobb, Lowell Collins, Bruce Conley, Steve and Wesley Conley, Bob Cooley, Ron and Barbara Cooper, Jimmy and Judy Counce, Donnie Cox, Mickey Cox, Mike and Beth Cox, Harold and Glenda Cozart, Jeff and Becky Crabtree, Jere and Diane Crenshaw, Al and Michelle Creswell, Blaine Cultra, Bob Cultra, Eddie and Judy Cultra, Pete Daniel, David and Bridgette Darnall, Sherry Daugherty, Jerry and Sandra Davis, Ken and Ina Davis, Leland Davis, Charles and Laura Denaburg, Mike and Patsy Dickerson, Willa Dickerson Carr, William (Will) King Dickerson, Sacchi Doss, Hal and Jackie Dodd, Ray and Mary Ann Douglas, Billy Dowell, Tim Doyle, Brother and Lindy Dunavant, Mary Dunavant, Barry Duncan, Brooks and Paula Duncan, Bill Dunlap, Nancy Dunn, Greg and Kris Dunn, John and Delana Easley, Larry and Betty Edmundson, Randy and Donna Eller, Harry and Rachel Ellison, Emily Elliston, Jim Emmons, Joanne Escarcega, Rogie Escarcega, Julius and Ellise Falkoff, Jimmy and Janice Faulk, Brian Ferguson, Bud Fisher, Keith and Anita Fisher, Bill and Susie Flood, David and Susan Fowler, Johnny and Janie Fowler, Mark and Sue Fowler, Pete and Charlene Fowler, Gordon Fox, Dan and Meredith Frankum, Dave and Amy Frankum, Sonny and Diana Frankum, Tim and Kelly Frankum, Lavene Fry, Lee and Connie Fry, Mary Ruth Fuller, Sandy Fuzzell, Janice Garrigan, Gary Gill, Ralph and Nancy Gilliam, Jo Glasgow, Jenna Glasgow, Steve Goodrich, Harry and Ruth Gorman, Alan and Linda Graham, Annie Laurie Graham, Bill Grasfeder, Fred Grasfeder, Helen Grasfeder, June Graves, Jim and Sue Greer, Mike and Debbie Greer, Ed and Glenda Griffin, Charlie Grooms, Jimmy and Laticia Gray, Jerry Gurien, Tiger Haig, Terry and Mitzi Hailey, Bill Hairston, John and Jane Hale (John and Pat are distant cousins), James Carl Hammond, Russ Hammonds, John and Linda Lou Harding, Mike Hardy, Joe and Mary Lou Harpole, Steve and Barbara Harpole, Jim and Linda Harrelson, Freemon Harris, James and Amy Harris, James and Sandra Harris, Jesse Harris, Jim and Michelle Harris, Myrtle Harton, Gussie Haskins, Kevin and Stacie Herrell, Jim and Ann Hibbler, Joe and Susan Hill, W. T. and Mary Ann Hime, David and Linda Hogan, Charles and Mary Sue Holland, Steve Hopkins, Gary and Marsha Houston, JoAlice Houston, Jack and Juanita Hudgens, Bernice Hudgens, Terry and Jane Huffstetler, Bob and Beverly Hunt, Charles and Martha Hutchinson, Amy Jackson, Bill James, Paul Jarnagin, Harold and Bettye Jenkins, Herman and Sandra Jenkins, Hal Jernigan, Leon Jessup, David and Teresa Johnson, David and Mary Hellen Johnson, Clint Joiner and Rebecca Russell, Abe and Velma Jolley, Jimmy and Barbara Jones, Trent Jones, Rob and Stacy Jordon, Rob and Lou Joyner, Paul and Pat Kasnow, Barry and Janet Keathley, Betty Keathley, Bryan and Angela Keathley, Barry and Josephine Keightly, Porter and Frances Keightley, Kenneth and Ann Kemp, Lee and Elizabeth Kendall, James David Kendall, Robert Kendall, Martha Lynn Kendall, Heath Key, Johnny and Shelvy Key, Jim Kincade, James Kinsey, Charles and Larrabee Kirkland, Hunter and Laurie Kirkland, Ken and Peggy Kirkland, Melissa Kirkland, Jim and Jan Kizer, Bill and Robbie Koupa, Doris Lanzer, Carol Latimer, Dorothy Latimer, Bill Lawrence, Roy Lawrence, Robert and Lois Lewis, Rodger and Sue Lewis, Francis and Jackie Lin, Mark and Lynn Lowrance, Grace Maddox, Martha Maness, Tony and Claudia Maness, Paul and Suzanne Marsidi, Joe and Joyce Martin, Bill and Frances Massengill, Gene McAdoo, Bob and Betsy McAnulty, Sam McCollum, Scotty McCullar, Jerry McCullough, Mary Whayne Miles, Randy and Melanie Mitchell, Bob and Amy Montgomery, Bill Moore, Greg Moore, J. R. Moore, Richard and Tricia Moran, Raymond Morris, Bruce Moss, Sam Nailling, Bob and Martha Carol Nichols, Tim and Carolyn Nipp, Allen and Lizzie Nohsey, Paul and Joy Olexa, Joe and Loretta O'Neill, Elwyn Oliver, Jack and Susan Parker, Nick Parker, Jerry and Jane Paschall, Kevin and Amy Paschall, Claud and DiAnn Perry, Ted and Brenda Perry, Billie Perryman, Leroy Perryman, Bill and Billie Petty, Terry and Gwen Petty, Jimmy Phebus, Dwight and Marsha Phillips, Jim and Nina Pierce, Phillip Pinion, Ken and Judy Pitts, Burnie and Suzanne Powers, Jon Ed Powers, Kelly Powers, Tripp Powers, Bill and Cathy Prather, David (Winker) and Leslie Prather, Phillip and Betty Puckett, Evelyn Quarles, Howard and Billie Ragsdale, Stephen Raines, Bobby and Jan Rankin, Karen Rawls, Terry Reed, Johnny and Jean Reeder, Ed and Rosemary Reese, Tracy Reese, Bob and Sharon Regen, Marion and Mary Lynn Reithel, Hal and Beverly Rice, Neal and Sarah Rice, Shea and Diane Riley, Shea Riley III, Heath Riley, Katherine Roberts, Allen and Phyllis Rogers, John Rogers, Virginia Roper, Art and Phoeba Ross, Kirk Ross, Kyle Ross, Marilyn Ross, Tab and Beth Ross, Paul and Charlotte Russell, Steve and Carol Russell, Bob Sanner, Matt Sanner, Grover Schleifer, Grover and

Fredricka Schleifer, Ken and Ethel Schneider, Allen Searcy, Bill Shanklin, Larry Shanks, Judy Shaw, Larry and Kim Sherwood, Joel and Bernice Shore, Shane Sisco, Travis and Linda Shumate, Mickey and Pam Smith, Tim Smith, Art and Tammy Sparks, Nan Sproles, David and Linda St. Clair, Bob and Joyce Stephens, Lenora Stephenson, David Stokes, Ed Lee Stone, Jeff Stone, Jim and Dora Stone, Smokey Stover, Jimmy Sutherland, Bill and Doris Tanner, Buzz and Carolyn Tanner, Rodger and Wanda Tanner, Raiford Tarver, Johnny Tate, Steve and Debbie Tate, Thel and Judy Taylor, Thel, Jr. and Kim Taylor, Beverly Terrell, Rob and Renea Terrell, Bill and Felicia Thompson, Jim and Rosalee Thompson, Joe and Jean Thompson, William (Bill) P. Thompson, Don Thornton, David Thorpe, Jim and Mary Thorpe, Corinne Tilghman, Winston and Martha Tipton, Leonard and Patsy Todd, Bill, Jr. and Martha Townes, David and Kristi Townes, Jeff and Teri Triplett, Farris Vaden, J. T. and Maggie Vaughan, Steve Vaughn, Larry and Beverly Vernon, Chris and Jenny Virgin, Eva Virgin, Gene and Barbara Virgin, Hugh and Winona Wade, Cliff and Terri Walker, Nina Walker, Russ and Lottie Walling, Mark Ward, Jack and Melanie Warner, John and Lelia Warner, Roy and Vera Wehman, Louise Welch, Phil and Cathy Wesner, Baxter and Carlyne Wheatley, Charles Whitby, Karen White, Phillip and Elizabeth White, Skipper and Lou Anne White, Vivian Whitehead, David and Beth Williams, Jerry and Brenda Williams, Roger and Juli Williams, Rick and Trisha Wilson, Butch Winter, Robert and Betty Wood, Kent and Heather Woody, Carlton Wright, Katherine Wright, Beulah Wyatt, Roy and Sherry Wylie, Ann Clark Young, Cheryl Young, George and Joann Zipp.

The names of some of the world's good people grace these pages.

Chapter Thirty-Seven

And Everything and All

Little Alice Dunlap and some other folks around here often wind up a sentence with an all-inclusive expression which would seem to indicate that the speaker wants the speakee to presume that he or she has been told everything that matters about the subject at hand. At least this is my impression of one of my favorite expressions, "and everything and all." This chapter is a catch-all for the winding up of my book and everything and all.

I received the following letter from an inmate in the Tiptonville prison who had formerly picked strawberries for me. The name is changed, of course:

"To Tom Wade From Joe Snigglefritz. Dear Tom Wade did you have a good crop of strorbaires this year i hope you did eveny iff i did not get to pick any for you i hope i will be able to pick some for you next your iff i am still in that the twon of Kokomo, Indiana at 101 Any Street one of my cusien died on me while i was away you probley did not want to here about it but i thot i wold tell you about it any way but my cancuren is do you need anyone to drive a traoeter for you iff you have anything to do on your farm write me back and let me no what kind of work it is so i will no iff i want to take the job or not ass i said earley that iff is always in the way but iff the job is not to hard i will take it From your Friend Joe Snigglefritz. That will be all for now write back soon and let me no what you got in mine for me Singed Sinely Yours From Joe Snigglefritz To Tom Wade."

In 1991 I read a fascinating story about an elderly New York City physician who ministered to the poor in Harlem. I wrote and complimented him on what he was doing. My letter was apparently on strawberry stationery, as he sent me a nice note addressed to Tom W. Strawberry, thanking me for my letter. The letter began, "Dear Mr. Strawberry." Some people might think this is appropriate.

The daughter of dear friends of ours had a date with a boy whom she had never before dated. He arrived to pick her up a little early or their family was eating a little late when he showed up, and the young lady's mother invited the boy to eat with them. His answer, "Nome, I done ate. I et afore I come." Though not grammatically correct, he succinctly got his point across.

One time the old maid aunt of a friend of mine took a three-week bus tour pretty much clear across the United States. My friend met his aunt at the local bus station when she returned home. He said, "Well, Aunt Flossie, how was your trip?" She replied, "To tell you the truth, Richard, it lacked a nickel being worth a damn."

Former Kenton Mayor Damon Cross recently told me an amusing story. When little one-row mechanical cotton pickers first came out, our fastidious cotton farmers had a hard time getting used to seeing so much of their cotton knocked out of the bolls and onto the ground. Hand picking got it all. A small conservative Mason Hall farmer could not find hands to pick his crop, so he arranged for a mechanical picker to pick it. He watched as the picker ran through his field picking and dropping cotton. Finally the cotton harvester had finished picking all but a few short point rows. As he started down to get those little rows the farmer said, "You needn't bother. I can knock that out with a stick."

The friend of a friend went into a beer joint in a town about 20 miles away from their hometown. My friend said to his friend, "Hey, Earl, what are you doing sitting here drinking beer instead of drinking at the Dew Drop Inn at home?" "Why, Ralph, beer's a nickel cheaper here." "But Earl, have you stopped to figure out how much the gas costs to get you from home to here and back?" "Yeah, Ralph, but you see, it's like this — I just keep on drinking here 'til I show a profit. But my head really is a thobbin' lak a redbird's tail!"

On another occasion when Earl was drinking a brand of beer that had a race car on the label Ralph asked him why he liked that particular brand of beer. Earl answered, "I just like to drink this here beer 'til that little race car goes 'round and 'round and 'round."

Tracy Griggs, who along with his brother, Tommy, and his nephew, Brent, farm some of my land and do a large amount of business with us, recently told me that his deceased father, Billy, told him about a Mr. Eddlemon who farmed around Mason Hall and who would occasionally proclaim, "I'd like to have some more land to farm, but I don't have any room for it." Guess he had a point.

After Mother saw her first "talkie," while walking back home (in Dyersburg) with a friend she commented that she did not think talkies would ever go over. The audio must have been mighty poor.

One of our little neighbors while we lived in Sherwood Hills was Felicia Hunt. She would knock on the door, and when it was opened she would ask, "Tuh tah tuh tin" which was her way of asking, "Can I come in?"

Years ago Union City had a world-class barbecuer, Charlie Moore. He and his wife at different times had a couple of restaurants where they also carried a small stock of groceries. One time Pat went out to pick up some barbecue and buns. Pat asked Mrs. Moore for some buns. Mrs. Moore asked Pat if she wanted a small package or a big package. Pat asked her how many buns were in each package. Mrs. Moore proceeded to tell her. Pat then said, "Give me a large package," to which Mrs. Moore replied, "We're out of buns." True story.

Mack Dove, who along with his brother, owns AAACooper, a very large trucking firm headquartered in his hometown of Dothan, Alabama, was a friend of mine at UT. He and I have in common the fact that I was a defeated candidate for Student Body President, and the same dubious distinction happened to him the very next year. Mack and I have seen each other occasionally through the years on football weekends, and we renewed our friendship at Johnny Majors' induction into the College Football Hall of Fame in New York (Chapter 17). Mack's daughter decided to come to UT, but her parents did not want her to take potluck on a dormitory roommate. There were several sharp Union City girls who were going to UT the same year, and one of them, Tracey Towater Kizer, did not have a roommate. Tracey was and is a very sharp girl. Mack and I worked out a deal whereby he and his wife and daughter flew up to Union City on one of their company planes and while Mack and his wife spent the weekend with us in our home, their daughter spent the weekend with

Tracey in the Towater home. The girls hit it off and roomed together at UT. Old friendships can have interesting ramifications.

I've always loved one of the old sayings around here, "Hit don't make me no nevermind."

Another one, "Ain't no harm in astin'."

Another one, "chored lark" is a nicer way of saying, "spoiled brat."

Old folks around here when questioned about why they were not eating more, often replied, "I'm eatin' a diet."

Another old folks expression when referring to late afternoon was "shank of th' evenin'."

One of my favorite sayings of Southerners is "a right smart." For you Yankee readers that means "a good bit."

Another good one is "fixin' to" which means, of course, "gettin' ready to."

A close friend's long-ago maid used the word, moderate, with emphasis on the last syllable, to express approval; i.e., "She moderated over it," which, translated, meant, "She liked it a lot." We use this verb quite often in our daily conversations. If you use this good word in this context over a period of time, it becomes easy on the ears. Try it — you'll like it.

It irritates me to no end when law enforcement officers and reporters refer to rapists, murderers, and those who have committed other heinous crimes as "gentlemen." This is now the norm rather than the exception.

Some pet peeves of mine include waiters and waitresses who bring my water or iced tea holding the glass by the top rim; chewing gum in church; people who use the phrase, "as far as," without the proper object, such as "goes" or "is concerned"; TV personalities around here who refer to "Western Tennessee." One of the neat things about Tennessee is the way we always gramatically incorrectly refer to West, Middle, and East Tennessee rather than Western, Central, and Eastern Tennessee. Our way of referring to the grand divisions of Tennessee is unique to us, and my fond hope is that it will ever be so; using an apostrophe before an "s" when the "s" is used for the purpose of making the word plural; using the word "Guest," as singular or plural — Tennessee sign painters need to be schooled on this one; drivers who do not signal before turning (most don't, which is an abomination to me); the use of the word "human" as a noun. I was taught that "human being" should be used when signifying a person, and "human" should be used as an adjective. "Human" is now used as a noun more often than not, and I presume this is now an accepted usage. The use of "healthy" when "healthful" is correct. We are healthy; our food is healthful.

I am an inveterate letter writer and have always been fascinated with statistics. I do not particularly like e-mails and can barely tolerate faxes. I continue to write letters, by hand or with my typewriter or dictated to my assistants, Julie Parker and Lilia Clanton. I enjoy receiving letters and like to think that others enjoy receiving mine, especially now that letters are no longer the ordinary. By far the largest group of recipients of my letters would be Pi K A fraternity brothers who have received letters from me that would number very close to five figures. Over the past twenty-five years I have received personal letters from the following: United States Presidents, a Vice President, Senators, Ambassadors, Congressmen, presidential candidates, a White House Chief of Staff, a White House Chief Counsel, Tennessee Governors, Tennessee Speakers of the House, Tennessee Speaker of the Senate, university presidents and chancellors, major college head football coaches, head basketball coaches, athletic directors, sports announcers, All-American football players and College Football Hall of Fame members, NFL players, coaches, and Hall of Fame members, U. S. Secretary of Agriculture, chairman of T.V.A., State Commissioners of Agriculture, Economic and Community Development, and State Parks and Environment, Chairmen and C.E.O.s of Fortune 500 companies, President of American Bankers Association, President of Metropolitan Museum of Art, Commissioner of the Southeastern Conference, Chairman of Augusta National, and chairmen and C.E.O.s of major banks.

Several decades ago when Prentice Cooper was governor of Tennessee, there was a political "boss" in an area of northeast Middle Tennessee named I. D. Beasley. In those days it was common to have political bosses in many places in Tennessee. Examples would have been E. H. Crump in Memphis and Jim Midyett in Kenton. Big and little places had bosses, people whom governors and the like could call on to get things "done" in the areas pretty much politcally controlled by these bosses. (I met Governor Cooper when he again ran for governor many years later, not long after my college graduation. My buddy, John Hoff, was a front man for his campaign. John would go into towns prior to Cooper's appearances and make arrangements necessary for campaign speeches, etc. Cooper lost; John cannot be blamed.) One day while he was governor, Cooper, a small, feisty man, was being driven through Beasley's territory when they came upon a roadblock where some highway repairs were taking place. They were stopped by a state highway employee, and the Governor's driver was told that it would be a few minutes before they could go through. The Governor, who was late for an appointment, jumped out of the car and exclaimed in no uncertain terms that they needed to get through immediately. The state employee said, "You will just have to wait your turn." The Governor said, "Do you know who I am?" "Nope," said the nonplussed flagman, to which Governor Cooper replied, "I am the Governor. Let me through!" The flagman, now visibly irritated, retorted, "Why, I wouldn't let you through here if you wuz I. D. Beasley!" I guess the Governor knew where he stood in the pecking order of that little corner of Tennessee.

Laura Joyce Howell Barton's mother, Mrs. Karon Howell, taught elementary school in Mason Hall and later in Kenton. While teaching at Mason Hall she boarded with somebody out there and came home on weekends. It's hard to imagine how unmanageable five miles could be back in those days. One time she had a little boy, we'll call him Johnny, in her class. Johnny and his folks had moved to Chicago and then had come home to Kenton. Johnny persisted in pronouncing his former home Chicargo, with an "r." Miss Karon finally decided to correct him once and for all so she wrote on the board, CHI-CA-GO, and then said to Johnny, "You see, Johnny, there is no car in Chicago." Johnny quickly retorted, "Ya ain't never been there, have ye, Miss Karon?" Miss Karon had to admit that indeed she had never been to Chicago. This story reminds me of one my Pat told me about a little jingle her grandmother, whom Pat and Bob called Bududa, recited. It went, "Chicken in the car and the car won't go. That's why you say, Chi-Ca-go!" I guess that makes sense.

During my lifetime I have known some unforgettable people. This is the story of an unforgettable couple Pat and I met at Coco Point on Barbuda. At Coco Point Pat and I met many friends of Robert and Jenny Kirkland, but our favorites were an older couple from New York, Julian and Hope Bach. Julian was a New York literary agent who was highly respected in his profession. Julian and Hope were charming, down-to-earth but urbane, witty folks. I invited Julian to John Michels' induction into the College Football Hall of Fame banquet at the Waldorf. That was the last time I saw Julian, as we have not been back to Coco Point.

Julian told us an amusing story about the great author, Pat Conroy. Conroy had never been published, and somehow he connected with Julian who was talking with Pat about his first book. In an early conversation Julian told Conroy that his publishing house was "thinking in terms of $1,500" (for an advance on Conroy's first book). Pat Conroy, having no knowledge of these things, thought that Julian meant that Pat would have to pay Julian's agency $1,500 in order for them to publish his book, rather than the fact that Pat would *receive* an advance. Pat said, "Mr. Bach, I don't believe I can come up with $1,500." Julian thought this was a scream, but to tell you the truth, I probably would have been under the same impression. I have just finished reading Conroy's latest great book, My Losing Season. He mentions Julian on pages 368, 391, and 401 of the hardback copy.

Scott Russell, a young man who headed Pi Kappa Alpha's Annual Fund for several years when I was chairman of the Fund, was a very good writer. Scott, an English major from the University of Kansas, upon learning that I knew Julian Bach, asked me if I would send Julian the first few chapters of a novel he was writing. It is very hard for an unknown writer to get a literary agent to read his work, but Julian read Scott's chapters and wrote me saying something to the effect that Scott was a good writer but that his writing was not out of the ordinary and his firm would not be interested in pursuing it further. Scott was very gracious and was delighted that Julian would read his writing. I read

Scott's chapters and thought his writing was pretty doggone good. Maybe Scott will get a break some day. Surely hope so.

A few years ago our Union City First United Methodist Church bulletin raved about the wonderful home cooked greens that Dr. Bob Cameron was bringing to the church every Wednesday night. We always go to Sunday School and/or church on Sunday mornings when we are in Union City, but I seldom go on Wednesday nights and it did not register with me that they had dinner at the church on these nights. My question to Bob the next time I saw him at church on Sunday morning was, "Bob, what do people eat your greens with?" He looked a little perplexed and finally replied, "Uhhhh, forks." Puzzled, my next question was, "What do they put your greens in?" He looked even more confused and said, "Uhhhh, plates." Somehow my mind's eye had him passing out cooked greens as people left church on Wednesday nights. I could just see him standing at the front door, ladling out greens to people who had their hands cupped and were somehow rapidly slopping them down as they left the church. When it dawned on me that the greens were part of a meal that folks had prior to church services, I felt like a penny waiting for change. During this conversation Bob never cracked a smile, apparently not wanting to embarrass me. He could tell that I was dead serious in my inquiries, yet he may well have thought that I had taken leave of my senses. It would have been remarkable if he had not thought so.

In his autobiography Sam Walton wrote about how, when he was a small-time Arkansas retailer, he would hitch a two-wheel trailer to his station wagon and drive to Union City on Sundays and load down his conveyances with dry goods purchased from the First Street wholesaler that was located on what is now the Commercial Bank parking lot. He called the firm, Wright Merchandise. Actually it was Rite Merchandise, and it was operated by the Altfeld ladies. Mrs. Altfeld was the mother of Jean Ray Altfeld Cohen. Jean Ray was an Obion County leader and a member of the County Court. She was married to the dentist, Merlin Cohen, who was a friend of mine at UT. Tragically, Jean Ray died of cancer at a young age.

For a long time I thought Olivia Newton John, the famous Australian singer, was a trio called, "Olivia, Newt, and John." Surely I'm not the only person in the world who thought this.

Dave Roberts, head of the UT alumni office, once wrote some letters on a piece of paper and asked if Pat or I could make any sense out of them. After a while we figured it out and thought it was a scream. Still do. Here 'tis.

M R DUCKS

M R NOT

S M R

C M WANGS

L I B

M R D U C K S

A little clue. Pronounce with an exaggerated Tennessee hillbilly twang.

The State of Tennessee recently passed a law making it legal to retrieve and eat roadkill. This could be a real coup for skunk aficionados who regularly travel Highway 45W between Union City and Kenton. Lots of these little black and white beasties bite the dust on our stretch of the road.

Here in the Bible Belt some of our little old ladies have ways of gossiping which they think will mitigate what they have just reported or are about to report. To wit, "Have you heard about Beulah getting a little tipsy at the quilting bee Thursday night? — Bless her heart." Or, "Tell me what it was that Clara did so I'll know what it is for which I need to ask the Lord to forgive her."

And everything and all!

INDEX

Hurt, Howard, 183
Hurt, Patricia, 156
Husselman, Tom, 271
Ivy, Cotton, 185
Jackson, Ida, 317
Jackson, Richard, 271
James, Tommie Faye, 217
Jarrell, Mabel Wade Senter, 393
Jenkins, Paul, 2, 8
Jenkins, Peggy, 8, 19
Jenkins, Richard, 19
Jenks, Janice Freeman, 391
Jernigan, Byrl, 39
John, Olivia Newton, 472
Johnson, Dan, 29, 266
Johnson, Dr. Joe, xi
Johnson, Frank, 419
Johnson, Fred, Jr., 325
Johnson, Gene, 28
Johnson, Mary Bishop, 141
Johnson, Pat, 278
Johnson, Rafer, 246
Johnson, Tom, 268
Johnson, Virginia Askew, 369
Johnston, Chips, 150, 163, 211
Joiner, Clint, 173, 220, 462
Jones, Cathy, 257
Jones, Eddie, 19, 49, 346
Jones, Nippy, 76
Jones, Spike, 110
Jones, Wade, 239
Jordan, Freddy, 66, 452
Jourdan, Louie, 112
Jowers, Danny, 362, 421, 453
Joyner, Lou, 462
Joyner, Rob, 217
Kaler, Shirley, 238
Kamehameha, King, 152
Kane, Ruth Wade, 61, 393, 396, 398
Karnes, Sarah (Bitsy) Bogle Karnes, T. C., 392
Keathley, Bob, 66
Kerr, Donald, 136
Kerr, Walker, 136
Kessling, Bob, 253
Key, Carolyn, 279

Kidwell, Dick, xii, 230
Kimbrough, Ben, 279
King, Lamar, 296
King, Mary, 57
Kinsey, Paul, 412
Kirkland, Carl, 171, 190, 217, 456
Kirkland, Carol, 278, 279
Kirkland, Chris, 175, 220
Kirkland, Jenny, 204, 207, 212, 217, 221, 230, 238, 242, 243, 260, 470
Kirkland, Ken, 240
Kirkland, Louise, 181
Kirkland, Turner, 284
Kizer, Tracey Towater, 467
Knepp, Ed, 76
Kurowski, Whitey, 75
Lacewell, Larry, 189
LaForge, Bill, 271, 351, 352
Lamb, Charles, 266
Lancaster, George, 265
Lancaster, Maggie, 48
Lancaster, Ron, 264
Lancaster, Sammie Lee, 317, 413, 444
Lane, Bruce, 406
Lane, Joe, 66
Lane, Will, 405
Lanier, David, 138, 145, 229
Lashlee, Carol, 257, 279
Latimer, Bill, 293
Latimer, Gail, 459
Lattus, Richard, 157
Lauricella, Hank, 249
Lawrence, Bill, 462
Lawrence, Peter, 213
Lee, Charlie Ruth, 317
Lee, Harper, 122
Leggett, Bob, 392
Leonidis, Valerios, 248
Levine, Jay, 98
Levy, Ron, 98
Lighty, Phil, 272
Linn, Tony, 294, 295
Lisher, John, 271
Little, Becky, 278
Little, Joe, 278

Murphy, Bill, 146
Muse, George, 98
Musial, Stan, 75, 76, 97
Myers, Adrian Baucom, 34
Narsh, Joseph David, 382
Neil, Luther, 67
Nelson, Lindsey, 253
Nelson, Margaret Pharr, 392
Nettles, Bert, 122
Newbill, Leonard, 47
Newmon, Andy, 295, 296, 347, 452
Neyland, Robert, 277
Nicklaus, Jack, 187
Nordman, Ernest III, 382
Nordman, Ernest, Jr., 381
Nordman, Lydabeth Tucker, 206,
    223, 348
Norvell, Joe, 28
Norvell, Louis G., 393, 395
Norvell, Louis G., Jr., 393
Oates, Warren, 183
Ofinger, Bob, 76
Ogle, Richard, 271
Oglesby, Judy, 177, 196, 248, 269
Oliver, Laura, 203
Oliver, Terry, 297
Orr, Delbert, 164, 252, 417, 418,
    444, 446
Orr, Susie, 278
Oswald, Lee Harvey, 89, 267
Owen, Tom, 310
Page, Andy, 298, 452
Pankey, Tom, 98
Papay, Al, 76
Pappas, Ana, 232, 238
Parker, Fess, 273
Parker, Julie, ix, 19, 441, 468
Parks, Hamilton, 271, 408, 423
Parks, Nate, 98
Parsons, Ann Nora, 232
Partee, Hunter, 99, 110
Partee, Willis, 99
Parton, Dolly, 179
Paschall, Lee, 47, 67
Pate, Joe, 57
Patterson, Robert, 412, 425

Patton, Arthur, 412
Patton, Buck, 412
Pauwel, Anita, 209
Pavarotti, Luciano, 232
Pease, Ed, 271
Peery, Harrell, 428, 440, 443, 447
Peery, Margaret, 437, 447
Pelham, Gordon, 80, 320
Pelham, Peter, 22, 32, 38, 41, 79, 80,
    93, 95, 96, 97, 98, 101, 102, 148,
    211, 273, 330, 332, 344, 391
Pellettieri, Buster, 103, 104
Penn, Ferris, 18, 405, 406, 408
Penn, Joe, 188
Penn, Joe Ferris, 15, 35, 391
Penn, William, 27, 134, 211, 250,
    391
Pennell, Frances Montgomery, 392
Penzner, Paul, 208
Perkins, Jeff, 297
Perryman, Lavan (Cotton), 24
Perryman, Mike, 298, 448
Person, Ed, 102
Pflueger, Nell, 309
Pharr, Betty, 390
Pharr, Bill, 389
Pharr, Elizabeth Josephine, 393
Pharr, Gus William, 387
Pharr, William C., 387
Phebus, Robert, 412, 425
Pieper, George, 419
Pierce, Dan, 57
Pittman, Flo, 127, 303
Pollett, Howard, 76
Porter, James, 297, 298
Porter, Joe, 297
Potter, Joe, 47
Powell, Gentry, 316
Powell, Jim, 251
Presley, Elvis, 152
Priest, Adam, 253
Priest, Tim, 253
Primrose, Jerry, 32
Prince, Richard, 228
Prothro, Tommy, 252
Prowse, Juliet, 130

ABOUT THE AUTHOR

Tom Wade. Jr. grew up in Kenton, Tennessee, pop. 892. He was educated in the Kenton school system, at McCallie School in Chattanooga, and The University of Tennessee, Knoxville where he received a B.S. in Business Administration. He and his family have lived in Union City, Tennessee for the past 40 years, and he goes to work in Kenton six to seven days a week. In Kenton he is a fourth generation farmer and third generation cotton ginner and grain dealer. He grows strawberries as have his Wade predecessors continuously for over 100 years. He has been very active in the affairs of his alma maters, his college fraternity, and his trade associations.

Tom Wade, Jr. has been equally as active in terms of his family and friends. He has kept in close touch with literally hundreds of these folks from coast to coast and for several decades he has compiled information about them for this book.

Printed in the United States
16428LVS00002B/31-255